Better Men

IN honor of the boys that died in Vietnam

Better Men

Coweta County, Georgia and the Vietnam War

Steve Quesinberry

ISBN: 9798357940759

"The person who has nothing for which he is willing to fight, nothing which is more important than his own personal safety, is a miserable creature and has no chance of being free unless made and kept so by the exertions of **better men** than himself."

John Stuart Mill
British philosopher, economist, and Member of Parliament, 1806-1873.

For them the task is done, the strife is stilled;
No more shall care disturb, nor zeal condemn;
And when the larger good has been fulfilled,
In coming years we shall remember them.

And far-off voices of the future sing,
"They shall remain in memory's diadem";
And winds of promise still are whispering
That same refrain, "We shall remember them."
--James Terry White

These boys gave their lives in Vietnam.

--Poem quoted in the Western High School Yearbook, 1968, as part of the dedication to Jessie C. Cofield, Jerry L. Smith, and J. Michael Watson.

To the sweetest woman I know, my wife Susan, and
our children, Stephen, Ashley, and David.

"In honor of the men and women of Coweta County
who served their country with dedication and bravery
during the Vietnam Conflict."
Thus reads the plaque on the west side of the
courthouse in downtown Newnan.
I couldn't say it any better.

CONTENTS

Section Two: Coweta County and the Vietnam War

Section Three: Appendix

FORWARD

I strode into the Media Center at Smokey Road Middle School, slightly apprehensive. I exchanged pleasantries with the Media Specialist, who pointed me toward a man at a table in the back corner. He had already stood and was moving towards me. He greeted me like we were old friends, though we were only acquainted as I had taught his oldest son the previous semester. Our meeting wasn't a casual get-together; this was a job interview for a position in the History Department at Newnan High School. The job that I had coveted since I had attended high school there. The man I gazed at across the table that day was the Chairman of that Department, Steve Quesinberry.

I began my Coweta career at Smokey Road Middle School, but my goal was always to return and teach at my alma mater. I knew that goal was within my grasp as I sat across the table from Quesinberry.

The interview that day did not proceed as I was accustomed to; Steve seemed more interested in why I loved history, my favorite time periods, what I was reading, and how I might improve their department rather than my expertise in pedagogy. While I do not recall every detail of our conversation, I do remember that I was more than a little stressed about my responses.

However, a week later, I filled out the transfer papers to go to Newnan High School.

Upon arrival at the school in the fall of 2003, I quickly moved to become an integral part of the team. The *Student-Vet Connect* program, still in its infancy, allowed me to see the possibilities of a new type of history education. Steve had recently started teaching an elective class listed in the course catalog as Modern American Military History, more commonly called "The Vietnam War." However, even that title is a bit misleading. His class was so much more than just a class dedicated to that war in Southeast Asia. Instead, it was a class that immersed the students in the era's culture, music, and history. The extraordinary thing about the course was the involvement of so many local Vietnam Veterans. They took great pleasure coming in, sharing their stories with the students, and, above all, they trusted Steve.

That class helped me see what could be done, and with Steve's help, I created a course based on the history of World War II; as far as either of us was aware, we were the only public high school in the state of Georgia that offered these two classes. Together, we spent countless hours working on ways to make these classes as fun and educational as possible, always focusing on those who served. As the years went on, with *Student-Vet Connect* and those classes as the backdrop, we became increasingly involved with the community and various activities involving our students and local veterans.

In the fall of 2011, Steve and the *Coweta Commission on Veterans Affairs* brought *The Wall that Heals* to Newnan. This traveling replica is the only Wall connected to the Vietnam Veterans Memorial Wall in Washington, DC. This was a week-long event, including helicopters, speakers, 24-hour access to the Wall, and recognition of those we lost from our hometown. This event was a catalyst for what was to come.

Many places in the United States have sent their best and bravest to war only to have them return in flag-draped coffins or not return at all. Coweta County is, unfortunately, among them. From World War 1 through today, Coweta County has buried numerous young men taken from us to defend this nation. If you travel the county, you will see roads and monuments bearing the name of these heroes. Regrettably, twenty-three of these local men were lost during the Vietnam War. As part of the *Wall that Heals* visit, Steve reached out to the families of those twenty-three. This led to the journey that became this book.

I watched as Steve hung the photographs of these twenty-three young men on the Wall in the back of his classroom and, every day, made sure that his students knew their names, their stories, and above all, the idea that they mattered. That dedication to those men makes Steve and this book so important. It is easy to find volumes of books on the battles, the controversies, the theories, and the famous people of the Vietnam War. However, the stories that need to be told are those of the men whom time has forgotten, but whose loved ones have not. That is what Steve has set out to do in the pages of this book. Over the last ten years, I have watched as he has reached out and followed even the most minor threads connected to these men. In this book, you will meet twenty-three American heroes who happen to be bound tightly by one of those threads; namely, they all resided in Coweta County. They come from very diverse backgrounds, but they represent the best in all of us, and Steve has, within these pages, done honor to their memories. Additionally, you will discover the details of Coweta's relationship with the Vietnam War during the 1960s and since, events that you have never heard about, and recent stories about Vietnam veterans, alive and dead, who have been honored and recognized for their service.

I am excited for people to read this narrative, relive these stories, and share in Steve's enthusiasm. I am proud to have witnessed Steve's journey of discovery and his drive to bring this book to life. Having Steve as a mentor and friend over the past twenty years has taught me many things. It has taught me how to be a better teacher, tell stories that matter, and relate the importance of knowing local history. Coweta County today is vastly different from the one these men and people in this book knew. It had no Walmart, no Target, no Chik-fil-A, and more dirt roads than paved ones, but the spirit of the people remains. We honor our fallen on Memorial Day, celebrate those who served on Veterans Day, and support those still serving on foreign shores and throughout the United States.

I am proud to be from Coweta County. I am pleased to continue the work that made Steve legendary by teaching the Vietnam War Class. This is not a book full of grand battles and epic historical moments; it is something more. It is a book detailing the lives of ordinary, local hometown boys who were taken too soon and who will, thanks to Steve, never be forgotten.

I am proud that my friend's hard work is now in print and that maybe, those twenty-three men are looking down and saying, "never forget."

Frankey Henderson
August 1, 2022

INTRODUCTION

When those boys are forgotten, that is when they really die.
—Elizabeth Crain

I stood in front of the bathroom mirror, talking to myself.

It was late October 2011. One of the most incredible weeks of my teaching career had recently concluded. The Vietnam Veterans Memorial Fund (VVMF) Wall That Heals had been at the Coweta County Fairgrounds for four days, and many local and out-of-town guests had visited to honor, remember, and pay respects to the men and women whose names graced that unique black granite. So many people, myself included, had worked to honor those who served and died in Vietnam. The week had been exhausting but exceptional.

I didn't want it to end.

In early 2010, local veterans Joe Brooks and Malcolm Jackson had asked me to serve on a new committee they had formed, the Coweta Commission on Veterans Affairs (CCVA*)*. General Brooks and Jackson had been part of our Student-Vet Connect program at Newnan High School and thought we should take that program "on the road." They wanted the community to have the same opportunity as Newnan High School students—to meet and learn from the men and women who had made the history of the twentieth century. Initially, I was skeptical. We had geared that program to bring to life what the students were learning in class. The kids loved it, but I was uncertain how adults would react. I was convinced to give it a go, so in October 2010, we took the show to downtown Newnan. We began the day by honoring Coweta's veterans with a ceremony at Veterans Memorial Park and a flyover by a UH-1 Huey. Downtown, Newnan High students past, and present helped with everything from setup to teardown. Many local veterans sat at tables on the Court Square, displaying memorabilia and talking history to anyone interested. It went well for the first-time event.

Within weeks, the group asked what should be done in 2011. We decided to attempt to bring the traveling Wall from the Vietnam Veterans Memorial Fund, The Wall That Heals, to Newnan. After reviewing the requirements for the Wall, we determined the only place that would fit all VVMF specifications was the Coweta County Fairgrounds. County officials were intrigued and agreed we could use the fairgrounds.

Six weeks later, with our confirmation letter from the VVMF, the committee began planning. This event would include activities for an entire week. Committee members took responsibility for some part of the week, and I volunteered to research Coweta's killed in action and locate their family members. These were the names memorialized on that black Wall that would soon visit Newnan.

Mounted on the west side of the historic courthouse in downtown Newnan is a plaque with the names of twenty-one men killed in the Vietnam War. That plaque was dedicated on Memorial Day 1988. On that solemn occasion, over 200 people, many of them family members of the slain, gathered to remember the men who died in Vietnam. Georgia Secretary of State Max Cleland, a disabled Vietnam veteran and a friend of local veteran G. D. Hendrix, served as the keynote speaker.

"It's my honor to be here with the families of those who have suffered in a deep and personal way," Cleland said that day, observing that a nation that has no heroes is poor. "Poorer still is the nation that has them and forgets them."

The local VFW, American Legion, and Troop E, 348th Cavalry from the local National Guard unit also participated. Angela Cole, sister of one of the Vietnam dead, read the names from the plaque, and taps was played to end the observance. It would be more than twenty years before another ceremony honored these men who had died in Vietnam.

This local plaque, then, was where I began my quest.

To find the families of the men listed on the plaque, I needed help. Local journalist Alex McRae of the *Newnan Times-Herald* wrote a twelve-part series on Vietnam and highlighted local vets in each article. He also wrote multiple articles about the Coweta KIA, which assisted me immensely in locating family members who were still nearby. I met a few of these families when they visited Newnan High School to speak with my students about their loved one. Between Alex's efforts through the newspaper and my early connection with some families, we made great strides in finding the family members.

I checked out the *History of Coweta County, Georgia* from the local library to see if I could find any helpful information. Instead, I found an interesting discrepancy between the list of deaths on the courthouse plaque and a list in the book, which contained three additional names. No one I spoke with knew anything about these three men. Homer Pease, Daniel Post Jr., and John Dozier would become a mystery and obsession over the next six months. Who were they?

By October, I had information on the three men and determined that two of them should have been included on the list. I presented my findings to the CCVA, and the members agreed with me. On the last day of the Wall That Heals visit, Daniel Post and John Dozier were part of the ceremony that honored those men and their families.

I failed to find family members for only one of the final twenty-three guys. The last family would be found a few weeks after the Wall visited Newnan.

As I contacted family members, they often shared something about their loved ones and the circumstances surrounding their death. Always a lover of a good story, I became engrossed by the story of these young men, the chronicle of their lives in Coweta County, and the tragedy that had befallen them.

As I stood in front of the mirror that day, I replayed those stories in my head. Someone needed to get these stories down, or these guys would be forgotten. So many family members and friends had passed away over the fifty years since the war. These stories would be lost unless I did something to preserve them. That day, in front of a mirror, I perceived that I was uniquely positioned to preserve this piece of local history. I had a starting point to learn about all of them.

But the clock was ticking.

I decided to write a book. I had collected and read history books my entire life and was familiar with what they looked like. However, this project turned out to be one of the most challenging ventures I had ever undertaken. It was highly frustrating but, strangely, intensely exhilarating. One day, I was raging about a problem, and the next day, I was pumping my fist after receiving new information.

More than ten years later, I'm finally finished. Those who knew the men in this book might find that what I have written may not jibe precisely with what they recollect or have heard from others. I would be shocked if everything I wrote was exactly the way they remember it. This book was created from military records, internet posts, books, newspaper and magazine articles, funeral home records, interviews with local historians and veterans, and my knowledge of the Vietnam War. However, the most crucial information comes from more than two hundred hours of interviews with families, friends, and Vietnam veterans who knew the men and were involved in these events.

First-person accounts as an author's primary source of information sound tremendous but are infused with peril for the writer and the reader. Often, they're incomplete and challenge people's memories and assumptions about the past. I was asking the interviewees to remember things that happened decades ago. Most of us can't remember what happened yesterday! Will their memories always be correct? Unlikely. I verified anything of a factual nature that I could. Will their memories always be the same as those of others? Again, doubtful.

It has been more than fifty years.

Regardless of how diligently I worked, these stories never seemed complete. Some men had few family members left. Some had family members who didn't want to talk about the war. Some events, regardless of how significant they seemed, had few people left who remembered them. These blanks were often impossible to fill. It was painfully obvious that the window on collecting these stories was slowly but surely closing.

Occasionally, I took some literary license and created a moment in someone's life based on military records or an interview. I didn't change the story but tried to describe the scene and the circumstances. I wanted the reader to feel that they were there with the young soldier or Marine. To do that, I needed to paint a picture and bring it to life. I wanted to tell a story, not just spout a collection of facts.

Some things in this book are probably inaccurate. Perhaps I was told wrong. Perhaps I needed to make a conjecture and got it incorrect. Hopefully, these are small items and don't take away from the story. I take responsibility for all errors in this book.

Each chapter contains an individual story. They're ordered chronologically, but they can be read in any order.

After teaching history for more than thirty-five years, I've learned that teaching history isn't about the textbook. It isn't about teaching students every imaginable detail. Instead, it's about engaging our students and community in a story about the world, our country, and our local area. Good and bad, the stories are always about people. These men and events from Coweta County, Georgia are part of that story.

They should never be forgotten.

CHAPTER ONE

A Brief Overview of the Vietnam War

We are not about to send American boys nine or ten thousand miles away from home to do what Asian boys ought to be doing for themselves.

Lyndon B. Johnson, President of the United States, 1963-1969

The Vietnam War is unquestionably the most divisive conflict in the history of the United States. Only the War of 1812 divided the country to the same degree. What follows is a brief overview of how we got to the place where American youth, and specifically young people from Coweta County, were going to the other side of the globe to fight a war that seemed unending. Most books about the war are individual accounts of the author's experiences, and many are excellent. However, if the reader is interested in tackling an extensive overview, those titles are limited. There are some available, including but not limited to Stanley Karnow's *Vietnam: A History*, Max Hastings's *Vietnam: An Epic Tragedy,* or even the Ken Burns PBS series, *The Vietnam War*. This overview will not be a detailed synopsis of the war and its background because that isn't this book's objective. Instead, this book is about a group of young men, a community in Georgia, and how national events impacted the lives of the people there.

Imperialism and the French

A simple definition of modern imperialism is the taking of countries or territories in various ways for the raw materials and markets those countries and territories can provide. While it's possible to trace imperialism back to the days of Christopher Columbus, the time frame of most interest to this story is the one that parallels the Industrial Revolution. As the factory system came to dominate the nineteenth century, more countries looked outside their borders to find the natural resources they needed to compete economically on the world stage. Often, that economic power also led to political power and national prestige. England became the most dominant global empire, with colonies that stretched around the earth. France, always England's fiercest competitor, also worked to build an empire. They colonized the same locations as the English: the Caribbean, South America, Africa, and Asia. In Asia, the French coveted the rubber of present-day Laos, Cambodia, and Vietnam. These countries collectively became French Indochina.

The French colonies were expected to turn a profit. When they did not, drastic measures had to be undertaken. Despite the French Declaration of the Rights of Man and of the Citizen, many Vietnamese were enslaved, and the population as a whole was treated miserably. When the Great War came along (1914-1918), Vietnamese laborers were sent to France to unload supply ships and perform other manual labor. Fortunately for them, they weren't sent to the trenches.

Twenty years later, when Nazi Germany conquered the French, Vietnam fell into the laps of the Japanese Empire, which was allied with Germany and Italy as one of the Axis Powers.

During World War II, a nationalist/communist leader named Ho Chi Minh organized the resistance movement against the Japanese, abbreviated Viet Minh (League for the Independence of Vietnam). American OSS agents worked with the Viet Minh and Ho Chi Minh against the Japanese, even though Vietnam was considered a backwater area of the global conflict. The OSS or Office of Strategic Services was the forerunner of the CIA.

When the Japanese surrendered on September 2, 1945, on the deck of the USS *Missouri*, Ho Chi Minh appeared before a jubilant crowd in Hanoi and declared Vietnam's independence. He quoted the American Declaration of Independence, comparing the Vietnamese situation to that of America 150 years earlier. He probably wanted to attract the sympathy of the United States, hoping that the most powerful country on the planet could keep its French colonizers from returning. Ho Chi Minh also quoted the French Declaration of the Rights of Man and of the Citizen and listed the abuses suffered by the Vietnamese at the hands of the same country that had once said, "All men are born free and with equal rights and must always remain free and have equal rights."

In other words, the French were hypocrites.

After World War II, and as the Western Powers began to slip into the Cold War, they needed a strong France back on its feet in Europe. So when the French decided to return to their colonies, their allies didn't object. In 1946, the French began returning to Vietnam. By 1947, the French were at war with the Viet Minh. The struggle continued for seven years, with the French making every effort to deal with the guerilla war at which the Viet Minh had become masters. By war's end, the United States was providing 80 percent of the financing for the French war effort, which amounted to approximately a billion dollars a year. The war concluded in the spring of 1954 with the famous battle of Dien Bien Phu. For three months that spring, the Viet Minh had surrounded, cut off, and whittled down the French Army so much that French commanders felt they had no choice but to surrender.

After this debacle, the government of France decided to cut its losses and negotiate a withdrawal.

The United States and Vietnam

The Cold War had been heating up as the French-Viet Minh War raged. China had fallen to the communist forces of Mao Tse-Tung, and Chinese soldiers had fought against the United Nations in Korea. The Truman Doctrine brought the word "containment" to the forefront of American foreign policy. The goal of containment was simple enough—to keep communism from spreading. The Western democracies could not and would not try to push it back from the places the communists already controlled, which could lead to a third World War. The Soviets' test of an atomic weapon in 1949 brought a threat of nuclear annihilation that became an undercurrent of all American policy and actions. The containment strategy had already been tested in Greece and Korea; it would become the policy of the United States for the next forty years.

The containment policy is the reason the United States financed the French during the Indochina war. Was Ho Chi Minh a nationalist? Absolutely. Was Ho Chi Minh a Communist? Undeniably. Trained in the Soviet Union, he was a founder of the

French Communist Party. Both the Soviets and the Communist Chinese had backed the Viet Minh against the French. The United States supported the French in containing the spread of communism in Vietnam and Southeast Asia. Then the French decided they were done trying to bring this colony into line. They wanted out, regardless of the Cold War. They met representatives of the Viet Minh in Geneva, Switzerland.

The Geneva Conference had begun just before the fall of Dien Bien Phu. That battle changed the dynamics of the conference in the communists' favor. When the agreement was finalized, Vietnam was temporarily divided at the seventeenth parallel, also called the Demilitarized Zone (DMZ). The Northern half was ceded to the Viet Minh, while the Southern half was left with a non-communist government set up by the French. The accords stipulated that the entire country would hold elections to choose a president then reunite in two years. The Americans refused to sign the agreement, seeing it as a concession to the communists and an infringement of the containment policy. Even though they didn't sign the accord, they grudgingly agreed to abide by it.

The elections scheduled for 1956 never took place, not because of the North but because of the South.

In the context of the Cold War, it was inevitable that Vietnam would become a hot spot. Immediately after the Geneva Accords, the Soviets and the Chinese began backing the North with military and financial assistance, while the United States matched their support in the South. The elections didn't occur because the government of South Vietnam, along with that of the United States, was convinced that Ho Chi Minh would emerge victorious, and the entire country would become communist. This might very well have occurred. If South Vietnam fell to the communists, it was believed that Laos, Cambodia, and possibly Thailand would follow suit and fall like dominos. The United States wanted to prevent this as part of the containment policy.

The North was unsatisfied with half the country; the nationalist side wanted the entire country reunited. Ho Chi Minh felt that the Viet Minh had defeated the French and should have been allowed to unite the country under his leadership. The communist side wanted the North and South joined as well, although their desire for unification revolved more around the spread of communism and the geopolitical chess match that was the Cold War. In 1959, the North began work on what was later nicknamed by the Americans as the Ho Chi Minh Trail. The trail went into Laos and continued into Cambodia, paralleling the South Vietnamese border. This allowed the Communists to bypass the narrow and heavily defended part of the country at the seventeenth parallel and move troops, weapons, and supplies through the two neighboring countries and enter South Vietnam anywhere they chose. The United States had shortsightedly promised not to send troops into Laos and Cambodia.

As the guerilla war against South Vietnam grew, abetted by the Ho Chi Minh Trail, the United States began sending advisors to the South Vietnamese Army, known as the Army of the Republic of Vietnam (ARVN). Those advisors assisted in combating the home-grown insurgents known as the Vietnamese Communists or, more commonly, the Viet Cong. During the Kennedy presidency, sixteen thousand American military personnel were in the country. That number was soon to increase.

On November 22, 1963, President Kennedy was assassinated, and Vice President Lyndon Johnson became president. Nine months later, in August 1964, two incidents occurred in the Tonkin Gulf of Vietnam. The first saw a US Navy destroyer attacked by North Vietnamese gunboats. The USS *Maddox* was not on an innocent sightseeing cruise down the coast of North Vietnam; it was on an intelligence mission. When it was reinforced two days later by the USS *Turner Joy,* it was alleged that once more, the two ships were attacked by North Vietnamese gunboats. This almost certainly didn't happen as described, and the two ship captains realized that soon afterward. Their requests to slow down while they investigated what happened that night were ignored, and soon, at the request of President Johnson, Congress passed what became known as the Tonkin Gulf Resolution. This gave the president a free hand to react to any provocation by the North Vietnamese in whatever way he saw fit. As Johnson said later, the resolution was like "grandma's nightshirt; it covers everything." While the war is frequently blamed on the Tonkin Gulf incident, if it had not happened, something else would have likely led to war.

Lyndon Johnson was elected president in November 1964. Early in 1965, the Viet Cong intensified their attacks on the ARVN. More American advisors and military equipment were caught in the crossfire or deliberately targeted. In March, President Johnson ordered the Marines into Vietnam to protect the airfields that held American aircraft and the crews assisting the South. The action was taken under the authority of the Tonkin Gulf Resolution. Soon, the Marines were on the offensive. By the fall of 1965, Army units had been ordered to Vietnam, including the First Cavalry Division. The deployment of these units set the stage for the action in the Ia Drang Valley at LZ X-Ray and LZ Albany, immortalized in the film *We Were Soldiers* starring Mel Gibson. Suddenly, American boys were nine or ten thousand miles from home, regardless of President Johnson's promises.

In the Ia Drang battles that continued for more than a month, more than five hundred American soldiers were killed. The communist losses were estimated to be more than 3,500. The Americans found out how determined the Viet Cong and North Vietnamese were, but military and political leaders thought they were easily beatable. So they decided to send even more troops.

Now, it was on. The Americans were confident; they were the most powerful country on earth. Yet they had learned little from the French experience. The American military used its firepower and technological superiority like a club. They felt the aircraft bombs, artillery, and naval bombardments would bring the Vietnamese communists to their knees. But the military people had been trained to fight World War III, which would have been a conventional war like World War II, not counting a possible exchange of nuclear weapons. But this was primarily a guerilla war, and the people they were fighting were ingenious, determined, and ruthless.

The guerilla war in Vietnam was characterized by tunnel systems, booby traps, and ambushes. The VC were reinforced by the regular soldiers of the North Vietnamese Army (NVA) that entered the South via the Ho Chi Minh Trail. Regardless of what the United States did to combat the communists, they couldn't degrade the enemy forces to the extent that they would feel that they had been defeated or that they would ask for peace. As Ho Chi Minh once famously said, "You can kill ten of our men for every one we kill of yours. But even at those odds, you will lose, and we will win." He was right.

American soldiers served a twelve-month tour in Vietnam. Marines served thirteen months in-country. One veteran said it wasn't a ten-year war but ten one-year wars.

At the end of January 1968, the communists launched a vast offensive during the New Year's holiday known in Vietnam as Tet. Every provincial capital, major city, and even the US Embassy was attacked by VC and NVA soldiers. The people of the United States were surprised. They were being told that there was light at the end of the tunnel. Over the next few months, the VC and NVA were decisively defeated on the battlefield. But that really was irrelevant. The most important result of the Tet Offensive was that many Americans were questioning the war and our reasons for being there.

As early as 1966 and 1967, protests were being held against the war and America's involvement. Chants such as "Hell no, we won't go" and "Hey, Hey, LBJ, how many kids did you kill today?" became commonplace, especially after the Tet Offensive. The country seemed to divide based on their support or lack of support for the war. The country was also divided by race, as the Civil Rights Movement continued its push for equal rights. Then 1968 was one of the most turbulent years in American history. The Tet Offensive led the incumbent president to withdraw from the presidential race. Martin Luther King and Robert Kennedy were assassinated. The Democratic National Convention in Chicago saw a pitched battle between the police and young street protesters. In this stormy atmosphere, Richard Nixon was elected president.

An experienced politician, Nixon had served in Congress and been vice president for eight years during the Eisenhower administration. When John Kennedy narrowly defeated him for the presidency in 1960, it appeared that Nixon's campaigning days might be over. But like the phoenix, he rose out of the ashes and eight years later won the presidency. He faced numerous issues after his inauguration, but the most critical issue was the Vietnam War.

Nixon's Vietnam policy became known as Vietnamization. He would gradually withdraw American soldiers and turn the fighting over to the South Vietnamese while negotiating with the

North Vietnamese. He hoped to calm the US anti-war movement and appear statesmanlike. His mantra was "peace with honor," and he was determined that the United States would get out of the war and look good while doing it. The negotiations dragged on.

The protest movement did slow down during the Nixon years, though it never stopped altogether. Protests exploded across the country in 1970 after the American invasion of Cambodia. Attempting to close the Ho Chi Minh Trail was military strategy 101. However, it should have been done years before. Militarily, the results were satisfactory, but domestically, the president had to deal with the shootings at Kent State University. Even so, Nixon was reelected in a landslide in November 1972. Shortly after the election and with the help of the most intense bombing campaign of the war, dubbed "the Christmas bombing," the North Vietnamese, South Vietnamese, and the United States agreed to terms. The Paris Peace Treaty was concluded in January 1973.

American troops were subsequently withdrawn, but the South Vietnamese were promised that if the North violated the treaty, American airpower would come to their rescue. In 1974, the Watergate scandal led to Nixon's resignation, and Gerald Ford became president. During the spring of 1975, the North Vietnamese blatantly broke the pact and invaded the South. Congress refused to allow American airpower to intervene as promised. They were determined to get out entirely and not let one more American boy die. South Vietnam fell to the communists on April 30, 1975.

It was over.

The impact of the war was tremendous. More than fifty-eight thousand young men and women had died in their country's service. On Veterans Day 1982, a new memorial opened in Washington, DC, quickly dubbed "the Wall." The names of the military personnel killed during the Vietnam War were on it. It quickly became the most visited and revered memorial in the Capital. On that black granite were the names of twenty-three young people who called a patriotic but sparsely populated county in western Georgia home.

This is their story.

CHAPTER TWO

Grady Lee Elder

Grantville, Georgia

Tragic tales rarely do make sense.
—Gwenn Wright

Thomas Winkles turned the key in his 1946 four-door Ford, and the engine roared to life. He rolled down the window. "C'mon! C'mon!" he yelled as several guys piled into the car. "Where's your money? C'mon, let me have it."

They slapped ten-dollar bills into his waiting hand. The Ford could carry seven people and was crowded on this trip from Fort Jackson, South Carolina, to Grantville, Georgia. It took twenty dollars' worth of gas to make the round trip. The rest was profit. Winkles, a Grantville native, liked to drive fast. The guys riding with him wanted to get to their destinations as quickly as possible, and he had no problem obliging. Not everyone was heading to Grantville. Winkles would drop people off almost anywhere between Fort Jackson and Coweta County, Georgia, if they had the cash. Winkles, who had some bookkeeping experience before being drafted, was a clerk in the Military Personnel Department (MPD). The office work allowed him to look over the personnel files for service members who might want rides along his route to Georgia. Winkles was anxious to see his girlfriend back in Grantville. Transporting riders paid for his trip and kept him awake. Grady Elder laid his ten-dollar bill in Winkles's palm and got comfortable for the six-hour trip home.

Grady joined the US Army in March 1954. He did his Basic Combat Training and Advanced Infantry Training at Fort Jackson in Columbia, South Carolina, and met Thomas Winkles, also from Grantville. They went home together on numerous occasions.

Winkles said Elder was "likable" and a guy who "appreciated getting to come home." Sometimes, Winkles was worried that the guys he ferried might decide not to go back to training, so he had to make sure they returned with him. He never worried about Grady Elder, who wanted to be there.

On May 11, 1936, Grady Elder was born to Mark James and Luella Elder. Luella had been born on a Seminole Reservation in Sweetwater, Florida, and had lost both of her parents. At eight, she was adopted by Robert and Merdice Smith, who lived in the Harrisonville community in western Troup County. Mark James had grown up in LaGrange. Grady was one of six siblings. Johnnie Mae was the oldest, then Grady, followed by Carolyn, Ernest, Virgil, and Annette. The Elders lived on Forrest Road between Grantville and Lone Oak and worked in the Grantville cotton mill in addition to caring for their land, raising livestock, and growing their own vegetables.[1]

Their children were expected to help at home, and all the children worked as soon as they were able. They milked cows, cleaned the house, and canned food for the winter. Johnnie Mae and Grady watched the other kids while the parents worked at the mill.

A tomboy, Johnnie Mae loved to climb trees and play outdoors. She and Grady enjoyed playing together. "We were raised to be pretty good children. There were too many switch trees out there," Johnnie Mae said with a laugh. "If Momma couldn't get to the switch tree quick enough, then she would get the brush broom. It was much different growing up in those days than it is now."

Grady wasn't interested in sports or hunting or fishing, preferring to stay around the house. One outdoor activity Grady enjoyed was riding horses. He especially enjoyed riding with a neighbor, Clifford Holtzclaw, who became his best friend.

"'Grady loved pranks,' Holtzclaw said. 'We had some ropes tied in trees outside Lone Oak, and Grady liked to swoop down on people, yelling like Tarzan. One boy ran home screaming about a wild man he saw in the woods'" ("Grady Elder 'saw a lot, did a lot' in Nam," Ray Coleman, *The West Georgia Beacon*, June 13, 2001).

"He was under mother's feet a lot but just a good kid," recalled Johnnie Mae. His sister Carolyn observed that while Grady wasn't always interested in playing ball, he was intent on becoming a soldier early on. She said he always liked his clothes to be perfect and for his trousers to be ironed with a crease, just like a soldier or Marine wore. He even paid Carolyn fifty cents to iron them that way for him.

Grady and Clifford started school in Lone Oak and might have gone to elementary school at Grantville Brown in Coweta County for a short time.[2] But the two ended up at Luthersville High School in Meriwether County. Grady quit school in tenth grade, and Holtzclaw quit then or shortly thereafter. Grady tried to join the US Army after dropping out of school, but they sent him home since he was only sixteen. When Grady turned seventeen, his mother signed for him to join.

When Grady entered the military, Johnnie Mae was married and living in Columbus, Georgia. Her mother called one day and said she had signed the papers for Grady to join the military.

"Seemed like a million pounds hit my chest because I just could not believe that he was going to be gone somewhere where I couldn't get to him in a few minutes," Johnnie Mae said.

Soon, Grady entered the gates of Fort Jackson, South Carolina, for Basic Training, where he met Thomas Winkles.

Thomas and Grady had many adventures on the two-lane roads connecting Columbia, South Carolina, and Grantville, Georgia. Winkles recalled an eerie moment on the road between Columbia and Augusta, a long, straight highway similar to the interstate that runs between those places today. At about 3 a.m., a group of soldiers drove up on a car, flipped over, wheels still turning, in the middle of the road.

"How they turned over on that stretch of road, I don't know," said Winkles.

The soldiers jumped out and rushed to the car to provide assistance. When they looked in the car, they saw no one. They looked up and down the road and on the side of the road. Again, they saw no one. They called out, hoping for a response, but saw and heard nothing. No other car had come down the road while they were there. They looked at the car again as the tires slowly stopped spinning. It was deathly quiet. Their car was still in the middle of the road, its headlights illuminating the scene. Spooked, they slowly backed toward their car and then quickly scrambled inside. Winkles cranked the ignition and hit the gas. The passengers didn't go back to sleep for a while.

One time, they followed another group of soldiers from Fort Jackson on US Route 78 west of Athens when the first car skidded off the road, and Winkles pulled over and stopped. The GIs in his vehicle piled out to help their comrades in the other car, whose back tires were in a ditch. A tow truck wasn't an option. Soldiers weren't supposed to go more than 150 miles from the base on weekend leave, and these soldiers were unquestionably going farther than 150 miles. If the news got back to Fort Jackson, all of them could face discipline. Someone thought he saw a police car coming, so they quickly improvised. With the smallest soldier in the driver's seat, the other riders pushed the car up and out of the ditch and back onto the road before quickly resuming their trip.

While Thomas Winkles was at Fort Jackson, he made fifty-four trips to Grantville, going as fast as possible and avoiding the police. Grady Elder was with him on many of these trips. During that time, Winkles received only one speeding ticket.

Grady completed Basic Combat Training in March 1954 and Advanced Infantry Training in May 1954 with an MOS of mortarman. It appears that after he took leave, he stayed in Fort Jackson until late July, then he was sent to Germany as part of the NATO shield against possible Russian aggression. He spent his first year in Germany assigned to the 22nd Infantry Regiment and his second year as part of the 373rd Armored Infantry Battalion. An armored infantry battalion is a group of infantry soldiers who go into battle in armored personnel carriers, allowing them more mobility and protection.

After Grady Elder finished at Fort Jackson, South Carolina, Winkles never heard from him again.

Winkles never saw Grady Elder because Grady was on the way to Germany, where he served for almost two years. Johnny Mae recalled that he planned to make a vocation out of the military. "He was going to be a lifer," she said.

The family received letters and occasional phone calls from Grady. "He loved Germany," his sister Carolyn said—until the day he witnessed something that he couldn't forget, the first tragedy in his young life.

Johnny Mae said he was working at an office on base in Germany, and he walked to his workplace each morning. Along the way, he had made friends with a German boy who started meeting him every morning as he walked. They would visit a local bar to get coffee. One morning after the youngster had met Grady and was on his way to school, he crossed the street without looking and was struck by a passing vehicle. Grady rushed to the little boy's side, but nothing was to be done.

"He was not himself for a long time after that," Carolyn said.

In August 1957, Grady returned to the United States and was assigned to the 29th Infantry Division at Fort Benning. A regiment of the 29th Infantry Division had been the first unit to land on Omaha Beach on D-Day, June 6, 1944.

More importantly, Grady was closer to home and a young lady he'd met in Grantville, Elaine Rigsby, who was commonly known as Sally. She had grown up around Grantville and apparently met Grady there. While the circumstances of their first meeting are murky, one family story has it that they met at the Grantville swimming pool. When Grady came home from Fort Jackson on the weekend, he often brought friends. They went into Grantville on Saturday night, and Grady and Sally might have met on one of these outings. Regardless of how they met, they must have stayed in contact while Grady was in Germany. On September 6, 1957, Grady Elder wed sixteen-year-old Elaine Rigsby in a double ceremony with his sister Carolyn and Tommy Floyd.

Tommy had served in the Army with Grady but had since left military service. Over the next nine years, Grady and Sally had five children: Cheryl, Steve, Tim, Donna, and James.

"Grady loved children," recalled Carolyn. "He loved my kids like he loved his, and there was a lot of love there."

In 1959, Grady was stationed at Fort Benning when his first child, Cheryl, was born, and a second tragedy shook his life. Sally had gone to Columbus to pick him up for the weekend, taking infant Cheryl with her. Grady had invited a friend home so they could go fishing. As they neared home, the guys stopped at a bait store. The men went into the store while Sally and the baby waited in the car's back seat. The car began to roll down an incline. Sally was frantic. Grady's friend, out of the store first, tried to get into the driver's seat to stop the car. But the vehicle rolled over on the incline and crushed Grady's friend, killing him instantly. Sally and the baby were shaken but unhurt. Grady was devastated after seeing another friend die in another freak accident with an automobile.

In 1959, shortly after this second tragedy in Grady Elder's life, the US Army sent him to Iceland. Grady returned in 1960 and was back at Fort Benning until 1962, where his next two children, Steve and Tim, were born. Then it was back to Europe. While in Germany, he added an MOS as an Armor Intelligence specialist. In 1964, he was at Fort Meade, Maryland, where his fourth child, Donna, was born. In 1965, he was transferred to Fort Knox, Kentucky, where he received his GED and became part of the 33rd Armored Regiment. His final child, James, was born at Fort Knox. Grady's military records indicate that during his military career, he served as an assistant squad leader, squad leader, personnel specialist, mortarman, and rifleman, even doing duty with the honor guard at Fort Meade.

American Marines entered Vietnam in March of 1965. They were there to help the Army of the Republic of Vietnam (ARVN) in their battle against home-grown communist insurgents (Viet Cong) and North Vietnamese Army (NVA) troops slipping into South Vietnam via the infamous Ho Chi Minh Trail. Initially, they defended airfields. However, unwilling to stay on the defensive, the Marines went on the offense. By the fall of 1965, the 1st Cavalry Division, the 173rd Airborne Brigade, the First Brigade of the 101st Airborne, and the 2nd Brigade of the 1st Infantry Division (Big Red One) had all been ordered to Vietnam. The war had begun. In March 1966, Grady Elder was stationed at Fort Knox, Kentucky, when he received orders sending him to the Recon Platoon of the 2nd Brigade of the 1st Infantry Division, located in and around Bien Hoa, South Vietnam.

Before shipping out, Grady took a thirty-day leave and caught up with all of his family before getting Sally back to Grantville with their kids. Grady had done a lot of office work in Germany, but he told Johnnie Mae that he would be in the field in Vietnam.

"The hardest thing that we ever did was to tell each other goodbye," Johnnie Mae said ruefully.

Grady left for Vietnam from the Atlanta airport. Johnnie Mae was living in Jonesboro then, so she went to the airport to see him off. Johnnie Mae couldn't find him. She had him paged, but he never showed. Later, he wrote her a letter saying he had heard the page, "but he just couldn't come. He couldn't say goodbye again."

Grady Elder left for Vietnam on May 25. Upon arrival in Vietnam on May 27, Grady was tasked as a squad leader in the Reconnaissance Platoon, Headquarters and Headquarters Company, 2nd Battalion, 28th Infantry Regiment of the 1st Infantry Division. The 28th Infantry was known as the "Black Lions of Cantigny" or just the "Black Lions." This name was acquired in World War I when the regiment captured the town of Cantigny from the Germans. The 1st Infantry Division was known as the Big Red One because of the red number 1 on their division patch. The Recon Platoon was considered a plum assignment, and the men assigned to it were top-notch.

From Hogansville, Georgia, Thomas Stewart Cameron arrived in Vietnam in December 1965, six months before Grady. He had attended St. Paul's AME Church in Hogansville and served as the junior Sunday school superintendent at the church while still in high school. Cameron attended and graduated from West End School, Hogansville's black school during the days of segregation, in 1964. While not a standout athlete, he worked as a West End basketball team trainer, was in the school chorus, and won a typing competition by typing more than one hundred words a minute (Coleman, 2001). After graduation, he joined the military and discovered he had what it took to be a soldier. Thomas was selected to be a 3rd US Infantry Regiment member and became one of the guards at the Tomb of the Unknown Soldier. As part of this unit, he was involved in various ceremonies at Lyndon Johnson's White House. However, in the fall of 1965, Thomas volunteered for Vietnam. In December 1965, he was assigned to the same Recon unit that Grady would be assigned to six months later.

Grady Elder would have little time to acclimate to Vietnam. "The day he joined recon, Grady went out on his first ambush patrol. We would leave just as it was getting dark, wait until it was pitch black, then move to our real ambush site," said Luther Kantner, another member of the Recon Platoon. "Waiting in an ambush site was worse than the fighting. The wait and nerve-racking silence was sometimes more than a man could handle" (Coleman, 2001).

> *'I remember Sgt. Elder was always joking, and that made things a little better,' Kantner said. 'In the few days he was there, Grady did a lot and saw a lot. The Recon platoon was in the field on operations for about 300 days [per year]. A lot of time would be humping the bush.'* ["Humping the bush" meant doing a lot of walking or patrolling through the jungles and/or countryside.] *'Grady was not one to mince words,' Kantner said. 'If you were doing something wrong, he would tell you. He took his squad leader position very seriously. We listened to him, even when we thought he was wrong. He would hear what we had to say, and if we were right, he would say okay, we will do it your way' (Coleman, 2001).*
>
> *'I remember one day, just before June 11, we were searching for VC. We came to a trail with hills on both sides. The lieutenant said to go down the trail. Grady didn't think this was a good idea and told the lieutenant that he thought if we went down that trail, we might get ambushed. The lieutenant didn't care, and he told Grady to get his a-- down that trail,' Kantner said. 'Grady said okay and told us to saddle up and hit the trail. The lieutenant watched us until we were out of sight. Grady held up his hand for us to stop and told us to get off of that trail. He said, 'Screw the lieutenant. I am not going to get any of my men killed,' Kantner said. A large force of VC was watching the trail, ready to ambush any troop foolish enough to go down it." (Coleman, 2001).*

The beginning of June 1966 saw intelligence coming in about a Viet Cong force planning to cut one of the all-important roads in the Binh Long province of III Corps, and Operation El Paso II began. "Both operations [Operation El Paso I and II] were in the same area around Loc Ninh. In the days before the battle, we patrolled the rubber plantation and the jungle that bordered it. We saw many signs of the VC and killed a few, and their booby traps took out a few of us,' said Kantner" (Coleman, 2001).

June 11 dawned with heavy fog. The plan was for units of the 2nd Battalion to conduct a sweep through the Michelin Rubber

Plantation northwest of Loc Ninh. Though the operation started late due to the weather, the Black Lions soon found the enemy. The Viet Cong were dug in on two hills outside the rubber plantation, Hill 177 and Hill 150. [The hills were numbered by their height in meters above sea level.] Company A was attacked first, and Company C moved to reinforce. The Recon Platoon was ordered to support Company C and assault Hill 177.

Kantner has written about the June 11 battle in the *West Georgia Beacon* and online at the Vietnam Virtual Wall. The battle that killed Elder and Cameron started about 7:30 the morning of June 11, with Company A taking small arms fire, which wounded three men. Company A and Company C were under heavy Viet Cong fire as the intensity of the battle picked up. The Recon Platoon had to be airlifted from their base in Lai Khe with ammunition to reinforce the other units. "Recon killed three VC on the way to drop off the ammo," Kantner said. "Recon linked up with Company C and began to move up a hill. The VC opened up with intense automatic rifle fire and grenades. With no cover to help shield them against the relentless fire, the Recon Platoon and part of C Company rushed toward a trench. Unbeknownst to them, Viet Cong still had a machine gun set up at one end of the trench, and the Recon soldiers died almost instantly" (Coleman, 2001).

"Kantner survived the June 11th battle only because he was knocked down and out by an enemy shell as he scrambled for safety in the VC trench. When he came to, lying behind some coconut trees, the eighteen Recon soldiers were dead" (Coleman, 2001). Kantner said a Sergeant Lofton, missing from Recon, was found dead tied to a tree with communications wire the next day. He had been tortured. Staff Sergeant Glen Lofton was from Lyford, Texas. (Vietnam Virtual Wall, Battle of Loc Ninh-Hill 177.)

Both hills were taken, and the American forces counted ninety-eight enemy bodies, but they were also forced to retrieve thirty-four American soldiers who had lost their lives. Eighteen of those soldiers were from the Recon Platoon. Five men were from Georgia, with one each from Troup and Coweta Counties.

The 1st Infantry Division Information Office issued this press release on June 18, 1966.

Troops of the 2nd Battalion, 28th Infantry recently accounted for nearly one hundred dead Viet Cong in bitter fighting north of the Loc Ninh airstrip.

Loc Ninh, a hamlet located in the northern sector of Binh Long Province, is a day's march from the Cambodia border. The center of a once busy and productive rubber plantation, Loc Ninh has an airstrip that is one of the last jumping-off places for allied operations against the Viet Cong in the area.

Increased Allied offensives from this airstrip against the already diminishing supply lines have forced the Viet Cong to make a desperate attempt to isolate this outpost. In the past, Loc Ninh has been protected only by a Special Forces camp.

From the Third Brigade Headquarters at Lai Khe, the Big Red One troops flew to Loc Ninh on Air Force C-130 troop transport planes. The primary mission was to defend the airstrip at all costs.

For nine days the 28th Infantry built fortifications, bunkers, barbed wire barriers and set out to guard against a surprise attack. The only sign of VC in the area came on June 4th when the Viet Cong dropped several mortar rounds on the airstrip inflicting light casualties and lightly damaging a few aircraft. On June 11th, Company A began a routine sweep to the north of the airstrip. After traveling some 1500 meters they were halted by heavy sniper fire. As the second platoon from Charlie Company moved forward to aid Company A, the firing subsided.

Anxious to maintain their contact, the men pursued the fleeing Viet Cong.

As Private First Class Michael B. Wegrzyn of Tulsa, Oklahoma, point man for Charlie Company's Second Platoon, led his column down a slope, 25 Viet Cong were spotted. "I opened up on them full automatic, and suddenly the whole woods screamed with rifle fire," Wegrzyn said.

The 1st Infantry troops fought with everything they had, including artillery. Soon an urgent call was sent back for ammunition, and the Reconnaissance Platoon was sent to resupply and reinforce. As the Recon Platoon approached the Viet Cong again ceased firing and pulled back. [Grady is in action with this sentence, bringing ammunition and reinforcing C Company.]

The First Platoon of Charlie Company and the Recon Platoon formed a skirmish line and pursued. As the two Platoons advanced, it became evident that the VC had been in the area for some time since trenches had been dug and fortified with rubber trees.

Halfway up the hill, the Viet Cong made a last-ditch effort to stop the advancing Americans. Through a volley of bullets and grenades, the Big Red One troops dived into a trench toward their front. Under a hail of hostile fire, Charlie Company's Second Platoon joined the men in the trench. [Grady's platoon is now in the trench with the Viet Cong machine gun at one end.]

For two and one half hours the battered force resisted valiantly. Wave after wave of Viet Cong were engaged and shattered. Then the artillery started again, and it was soon over.

In the eerie silence that followed the battle, the men of the 28th Infantry counted ninety-four Viet Cong dead and indications that many more dead or wounded troops had been dragged away.

"Yes we got our nose bloodied," Pfc. Wegrzyn mused as he nursed his own wound the next day. "But we hurt them, we hurt them bad."

While the machine gun killed most of the Recon men sheltered in the trench, Grady Elder died of fragment wounds to his head, likely resulting from an artillery or grenade explosion, either as he scrambled into the trench or after he had already settled into it.

Gary Kellerman, a member of the Black Lions, left a commemoration of the Recon Platoon on the VVMF website dedicated to one of the platoon's members who also died that day, Tommy Chatburn of Oregon.

Tommy was with the Recon Platoon, and the day he died,

> *the Recon Platoon was ambushed and most of them were killed. It was a terrible shock to the men of the Black Lions because too many a new member* [of the Black Lions] *the Recon Platoon was larger than life, they were every man's dream of what a combat soldier should look like, as well as act like, and if they could be ambushed, or, worse yet, killed, then the rest of us were in real trouble. It was a harsh eye-opener to start a one-year tour of duty in a front line infantry battalion in Vietnam in 1966.*

Grady Elder had been in Vietnam for only twelve days.

On Sunday, June 12, 1966, soldiers visited the Elder family home outside Grantville. Carolyn had just returned from church. As she entered the house, a neighbor told her that her phone had been ringing. As she spoke with her neighbor, the phone rang again. It was her father with the news.

A week later, Grady returned home. Johnnie Mae desperately wanted to greet his body when it got to the Atlanta airport, but her family wouldn't let her go, worried about how upset she might be seeing her brother that way since she was pregnant. Nevertheless, shortly after Grady's funeral, she lost the baby.

The casket lay in the Elders' home for twenty-four hours before the funeral. It was covered by glass, and the body wasn't recognizable to family members since gauze was all around his head and over his eyes. Carolyn's husband, Tommy Floyd, got the casket open and pulled the glove off Grady's right hand. Grady had lost part of his index finger in an accident when he was growing up, and the family wanted someone to make sure it was him. Unfortunately, they confirmed what they already knew.

There was no doubt about his death, and five children were now fatherless.

On Sunday, June 19, 1966, the funeral was held at Asbury United Methodist Church in Harrisonville in western Troup County.

"Clifford Hotzclaw could not bear to attend Grady's funeral" (Coleman, 2001). Grady Elder was laid to rest in Myrtle Hill Cemetery in Hogansville. His tombstone read, "He gave his life for others near Loc Ninh, South Vietnam." Grady Elder was thirty years old.

On the other side of Hogansville, another family was also mourning. Another son had fallen on June 11 from the same area of Georgia. Thomas Cameron, who had also scrambled into the trench that day to be greeted by bullets, returned to Hogansville the same day as Grady.

"Louella Elder, Grady's mother, visited Althea 'Sweetenin'' Cameron, Thomas's mother, before their sons' funerals. No one knows what the two mothers said to each other. The Elders sent a heart-shaped wreath of white roses to the Camerons, like the one they purchased for Grady's funeral" (Coleman, 2001).

Three years later, Sally Elder bought a house and moved her family to Franklin Highway in Newnan. She took a job in a textile mill, met Charles Turner, and remarried. The marriage didn't work out, and they quickly separated. In June 1969, Sally went to Florida with a friend for a short holiday. They were heading home north on Interstate 75 near Perry, Georgia. It was 4:30 a.m. It's unclear who was driving, but officers believe the driver fell asleep. The car went down an embankment, and both occupants were thrown, although the friend survived. Three years and twelve days after Grady's death, Sally, twenty-eight, was dead as well. The accident left five children without either parent.

The children were briefly in foster care before Grady's parents secured custody and brought them back to the land where their father had grown up. Although James died in 1972, Luella continued to raise the children. As of 2021, Grady and Sally Elder had eleven grandchildren.

Grady and Sally are both resting at Myrtle Hill Cemetery in Hogansville. Just down the road, Thomas Stewart Cameron is buried at West View Cemetery. The two cemeteries are 1.7 miles apart—four minutes by car, twelve minutes by bicycle, and a thirty-three-minute walk. One of the many tragedies of their story is that although Grady and Thomas could die together in the same trench in South Vietnam, they couldn't be buried in the same cemetery in the United States.

"Tragic tales rarely do make sense."

** See end notes in the appendix for additional details.*

***Born**: May 11, 1936*
***Home of record**: Grantville, Georgia*
***Died**: June 11, 1966, in Binh Long province of South Vietnam*
***Coweta servicemen who died in the same province**: None*
***Unit on death**: Recon PLT, HHC, 2nd BN, 28th Infantry, 1st Infantry Division*
***Decorations:** Purple Heart, Good Conduct Medal 2nd Award, National Defense Service Medal, Army of Occupation Medal, Vietnam Service Medal*
***Buried:** Myrtle Hill Cemetery, Hogansville*
***Vietnam Memorial, Washington, DC:** Panel 8E Line 36*

Sources
Interview with James Elder, son
Interview with Carolyn Elder Floyd, sister
Interview with Johnnie Mae Elder Melton, sister
Interview with Deborah Olmstead, niece of Elaine Rigsby Elder
Interview with Ernest Elder, brother
Interview with Thomas Winkles, US Army
Assistance from Chris Swanson, Newnan High School History Department
Assistance from John McKibben, McKibben Funeral Home, Hogansville
Assistance from Ray Coleman, researcher
Assistance from Marty Hohmann, journalist

References
The Virtual Wall Vietnam Veterans Memorial. "Battle of Loc Ninh-Hill 177." Accessed January 10, 2022. http://www.virtualwall.org/units/BattleofLocNinh1966.htm
Vietnam Veterans Memorial Fund. "Wall of Faces: Thomas Chatburn." Accessed January 10, 2022. https://www.vvmf.org/Wall-of-Faces/8815/THOMAS-W-CHATBURN-III/
Headquarters: 1st Infantry Division Information Office, June 18-19, 1966,
Staff Reports. "Viet Nam Widow Killed in Auto Accident Here."

Houston Home Journal, June 26, 1969.
https://gahistoricnewspapers.galileo.usg.edu/search/pages/results/?proxtext=Houston+Home+Journal%2C+June+26%2C+1969
Coleman, Ray. "Cameron saw Vietnamese as people seeking Liberty." *The West Georgia Beacon*, February 28, 2001.
Coleman, Ray. "Grady Elder 'saw a lot, did a lot' in Nam." *The West Georgia Beacon*, June 13, 2001.
Coffelt Database, "Grady Elder." Accessed April 5, 2019.
http://coffeltdatabase.org/index.php

CHAPTER THREE

Daniel Zachary Post

Newnan, Georgia

Zack, a day has not passed that I haven't thought of you in 46 years. All those firefights and patrols, I never worried about my back or flank, I knew you would be there, and you were. I left 6 4-66, and you were KIA 6-31-66. Buddy, it still eats at me.

—Corporal Gary Taylor

Twelve miles from the South Vietnamese city of Danang sits a hill designated as Hill 22. The hill was not large or particularly impressive. In reality, it was only called a hill because of the seemingly limitless number of flat rice paddies surrounding it. In 1965, Hill 22 had been the center of a brutal struggle between the 1st Battalion, 1st Marines, and the Viet Cong. As a result, it already contained an extensive set of bunkers and trench lines. Nevertheless, Corporal Post and the rest of the 2nd Platoon of M Company, 3rd Battalion of the 3rd Marine Division, set up on Hill 22 in late June 1966.

Corporal Daniel Post, one of the squad leaders in the 2nd Platoon, was a natural leader. He was known for giving his opinion on any plans involving his squad and then following orders, regardless of whether he agreed with them. The 2nd Platoon's mission was to patrol the area and secure the west side of M Company's area of responsibility. The 2nd Platoon was joined by a security platoon, a light section of tanks, and an engineering team that swept for mines. Corporal Post was about a month away from rotating home when the 2nd Platoon settled in on Hill 22. The move to the hill was good for his platoon, as they had moved around frequently and were ready to settle down in a secure spot. As Post's platoon set up perimeter security, checked defensive positions, cleaned their weapons, and started to break out their C-rations, it would have been extraordinary if he had not started thinking about going home. Corporal Post, in Vietnam parlance, was "short"—extremely short. He was so short that he used a rifle-cleaning patch as a poncho, as soldiers used to joke in Vietnam. He didn't have much time left before he boarded the "freedom bird" and headed back to "the world." The "world" was the land of the big PX and flush toilets, otherwise known as the United States of America!

Daniel Zachary Post Jr. was born on January 16, 1943, to Daniel Zachary Post Sr. and Jane Ansley Manget of Newnan. Exactly which Daniel Post fathered the boy is a genealogical mystery. One graduated from Newnan High School, probably in the class of 1932. Some family members believe the Newnan High School graduate was not the Daniel Post who married Ansley Manget but was part of another Post family who also lived in Coweta County. Ansley was the daughter of Victor and Lucille Manget. In Newnan, the Manget family were farmers and cotton brokers. Victor Manget was a prominent farmer from one of the older families in Newnan. He and his brother had a cotton brokerage next to the present-day downtown Newnan post office.

Daniel and Ansley appear to have had a stormy marriage, even after the birth of their oldest child, daughter Danna. Three years later, Daniel came along, but that didn't solve Daniel and Ansley's troubles. Shortly after Daniel's birth, the couple left Newnan and moved to Brownsville, Texas, to work in the cotton business and perhaps get a fresh start.

After several years in Brownsville, Dan and Ansley had a third child they called Lady Ansley.

Little is known about Daniel's life between the family's move to Brownsville and the time he turned sixteen. A family story circulated that Dan didn't speak until age two, perhaps due to the unrest in the family or some developmental issues. Regardless, the family's experience in Brownsville was hard to pin down until Danna turned eighteen and Daniel sixteen, when their family made a move that would dramatically change the two teenagers' lives.

In 1959, Daniel Sr., Ansley, and Lady Ansley headed south to Mexico City. It appears they were still following the cotton business, but for whatever reason, they didn't take the two older siblings with them. While Lady Ansley went with her parents to Mexico, Dan headed to Staunton Military Academy in Staunton, Virginia. Danna ended up in Newnan, Georgia, and was a senior at Newnan High School. Danna settled in with her widowed grandmother, Lucille Manget. Her paternal grandmother, Nell Kernan, also moved into the house to assist.

Danna tried to adapt to Newnan High School. A small, attractive girl with a dark complexion, she immediately caught the attention of the school's young men. Elizabeth Farmer, Danna's third cousin and a year younger, remembered her coming to Newnan High School and "fitting right into the innocent mode with the rest of us, but we just knew that she was a little wilder than we were." Elizabeth recalled that Danna's family was never discussed. "The little time that Danna was here, she never seemed to miss them at all. She never mentioned her parents or her brother or sister. I think Danna was looking for security from her family situation," Elizabeth said. "It was strange, looking back, that neither her family nor Dan ever came to visit."

Midway through her senior year, Danna dropped out of school and never graduated.

Daniel went in a completely different direction by entering one of the most prominent military schools in the southern United States, Staunton Military Academy. Daniel followed in a long line of distinguished graduates from the school's 116-year history. While the events that took Daniel to Staunton Military Academy are unclear, it appears that he thrived while there. The 1962 yearbook had a senior picture of Daniel in uniform. Each graduate also had a personalized inscription. His read,

Daniel Zachary Post, Jr., 'Dan,' Sergeant C Company; Military Ribbon 1. The quotation underneath read,

"Dan liked basketball but did not like to get up for reveille... algebra II was his best subject, but he found biology hard... his ideal at SMA was Captain Odell... future plans include Texas Christian University."

Daniel graduated from the school in the spring of 1962. It is unclear where he lived, what he did for the next five months, or what happened to his plans to attend TCU, because on October 29, 1962,

Daniel Post became a United States Marine and started his career with the First Recruit Training Battalion in San Diego, California. He remained in San Diego until January 1963, when he reported to Camp Pendleton. Like all Marines, he first trained as a rifleman and became an assistant automatic rifleman, a Marine who carries extra ammunition for the machine gunner. In June 1963, he was assigned to Company B, 1st Battalion, 4th Marines, 1st Marine Brigade at Kaneohe, Hawaii. In March of 1965, Daniel was promoted to corporal and given command of a fire team, the four-man unit that is the smallest in the US military. A Marine squad of twelve men would include three fire teams.

Daniel deployed to Chu Lai, the Republic of Vietnam, on May 28, 1965, a few months after the first Marines went ashore at Danang. On June 7, he transferred to the 3rd Marine Division headquarters security platoon. August 11 found Daniel back in California and the Marine Corps base at Barstow. Daniel's enlistment would have been up in October, but it appears that he was involuntarily extended. While such extensions were usually avoided, the military can prevent someone from leaving service at the end of his enlistment if he has specific skills or they require additional men for whatever reason. So the end of October found Daniel a fire team leader in the 2nd Platoon of M Company, 3rd Battalion, 3rd Marines, and back in Vietnam. Company M made its headquarters in the village of An Trac southeast of Danang and was involved in Operation Georgia in May of 1966.

A month-long operation around An Hoa, Operation Georgia involved helicopter insertions and foot patrols to track down the elusive yet deadly military arm of the National Liberation Front (NLF), nicknamed the Viet Cong (Vietnamese Communists). Once the unit stood down from this operation, M Company became part of the Danang airport's security element. They provided relief to the company with hot meals, guard duty every third day, training, and rest. However, this stand-down was interrupted by problems with the local ARVN forces, and the Marines were forced out to protect the bridge east of Danang to ensure its safety. The Marines couldn't have this bridge destroyed, as it would cut off the most direct route into Danang and the Marine headquarters and reinforcements. Shortly after the Marines' relief from bridge duty, in late June, they moved to secure Hill 22. The Command Summary of the 3rd Battalion, 3rd Marines almost monotonously communicates the actions the unit was involved in during this period—ambushes, various mines and booby traps, sniper fire, American artillery and mortar fire, incidents with small groups of Viet Cong, and interaction with civilians. The Command Summary can't convey the camaraderie, the focus, the insects, the weariness, the fear, the heat, the smell, the noise, and the death. Paper and pencil can never do those things justice; the only people who can describe those things are the people who were there.

Corporal Post was a fire team leader and, at other times, a squad leader. Patrick Kahler, 2nd Platoon leader and company executive officer (XO) in 1966, explained that the movement depended on rank. Corporal Post was designated squad leader on February 1, 1966, when no qualified sergeant was available to fill the slot. When Sergeant Dacey joined the platoon, Post returned to being a fire team leader, as a sergeant typically commanded a squad.

Dennis Ray arrived in Vietnam in January 1966 and was soon assigned to Corporal Post's squad. He described Post as a "real professional." He remembered Post as a baseball fan, especially of the Los Angeles Dodgers. Ray believed that Post became a Dodgers fan while stationed at Camp Pendleton in California. Post constantly checked the *Stars and Stripes* for baseball scores and statistics. Ray said that one of the other squad leaders, a man named McCloud from Alabama, used to call Daniel "Wally Post," a reference to a 1950s baseball player.

Ray vividly remembered his first-night ambush with Post as the squad leader. Daniel had eight to ten Marines, half of whom were "newbies." He set them up along a berm in a rice paddy so they would be in the water. He set the watch, and the squad settled in for the night. Around 2 a.m., Ray awoke to the sound of screaming and gunfire. One of the newbies, a radiotelegraph operator or RTO, had opened up on some Viet Cong moving through the area without waking everyone else first. Post was most unhappy. He lambasted the new RTO and vehemently instructed him on how an ambush should be conducted. Post wanted to ensure that the lesson was understood. Lives could depend on it.

Gary Taylor also served with Post. He painted Post as a

courageous young American.

> *The patrol moved out, leaving the village perimeter, staying on the village trails through a few villages about 2 or 3 klicks. As we exited the last village, a large rice paddy was to our front, 400 or 500 yards wide. We decided not to cross the wide paddy, for they were wet and flooded, the mud was waist-deep. Deciding to stay on the dikes and close to the village woodline we had just exited. As the patrol began zigzagging the dikes approximately 100 yards out, we started taking flanking fire (small arms) from our left flank. Not wanting to be pinned down, we continued to move; the S/Sgt called artillery and then yelled "arty on the way." I heard the incoming and yelled, "Artillery—!" I never got "in" out. Two rounds landed 30 yards to our right flank, fortunately in the waist-deep mud. Unfortunately, we were using old French maps and were known to be off several 100 meters. We did take two casualties; CPL Johnson was hit in the jaw just in front of the ear. I was hit across the bridge of my nose, impairing my vision for a few moments.*
>
> *CPL Johnson had a two-inch hole in his jaw and needed to be Med Evacuated quickly. Knowing this, we decided to make for a burnt out pagoda location on some high ground and would provide a LZ for the chopper. The pagoda was some 100 yards away to our right front. Knowing this, we would have to run the paddy dikes and the last leg of the run towards the pagoda. We started taking frontal fire in addition to the left flanking fire.*
>
> *To compound matters, the other new men had hunkered down and were not returning fire. We did not have suppression fire. I climbed out of the trench and went behind them, standing I yelled telling them they were United States Marines and if they didn't start returning fire, I would shoot every son-of-a-b--- there! Needless to say, they began returning fire and providing some suppression fire. I went back to the trench, I muttered something to Sanchez, dropped my rifle, and started running out to Bates. I felt someone kick my foot, but never looking back, I/we ran to*

> *Bates. I approached his left side while the other Marine approached Bates' right side. I looked in the eyes of the Marine with me, as we grabbed Bates and said, "This f----- sucks" - it was CPL D. Z. Post. The two of us, along with Corpsman Seavers, carried Bates back to the pagoda position with rounds landing all around us, hitting the dikes and paddy.*

This dramatic incident wasn't Taylor's only experience with Post. He continued:

> *We were out on patrol, and our orders were to set up an ambush it was the rainy season, and the word rain doesn't begin to describe it. You couldn't see your hand in front of you, it was pitch dark nor could you hear anything, you try to walk heel to toe in the event you step on something you may be able to retrace your step. Being the squad/platoon point man I had walked point literally hundreds of times (discovering numerous booby traps and leading the Platoon into only one ambush) however this particular night I couldn't do it, I had the shakes, I literary was trembling and I could not control myself. When I stopped the patrol I called Sgt. Darcey up along with Zack. I told Darcey I couldn't lead the patrol, Sgt. Darcey was new, really didn't know us and he was giving me a hard time and insisting on continuing to lead the patrol and it got rather heated, Zack stepped in on my behalf and informed Darcy that I had led many patrols and not to question my ability. Zack then called his fire team up and told me to take the rear. This is just another example of Cpl. Post's leadership. Zack and I never did talk about the incident because we both knew and had the highest respect for each other's ability as United States Marines. I was known as a joker of sorts and I did at times harass Zack but he always took it in stride, he gave as well as he took.*

Lieutenant Kahler, Daniel's platoon leader, described the usual routine for a twilight patrol.

> *Later in the morning, the patrol activity for the next day was briefed. Late in the afternoon, before sundown and the departure of night patrols, we played volleyball. The volleyball game was organized by the ARVN Sgt. Major who was our liaison with ARVN forces; he was at the most 5'4" tall and a parachutist who had jumped into Dien Bien Phu with the French Forces and was later captured and was a Prisoner of War, then released to South Viet-Nam. He returned to the military and had only known a lifetime of war but he loved volleyball. Different squads played each afternoon a much-needed break from the reality of war.*

On July 31, 1966, Corporal Post's fire team was assigned to one such late-afternoon patrol to prevent any infiltration of the company area. Sgt. Lacy was unavailable to lead the squad that day, so Post stepped into his place. Dennis Ray said that "Corporal Post was killed on this patrol. He found a 'CAM VAO' [keep out] sign but couldn't find the booby trap and reached over to pull out the cardboard sign, and in doing so, he stepped on the device."

Lieutenant Kahler recalled it being an M-26 grenade with a fifteen-feet bursting radius. Since Daniel was right on top of it when it went off, he was critically injured. The medic assigned to Post's platoon was William "Doc" Thomas. He described his memory of that day.

> *After processing, I was finally sent to "M" Company, 3rd Bn, 3rd Marines for duty. That's when I met Dan. I was assigned to his Platoon (2nd). He and I hit it off pretty quick. We were usually on the same patrol about every 2-3 days. As a corpsman, I always had to stay with the patrol leader and the radioman, in the CP [Command Post] group. Dan was usually somewhere toward the rear in charge of a fire team. On the day he died we were on a patrol in Quang Nam province about 5-6 miles outside Da Nang. We stopped for a smoke break, so I walked back to where he and another friend (Smith, I think) were sitting and we took our break together. I left the two of them when the order to saddle up came through and the patrol resumed. In just a few minutes*

there was a loud explosion to the rear and then I heard 'corpsman up.' I made my way to the rear of the column and found it was Dan. He had stepped in a pit that was rigged with a grenade and a trip wire attached to the pin. The booby trap (pit) he stepped on must have been maybe to the side of the trail because several people had to have passed by it. He had major damage in the upper torso, head, neck, and arms. Died on me a couple of times but we were able to get him back long enough to call in a medevac chopper. He was breathing when we loaded him out but we were told later he passed away while in surgery at Da Nang. I think of him often. He told me when we first met he heard I was a good doc and asked if I would stay close to him because he was a short-timer. I think he only had 2-3 weeks left and would be going home. Was planning to enroll in some junior college that fall. As far as I know, he was the only Marine I lost. I left the company on November 20th after falling and breaking a wrist. Dan and I only served together for 5-6 weeks but I will always remember him.

Dennis Ray recalled hearing and seeing the explosion in the distance then watching as they placed Post on a medical evacuation helicopter. He heard later that Post had died at the Naval Hospital in Danang.

He had been my squad leader and team leader until the day I was put in Sgt. Kelley's squad as a team leader. Corporal Post had been on R&R in Hong Kong and had bought five or six suits as he planned to attend college [Texas Christian University] after Vietnam. He was extended 120 days and had only a few days left in the Marine Corps. His grandmother had already paid for his college. Corporal Post loved the Los Angeles Dodgers; he was always checking the Stars and Stripes *for the box scores and would talk about Wills, Koufax, and Drysdale; he was the original fanatic. I had great respect for Corporal Post, as did everyone in the Platoon. His death was a heavy loss to me and everyone who had served with him.*

According to Lieutenant Kahler, "Corporal Post was on his last patrol as he was to return to the Battalion rear the next day for processing and transfer to the United States. To have served so well and so long, his death was doubly tragic for all of us."

Daniel's death made the front page of the *Newnan Times-Herald* on August 11, 1966. Though Daniel had not been in Newnan for many years, most of his relatives still lived there. On August 18, 1966, his obituary ran in the Newnan paper.

> *Corporal Daniel Z. Post of the United States Marine Corps, died July 31 in Viet Nam, after being wounded while engaged in active duty. Graveside services were held on August 13 at Oak Hill Cemetery, with the Reverend Roger McDonald, pastor of Central Baptist Church, officiating.*
>
> *Corporal Post, who was born in Newnan in 1943, graduated from Staunton Military Academy in Staunton, Virginia. He volunteered for service in the U.S. Marine Corps in 1962 and was completing a year's tour of duty in Viet Nam. He had chosen to make a lifetime career in the Marine Corps.*
>
> *Survivors include his parents, Mr. and Mrs. Daniel Z. Post Sr. of Mexico City, Mexico; two sisters, Miss Lady Ansley Post, Mexico City, and Mrs. Danna Wilkinson, Winter Park, Florida; grandmothers, Mrs. V.E. Manget Sr. and Mrs. F.J. Kernan, both of Newnan.*

Daniel had finally returned to his birthplace but not to a reunion or celebration but rather to mourning. The day before Daniel was to return home to American baseball, his car, possibly college, or a career in the Marine Corps, he was tragically killed. Unbelievably, the family tragedy wasn't yet over. Before Daniel's death, Danna Post had married John Wilkinson of Hogansville. The two lived in Hogansville for a short time, but at the time of Daniel's death, Danna's address was Winter Park, Florida. She had gotten divorced at some point before Daniel's death, and in November of 1966, her grandmother Lucille Manget died as well. A son was born to John and Danna during their marriage, and his status is presently unknown. On February 12, 1967, more than six months after Daniel's death, Danna committed suicide. The circumstances that led to Danna's last desperate act are unclear, although 1966 had undoubtedly been a tough year for her. Conceivably, a combination of things sent her down this route: a rough childhood, separation from her parents, marriage, pregnancy followed by divorce, Daniel's death, and finally, her grandmother's death. Elizabeth Farmer felt like Danna's "world had fallen apart."

"The young people who gave it all over there never got to live out the life they wanted," said Doc Thomas. "I'm sure Dan would probably be a granddad or great-granddad by now as I am."

Today the two siblings, Danna and Daniel, are buried in the Manget family plot, along with their grandmother Lucille, in Oak Hill Cemetery in Newnan.

Born: *January 16, 1943, in Newnan, Georgia*
Home of record: *Brownsville, Texas*
Died: *July 31, 1966, in Quang Nam province of South Vietnam*
Coweta servicemen who died in the same province: *Bill Thomas, Mike Watson, Larry Pinson, and Jerry Smith*
Unit on death: *M CO, 3rd B.N., 3rd Marines, 3rd Marine Division*
Decorations: *Purple Heart, Good Conduct Medal, National Defense Service Medal, Vietnam Service Medal, Republic of Vietnam Gallantry Cross with Palm, Republic of Vietnam Campaign Medal with Device*
Buried: *Oak Hill Cemetery, Newnan*
Vietnam Memorial, Washington, DC: *Panel 09-E Line 93*

Sources:
Email and oral interviews with Elizabeth Farmer Crain, cousin
Email and oral interviews with Dennis Ray, USMC
Email interviews with Patrick Kahler, USMC
Email interviews with Gary Taylor, USMC
Email interview with William Lynn Thomas, Navy Corpsman

References
Coffelt Database, "Daniel Post." Accessed June 15, 2016. http://coffeltdatabase.org/index.php

Daniel Post, second from left

Photos courtesy of Staunton Military Academy Alumni Foundation and Patrick Kahler.

CHAPTER FOUR

Donald Steven Lowery

Newnan, Georgia

Newnan High School was so big from what we were used to. We were scared to death the first day. The first day you went to the auditorium, they told you where you went to homeroom. The auditorium was filled with kids, and it was just like...wow! We were in shock, culture shock. And that was when Newnan High School only had 900 kids. It was just a big deal for little ole country kids.

—Susan Powers Smith

The heat was unbearable. The asphalt in the parking lot seemed to absorb and radiate the heat so much that customers must have felt like they were baking in an oven. Donald Lowery had just exited the store's front door with carts of groceries, waiting as each car pulled up to be loaded. Each cart was numbered, and each woman in a vehicle had a ticket for her cart. Sometimes the women were elderly. Sometimes they were middle-aged. Occasionally, the women were young with small children. It didn't matter to Donald. He smiled and chatted with them as he loaded items into their cars. He didn't enjoy the heat, but he enjoyed helping people, even with their groceries. Not loud or boisterous, he was more composed and unassuming than most teen males. But his smile was captivating, and thanks to his upbringing, he moved easily in the adult world.

Donald Lowery worked at Colonial Grocery Store on Greenville Street, not far from the square in downtown Newnan, on the property where the Coweta County Justice Center sits today. He was heading back into the store that summer day when something across the parking lot caught his eye. It looked like trash; the wind blew it slowly across the asphalt. But there was something different about how the breeze blew the object that caught his attention. Donald ambled over to pick it up. He reached down then froze. He fingered the item and slowly brought it closer to examine it. He looked around the parking lot and saw the woman he had just assisted with her groceries. As she pulled away from the curb, Donald ran to the car and knocked on the driver's-side window.

"Ma'am," he gasped, trying to contain his excitement. Donald held up the twenty-dollar bill he had just retrieved. "Did you lose this?"

A smile broke across her face. "No, son. It looks like it might be your lucky day." She rolled up her window, drove out of the parking lot, and turned onto Greenville Street. Donald watched her go and then, clutching the bill tightly, strode into the store.

Johnny Wilson worked there as a cashier and stock boy. Already twenty-one, he was almost three years older than Donald. Johnny attended West Georgia College and worked part-time at Colonial. He had graduated from Newnan High School with Donald's older brother, Joe. Regardless of their age difference, they had quickly become friends.

"I didn't know him before he came to work at Colonial, but we just sort of hit it off," Johnny said. So seeing Donald suddenly come back into the store wasn't unusual, as Donald came in and out all the time. But that day was different.

"He came running in one day and told me to look," Johnny said. "He had a twenty-dollar bill in his hand. This was in the mid-1960s. Twenty dollars was big money then. I asked him where he had found it. He said he had found it lying in the parking lot."

The young man turned the money in to the manager, Bill Griggs, who said the money would belong to Donald if nobody claimed it.

Donald turned to Johnny with a grin. "I want you to have half of it if nobody claims it."

Johnny protested, insisting that Donald had found it and should keep it if it was unclaimed, but Donald was adamant that he would share it.

"Why do you want to give me part of it?" Johnny asked.

Momentarily taken aback, Donald looked intently at Johnny. "You are my friend."

That settled it. A few weeks later, with no claimant for the money, the manager awarded the prize to Donald. He promptly made change at a cash register and gave Johnny ten dollars, just as he had vowed to do.

"That just goes to show what kind of person he was," Johnny said.

"What kid would have told the manager he found twenty dollars in the first place?" asked Johnny's wife, Penny, as she shook her head.

Another childhood friend, David Brown, said, "You could trust him with the keys to your car."

Donald was born on July 29, 1947, to Merrell and Pat Lowery of Newnan. They didn't have a large house, but they certainly had a large family. Donald was the third of six children, who also included Elaine, Joe, Nancy, Walter, and Russell. The Lowerys lived on Happy Valley Circle, a dirt road in the Madras community of Coweta County. A farming community, Madras was extremely rural. People grew their food, kept chickens and various farm animals, and typically saw their neighbors only when visiting the local post office. Most people had at least one cow, and some made their living on a dairy farm.

"No one slept with their doors locked. A front door would be wide open at night, and no one thought anything about it," said Scotty Scott, another of Donald's childhood friends. "Everyone knew everyone else."

"Donald and I grew up together," said Bobby Jacobs, another friend. "We were country boys. We lived on Happy Valley Circle. It's about nine and a half miles around, and if I can remember, there were only ten, maybe twelve houses on the whole circle."

The Lowerys owned ten acres on Happy Valley Circle and had a milk cow, a chicken house, and a large garden. Merrell, a mechanic at Roadway Express in Atlanta, did paint and bodywork on the side at a shop in Newnan. Pat was a nurse's aide at Coweta General Hospital.

Donald's friend David Scott said that Merrell "was real mechanically inclined. He worked all the time."

As the Lowery boys grew up, they first and foremost enjoyed playing in the woods surrounding their home. Cedar Creek—a big, wide creek—was on the backside of the Lowery property, and the boys and their friends enjoyed the water during the summer.

"We loved going over there," said Scotty Scott. "We lived in that creek. You could float on an inner tube in that creek."

Joe Lowery, Donald's older brother, remembered spending time with his brother at the creek. "We would be kinda close to the road here and climb a tree and go way down into the swamp without even getting on the ground, make a loop and come back and never touch the ground, just swinging from tree to tree."

Buddy Titshaw, Donald's cousin, lived half a mile from the Lowerys. Donald was one year older than Buddy, who played with Donald and his brothers every day during the summer, climbing trees, playing army, riding bikes, hunting rabbits and squirrels, and fishing at Cedar Creek. The Lowerys also enjoyed traveling through the woods to the home of their friend Tim Cole, who liked playing in the woods as well.

"We just loved to be in the woods," said Joe Lowery. "Tim Cole was one of our best friends."

This love of the outdoors was widespread in Madras and led many boys from there into the Boy Scouts, including Donald. Camping with the Boy Scouts or just camping was always a big event.

If the boys weren't in the woods, they were playing ball. Team sports were the favorite, especially baseball, basketball, and football. The kids enjoyed the comradeship as much as playing the game. Donald wasn't big, but his childhood friend Phillip Smith described him as "a good little athlete who was really fast."

On fall days after church, the boys had to get their chores done before going out to the Sunday afternoon football game, wherever it was being held. On Saturdays in summer, someone in a pickup would get all the boys and take them to Madras school to play baseball.

"We filled that truck up," said Joe Lowery. He was usually the pitcher, and Donald was the catcher. They played teams in different areas of Coweta or southern Fulton County.

The Lowery boys also enjoyed anything transportation related. They rode bicycles in the woods and around Happy Valley Circle. Their father was a good mechanic, and the boys picked up a little of his talent. The Lowerys had an old "jalopy" in their yard. It consisted of a car frame and an engine but had no sides and no hood.

"We were all the time in the backyard, putting this old jalopy together for us to ride around in," said David Scott. "Donald and I used to take turns driving it through the backyard."

The kids also liked running to the post office to watch the train come through Madras. There was no train station in Madras, and the train barely slowed down as it went through the community. As it neared the post office, the railroad post office clerk on board would kick a bag of mail out of the train while also picking up the bag of outgoing mail from the mail crane posted alongside the track.[1]

"There was no such thing as sitting in the house watching television and playing video games. You had to invent something to play with," said Joe Lowery. "It was a good life."

During the 1950s and 1960s, Madras School encompassed first through eighth grades, and those students headed to Newnan High School for ninth through twelfth grades.

"You knew everyone in your class. You stayed with the same group for all eight years," Phillip Smith said. There were never more than 150 students in the entire school. Donald's class at Madras had thirty-one students, which was considered a large class. That group was part of the class of 1964 at Newnan High School.

When the Madras students got to Newnan High School, they were stunned by the size of the school—not only the facilities themselves but also the number of students was overwhelming. They had never seen that many students in one place before. Also, students from Madras weren't always prepared for the academics and discipline that Newnan High School demanded, as Phillip Smith explained.

> *When you went to Madras, eighth grade was a dead year because the principal was the teacher. They didn't have enough money to have a teacher for every grade, so the principal taught the eighth grade. Usually, during that last period of the day, right after lunch, from 1 p.m. until the buses arrived at 4 p.m., students were left to look after themselves. The principal would say, "Look, I got some stuff that I got to do. Y'all get a basketball, go on outside, don't*

get in no trouble, I'll check on you." You never saw him the rest of the time. Of course, kids pretty much did what you told them then.

I remember one time when I was in eighth grade, the principal said, "Hey, I need this letter mailed. Y'all walk up to the post office and mail it for me." So, me and another boy walked all the way to the Madras Post Office... It was probably a mile from the school, so we walked up Route 29. Of course, there was not near the traffic there is now, but you wouldn't dare to send a kid down the road like that today. So, of course, we piddled away the whole day, we threw rocks, and we weren't in any hurry to get back. I think we got back about lunchtime.

When David Scott was about ten, he was eating dinner with the Lowerys one day and inadvertently used the word "hell." He didn't think anything about it. Mrs. Lowery got up and asked Donald to step into the other room. When they returned, Donald tapped David on the shoulder and asked him to step out onto the porch. There, Donald told David his mother was unhappy because he'd used a cuss word at the dinner table. David was confused. This word wasn't a big deal at his home. Donald said that David wouldn't be invited back and they wouldn't be able to play together unless he apologized. David did so immediately. When he apologized, Mrs. Lowery waved her finger in his face and told him he should never do that again or he wouldn't be welcome in their house. David Scott never did that again.

Donald Lowery ended up at Newnan High School as a freshman in 1961. Buddy Titshaw arrived the following year. He occasionally saw Donald in the hall, but they didn't take classes together since they weren't in the same grade. Neither boy participated in extracurricular activities.

"Back in the early sixties, if you lived on Happy Valley Circle, there was just no way to get home from Newnan High School unless you walked, so we weren't involved in a lot of stuff," Titshaw said.

Johnny Wilson, recipient of the ten dollars Donald had so generously given him, said, "We got to be buddies." They occasionally went to parties or did the Newnan teen cruise. "On

Friday and Saturday night, you would get in your car and cruise around the Brazier Burger (Dairy Queen) and see who was there, and then you would go out on Temple Avenue and cruise around the Burger Chef and see who was there, then go back down to Brazier... just ride all night. That was about all there was to do."

When Donald turned sixteen, he got a 1950 Chevrolet Coupe with a V8, while Joe purchased a 1955 Chevrolet Bel Air. Donald and Joe enjoyed working on their cars together, recalling their younger days with the jalopy.

After Donald turned sixteen and before he left for military service, he worked at High-Brand Foods in Peachtree City and the Colonial Store in Newnan. He likely did the same work at both locations, bagging groceries and taking them to customers' vehicles.

Joe graduated from Newnan High School in 1963, moved to Marietta, and took a job at Lockheed. He joined the US Army in 1965. Donald had some trouble at Newnan High School during the 1963-1964 year and didn't graduate, although the reason for this is unknown. As Donald reported back to school in 1964-1965, many changes were happening at Newnan High School. First, longtime principal O. P. Evans was promoted to superintendent of schools. Second, Mr. Tom Hutcheson, a former Newnan High School teacher, had returned and became the next principal. Perhaps even more significant, Drake Stadium was completed in 1966. The days of playing football at Pickett Field were over, and Newnan High School would inaugurate the stadium that fall. Donald graduated with 157 of his classmates in the auditorium at Newnan High School in June of 1966. Two weeks later, he reported for Basic Combat Training at Fort Benning.

Donald was drafted during his senior year at Newnan High School. Joe was already in the military and was at Fort Bliss in Advanced Infantry Training when he got word about Donald.

"I came home on leave to see him before he went in, and that was the last time that I saw him," Joe said. After his training, Joe joined the NATO forces stationed in Germany.

Donald took the same training path as many young men on their way to Southeast Asia: Basic Training at Fort Benning during the summer of 1966 then Advanced Infantry Training at Fort Polk, Louisiana, during September and October of that year. Once he completed AIT, he returned home for a thirty-day leave before shipping out to Vietnam.

Martha Lee, who graduated with Donald from Newnan High School, thought Donald wanted to join the Army and be like his big brother Joe. "He was a great guy. Just a really nice, nice young man," she said.

While on leave, Donald spent time with his family and visited old haunts.

"Before he left, he came to visit and told me, and I guess my whole family, that he wouldn't be coming home," said Buddy Titshaw. "Maybe some people have a premonition."

The day before Donald left for Vietnam, he visited the Colonial Store. He hugged all the ladies he'd worked with.

"That was the last time that we saw him," said Elaine Moore.

Johnny Wilson remembered that visit to Colonial. "He told me, 'I'm not coming back.' I said you are, too, Don! He replied, 'I just have a strange feeling about this that I am not going to come back.' He told me that."

Jimmy Davenport, a Newnan police officer at that time, ran into Donald while he was home before going to Vietnam. As part of his patrol, Davenport checked on the skating rink behind Wadsworth Auditorium. When he went into the building one day, he saw Donald. After the initial pleasantries, Donald said, "Jimmy, I want to buy you a Coca-Cola." Jimmy remembered thinking he was the one who ought to be buying, but he let Donald buy him a soft drink. Jimmy never saw him again.

The week of Thanksgiving 1966, Donald reported to B CO, 1st BN, 27th Infantry Regiment, 25th Infantry Division. The 27th Infantry Regiment, known as the "Wolfhounds," had a long and distinguished history. Constituted in 1901, its soldiers fought during the Philippine Insurrection (1899-1902) and were sent to Siberia to help guard the Trans-Siberian Railroad as part of the Allied Expeditionary Force between 1918 and 1920. According to the Global Security website's history of the 1st Battalion, 27th Infantry Regiment, the unit got its nickname in Russia "because of its aggressive pursuit of retreating Bolshevik forces." The 27th Infantry was brought under the 25th Division's umbrella just before the attack on Pearl Harbor and fought against the Japanese onslaught that infamous Sunday in December 1941. The 25th Division fought through the Southwest Pacific during World War II and was part of the occupation of Japan after the war. They fought heroically during the Korean War (1950-1953).

When Lowery arrived in Vietnam, the 27th Infantry Regiment had been in-country slightly less than a year and was based in Cu Chi.

Lowery joined the Wolfhounds as a replacement for losses suffered in their most recent operation, code-named Attleboro. Attleboro was a massive search-and-destroy mission involving several American units. Search and destroy became one of the most significant tactics during the Vietnam War. Land troops in an area, frequently with helicopters, searched for the enemy and destroyed them.

The Wolfhounds had acquitted themselves well during the operation, especially during a three-day battle with the communist forces in late October. The operation was just wrapping up when Lowery arrived in Vietnam. He was thrown into combat a short time later and was part of Operation Cedar Falls in January of 1967. This hammer-and-anvil operation was largely successful. This tactic involved placing a unit in a defensible position, the anvil, then having another unit, the hammer, drive the enemy into the anvil unit.

Lowery was slightly wounded in December 1966 or January 1967 and received a Purple Heart. He didn't tell anyone at home about his injury, so it must be assumed that it wasn't serious. Joe Lowery thinks the injury had something to do with Donald's leg, but on February 1, he was out on patrol with no known complications.

That day, Donald Lowery was the point man on a patrol when a sniper ambushed them. Donald was shot in the neck, and after contact with the enemy was broken, he was evacuated by helicopter to the Third Field Hospital in Saigon. Unfortunately, the round traveled through his spine, and he was paralyzed.

The Red Cross notified Joe, with the US Army in Germany, about Donald's wound. The Red Cross promised to keep him posted on Donald's condition. The family also received notification, but no one in Newnan heard from Donald while he was in the hospital. That news arrived soon enough. Donald had died on February 15. Joe was sent home from Germany and arrived in Newnan at the same time as his younger brother.

News of Donald Lowery's death swept through Newnan. The town was stunned.

"Somebody came in the [Colonial] store and told us about his death. It was really sad," said Elaine Moore.

Phillip Smith heard about it while attending West Georgia College.

Nine months before, Donald Lowery had been attending Newnan High School. Now, people were coming to McKoon Funeral Home to pay their respects.

"I didn't want to believe that it was him," said Buddy Titshaw. "So when they got his body home, he was at McKoon's, and they let immediate family see him. I wanted to see, so… it was him. It was bad."

"I remember going to the funeral home when they had his wake," Johnny Wilson said. "I remember how distraught his mother was. I stayed a couple of hours because there were so many people. I remember seeing kids from the store and his family there."

Donald Lowery had a military funeral on Wednesday, February 22, 1967, and was interred at Oak Hill Cemetery.

Bobby Jacobs, one of Donald Lowery's childhood buddies, had gone into the Navy at age seventeen and had done three tours of duty off the coast of South Vietnam. "When I was off the coast of Vietnam, I got a letter from a friend and a picture telling me that Donald had been killed. They sent me a picture of the gravesite." Jacobs was bewildered at the loss of his friend at such a young age.

When he moved back to Newnan in 1998, Jacobs learned that the gymnasium at the old Madras school had been dedicated to Donald. When they built the new school, they didn't move the dedication plaque or rededicate the gym. That didn't sit well with Jacobs, who felt the schools had forgotten Lowery. That was when he decided to do something.

Jacobs proceeded to gain the support of the local VFW and American Legion. He contacted the school system but couldn't seem to make any headway. Then he contacted Randolph Collins, the county commissioner for that part of Coweta. Collins worked to get Happy Valley Circle dedicated to Lowery and Tim Cole. He then continued to pursue the Madras school issue with the school board.

He attended multiple school board meetings, trying to get the Lowery dedication brought up, without success.

> *I could see the writing on the wall; something just wasn't right. I think it had to do with the superintendent. He had in his mind that we wanted to name the gymnasium Lowery something, and he didn't want to do that. And I could understand. I went down and talked to him and explained it, we just wanted a rededication, the picture, the plaque, and then I had his support.*

Thanks to Bobby Jacobs and others, the Madras Middle School gymnasium was once again dedicated to Donald Lowery. Happy Valley Circle is now much less rural and with paved roads but in many ways still the same place where Donald Lowery grew up. Now dedicated to Donald Lowery and Tim Cole of Madras, the road recalls their sacrifice for this country.

** See end notes in the appendix for additional details.*

***Born**: July 29, 1947, in Newnan, Georgia*
***Home of record**: Newnan, Georgia*
***Died**: February 15, 1967, in Hau Nghia province of South Vietnam*
***Coweta servicemen who died in the same province**: Leavy Solomon*
***Unit on death**: B CO, 1st BN, 27th Infantry, 25th Infantry Division*
***Decorations:** Bronze Star, Purple Heart (2), National Defense Service Medal, Vietnam Service Medal, Vietnam Military Merit Medal, Vietnam Gallantry Cross with Palm, Republic of Vietnam Campaign Medal*
***Buried:** Oak Hill Cemetery, Newnan*
***Vietnam Memorial, Washington, DC:** Panel 15E Line 33*

Sources
Interview with Joe Lowery, brother
Interview with Buddy Titshaw, cousin
Interview with Bobby Jacobs, childhood friend
Interview with Scotty Scott, childhood friend

Interview with David Scott, childhood friend
Interview with Phillip Smith, childhood friend
Interview with Susan Powers Smith, childhood friend
Interview with Johnny Wilson, childhood friend
Interview with David Brown, childhood friend
Interview with Elaine Moore, childhood friend
Interview with Martha Lee Child, childhood friend
Interview with Jimmy Davenport, Newnan native

References

Global Security. "1st Battalion, 27th Infantry Regiment 'Wolfhounds.'" Accessed January 19, 2022. https://www.globalsecurity.org/military/agency/army/1-27in.htm
History Central. "Operation Cedar Falls." Accessed January 20, 2022. https://www.historycentral.com/Vietnam/cedarfalls.html
Coffelt Database, "Donald Lowery." Accessed January 12, 2022. http://coffeltdatabase.org/detreq2.php

Lowery at Newnan High School and in Vietnam.

CHAPTER FIVE

Jessie Clifford Cofield

Newnan, Georgia

He was always my big brother no matter what.

—Betty Ann Cofield Acree

"We grew up with a simple life. We had fun. We didn't have a whole lot. Grandma made the boys' shirts and my dresses out of flour sacks and anything like that. We had our own garden. We had goats, chickens, and all kind of stuff like that," said Betty Ann Acree. The Cofield children wore shoes only when they went to school. They had no indoor plumbing. "We had each other. That was the most important thing," she said.

J.C., Betty Ann, and James Cofield were born in the Arnco mill village since their parents, Thomas and Kathern, worked at the mill. As they got older, the children had specific responsibilities each day. They drew water from the well and put it in the house or the washtub, which was in the yard so the sun would warm the water for baths. The children also brought in kindling for the wood-burning stove and fed the chickens and goats.

But it wasn't all drudgery for the youngsters. The boys had bicycles, and Betty Ann had a baby carriage, although she also played cowboys and Indians with her brothers. She hid in the fields and woods, and the boys did Indian whoops as they tried to find her.

J.C.'s cousin, Millard Floyd, called J.C. a "good ole country boy." When the two boys were between eight and twelve, Millard would play at the Cofield house. They hunted and fished together. J.C. had a BB gun and later a .22 caliber rifle, so they hunted squirrels and rabbits. The pond behind the house was a beacon for fishing but not swimming due to the snakes. If they weren't hunting or fishing, they were playing ball.

Second cousin Danny Cofield of Cofield Road—named after the Cofield family and located near O. P. Evans Middle School—was about six years younger than J.C. and also fished and played at J.C.'s house. They played baseball with a golf ball. Danny remembered one time when J.C. was pitching and Danny's brother was batting. He whacked the golf ball hard and hit J.C. in the thigh, dropping him to the ground. "Lord have mercy, I thought he had killed that boy," said Danny.

J.C. had a big knot on his leg, but he was soon playing again.

The Cofields eventually built a house in Welcome on land owned by J.C.'s grandparents, and they moved there as J.C. entered his teenage years. They had a small black-and-white television at this house and a telephone "party line," a circuit they shared with five neighbors, so they might have to wait for them to hang up before making a call.

"You couldn't get on it," Betty said with a laugh.

Once J.C. moved to Welcome, he befriended Charles Stanford. Charles remembered riding with his father to feed some horses they owned near J.C.'s home. When they passed by, Stanford shook his fist at J.C. if he was outside as they passed, and J.C. shook his fist in return. "It was a game," Stanford said.

Stanford and Cofield attended a local school, Western, for grades one through twelve. The school had no kindergarten back then. Today, that spot is the home of Western Elementary School. J.C. enjoyed shop class but otherwise didn't do well in school. He repeated seventh and ninth grades. It's unclear whether he passed ninth grade the second time, but since he was already sixteen, he left school.

While J.C. didn't like or do well in school, he was intensely interested in cars, as were many young men of his era. His first car was an old Chevy Coupe that he had to push to get started. He put a Woody Woodpecker decal on the side of the vehicle. His father told him that the car was to sit still while he was at work. Naturally, J.C. decided to give his sister and brother a ride. He got his siblings into the car, began to push, and promptly ran over a cedar tree that his father had planted. When he pulled the car off, the tree was broken, and when his father returned home, he would undoubtedly notice the tree. J.C.'s solution was duct tape! Initially, his father didn't see that the tree had been damaged, but gradually, it began to die. When that happened, his father noticed, although his reaction hasn't been recorded.

According to Millard Floyd, J.C. had an Edsel for a while. As he got to driving age, one of his early cars had "cutouts" on the manifold, which made the car noisy. Caps could be put on them to quiet them down, but J.C. wasn't interested in being quiet. He was known for making quite a racket on Welcome Road, so much so that the sheriff's deputies were looking for him. He was never caught.

Along with Charles and Jerry Smith, J.C. enjoyed driving and riding around town. Local teens drove their cars three places during those formative years: Temple Avenue, through downtown, and on to Greenville Street where they arrived at the Dairy Bar, which was also known as Big John's, located across from the intersection with Sewell Road. Stanford remembered that Big John's had speakers in the trees playing "Ring of Fire" by Johnny Cash. When they left there, the teens went back through downtown past the Wadsworth Auditorium to the Brazier Burger, hung out there awhile, then went down Temple Avenue to the Burger Chef near the intersection with Franklin Highway. They would circle Burger Chef, perhaps staying there, or they might start the ride all over again, beginning at Big John's. Stanford said they might ride all night long.

Every teen had a scarf hanging over the mirror, and guys would swap cars and ride with different friends.

Stanford worked at the Pontiac-Cadillac place next to Goodyear on the South Court Square in downtown Newnan. He recalled Cofield hanging out there and watching the body man paint cars.

J.C.'s parents moved out of millwork to work at Bonnell, one of the oldest businesses in Newnan. The couple divorced in 1960 when J.C. was fourteen. The children stayed with their father. In 1963, the father died of a massive heart attack, and the Cofield children went to live with their grandparents. The grandfather made a living by sharpening blades and fixing watches or whatever needed repairing. The grandparents were extremely strict with the children, and J.C. rebelled. In due course, a bitter breakup with the grandparents involved the younger siblings as well. All three kids wound up back with their mother.

Millard Floyd recalled double-dating with J.C. a few years later when they were about eighteen or nineteen. J.C. had a girlfriend named Diane Posey, and he was crazy about her. Stanford said she worked at one of the local banks, and J.C. met her one evening on their ride around town.

According to J.C.'s cousin Danny Cofield, his cousins "had a different lifestyle," and while they were good people, "They were just old-fashioned. His grandma and grandpa, who they stayed with most of the time, still cooked on a wood stove." Even when Cofield was a kid, the family had no indoor plumbing. "They pulled water out of the wells," Danny said.

J.C. Cofield took his Armed Forces physical on July 25, 1966, and entered the military on September 13, 1966. He enrolled in Basic Training at Fort Benning and Advanced Infantry Training at Fort Polk, Louisiana, a known stop for young men headed to Vietnam. Millard Floyd, already serving in Germany, heard from his grandmother that J.C. was entering the service. Later, he got a letter from J.C. saying he hoped to end up in Germany. Unfortunately, Germany wasn't in his future; J.C. and many others like him were heading to Southeast Asia. Most of the information about Jessie Cofield's military experience has come from letters he sent to family and friends.

J.C. came home on a thirty-day leave at the end of his training. He visited Danny Cofield's home sometime that month to say goodbye. Stanford noticed that J.C. didn't go out with Diane while on leave. He doesn't remember J.C. ever mentioning her. Neither Stanford nor Millard Floyd knows what transpired between the couple.

One day during the leave, J.C. and Charles got in the car to do the Newnan teen cruise (Burger Chef, Dairy Bar, Brazier Burger), and Charles observed that J.C. just wasn't himself. "He was just…he just wasn't J.C. I don't know if she broke up with him that day or broke up with him before, wouldn't go out with him or what it was, but they had went together for a while." Stanford said he and J.C. might have met up with some people from Western on the Court Square that evening. Whatever happened or didn't happen with J.C. and Diane, the couple was in contact while he was in Vietnam.

Stanford felt that J.C. sensed that he wasn't coming back. J.C.

told him, "You know, I think it might be better to get killed on foreign soil than this soil over here."

Stanford was puzzled. What was he talking about? "Don't say stuff like that. We have a heap more fishing to do," he finally said.

J.C. Cofield arrived in Vietnam sometime around February 22, 1967, and headed to the 5th Battalion, 60th Infantry Regiment, 3rd Brigade of the 9th Infantry Division in the Mekong Delta. The 5th Battalion had arrived in the Delta in December of 1966, establishing a base camp in Rach Kien in the province of Long An in the IV Corps Zone. They moved to secure that position and pushed against the communists in their area. The 5/60 was a Mechanized Unit. It is unclear when J.C. was trained to operate in a Mechanized Unit. He either got training in the United States or was taught when he arrived in Vietnam.

The grammar and spelling, copied verbatim from Cofield's letters, reflect his lack of education and the rush in which they were frequently written. J.C.'s letters home included many mentions of his car. When he left for Vietnam, he is thought to have owned a Ford Fairlane and a 1964 Dodge Dart. His sister, Betty, drove his Dodge to work at Burger Chef so it wouldn't be sitting all the time. One day when she left work, she was in a minor accident. "I was scared," she said. "I got it fixed in a hurry!"

On March 6, 1967, J.C. wrote to his mother, Mrs. Kathern Gaddy, from Vietnam. Excerpt.

> *I ought to make sp/4 in two more months and hope I do. My job own the track write now is machine gunner. I like it pretty good. May starts the rainy season over here. It rains for 6 &7 months. By the time it ends I will be just about ready to come home.*

Stanford recalled getting letters from J.C. asking about things in Newnan. At one point, J.C. mentioned that his unit had been on an ambush and killed five Viet Cong.

Also on March 6, 1967, Miss Diane Posey sent a letter to her friend J.C. in Vietnam. Entire letter.

> *Dear JC,*
>
> *I got your letter today and was very happy to hear from you. I got your card from Japan, and it sure was pretty. I*

thought you wasn't going to ever write me anymore. I couldn't really blame you. I'm not really important anyway.

You don't have to get me anything if you don't want to. It has been really stormy all day today. Tornado warnings were out all day today. I hate this kind of weather. I didn't do anything last weekend. Me and Carol went uptown for awhile Friday night. Then Saturday night I went to the Burger Chef and ate a hamburger and then I went to the show by myself because Carol went to Atlanta to see Marie Sharpton (big mouth.)

After I got out of the show I rode around with George Moore and drove his car and he gave me a beer. I believe you know him. He walks on crutches all the time. Then Sunday I went uptown and drove George's car again because I didn't have anything else to do. I wrote Millard last week and haven't heard from him yet. I haven't heard from Billy in about a week. I guess he has forgotten about me. Did you go to Hawaii too? You are getting to see the world just about aren't you. I am so glad I don't have to work tomorrow because I am so tired. I'll probably sleep real late in the morning. You didn't sell your car before you left did you.

Do you want me to send you a Times Herald every week. I will if you wan't me to. I don't mind. Then you can know what's going on in Newnan. I hope you don't get bored with this letter. I know a little about being away from home and wanting long letters from somebody because I wanted them when I was at North Georgia.

Bob Cook, Billy Cooks brother was trying to get me to buy his Corvair Sunday night but I wouldn't have it. It's hard to get parts for a Corvair. I don't want a Corvair anyway. I'm not sure yet what kind I want.

I think we will be in our new church by Easter. It sure is pretty. JC, don't get mad at me when I ask you this question but I have always wanted to know. Have you ever been saved or joined the church? Every night before we go to bed I pray that you will be safe and that someday you will get in the church. Please don't get mad at me for asking you that. I'm not trying to be nosey. I've already started missing you. I know you don't miss me. You probably miss Emily but not me. Where is Jerry Smith now or do you know? Write me and tell me what you will be having to do if you can tell me. Well I've run out of things to say. Just let me know if you want me to send you a Times Herald every week.

Write me real soon.

Love,

Diane

On April 14, 1967, J.C. was in Vietnam when a young woman named Linda from the House of the Good Shepherd children's home in Utica, New York, wrote to him. Linda was a friend of J.C.'s buddy Johnny in Vietnam, and she wrote to J.C. without personally knowing him. Back then, it was common for a girl to write a serviceman to boost his morale and allow him to receive more mail. Entire letter.

Dear JC,

Hi, well here I am to answer your letter you wrote to me. If you forgot I'll tell you. I'm Linda! Sure I'll write to you if you write to me. Well there is one thing, I don't know what to call you, unless you want me to call you "JC."

Will, I'm 5'4, blonde hair (not the bright blonde, a dirty blonde) blue eyes and medium long blonde hair. I really don't know what to tell you other than that. I just looked to see if I had any pictures of me but the only ones I have of myself are in a bathing suit. I'll get some other taken of me.

So, how do you and Johnny get along? He's a good kid. He's a very true friend and you can trust Johnny with anything. By the way, will you do me a favor? Tell Johnny to write back to me. Thank you! Johnny and I are very close friends.

Well you can tell me whatever you think I'd like to know! Are you going with any girls?

How do you like Vietnam? My brother might go over in Vietnam also. Right now he's in Germany.

Well, I hope to get to meet you, you sound like a nice guy. Do you like it in Atlanta, Georgia? I live in Coeymans, New

York. It's right outside of Albany.
When I leave the house maybe next year I'm going to live in Flordia.
Well, I hate to say this but I have to go for now so I'll close this but never my heart to you. May God bless you and protect you.
Love Always,
Linda
P.S. Write back soon
PSS. I would like to have a picture of you if you'd send me one. (Hint!)

On June 8, 1967, J.C. wrote to his sister, Betty Ann, from Vietnam. Excerpt.

I just came in off a allnite mission I'm sure am tired.

The way I figure it I will leave here just after Christmas of the [illegible]

and go back to rear until I leave Viet Nam. They usually leave pull you out your unit 30 days before you leave your unit. When I do come home and buy my new car and after I get out of the Army in September I'm going to finished school or go to a trade school. I should have something like $2500 dollars when I leave this hole over here. The first thing I'm going to do is by me a new car because that is all I think about now.

Do you ever see Diane much tell her I have wrote her three letters and haven't heard from her in a month now. Oh, yes, by the way I'm writing a girl from New York and she and I are getting in[illegible]think but don't tell Diane about it. Do you ever see her out with anyone do or do you work all the time. If you and James or mom takes care of my car and things while I'm gone I will take of [illegible].

In July 1967, J.C.'s mother, Mrs. Kathern Gaddy, wrote to him in Vietnam. Excerpt.

I guess Betty Ann told you she was getting married. I guess she is old enough to marry. Tomorrow she will be 19 years old the 1st of July. You no it want be long before you

will be 21. A man of your own.
We washed your car today. Millard drove it around the block and back.

July 25, 1967. Letter sent from Miss Diane Posey to J.C. in Vietnam. Excerpts.

I'm going to send you a 5 by 7 picture of me this weekend. You can throw it away if you don't want it. I haven't seen your sister in quite awhile. I heard she was working at Color Craft. Has your brother still got your car? Guess what? I got a two piece bathing suit this year. I haven't been swimming any so far. Have you wrote Millard lately? If you find time write him. He sure is sweet and so are you.

July 28, 1967. J.C. was in Vietnam. Letter sent to his mother, Mrs. Kathern Gaddy. Excerpts.

I'll be going on R&R next month. I'm going to Tokyo Japan. I'll leave hear on the 27th of August and wont half to be back until the 3rd of September. I'll try to call home but cannot promise you anything.
"I have been hear six months and it seems like 6 years."

September 3, 1967. J.C. was in Vietnam. Letter sent to his mother, Mrs. Kathern Gaddy. Excerpts.

Just a few lines to let you know that I'm alright. Well pretty soon I will have a year in the Army and 20 more days I will start on my eight month and have just 4 to go boy does that sound good.
How is your new son in law getting along with you. Where is him and Betty Ann living at.
I guess James is in school by now or did he quit.

I am going to start to send you from 50 to 100 dollars a month after this month because I made Sp/4 this month. By the time I leave hear I will be a sergeant.
I'm going to NCO school in about a week or two.
Well, I guess that all for now. Write soon.

September 12, 1967. J.C. was in Vietnam. Letter sent to Mr.

Charles Stanford. This was the last letter Jessie Cofield would write since he died in combat the next day. Entire letter.

> *I got your letter today and was glad to hear from you. You bet I'm getting tired of this place. In 10 more days I will 8 months in this hole and have four to go. I'll get to the states about the 20 & 21 of February.*
>
> *So old uncle sam is after your ass. Well you had better look out. Because I read in the paper we get that they are sending 45,000 troops over hear by July of next year. You might be the one who takes my place.*
>
> *Charles remember when I told Buster that would not last with that girl. Tell him he lost his bet. He bet me a dollar he would last with her until he married her. Well tell Buster I will collect that dollar he owes me when I get home. Tell him he thinks he has something that will run pretty good. Tell him when I get moved I will spot him a mile and run him.*
>
> *Tell Buster to write me a letter I have a few things to tell him.*
>
> *Well, I guess that all for now write soon.*
>
> *J.C.*

According to Danny Cofield, J.C.'s mother woke up one night about a week before J.C. was killed. She had a vision of J.C. standing at the foot of the bed. He looked at her and said, "Momma, I'm coming home."

On September 12, 1967, the 5th Mechanized Battalion, 60th Infantry kicked off an operation north of their base at Cai Lai called Coronado V. According to the 5th Battalion, 60th Infantry Association website:

> *Fifty of the enemy died the 13th of September in one fierce encounter along the Rach Ba Muong River, four miles southwest of Cai Lai.*
>
> *The action began at 11 a.m. when two platoons from Company A, 5th-60th, and two platoons from Company C, 3rd-60th were hit by machine gun fire from four bunkers concealed in a wood line along the river.*

The infantrymen turned in to attack and called in the 5th-60th reconnaissance platoon for reinforcements.

Reports initially listed the enemy force at squad size but as the fight became more intense, officers at the scene radioed that the VC strength was much greater than originally estimated.

In the late afternoon recon platoon leader First Lieutenant Robert L. Brechinor of Bakersfield, Calif., launched a swift attack against the bunkers and found they were only part of a much larger complex.

A heavy volley of anti-tank round and automatic rifle fire answered the probe.

Artillery pounded the enemy position throughout the night though ground contact was broken at nightfall.

A sweep the next day revealed the 30 enemy bodies.

Lieutenant Colonel William B. Steele of Carlisle, Pa. 5th-60th battalion commander praised the performance of his men against a well-equipped and well-entrenched enemy.

According to the US military, fifty of the enemy died on September 13. So did ten young Americans, including one country boy from Newnan, Georgia. The circumstances of Cofield's death are unknown, but military records indicate that he was hit by small arms fire one year to the day that he entered military service. He might have been on the machine gun of the vehicle, or he might have been outside the personnel carrier altogether.

Betty Ann, who was nineteen back then and recently married, recalled a car pulling up to the curb and a man coming to the door. Both she and her husband answered the door. The car had already been to her mother's home, and her mother sent them on to Betty Ann's house. "When he came to that door, I was so devastated, but I will never forget that man. I know that is their job, but I don't see how they do it," she said.

Doyle and Harriet Steele recalled the gathering at J.C.'s mother's home. After hearing the news, family and friends converged on the house with food. Cars were parked everywhere. A solemn Travis Eidson, then pastor of Arnco Baptist Church, was present to comfort the assembled group. (Eidson was considered a surrogate father to everyone in the western part of the county. US 27 in western Coweta County is now dedicated to Travis Eidson.)

The casket was flown to Atlanta and brought to Hillcrest Funeral Home in Newnan. Instructions from the Army were that they should not open the coffin. However, Cofield's mother wanted it opened to ensure it was her son. Cofield's stepfather went to identify the body and took J.C.'s little brother, James, who had insisted on going along. Viewing his brother's body seemed to affect him a great deal, and he committed suicide seventeen years later, in the same month his brother died. Whether J.C.'s death led to his brother's suicide will never be known.

Charles Stanford said Cofield's mother contacted him about being a pallbearer. He wanted to do it but at the same time didn't want to. In the end, the Army supplied pallbearers.

"I couldn't imagine losing one child, but when you think about losing two children, I mean, how could you handle that? And knowing one was way over [in Vietnam]. 'I am coming home, Mama. I am coming home. Don't be afraid for me,' he used to say. I don't know how anybody could stand that. It just run Momma crazy," recalled Betty Ann.

On Memorial Day 2011, the City of Newnan honored J.C. Cofield at its annual ceremony. The *Newnan Times-Herald* quoted Floyd as saying, "He was not a great scholar. He was not a great athlete. But he was a great American who gave the ultimate sacrifice for this country."

"He was always thinking about his family and his country," said Betty Ann Acree. "He gave the ultimate sacrifice. He gave all he had to give."

"Think about a little ole feller that comes from the country, didn't have anything extra, just had what he had, to go on the far side of the world and had never been any further than Alabama out of the state of Georgia and to go over there and die on foreign land like that, being afraid every day," said Betty Ann. "He was a humble person. He never stole anything from anybody. He would give you the shirt off his back. He is still my hero. He will always be my brother, and I am proud of those who went with him too."

**To see the catalog of original letters to and from J.C. Cofield, visit www.bettermencoweta.com.

Born: *August 2, 1946, in Newnan, Georgia*
Home of record: *Newnan, Georgia*
Died: *September 13, 1967, in Dinh Tuong province of South Vietnam*
Coweta servicemen who died in the same province: *None*
Unit on death: *A CO, 5th BN, 60th Infantry, 9th Infantry Division*
Decorations: *Purple Heart, National Defense Medal, Vietnam Service Medal, Republic of Vietnam Campaign Medal*
Buried: *Oak Hill Cemetery, Newnan*
Vietnam Memorial, Washington, DC: *Panel 26-E Line 65*

Sources
Interview with Millard Floyd, cousin
Interview with Danny Cofield, cousin
Interview with Charles Stanford, friend
Interview with Harriet Steele, cousin, and her husband, Doyle
Interview with Betty Ann Acree, sister
Assistance from Mark Darrow and Pam Beavers

References
Wikipedia. "Operation Coronado V." Accessed October 15, 2021. https://en.wikipedia.org/wiki/Operation_Coronado_V
5th Battalion, 60th Infantry Association. "Operation Coronado V." http://5thbattalion.net/operation-coronado-v/
Coffelt Database, "Jessie Cofield." Accessed July 21, 2019. http://coffeltdatabase.org/index.php

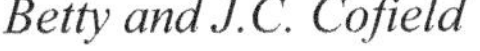

Betty and J.C. Cofield

J.C. Cofield

Millard Floyd, left, and JC Cofield.

CHAPTER SIX

Thomas Pate Huddleston

Newnan, Georgia

The true soldier fights not because he hates what is in front of him, but because he loves what is behind him.
—G.K. Chesterton

Principal Jerry Singleton strode down the Newnan Junior High School corridor, making for his office. Inside sat Sue Huddleston with her son, Tommy. The school counselor slipped into the meeting. The school was located on the corner of Temple Avenue and Jefferson Street next to McKoon Funeral Home, and it operated much differently than a public school would today. Mischief wasn't tolerated.

Tommy was in trouble again. This time, he had used too much soap in the bathroom. The counselor asked Mr. Singleton if there was a limit to the amount of soap students could use.

The principal responded curtly, "No, but you don't need to be wasteful either."

When the counselor asked if Tommy was the only student in the bathroom, she was surprised to discover five students had been in the bathroom at the same time. Only Tommy, however, had been taken to the office.

Tommy's sister, Melissa, said, "I remember Mother saying that every time she turned around, Tommy was in trouble." Melissa recalled that "he hated school, I mean hated school."

Sue would drop him off, and he would almost beat her home. That day in the office, Mr. Singleton looked Tommy in the eye and asked him what he wanted out of life.

Displaying his combative nature, Tommy replied, "I want away from you and this school." That was Tommy Huddleston's last day at Newnan Junior High and his last day of formal education—ever.

Tommy Huddleston was born in Roanoke, Alabama, on *September 4, 1946*, to Robert and Sue Huddleston. Tommy's father was on the wild side when he was young, working as a mechanic but hauling moonshine in his spare time. Robert was nicknamed "Shorty" because he was short and stocky, characteristics that Tommy also displayed as he got older. Dennis Madaglia, Tommy's cousin, remembered the summers in Roanoke when they were growing up. The two of them hung out with Tommy's brother Daryl and another cousin, Terry Lewis. Daryl and Terry were older, so while the adults were at work, they were responsible for what happened during the day. They picked blackberries and sold them to earn money for the movies. They enjoyed playing ball, and Tommy was a good baseball player. His uncle Jake had played first base for the Brooklyn Dodgers during the 1930s, and that heritage seemed to have rubbed off on young Tommy. He was quite good at second base and shortstop. Tommy was so accomplished that he usually played ball with the older guys.

Lewis recalled, "He was always the best in his age group."

The boys liked to catch fireflies at night. Madaglia remembered Tommy getting a jar to put the fireflies in. Once, Tommy punched small holes in the jar's lid using an ice pick and stabbed his palm.

"It hurt him, I know, but he didn't say much," Madaglia said. "He was worried about how much trouble he would get into when his mom and dad got home. But Tommy wouldn't let us pull it out because he was afraid it was going to hurt. So he went around with it for part of the day. He finally jerked it out and never even told his parents. He put something on it and never went to the doctor or anything."

By the time the family arrived in Newnan by way of LaGrange, there were five Huddleston children—Daryl, Bobby, Danny, Tommy, and Melissa. The moves involved the father's job. Robert came to Newnan to work at Bonnell Aluminum then moved to the W. P. Woodall Company, an asphalt company in Tyrone. Sue landed a job at Playtex.

They originally lived on Greenville Street just past Sewell Road then moved to Helm Street near the water tank. The house on Helm Street became the base for Tommy, his brothers, and his friends. The house had three bedrooms—one for Robert and Sue, one for Melissa, and one for the four brothers.

Melissa recalled the place being full of boys and the testosterone level always extremely high. Tommy, for instance, one day decided to climb the Newnan water tower not far from their home. At the top of the tank was a globe that Tommy took to prove he had made it there. He was proud of that globe and kept it in his bedroom. It signified an achievement that his siblings and friends couldn't possibly overlook. Once, when Robert and Sue had a heated argument, Sue grabbed the globe and threw it at her husband. Melissa recalled Tommy's look of horror.

"Mom, couldn't you have picked up anything but that globe? I climbed the water tank to get that!" he said.

Tommy had never been a fan of school and managed only average grades until he left.

"Back then, we didn't strive much. We just strived to get out of school," said Terry Lewis.

Millard Floyd, J.C. Cofield's cousin, knew Tommy and described him as "a very likable guy, but he was always into something."

"He was the class clown," said his sister, Melissa. "He used to tell Momma that he would just walk into the class, and they just laughed at him. He was just the kind that everybody loved. He was always doing something to make everyone laugh."

Archie Slaton met Tommy in junior high. They ran track together because they ran about the same speed. They didn't wear shorts to school, but they wore gym shorts for Physical Education and Track after school. When Archie forgot his shorts one day, Tommy gave him an extra pair he had.

"That made us friends forever," Archie said. He described Tommy as "a little cocky but real generous." Over time, the two became close friends, "as tight as two guys can be," and hung out at each other's house after school.

Another friend, Larry Hayes, got to know Tommy at the local teen hangouts—the pool room on Madison Street, the Brazier Burger, the Alamo Theater, the drive-in theater on Route 29, and

Spencer's Skating Ring. Tommy and his brothers also enjoyed visiting their cousin, Johnny Calhoun, who lived off Poplar Road.

For some males in Newnan in the 1960s, there was a "culture" of fighting. Tommy Huddleston was well known for his ability in this arena.

Terry Lewis said Tommy was an outstanding athlete and fighter. "Guys three to four years older would not mess with Tommy. Some of them tried him because he got a little bit of a reputation, and after they tried him, they backed off."

Larry Hayes said, "He was a short guy, but he could really go. He would fight a bear."

"We had these little rivalries, and we'd get into a fight every once in a while, over girls, whatever, but Tommy would always jump in and take care of me. He would never let me fight," Slaton said. "I wanted to fight my own battles, but he would always jump in and take care of me. I guess that we were just that close. I remember one time, a guy wanted to just get on me really bad, but Tommy took him and really just wore him out. Tommy was a medium-built guy, strong as an ox. I promise you, and I have never seen any fight, and I have been to quite a few, that he didn't win. He was just one tough cookie. He could fight. I'm not talking about guns or stabbing you. I am talking about fist fighting, face to face, toe to toe. We used to go to the bottom of Armory Road at night, and that is where the cars would round up, and that is where you watched the fight. The way I see it today, that is probably what got him killed. He was just so into protecting other people, especially if he made you a friend. I never saw him start a fight, but I never saw him back down from one either."

Melissa recalled her brother's fighting instincts as well. "I used to say that my brother Bobby could get a fight started, but he wanted Tommy to finish it. You know, Daddy was the same way. Daddy didn't start a fight, but he would be the one to finish it. And Tommy was the same way as Daddy."

One of Tommy's most famous fights was with a boy named Billy Joe, who was much larger than him. According to one eyewitness, Tommy and Billy Joe had an altercation in one of their homes. They decided to take it outside.

Larry Hayes recalled, "Billy was bigger, but Tommy got the best of him out at Spencer's Skating Rink."

The skating rink was one of the biggest teen hangouts during the 1960s, a place where kids could cut up, flirt with members of the opposite sex, have fun, and skate! Many Newnan teens, including Tommy, loved roller skating at Spencer's. He became a superb skater and at one point told his mother that he wanted to get into roller derby.

Archie Slaton recounts, "In Newnan when we were coming up, we had little skating clubs. Tommy was an excellent roller skater. One of the best. I have seen him do tricks I didn't think any human could do." In addition, Tommy taught his siblings Danny and Melissa to skate.

"I had a wonderful teacher," Melissa said. "I could skate forward, backward, sideways. I doubt that I could do that good now, but I believe that I could still skate today."

Melissa said Tommy had a knack for being in the right place at the right time. Once, the electric fan in their home shorted out and began smoking. Tommy smelled it immediately and pulled it out of the socket and out of the house. When Melissa was in elementary school, she was in a Christmas play. While the family attended the performance, a light came off the family tree and burned through a flannel shirt, a gift for their grandfather, then through the cloth skirt around the tree, and finally, it scorched the floor. Tommy came home and found it.

"He said he had to come home and save the house from burning down," Melissa said with a laugh.

After leaving school, Tommy got a job at the local grading and asphalt company. He lied about his age to get his driver's license. At that time, it wasn't necessary to show the examiner a birth certificate. Soon, Tommy worked at the asphalt company, driving heavy equipment at age sixteen and possibly even working at the construction site of the original Atlanta-Fulton County Stadium.

But Tommy's life changed when he lied about his age to join the Army, and he entered the service at seventeen.

"Mother begged him not to join the Army," Melissa recalled. "She said that she would tell on him and take his birth certificate to the Army. He said that he would just run away. He was so adamant about wanting to defend his country. When I was six or seven and living on Helm Street, we were out flying a kite one day, and he told me, 'When you get nineteen years old, they're going to be dropping bombs around here.' I can remember that so well. I know in his mind, he had to do everything he could to defend his country, and he did."

Tommy could have gotten into the Army at seventeen had his parents agreed and signed the papers, but that wasn't what happened.

According to Tommy's friend Millard Floyd, about thirty young men from Coweta County entered the US Army at the same time in March of 1966. The men who trained at Fort Benning were frequently given weekend passes and immediately headed to Newnan. Floyd said the platoon sergeant joked with them by saying, "Guess you guys are all going to Newnan."

Tommy would return home and enjoy seeing friends and family. Floyd also recalled an incident when Tommy was still at home on a Sunday afternoon, a few hours before he needed to be back at Fort Benning. Tommy strode into the Burger Chef on Temple Avenue, wearing his formal uniform and all sorts of medals. He created quite a stir. Where the awards came from is unclear, as Tommy was still in Basic Training and didn't have any!

Once, after a weekend leave, he showed up on Monday morning in his khaki uniform with blood all over it. He just wasn't afraid of anyone.

"He was the kind of guy you would want to go to war with because he was fearless," said Floyd.

According to his military records, Tommy finished Basic and Advanced Training at Fort Benning then trained in artillery at Fort Sill, Oklahoma. At some point, he volunteered for the Airborne.

According to Archie Slaton, Tommy always wanted to go into the Airborne and "always wanted that little danger." Slaton thought Tommy loved the look of a paratrooper, the elite soldier.

"It was a big thing when we found out he was going to jump out of airplanes. When you're kids, it doesn't take much to fascinate you," Melissa said.

Tommy's life changed when he met a young lady named Laura Lee, perhaps at the skating rink. They began dating before he left for Basic Training at Fort Benning. While Tommy was training, Laura desperately wanted to see him. She called the Huddleston house, wanting to know the next time they would be going to Columbus. Laura's parents, however, had called first and told Sue Huddleston that they would prefer that Laura not see Tommy. A month later, Laura's parents called back. They would allow her to see Tommy the next time he came home, as Laura was pregnant.

They were married the next time Tommy came home. The ceremony was performed at a courthouse in Wedowee, Alabama. Roger Huddleston was born on November 16, 1966.

Tommy Huddleston arrived in Vietnam in early February 1967 and joined the 173rd Airborne Brigade. The 173rd had been activated in 1963 and become the first significant unit deployed to Vietnam in May 1965. The brigade's nickname, "Sky Soldiers," came from a Taiwanese unit with whom they had trained. The Sky Soldiers were proud of the handle.

Tommy arrived at an exciting time. On February 22, the 173rd made the only combat jump of the Vietnam War as part of Operation Junction City, one of the most extensive operations of the war. According to the Vietnam War 50th Commemoration Website:

> *Elements from multiple US Army, US Air Force, and South Vietnamese army units take part in Operation JUNCTION CITY. The operation is the primary offensive of the overall campaign in III Corps. Its objective is to encircle and destroy the Viet Cong 9th Division, which controls the area northwest of Saigon near the Cambodian border. JUNCTION CITY represents one of the largest helicopter actions of the war, and the offensive begins with the only major parachute assault of the war.*

While there is no evidence that Tommy Huddleston got there in time to make the jump during Junction City, he certainly would have been involved in Junction City during its four-month duration.

David Brown graduated from Newnan High School in 1964. He played on Newnan's football team along with Tommy's brother Daryl. After graduation, David entered the military and lost track of everyone in Newnan. He went to airborne school and eventually was assigned to the 4th Battalion of the 173rd Airborne Brigade.

Huddleston was in the 2nd Battalion. Therefore, it was a surprise when David ran into Tommy in Vietnam.

David was in the enlisted club in Ben Hoa when Tommy walked in the door, and they immediately recognized each other. David recalled it this way:

> *We were sitting there drinking a beer, I saw him, he knew me, and I knew him, we sat down at a table, we got to talking. He told me about his wife. Her name was Laura Lee, Laura Lee Huddleston back then. I knew her, had dated her. He was telling me that he was married to her and had a child by her. Back then, Hawaii was off-limits to enlisted men [for R&R]. Only the officers could go. He told me- man, I am going to do what I ain't supposed to do. He was always an aggressive boy. He wasn't a troublemaker. He was just like me and everybody else, just a fun-loving guy. He had a great time wherever he went. He told me he was going to Hawaii. He had already talked to Laura Lee, and she is going to meet him. There again, he wasn't supposed to do that.*

Huddleston's R&R was legendary in Huddleston family lore. At the midway point of their one-year tour, service members could choose a place to visit during their rest and recuperation. Locations included Japan, Singapore, Thailand, Australia, Hong Kong, Taiwan, and Hawaii. Hawaii was the destination for most married men, as their wives met them away from the war for their week. The military flew the servicemen to the chosen location and gave them vouchers to stay in approved lodging. Tommy planned to meet Laura in Hawaii, but for some reason, their plans changed. According to Archie Slaton, Tommy won some money in a poker game and decided to fly from Hawaii to Newnan in hopes of seeing his wife, son, and family.

Service members were forbidden from getting on a commercial aircraft and flying to the United States, but somehow, Tommy managed to get on a plane to the mainland. His sister said he might have posed as a student.

Tommy arrived in Newnan on a Monday morning. Melissa was in school at Atkinson Elementary when her brother Bobby stopped by and picked her up. Bobby explained that they were going to their grandmother's home in Roanoke. Melissa thought it odd. They had just been there on Sunday, and she had never been picked up in the middle of a school day. When they pulled up at the home, Tommy was there. They did go to their grandmother's house that afternoon.

"Tommy was notorious for sneaking home," Melissa said. "If there was any way to get home, he was coming home."

Shortly after his triumphant return to Vietnam from R&R, Tommy encountered Hill 875.

"They underestimated the force up on that mountain," said Terry Lewis. "When it came to a scrap like that in Vietnam, you would think if anyone came out, he would come out."

The Vietnam Reflections-Fallen Heroes page on Facebook gives a good summary of the lead-up to what Tommy faced in November of 1967, three months before he was to return home.

> *The battle of Dak To was a series of major engagements of the Vietnam War that took place between 3 and 22 of November 1967 in Kontum Province, Central Highlands of Vietnam. Dak To lies on a flat valley floor, surrounded by waves of ridgelines that rise into peaks, some as high as 4,000 feet, and stretch westward and southwestward towards the tri-border area where South Vietnam, Laos, and Cambodia meet. One of those peaks was Hill 875.*

The 173rd got orders to assault Hill 875, which they proceeded to do. However, the assault ground to a halt as the Americans encountered an extensive enemy bunker system. Tommy Huddleston was there.

So was Lester Daughtridge, another member of the 173rd. He supplied this account of what happened on Hill 875.

> *As for Hill 875, I didn't know, and I don't think anyone knew the true capabilities of the enemy forces that day. My squad was to secure the Company Command Post (CP) when we started up the Hill. I am sure second platoon led the way up the finger with the CP Attached. On first contact*

Charlie Company [Tommy Huddleston was in Charlie Company] was to assault on line on the right side of the finger (ridge line going up the Hill) and Delta Company was to assault the left side of the finger. Alpha Company was to our rear in reserve. Alpha was tasked with securing the rear and clearing an LZ [Landing Zone for helicopters] to receive supplies and transport wounded. They were also charged to support the assault elements.

We could hear the artillery prepping the Hill as we were going up. I remember one shot and the second man in the column was hit. We all deployed to the flanks my squad was to secure the CP during the assault. Once the assault began all Hell broke loose. We were close to their first trench and bunker system. They were sniping us from the trees, but we continued a slow assault. We were so occupied with the assault we didn't realize what was happening in the rear with Alpha. We were practically throwing grenades back and forth at each other. I heard later on there was actually hand to hand taking place in some parts of the assault line.

I remember going forward and dragging wounded sky soldiers back in our lines. So much happened and time seemed to be still the entire battle. Every detail of the battle connected concurrently without pause.

Just as the sun started setting, we started digging fighting positions to protect us. You guessed right. Our entrenching tools and food and extra water was lost with the fall of Alpha. We dug using bayonets and steel pots. One guy dug while another watched the front (still fighting). I was digging and Specialist Northern was watching. I remember my ears screamed in pain and I was flying through the air. I think I was slammed face first into the root system of a giant tree. It held me there for a few minutes, seconds, who knows and then released me. I grabbed my chest and said My God I can't breathe and passed out.

I guess a couple of hours later, I know it was later because it was dark when I regained consciousness. I was on my knees staring at the blood dropping from my hand wondering what happened. All I could hear was the screaming. I learned from the Canine Handler two 500 Lb bombs fell on us. They landed right on the CP and the place we were bringing the wounded. I went from position to position trying to help the wounded. I can't explain to you what I saw that night.

The next day we fought for our lives repelling attack after attack. All the officers and medics in my company were dead. SFC Kratzow was leading at this point. That night again just before Day break Bravo Company 4th Battalion was able to get up to us and help fortify our defenses.

Fourth Battalion Assaulted the Hill for the next three days taking it on Thanksgiving Day 1967. I was evacuated the evening of the third day for wounds suffered from the bombs.

This account would have to be close to what Tommy Huddleston experienced on Hill 875 as a C (Charlie) Company member. It is known that he fought bravely and heroically. His citation for heroism reads:

Citation: Bronze Star Medal for Heroism Date Action: November 19, 1967

For heroism in connection with military operations against a hostile force: Specialist Huddleston distinguished himself by exceptionally valorous actions on November 19, 1967, in the Republic of Vietnam. On this day, Company C, 2nd Battalion (Airborne) 503rd Infantry, made contact with a large force of North Vietnamese soldiers. Specialist Huddleston charged forward and began to engage the enemy despite the fact that he was exposed to heavy automatic weapons, mortar, grenade, and rocket fire. Seeing one of his comrades hit, Specialist Huddleston dashed in front of the lines and dragged him to safety, completely ignoring the intense fire directed at him. As soon as he had secured medical attention for him, Specialist Huddleston returned to his position and continued to inflict heavy casualties on the enemy until he was mortally wounded. Specialist Huddleston's outstanding

> *display of aggressiveness, devotion to duty, and personal bravery were in keeping with the highest traditions of the military service and reflects great credit upon himself, his unit, and the United States Army.*

This citation seemed to explain what happened to Tommy Huddleston. The information about how Tommy was "mortally wounded" is rather vague, as these sorts of documents tend to be. It doesn't seem to cover what really might have happened to him. Lester Daughtridge described in his account a "friendly fire" incident on Hill 875 involving a Marine Corp A-4 Skyhawk bomber aircraft. On the VVMF website, researcher William Killian posted this account of what happened on November 19, 1967, on that lonely hill in the Republic of South Vietnam.

> *On November 19, 1967, during the Battle of Dak, one of the worst friendly fire incidents of the Vietnam War occurred when a Marine Corps fighter-bomber dropped two bombs into the perimeter where officers and noncommissioned officers of 2nd Battalion, 503rd Infantry had set up a command post with their radio operators. The soldiers of the 173rd Airborne Brigade were dug in on the steep southern slope of Hill 875, fighting beside napalm fires and exposed to the guns of the North Vietnamese Army shooting from tunnels nearby. Just past dusk, after making three dry runs over the battlefield, the Marine Corps A-4 attack jet descended to 1,000 feet above the jungle and released two 250-pound Mk-81 bombs fitted with Snakeye fins. Barreling in on a shallow 10-degree angle at hundreds of miles per hour, the two bombs from the A-4 hit the ground. One was a dud. The other exploded in a huge orange fireball. Instead of hitting the North Vietnamese, the bomb struck the branches of a lone tree along the Americans' perimeter, under which the Battalion had set up their command post. It was also a casualty-collection point where the most badly wounded soldiers were being treated by medics while awaiting medevac helicopters to take them off the hill.*
>
> *The bomb killed 21 men and wounded 10 more, including*

most of the remaining senior leaders and medics. A single radio operator was spared when he was protected by a pile of broken tree trunks that absorbed deadly fragments. The dead included MAJ Charles Watters, a 40-year-old Catholic priest who served as the Battalion's chaplain. Earlier in the battle, Watters had ventured out past the perimeter several times to rescue wounded soldiers, carrying or dragging them to safety, providing first aid, and administering last rites to the dying—actions for which he was later awarded the Medal of Honor. After witnessing what happened below, a crewman on a US Air Force AC-47 "Spooky" gunship flying in a slow circle 3,000 feet above the dead and wounded troops tossed parachute flares out the back of the plane to help survivors on the ground see in the darkness.

A January 1968 US Air Force investigation into the incident was inconclusive, declaring that "there is insufficient evidence to determine the exact cause of the short round" before blaming "improper release conditions." The investigator recommended that pilots undergo remedial training and that the investigation be closed, as it had revealed "no gross personnel errors nor evidence of equipment malfunction" (Ismay, 2019).

David Brown of Newnan, who had run into Tommy in the enlisted men's club a few months before, was also involved in combat on Hill 875. He was too busy trying to stay alive to even think about Tommy. David was wounded and in the hospital. "They came on the radio and said that the 173rd had just taken Hill 875. It was later that I thought about Tommy being on that hill."

The week of Thanksgiving in 1967 started eerily in the Huddleston home on Helm Street. That Monday, Sue Huddleston thought she heard someone calling her.

"Momma!" the voice called. "Momma!"

She asked everyone in the house if it was them or if they'd heard it. They had to send her to the nurses' station at Playtex, where she was at work that Tuesday, because the voice had gotten so loud. Sue was convinced that the voice was Tommy's and that he was calling to her.

Melissa remembered her mother saying that "it was like Tommy was right there beside her, calling to her."

On Wednesday, Sue stopped hearing the voice.

As the family sat down for Thanksgiving dinner that Thursday afternoon, she saw the military car pull up.

"She said she didn't need them to tell her anything. She knew," said Melissa, who was eight at the time.

As the family waited for the country to return their boy home, they worried. A story circulating at that time seemed to impact the Huddleston family. An American boy's family had supposedly been notified that he had been killed in Vietnam. The casket went home with instructions for the family not to open it. The military frequently gave such guidance when they felt the body was so disfigured that it would be disturbing to the family to view. The family in the story did not open the casket and held a funeral for their son. A few months later, they received a call from their boy, who was very much alive.

While this story was certainly possible, it was also improbable. These early "urban myths" provided a false sense of hope to grieving families. Nevertheless, the stories made a circuit of families with loved ones in Vietnam and influenced many to check inside a casket they had been instructed to leave closed.

As Tommy's body returned to Newnan, the Huddleston family continued to grapple with the idea that their youngest son was gone. Terry Lewis said they all had difficulty believing it could be true. "Somebody was going to have to see the body in order for them to believe it."

Daryl, the oldest brother, insisted they wouldn't bury this coffin and put his mother through this ordeal until he was sure it was Tommy. Finally, Daryl got his chance and confirmed it was his brother. But viewing the body shook him to the core. Stories about the viewing of Tommy's body continue in the family today, suggesting that he was missing an arm and leg or even that the arm and leg were in the coffin with him. These are stories that no family should be required to endure.

The year 1968 saw the Huddleston family moving to a more rural part of Coweta County, off Poplar Road. The father had a shop in the garage behind the house, where he placed many photographs of his son.

"He and his dad were real close, and it really affected his dad something awful. I don't think he ever got to where he could deal with it," said Archie Slaton. "I remember when the house out on Poplar Road burned [in 1969]. I remember it burned all the pictures and everything they had of Tommy. That right there probably bothered him more than anything. That was the only memories they had of him."

Tommy was buried in Oak Hill Cemetery. A cousin, Johnny Calhoun, who would die four months later, returned from his tour in Vietnam to attend the funeral. (See Johnny Calhoun, Chapter 10.) Mike Watson, a friend of Tommy's who had one month to live, also attended. (See Joseph Michael Watson, Chapter 8.)

"I have thought about him a lot, he and some other friends," Slaton recalled. "There were a lot of guys from Newnan that were killed. I think constantly about Tommy, and I will never forget those guys. Tommy was my friend, my bud, and you don't ever forget. I still believe today that what got him killed was trying to protect someone else. In my eyes, he was a hero. Actually, he was a hero before that, as far as I'm concerned."

"He was just a unique fellow," said Melissa. "You look back, and you think at nineteen years old, how young. Now that I'm older, how young that really is. He didn't really have time to enjoy life."

After David Brown got home in April 1968, he visited Tommy's wife, Laura. "I probably was the last guy from Coweta County to see Tommy alive, and I just want you to know that he talked about you and that he loved you," David told her.

Tears came to her eyes as she introduced David to Tommy's son. David hugged him and told him, "You can be proud of your dad. He died a hero."

The Huddleston family sacrificed four men to the Vietnam War—Tommy, Johnny Calhoun, and two uncles. Melissa has visited the Wall in Washington, DC. "If you don't feel something in your heart, you don't have one."

Born: *September 4, 1946, in Roanoke, Alabama*
Home of record: *Newnan, Georgia*
Died: *November 19, 1967, in Kontum province of South Vietnam*
Coweta servicemen who died in the same province: *Arthur Hines,*

Stevan Pittman
***Unit on death**: C CO, 2nd BN, 503rd Infantry, 173rd Airborne Brigade*
***Decorations:** Bronze Star, Purple Heart, National Defense Service Medal, Vietnam Service Medal with Bronze Service Star, Republic of Vietnam Cross of Gallantry with Palm Citation, Republic of Vietnam Campaign Medal*
***Buried:** Oak Hill Cemetery, Newnan*
***Vietnam Memorial, Washington, DC:** Panel 30E Row 27*

Sources
Interview with Melissa Huddleston Warren, sister
Interview with Terry Lewis, cousin
Interview with Dennis Madaglia, cousin
Interview with Archie Slaton, childhood friend
Interview with Larry Hayes, childhood friend
Interview with David Brown, childhood friend
Interview with Millard Floyd, childhood friend
Email interview with Lester Daughtridge, 173rd Airborne Brigade
Research assistance from William Killian

References
Vietnam War Commemoration. "Operation Junction City Begins." Accessed December 8, 2021. https://www.vietnamwar50th.com/1966-1967_taking_the_offensive/Operation-JUNCTION-CITY-Begins/
Facebook. "Vietnam Reflections-Fallen Heroes." Accessed December 10, 2021. https://www.facebook.com/groups/506918322782909/
Wall of Faces. "Thomas Huddleston." Accessed December 10, 2021. https://www.vvmf.org/Wall-of-Faces/24499/THOMAS-P-HUDDLESTON/
John Ismay. "The Secret History of a Vietnam War Airstrike Gone Terribly Wrong." *New York Times*, January 31, 2019.
Coffelt Database, "Thomas Huddleston." Accessed November 20, 2020. http://coffeltdatabase.org/index.

Tommy Huddleston

Tommy and his father, Robert.

The Huddleston family receiving Tommy's bronze star medal.

CHAPTER SEVEN

Jerry Lynn Smith

Newnan, Georgia

I remember him today the way he went into service—young. I mean, he will always look young to us, even though it has been forty-three years since he's been gone. To me, he is still my little brother.
—Jackie Smith Stanford

The door to the classroom opened, and in walked Jerry Smith. An immaculate dresser, he emanated confidence. In his hands was an eye-catching box of valentine chocolates with beautiful lace and a red bow. Jerry had a broad smile on his face as he strode toward the teacher, who was standing behind her desk. He hesitated then presented her with the gift.

This scene is a vivid memory for Susan Rowe, a member of the Western Class of 1968.

> *Jerry came to Western when we were in sixth grade, as I recall [1962]. He was a few years older than us. Lucky for him, we had Mrs. Melson Beavers as our teacher that year. Mrs. Beavers had a sixth sense where her students were concerned. Being a mother of two boys herself, she always made us feel like we were part of a big family. She was very calm and maternal. That was probably why the principal put Jerry in our class.*
>
> *Jerry was a very quiet and kind person. He always had a shy smile and was well-mannered and easy-going. It was the time of penny loafers, buttoned-down collars, and pinstriped shirts. The boys didn't wear jeans. They wore slacks. Jerry was always ironed and creased and neat as a pin with*

loafers shining! I remember being in awe of him and being glad he was in our classroom.

Our school year began rather uneventfully that year, but by October, we had come face to face with the Cuban Missile Crisis! It was the year that every night at the supper table, the local news (WCOH radio station) would repeat the warnings from Russia! Most of us had written, 'I hate Nikita Khrushchev' on our Blue Horse notebooks! The Cuban Missile Crisis scared us all to death, but by the end of October, it had ended. There were a lot of history-making events during this time period, but we thought the worst was over. How could we have foreseen that the Vietnam War was just around the corner?

The school year rocked along, and finally, Valentine's Day arrived. We were so excited! None of us were old enough to have a boyfriend or girlfriend, but we pretended that we were anyway! But the big event that day, for me, was when Jerry Smith came in the door that morning with a big heart-shaped box of chocolates! It was covered in red and white lace with a red bow on top. It was so ornate and beautiful! A real store-bought box of candy! It was a first for a lot of us. For me, everything seemed to instantly switch over to slow motion as Jerry walked across the room to Mrs. Beavers's desk and handed her the box of candy. He had the sweetest smile on his face, and she was so gracious and humble as she accepted it. I knew then that I would remember it forever.

Many, many years later, I was asked to introduce Mrs. Beavers at our yearly Honor's Day program at Western Elementary School. Back then, we honored many of the former teachers of Western High School and gave an individual award in their names. It was always a big event! It was easy for me to share a story about Mrs. Beavers because she had held a special place in my heart since sixth grade. She still does! This particular year, I shared with the audience the story about Jerry Smith and the valentine box of chocolates. I described how pretty and ornate the box was, but mostly, just how proud Jerry was to present it to her. It was still a sweet memory for me, and I enjoyed sharing it! I think the audience did, too!

As Mrs. Beavers approached the podium to speak, I took the opportunity to ask her if she remembered that Valentine's Day and the box of chocolates. She answered in her usual calm and gracious voice. "Oh yes," she said, "I still have it." Jerry would have been so thrilled to know that his gift had meant so much to her. She had meant that much to him!

Western School was a small community school in the rural, western side of Coweta County. Students attended for grades one through twelve. They had one teacher for all subjects until they got to the eighth grade, where they started changing classes and teachers.

Female students at Western were required to take two years of Home Economics. All male students were required to take two years of Shop class. Hugh Beavers, the son of Jerry's teacher, had befriended Jerry, and they were good buddies at Western. In Shop class one day, the two friends became angry. Things got so heated that they used hammers to destroy each other's wood projects. As soon as they finished, the disagreement was over, and they returned to being chums. No one remembers what precipitated that uncharacteristic outburst.

Rowe said that as the bus dropped Jerry off at his home each day, his sister June was waiting for him in the driveway. Jerry would run over and hug her.

Jerry lived in a "perfect neighborhood," according to Steve Pierce, "because there were a lot of guys my age that all liked football, we all liked baseball, we all liked camping out, so the neighborhood was perfect because there were other kids my age here. We always enjoyed summer because we got to do everything." The neighborhood off Franklin Highway had four to five boys. Jerry lived on Wynn Street.

"Jerry enjoyed playing outside because he was a boy, and he had a house full of sisters," said Pierce. "We spent a lot of time camping down past the next street, Gordon Street, that was wooded, you know. In the summertime, we just camped out the whole weekend, making our forts and tents and things like that. There was a creek there. We used to play in that creek. We used to have BB gun battles. I remember that. That was fun. We divided up into teams, and we had BB gun battles. They sting a little bit, but we were playing war and playing Army and learning the benefits of having the high ground, things like that, because there were some hilly places down in the woods."

Pete Turner, another friend who lived across Wynn Street, said the guys loved to build forts in the woods. "Wood [to build forts] always managed to end up back in the woods with us. Not sure how it got there, and somehow or another, there was always some beer that ended up back there [as they got older]. I don't know where it came from, don't know where it went."

Turner said Jerry could play almost any game that involved a ball, and Pierce agreed. They said Jerry had good "power" with a bat when they played Little League. They enjoyed playing home run derby and basketball. They played football at Peter Turner's house because it had softer grass than the other boys' yards. All of Jerry's friends called him Smitty.

Turner recalled Jerry as tough but mild-mannered. Walking home one day, a boy threatened to jump on Jerry and pushed Turner aside. Turner jumped in the way and told the boy, "Before you get to him, you go through me."

Jerry was the same way.

"That's how close friends we were. You mess with one, you mess with both," Turner said. "Me and Jerry never had a cross word in our lives. He was a guy you could always count on."

Jerry was born on August 12, 1947. His mother, Ruby, worked in the home. His father, Lynn Smith, worked in the cotton mill when the kids were small. He typically got his hair cut at the barbershop run by Tom Holloway in downtown Newnan in the space above present-day Morgan's Jewelry. Holloway offered him a job, and Lynn found his calling as a barber.

The family had five children—Cecil, Jackie, Janice, June, and Jerry.

"He was a happy child," said sister Jackie. "He was the baby of the family. We all kind of gave in to him. Of course, my mother just thought he was all there was. Anything he wanted, she tried to see that he got it. She felt like he would go into the service when he grew up. So she tried to make him happy as much as she could."

His sisters said he always had a smile on his face and was forever teasing them. June said, "He came home one day and had this green snake wrapped around his hand, and I wouldn't let him come in the house. It was just me and him. He said, 'Awww, it's dead.' So I was going to unhook the screen and saw that head stick up. I slammed that door and locked it and wouldn't let him come in until our older brother got home from work."

Jackie got married when Jerry was twelve, and her groom was also named Jerry. He became "Big" Jerry, and her brother became "Little" Jerry. Big Jerry would take Little Jerry fishing and to play ball, which Jerry enjoyed.

Miriam Horton encountered Jerry in seventh grade at Western and found him quiet, shy, and very friendly.

Pete Turner asked her one day, "Did you know that Jerry Smith likes you?"

Miriam and Jerry started sitting together on the bus and attending basketball and baseball games. They went to the movies and the fair. Jerry sat behind her in class, called her on Sunday afternoon to talk, and gave her a Valentine's Day card and candy. Jerry also gave Miriam a US Army ring and a photograph. He told her that the ring was given to him by his brother.

Miriam described Jerry in her seventh-grade diary.

> *His name is Jerry Smith. He is about 14. About 5'8" or taller, weighs about 135, he has brown hair and green eyes; he is very cute to me. His favorite color is blue, his favorite sport is football, his favorite song is Jimmy Come Lately. He has brown skin. I got his ring on May 29, 1962; the ring says United States Army. His brother gave it to him before he went away. It is a very pretty ring; it fits him perfectly.*

Miriam doesn't remember what happened and why they broke up, but she knows that the relationship ended the summer of her eighth-grade year. She recalled that his brother Cecil came in where she worked after Jerry's death and said, "You were the one that Jerry used to like when he was younger."

Miriam Horton still visits Jerry's grave.

Jerry Moore, about seven years younger than Jerry Smith, recalled the impression that Jerry left on a young boy. On the Western High School Facebook page in 2020, he described an encounter with Jerry.

> *Jerry Smith was sweet on one of my sisters. I don't know which one. [The sister was Susan.] One day while on the bus (I guess he learned I was a little brother) he let me know that if I needed anything or anybody bothered me to just let him know. I don't know what year it was or how long after that we lost him. I never forgot what that made me feel like. To sit tall beside such a guy. And know he had my back. We made friends that day on the bus. And as the story unfolds, he did have my back and all the rest of us. A true hero.*

"He always looked sharp and snappy. Somebody you would always want to grow up to be, and that left a big, giant impression on me," said Moore.

Jerry attended Western until he turned sixteen, when he left school permanently. Steve Pierce said he and Jerry hung out at the skating rink off the square in downtown Newnan. Buck's Pool Room was next door, but they couldn't go in until they turned sixteen. Eventually, they got into Buck's. They were both excellent at pool and enjoyed playing together. This freedom marked the beginning of the boys entering the "adult" world, always attractive to teenagers. As they got older, however, they drifted apart.

Like many young males, Jerry wanted to purchase his own vehicle. He worked the night shift at Bonnell Aluminum on Temple Avenue. Jerry got off work around 11 p.m. and often went to the Oaks Motel on Route 29 with Pete Turner, who worked the same shift at Bonnell, to get something to eat. One night as they drove toward the motel, they cut through Armory Road beside Newnan High School. As they gunned it up Sewell Road, a Newnan police car came by them, going the other way. They had beer in the car. They saw the police car begin to turn around, so they turned right onto Greenville Street. The policeman caught up and pulled them over on Greenville Street, but there was no beer in the vehicle.

Afterward, the two went to the Oaks, where they ate and chatted with other customers. When they finished, they went back to Sewell Road and looked for the beer. They found all of it!

Jerry worked at Bonnell from 1964 to 1965. Pete Turner, a year older than Jerry, was married at Mills Chapel Baptist Church in 1965 with Jerry serving as best man. Jerry, however, couldn't be outdone in the romance department. Handsome and athletic, he had a smile that put girls at ease. Never loud and boisterous, he was generally quiet in a crowd but talkative with friends. He rarely got upset and never judged the people around him.

Carolyn Pittman and her family lived on Murray Street in Newnan, and Jerry had a buddy named Larry who lived across the street.

"Where I lived," said Carolyn, "there was a guy that lived across the street, and I didn't know it for a while, but Jerry would go see him and sit outside so that he could see me because he didn't really know me, but he wanted to ask me for a date, and he didn't know how." She laughed. "He finally got up enough nerve to ask me to go out with him."

Jerry made quite an impression on that first date when he drove into a post at the drive-in theater. He worried that Carolyn's father wouldn't let her go out with him again.

"My dad was very strict, but he told him, 'It's OK, accidents happen, and you're both OK, so there's no problem,'" Carolyn said. She was two years older than Jerry, and he didn't want to tell her his age because he was afraid she would refuse to go out with him. When he finally told her, she just laughed. Carolyn liked Jerry, and his age made no difference. She worked for the Manufacturers National Bank then the First National Bank on the square in downtown Newnan. She ran a proof machine and was responsible for using it to review transactions for accuracy. She then worked as the bank president's secretary.

Jerry and Carolyn dated for about three years. They went to the movies, out to eat, and did the Newnan teen cruise—Burger Chef on Temple Avenue, Brazier Burgers on the north end of Greenville Street, and the Dairy Bar (Big John's) on the south end of Greenville. They visited each other's homes, and they did things with Jerry's sister Jackie and her husband. They double dated with

J.C. Cofield and his girlfriend, Diane Posey. When Diane was unavailable, J.C. occasionally joined Jerry and Carolyn for some fun. "We were going to get married whenever he got back from Vietnam," said Carolyn. (See Jessie C. Cofield, Chapter 5.)

Jackie Stanford said Jerry had a girlfriend, Carolyn Pittman, when he went into service. "She worked at the bank here," said Jackie. "This was the special one. I know that they would have gotten married. He even toted her checkbook around. She just turned everything over to him."

Jerry finally got the car that he desired, a 1965 Red Chevrolet Impala. Carolyn was enamored with it as well. Charles Stanford enjoyed riding around town in the car. Jackie said Jerry even took her little girls for rides. However, it wasn't long before the adult world intruded on Jerry's seemingly idyllic life.

Pete Turner was drafted into the military in January 1966, and Jerry followed six months later. He entered military service in September 1966. Charles Stanford was working part-time at the Westside Service Station on Temple Avenue and recalled Jerry coming by the station to say he'd gotten his draft notice.

"You could tell that he was down in the dumps. He said that he knew his time was coming to go, but he said, 'I just got my brand-new car… sure would like to ride around some more before I went into the army.'" Stanford replied, "You'll be back before you turn around."

"We didn't like it, but he was willing to go for his country. He was ready to go when they called him," Jackie said.

Jerry Smith was eighteen years old.

Jerry did his Basic Training at Fort Benning in Columbus. Stanford and a few other guys from Western went down to visit Jerry, and some others they knew were there on the weekend. His family attended his graduation. After that, he came home on leave, got his car out, and rode around. Then he was off to Fort Polk, Louisiana, for Advanced Infantry Training. When he finished, he got thirty days' leave and returned home. He got the car out again and rode around, visiting with friends.

"Jerry seemed to have something heavy on his mind," said Stanford. "I told one boy that didn't seem like the Jerry Smith I knew."

The day Jerry was to catch a plane for Vietnam, he visited Stanford at the service station. One of Jerry's uncles was with him and started giving him advice; Uncle Reuben was a World War II veteran. Jerry told him, "I ain't coming back."

Uncle Reuben quickly responded, "Boy, don't talk like that. You will make it back."

Jerry said, "He had that gut feeling that he wasn't coming back."

Before Jerry caught the flight, he visited Carolyn. She'd been sick with the flu, and she and Jerry hadn't been able to go out the night before. He left her and went to the airport, but the flight was delayed, so he returned to Newnan and checked on his sweetheart. That afternoon, Jerry left on a flight out of Atlanta.

"He came back," said Stanford, "but he didn't come back alive."

Carolyn felt that Jerry's coming back to see her was a cause of his later misfortune. "I felt it was bad luck," she said.

Pete Turner was assigned to a unit in Germany. Steve Pierce ended up in the combat engineers and headed to Vietnam. He was there about the same time as Jerry, but they never had any contact.

"I kept in touch with what he was doing through my parents because my parents lived here, and he lived six to eight houses down the street," Pierce said. "I figured he was in danger most all the time being in the infantry. I wasn't in the infantry and experienced some of it but not like those guys. I mean, those guys are my heroes. They're the ones that didn't know if they would live from minute to minute. I was in combat engineering and got a Purple Heart from being wounded. It just wasn't that bad. There were times that I feared for my life, but it couldn't have been anything like those guys were facing every day. So that's why I have a lot of respect for World War II veterans, you know? Those guys are the heroes. What I did was nothing."

When Jerry Smith arrived in Vietnam, he went to the First Cavalry Division with the military occupational specialty (MOS) of 11C, an indirect fire infantryman. That specialty typically worked with mortars. Jerry, however, appears to have ended up as a machine gunner.

The headline of an undated article in the *Newnan Times-Herald* reads "Jerry L. Smith Participates in Viet Operation." According to the press release from the US Army in Vietnam, "Army Private First

Class Jerry L. Smith, son of Mr. and Mrs. L.A. Smith, 12 Wynn Street, Newnan, Ga., is participating in 'Operation Pershing' in Vietnam. Pvt. Smith and other members of the 1st Air Cavalry Division have evacuated more than 19,000 refugees from coastal areas to numerous refugee centers in secured areas as well as inflicted heavy damage on the Viet Cong. During the search and clear operation, Private Smith has been engaged in dragging the VC from their vast network of tunnels and bunkers. They had been driven underground by constant US artillery and airstrikes. Private Smith is a machine gunner in Company D, 2nd Battalion of the division's 12th Cavalry."

Operation Pershing started in February 1967, about the time that Jerry Smith arrived in Vietnam. The operation went on for eleven months in the Binh Dinh province, located along the coast of the II Corp region of Vietnam. The First Cavalry Division attempted to sweep the North Vietnamese and Viet Cong from the area. According to The American Warrior website:

> *Operation Pershing triggered eighteen major engagements and countless skirmishes as the troopers of the 1st Cav struggled to clear tunnel and cave complexes on the Bong Son Plain and its environs. The battles in Binh Dinh Province have been overshadowed by the Ia Drang Valley campaign of '65 and the 1st Cav's role in it, but the battles fought there in 1967 inflicted heavy casualties on the NVA and VC (almost 8,000 killed or captured) and became the longest single operation of the division's experience in the Vietnam War.*

Though Jerry never mentioned Operation Pershing in his letters home, he was involved and described some of what he did during that operation.

Smith wrote home to his siblings and his girlfriend, Carolyn. He also made sure to write his mother frequently, and his odyssey in Vietnam is chronicled in his letters to her. The grammar and spelling, copied verbatim from Jerry's letters, reflect his lack of education and the rush in which they were frequently written. However, Jerry had excellent handwriting. Interestingly, Jerry talked about becoming a radio-telephone operator in Vietnam, not a machine gunner. While his accounts were often incomplete, they give a glimpse into Jerry's daily life in Vietnam in 1967.

September 17, 1966. Jerry was in Basic Combat Training at Fort Benning. Letter to his mother, Mrs. Ruby Smith. Excerpts.

Hi Mom,

Just a few lines to say hello and to let you know I'm fine. We got to Fort Benning last night about 8:30. I hadn't been doing much but marching and cleaning up this damn place.I got my hair cut off Friday morning and I look like a bald eagle. We hadn't been working to hard except for getting our clothes. That was the hardest thing I've done yet. We plan to start training Tuesday morning.I have had guard duty two times since I've been here and KP [kitchen police] once. It not so bad. I think I will like it once I get in basic training.

Mom have you heard from Carolyn since I left. I haven't had a chance to wright her yet. This is the first chance I've had to wright anybody.

October 25, 1966. Jerry was in Basic Combat Training. Letter to his mother, Mrs. Ruby Smith. Excerpts.

Well Moma we went out to the rifle range today and I shot reall good I got 46 out of 56 targets it was about third in the Co. of about 220 men. So I thing I done real good. I just hope I can do that good tomorrow. I need 14 out of 28 targets to shoot expert. I sure hope I can do it. I would like to have one of those expert badges. [Based on a photograph of his military awards, it appears that he attained the Expert rating.]

November 24, 1966. Thanksgiving Day. Jerry was in Advanced Infantry Training at Fort Polk, Louisiana. Letter to his mother, Mrs. Ruby Smith. Excerpts.

Hello Mom,

Just thought I would wright a few lines while I wasn't doing anything. This is the first time I have had a few hours off sence I've been here. We start training at 6:00 every morning and it is 8:30 or 9:00 before we get off. So I don't have much time to wright. We got off at 10:00 this morning and put on our class A and went to church. After church we ate Thanksgiving dinner you should have seen the mess hall it was really beautiful the way they had it fixed up. It was the best meal I have had sence I've been in the Army. I just wish I could have been home to eat dinner with you and all the rest.

Moma, we are suppose to leave here this 16 or 17 of Dec. for our 14 day leave. I don't know how I will get there. I wanted to fly but I don't know [illegible] I will have enough money or not and even if I have enough money I don't know where I can get reservations but I will get there some way if I have to walk all the way.

March 2, 1967. Jerry was in Vietnam. Letter to his mother, Mrs. Ruby Smith. Excerpts.

Hello Mom,

Well mom I finally got what I wanted ever since I have been in the Army I have wanted to be in the 1st Cav. and I finally got it. I think I am going to like it here now. Everyone is real nice here it don't seem like the Army over here. The country is really beautiful here. I am in the northern part of Vietnam at a place called An Khe. There is nothing but mountains and more mountains. I think I am going to really like it here.

March 2, 1967. Jerry was in Vietnam. Letter to his mother, Mrs. Ruby Smith. Excerpts.

We are LZ Two-Bits they said we would be here about five days. I sure hope so because we don't do anything but eat and sleep.

Yes, mom- I am getting your mail and I have been getting it for about three weeks now, so I wish you send my glasses. I got a letter from Steve yesterday he's at Cu Chi its south of Saigon and I'm about 85 miles north of Saigon. I am going to try to go down there and see him in a couple of months during my in country R & R. He said in his letter that John Smith was in Saigon. I sure would like to see both of them.

[It seems likely that the Steve referenced in this letter is Steve Pierce, as they were in Vietnam at the same time. However, Steve doesn't recall having any contact with Jerry while in Vietnam.]

March 3, 1967. Jerry was in Vietnam. Letter to his mother, Mrs. Ruby Smith. Excerpts.

Well its about 6:30 and I'm sitter at the EM [enlisted man's] *Club, drinking a cold Blue Ribbon. We get off work at 4:30 every day and I come over here and drink a few beers because there is nothing else to do. My company is going out to the field the 7th of this month and wont come back in until May. But I wont leave with them because I have got 3 days of training so I guess I will leave about the 12th to go out. Everyone says the time goes by a lot faster while you are in the field.*

Moma, I think I am going to Hawaii in July on my RR They will pay my way their and back. I would like to have about 3 or 4 hundred dollars to spend while I am their. I should have about that much sent home by then. I'll just have 7 days but I want to live it up while I am there. Well, mom its getting late and I've got to write Carolyn before it gets dark. So be good and don't worry about me. Ans. Soon
Love, Jerry

April 5, 1967. Jerry was in Vietnam. Letter to his mother, Mrs. Ruby Smith. Excerpts.

I had my picture made Sat. and it should be in the paper in about two weeks. I wish you would send me a copy of it. I know it will look terrible because I hadn't shaved or took a bath for a week and I hadn't changed clothes for about three weeks.
Well, I got a new job last week I'm a R.T.O. [radio-telephone operator] *it about the same thing I've been doing but I like it a lot better. I don't know much about it now because I never went to school of* [for] *it. Most of the RTO went to school for nine weeks but I hope I can learn everything about* [it].

April 27, 1967. Jerry was in Vietnam. Letter to his mother, Mrs. Ruby Smith. Excerpts.

Hi Mom

Just thought I would write a few lines to say hello and to let you know I'm still alive. I know its been about three weeks since I've wrote a letter but we have been working pretty hard lately.

Mom, you keep asking me if I have got my glasses well I got them about a month ago and I finally got one of the boxes candy you sent. The boys in my sq. [squad] *really enjoyed it. I still haven't got my camera yet. I guess its back in base camp. We should be going in about four or five days. I sure hope so we have been out in the field for almost six weeks and I'm tired of sleeping in the woods. I hope you didn't pay 5.75 for that picture because I know its not any good. You asked me if I had to wear all that junk I had on. Well, that just about half of the junk I have to carry. That was just my fighting gear. I have to pack and a radio to carry the radio weights about 27lbs and the pack is about 30lbs but its not all that heavy.*

Moma, I thought you was going to send me a paper every week. I got one paper about three weeks ago and I've been looking for one every since then. If it not too much trouble I wish you would send me one every week.

May 1, 1967. Jerry was in Vietnam. Letter to his mother, Mrs. Ruby Smith. Excerpts.

Hi Mom,

Just a few lines to say hello and to let you hear from me. Well, how is everyone back in the world. As for me I'm OK as usual. We haven't been doing anything for the last 7 days but sitting on our fat ass and taking it easy. The old man told us yesterday that we would be going in June 1. I sure hope so I'm tired of being in the field all the time. I was reading in the paper yesterday that a friend of mine I took AIT with was killed about three weeks ago. I sure did hate to hear it but you have to expect that in a place like this. Monday morning about 10 oclock A Co. caught 27 VC [Viet Cong] *taking a bath in a stream and they didn't have to fire a shot. It was only about 1 1/2 miles from where we are at. We are in An Lao valley now if you watch the news you should hear about this place.*

May 24, 1967. Jerry was in Vietnam. Letter to his mother, Mrs. Ruby Smith. Excerpts.

Yesterday we were on a patrol and killed one VC and captured another one. We also found a VC hospital and burned it. They said we done a good job so they gave us the day off.

Well, we have been out in the field for 69 day now I'm beginning to wonder if we are every going in. Moma when we do get back to base camp I am going to try to call you if I can. I think I am going on R&R about July if nothing happens. I have been thinking about going to Tokoyo or Hawaii but I don't care where I go I just want to get out of this place for awhile.

July 26, 1967. Jerry was in Vietnam. Letter to his mother, Mrs. Ruby Smith. Entire letter.

Hello Mom,

Just a few lines to say hello and to answer you letter I got today. I was really glad to hear from you as usual. Yes mom I got the money about a week ago but this is the first chance I've had to write. I got back to base camp Monday and it sure does feel good to get back. It was the first time I have seen this place for over four month. Mom I never did get the film you send. They must have got lost on the way. Well, if nothing happens I will leave for Bangkok Friday and I sure will be glad I really do need a rest. A good friend of mine that got over here the same time I did is going with me. Would you believe I mad SP/4 the 17 of this month it means about $50 more a month and I can sue the money. Well Mom, I hate to make this short but its chow time so I will close for now. I will call you when I get to Bangkok. Ans. soon.

Love,

Jerry

August 4, 1967. Jerry was in Vietnam. Letter to his mother, Mrs. Ruby Smith. Entire Letter.

Hello Mom

How are you today? Fine I hope as for me I'm OK! Except tired. We got back to Cam Ranh Bay yesterday about 2:00 and I have been sleeping most of the time. We were supposed to leave for An Khe at 6:30 this morning but we wanted to stay here for two or three days to rest up after our R&R. I really had a wonderful time while I was there but I think I spent too much money. I spend over $500 in four days and five nights. Four boys from my company went with me. I had five suits made and they are really beautiful. I am going to send two of them home when I get back to An Khe. I haven't paid for the other three yet but when I get paid next month I am going to send the money to the man and he will send the suits home.Mom, I want you to pay for that telephone call out of my check because I know you can't afford to pay for it. It should be about $70 or $80 dollars and I want you to take it out of my check. OK!I am sending you a few pictures we took while we were there they are not very good but what can you expect.Well mom, I think I will close for now and go over to the club. Tell everyone I said hello. Ans. soon.

Love,

Jerry

September 29, 1967. Jerry was in Vietnam. Letter to his mother, Mrs. Ruby Smith. Excerpts.

Thanks a lot for the package it sure was good. But next time don't send that much fruit, one can of peaches is enough. I hope you are keeping enough money out of my check to pay for it. I was really sorry to hear about JC but I try to not let anything like that bother me. [J.C. Cofield was killed on September 13, 1967.] I have seen too many men killed and hurt bad over here and I just can't aford to let something like that get to me. Well that's enough of that. Did I tell you I got my air metal and CIB last month? They can keep all of their damn metals as long as I get out of this hell

> *hole.*
> *Mom, I think Carolyn has got a birthday coming up about the last part of Oct. I wish you would find out when it is and send her about two dozen yellow or red roses.*

November 11, 1967. Jerry was in Vietnam. Letter to his mother, Mrs. Ruby Smith. Excerpts.

> *Did you know I've only got 102 days left in this place. I just hope the next three months goes as fast as the first 9 months.*

November 20, 1967. Jerry was in Vietnam. Letter to his mother, Mrs. Ruby Smith. Excerpts.

> *Well, I'm on my way to Penang now. We left Cam Rahn Bay about 1 hr. ago and we will be in Penang in about 1 1/2 hrs. I didn't care nothing about going to Tokyo so I thought I would go back to Penang. I really had a good time the last time I was there.* [Penang is in Malaysia, not far from Thailand. Perhaps Jerry visited there on his last R&R.]

December 27, 1967. Jerry was in Vietnam. Letter to his mother, Mrs. Ruby Smith. Excerpts.

> *Well, I hope everyone had a Merry Christmas it wasn't too bad over here. We had the day off and a hot meal and that was all I wanted. Well mom, I've got 56 DAYS left over here.*
> *I got 17 packages last week from all over the states. I don't know how the people got my name and address, but I was glad to get the packages. Mom I got the pound cake yesterday and it sure was good.*

According to his sister Janice, Jerry called home at least once during the year.

"I answered the phone and talked to him a little bit. We always picked on each other about weight, and I asked him if he had lost any weight. He said yeah, and I said maybe I should come over there. He said you don't want to come over in this hell hole." She gave the phone to her mother, who started crying.

Toward the end of 1967, the First Cavalry sent Jerry and his Company north to Firebase Leslie (Hill 138), a firebase that contained both US and South Vietnamese troops not far from the ancient city of Hoi An. In Vietnam, a firebase provided artillery and mortar support for US infantry soldiers in that particular area. The hill was occupied by D Company, Jerry's company, and a platoon from A Company. On January 3, 1968, four firebases in this valley were struck hard by North Vietnamese rockets and mortars. Ground attacks on firebases Leslie and Ross followed. At Firebase Leslie, NVA soldiers penetrated the base that morning and attacked bunkers using satchel charges and flamethrowers.

Jerry was killed that morning by shrapnel, perhaps in the initial volley of rockets or mortars. Conceivably, it was later in the morning. According to Pete Turner, Jerry was on his machine gun and was killed by a mortar. He had been promoted to sergeant but had not gotten the news yet; the schedule showed him going home in six weeks.

In Newnan, Jerry's family believed his tour was ending. Carolyn was getting three or four letters a week from him. He was already sending some things home. Consequently, the family was expecting Jerry home soon when "those two soldiers showed up at the door. It was terrible," Jackie said.

After the soldiers visited the Smith home, Jerry's parents sent them to Carolyn's house. She was eating dinner with her parents when there was a knock on the door. When she opened it, two soldiers stood there in dress uniforms. She fainted.

"Evidently, I passed out and hit the floor because when I woke up, I was in the hospital," she said. "Mother and Daddy said they heard me hit the floor and went running in there. I remember Daddy telling me that the two soldiers said, 'We didn't do anything to her, sir. She just opened the door and passed out.' I knew what they were there for."

Steve Pierce recalled having "a hollow feeling" after hearing the news. "I had probably been sheltered my whole life. Not a lot of death, things like this except distant relatives… It just didn't seem real that someone I knew and had grown up with is now gone." When Jerry died, Pierce was deciding whether to extend his tour or get out of the military. Then the letter about Jerry arrived from his parents, who worried that this could happen to him. "Since I was on the fence anyway, I just decided not to reenlist."

Someone called Pete Turner and told him about Jerry. He remembered their plan to go squirrel hunting when Jerry got back. "It was like a part of me died too," Turner said. "Jerry was a friend that everybody wanted. That is the kind of friend that you would like to have. I think about him all the time. You know, he was my brother."

Jerry was listed as Missing in Action for a few days, then the military changed his status to Killed in Action. The family waited eighteen days for his body to come home. Jerry's personal effects were sent to his family, but many things that came home weren't familiar. The military had mixed up his effects with those of another Jerry Smith, possibly Jerry Walton Smith of Orange, Texas, who was killed in February of 1968.

The blast that killed Jerry focused on his head and face, with the rest of his body seemingly undisturbed. The military wanted the coffin to remain closed; the family opened it anyway. His brother Cecil told others that the family didn't recognize him. No one wished for Jerry's parents to see him, but Jerry's sisters believe they did so at some point. Carolyn wasn't allowed to view the body and remembers little about the funeral.

At Jerry's home on Wynn Street, two soldiers stayed with him, one at the head of the coffin and the other at the foot. Hillcrest handled the funeral, and Mills Chapel Baptist Church held the service on East Washington Street. Jerry was laid to rest near his friend J.C. Cofield in Oak Hill Cemetery.

After the funeral, Jerry's mother stayed in bed for several days. Eventually, they called a doctor to see her. His father wouldn't sell Jerry's Impala and kept it in the garage.

"Mom and Daddy never really got over him being killed over there. Our family changed. Our mama wouldn't put up a Christmas tree or anything for the longest time. We just didn't celebrate no more," Jackie said. "They used to go over to the cemetery and just sit there all day. It was awful. Daddy only lived for a couple of years after Jerry got killed. He just kinda grieved himself to death."

After Jerry's funeral, Carolyn received a letter from him postmarked from Vietnam. Hope sprang forth, and she insisted to her parents that the military had made a mistake and Jerry wasn't dead. Her parents gently showed her the postmark and explained how she had gotten the letter after Jerry had been laid to rest. "It took me a long time to accept that," she said.

A couple of years later, Carolyn got married.

"Carolyn told Mamma that she found somebody. She found somebody as close to Jerry as she could find, and she said she was going to marry him, but it didn't work out," Jackie Stanford said.

"We often wonder what his life would be like if he were still alive," she said. "We keep his cemetery up. You can go there any time, and there will be flowers. If they start fading, we change them. He was willing to go for his country, even though I'm sure he was scared and didn't want to, but he never said he wouldn't go. He was right ready when he was called. And that made us very proud of him too. He is the sweetest boy that ever lived, and I'm not just saying that bragging. He really was."

The same week that Jerry died, Charles Stanford got his draft notice.

**To see the catalog of original letters to and from Jerry Smith, visit www.bettermencoweta.com.

***Born**: August 12, 1947, in Newnan, Georgia*
***Home of record**: Newnan, Georgia*
***Died**: January 3, 1968, in Quang Nam province of South Vietnam*
***Coweta servicemen who died in the same province**: Daniel Post, Bill Thomas, Mike Watson, and Larry Pinson*
***Unit on death**: D CO, 2nd BN, 12th Cavalry, 1st Cavalry Division*
***Decorations:** Purple Heart, National Defense Medal, Vietnam Service Medal, Republic of Vietnam Campaign Medal*
***Buried:** Oak Hill Cemetery, Newnan*
***Vietnam Memorial, Washington, DC:** Panel 33E Line 32*

Sources

Interview with Jackie Smith Stanford, sister
Interview with Janice Smith Wolfe, sister
Interview with June Smith Bowman, sister
Interview with Charles Stanford, childhood friend

Interview with Pete Turner, childhood friend
Interview with Steve Pierce, childhood friend
Interview with Miriam Horton, childhood friend
Interview with Donna Moore, classmate
Interview with Susan Rowe, classmate
Interview with Carolyn Pittman Wilbanks, fianceé
Assistance from William Killian, researcher
Assistance from Pam Beavers and Joe Loadholtes, US Army

References

Coffelt Database, "Jerry Smith." Accessed September 20, 2021. http://coffeltdatabase.org/index.php

John Bruning. "Operation Pershing: They Rode with Custer's Ghost." The American Warrior, https://theamericanwarrior.com/tag/operation-pershing/

Jerry Smith, 8th grade, and in Vietnam, 1967

MR. AND MRS. LYNN A. SMITH, 12 Wynn Street, solemnly display the medals awarded posthumously to their son, Sgt. Jerry Lynn Smith, who was killed in action against a hostile force in the Republic of Vietnam on January 3, 1968. Sergeant Smith was posthumously awarded the Bronze Star, the Air Medal, the Purple Heart, Vietnam Service Medals, and other individual military badges.

Ruby and Lynn Smith, with Jerry's medals.

Photos courtesy of Jackie Stanford.

CHAPTER EIGHT

Joseph Michael Watson

Moreland, Georgia

Death leaves a heartache no one can heal; love leaves a memory no one can steal.
—From an Irish headstone

It was the third week of January 1968. The United States had yet to be shaken by the Tet Offensive. The assassinations of Martin Luther King and Bobby Kennedy were still to come. Sandra Jordan had no clue what the future held as she forced herself to get up early that morning and don her winter gear; it had snowed in Newnan, Georgia.

Her boyfriend, Mike, had wanted her to take photographs of the flakes, as it snowed so seldom. She grabbed her camera and headed outdoors, walking up a small hill behind the house where she might be able to get good pictures. Once satisfied that Mike would be pleased with her efforts, Sandra planned how to get them developed and sent to him. Stomping the snow off her boots and in a bit of a trance, she reentered the house. The phone rang incessantly. Her mother finally answered and, looking puzzled, motioned her over. When Sandra answered, she realized it was Mike's mother, and her voice sounded peculiar. Why was Mike's mother calling her?

In a flash, it became abundantly clear. Sandra let out what was later described as a "blood-curdling" scream. Family members ran into the room, but Sandra couldn't speak. She tried, but nothing came out. Finally, she gave the phone to her mother. Her boyfriend, Mike, was in Vietnam, and she had just realized that her teenage dreams would never come true.

"Later," Sandra said, "Mike's mother came to the house and visited with my mother for a long time. I went home with her and got up the next morning when she and I, along with this guy she had living with her, went to tell Charles (Mike's brother) that Mike had died. We were over at his grandmother's house by the railroad track near Salbide Avenue when Charles locked himself in the bedroom. He wouldn't eat. There was no way they could get that door open. The house was an old one with high ceilings and heavy locks on the doors. He finally came out after two days."

Mike Watson returned to Newnan on a day of severe January weather, and winter storms threatened to delay the body's return from the airport. When Sandra got to Hillcrest Funeral Home that day, she counted the steps going up and into the beautiful antebellum home. They were greeted at the door and taken to the room where the casket lay.

"I just looked at him and said, 'That's not Mike.' When the thing blew up, it had burned his hair off of his eyebrows and eyelashes. He had been dead for two weeks, and he was swollen, and he didn't look like himself at all. From that time, his mother and I never left the funeral home. We just told them that we were staying. The first night, about one a.m., there was someone at the front door of Hillcrest, tapping on the door because the door was locked. I looked, and it was Archie Slaton and Phil Tucker. They came in, and we all just held each other and cried. Janie [Mike's mother] had taken something to help her sleep, and she was sleeping on the sofa in that room. We pulled some chairs up close to Mike, and we could see the side of his face. I went to the bathroom, and when I came back in, I caught a glimpse of the side of his face, and it looked like Mike. That's the first time that it looked like Mike."

Archie Slaton, Phil Tucker, and a few more of Mike's friends had been at a local restaurant when they heard that Mike's body had returned to Newnan that day. Archie was distraught. Mike had just been home on leave. What had happened?

The day of the funeral arrived. Sandra's mother brought her a change of clothes. She went to dress in something more appropriate and ran into the military honor guard, waiting for the funeral to start. "I couldn't breathe," Sandra said.

The funeral finally began, and numerous young people attended.

"I don't remember the preacher. I don't remember the service whatsoever. I was just so fixed on him," said Sandra. "I couldn't hear. I couldn't feel the cold at the cemetery. In fact, I got up and walked out without my coat. Someone chased me down at the cemetery and got it on me. It was like we were dazed. It was like it was not real. I have lost people that I loved, but I have never experienced anything like that."

Archie Slaton said he and the other soldiers were always proud to be in the military but didn't quite understand what they were there for. "There was also a lot of rebellion going on at the time, but living in Newnan, which was a small town then, you didn't think much about it," he said. "But we realized that this thing was real. A lot of our guys wanted to join, and some of them did, I think just out of pure curiosity. That was just the way we were. We thought we were ten feet tall and bulletproof."

From the end of November until mid-January, three young men from Coweta County had been killed in Vietnam and laid to rest in Oak Hill Cemetery: Tommy Huddleston (Chapter 6), Jerry Smith (Chapter 7), and now Michael Watson.

Joseph Michael Watson was born on February 28, 1948, in Moreland.[1] His father, John Watson, was one of his mother's many boyfriends and wasn't around as Mike grew up. His mother was Janie Conley. Mike had two older sisters, Carol and Sandra, and an older brother, Billy, all of whom had been adopted by other families. Mike never knew them. Mike had a younger brother, Charles Entrekin, born a few years after Mike and by a different boyfriend.

Mike, Charles, and their mother moved around during Mike's childhood, never staying long in one place. The family moved to Valdosta then to Griffin for a short time before returning to Newnan, where they rented a house on Welcome Road. His mother was a waitress and tended bar at truck stops and other establishments. Eventually, she and her two boys settled in Mike's grandmother's large white house at the intersection of Robinson Street and Salbide Avenue. Mike always took care of his little brother.

"He watched after that kid. He really did," said Sandra.

Judy Proctor, a friend of Mike, said Charles was "a very cute little boy when he was younger." Mike became his protector.

As Mike Watson became a teenager, he had little supervision

from home. Larry Hayes befriended Mike at Atkinson Elementary School. As they grew older, they hung out at Union Station, the train station a few blocks from the old train depot on East Broad Street. Union Station was at the intersection of Savannah and Dunbar Streets, a few blocks from Mike's grandmother's home. This station was the hub of passenger and cargo trains that went through Newnan during the 1940s, 1950s, and 1960s. They liked to hang out here because they could smoke in the station's bathroom.[2] They also enjoyed hanging out at the Alamo Theater. They didn't hang out very much at Mike's grandmother's home, as Larry felt that Mike's grandmother was mean.

"I don't think she liked me very well," Larry said, "and I don't know that she liked Mike that much either. My mother and grandmother liked Mike. They really did. The only time Mike got into trouble with my grandmother was when he would come to the house, and we had a peach tree, and he would pick the peaches green and eat them. My grandmother used to get mad at him about that."

Larry felt that since Mike didn't appear to have much support at home, he was forced to fend for himself. His education was erratic at best. When the family lived in the Welcome area, he attended Western. When Mike came to live with his grandmother, he attended Atkinson. Larry believes that Mike attended Newnan Junior High on Temple Avenue for a short time before dropping out altogether.

"He had nobody to encourage him to go to school, nobody to set a role model for him," said Judy Proctor. "It would have been interesting to see what would have changed after he came out of service if he had lived."

Mike's family always had money problems. Janie didn't make a lot with the jobs she usually worked. Larry recalled getting a monthly haircut from a barber above Morgan's Jewelry in downtown Newnan, but Mike didn't have the money to go every month. Larry also reminisced about going to Colonial Grocery Store, where they traded glass bottles for a couple of cents. The store stashed the bottles behind the building, and Larry and Mike would walk around, get the same bottles, and trade them in again, actions that embarrass Larry today.

"We just didn't have any money," he said.

Judy Proctor said that while Mike had little money, "he always tried to dress nice."

As a teenager, he got a job at the U-Save-It grocery store on Jefferson Street. His mother likely took most if not all of his paycheck for living expenses. Despite the precarious state of the family's finances, Watson was interested in cars early in his teen years, an interest that continued as he got older. Larry Hayes recalled them going to Fairburn for car races. And while there's no evidence that Mike could ever afford a car, he did seem to enjoy working on them.

Mike Watson was part of a group that called themselves the "Farmer Street Boys" because they all lived on or near Farmer Street. He was friends with all of them, but Mark Abercrombie, Delma Morrow, Phil Tucker, Archie Slaton, and Tommy Huddleston were especially close friends. There on Farmer Street, they hung out at the front of Hewlett's Store, a small mom-and-pop grocery with a sandwich counter. They respected the owner and called him "Uncle Hewlett." He had a soft spot for the young men.

"He was a very sweet man who seemed to enjoy the young people," Sandra said.

Spencer's Skating Rink was one of the great teen hangouts of 1960s Newnan. It ranked alongside the car cruise that ran from Burger Chef to Brazier Burger and the Dairy Bar (Big John's). Mike Watson encountered some of his greatest teenage glory in that rink.[3]

Judy Proctor and Sandra Jordan remembered him as a good skater. Larry Hayes said he and Mike loved to skate and meet girls at Spencer's.

"We would go to the skating rink, cruise the burger joints, Brazier and then Burger Chef on Temple Avenue, then to the Dairy Bar at the intersection of Greenville Street and Sewell Road. We always called it Big John's [John was the owner and actually a little guy]. We would get together there or another place after a date to talk and hang out," said Archie Slaton.

Mike likely met or certainly socialized with Tommy Huddleston here, as Tommy was also an excellent skater.

Despite Mike Watson's family situation, people genuinely enjoyed being around him. "Mike was one of those guys you just connect with real easy," said Archie Slaton.

Larry Hayes said that "people were drawn to him. He was just a big-hearted person."

"Everybody liked him. He was just so funny and likable," said Sandra Jordan. "I never heard anyone talk bad about Mike, and I'm not saying that because I loved him so much but because they always talked good about Mike. He had that kind of personality, and he was very smart. If he had a chance to go to college, he could have done just about anything."

Archie Slaton noted, however, that "you could go to his home and tell that he didn't have a dad there, and it bothered him a lot, you could tell."

Sandra Jordan first met Mike when he moved into the house next to her family on Welcome Road. She saw him chasing a dog with a couple of friends out near the street. She went out to offer assistance and spoke to him for the first time, soon developing a crush on him. She was twelve, and he was sixteen.

He moved to his grandmother's house, and they lost contact shortly afterward. She saw him again from the window when he and Tommy Huddleston came to Huddleston's cousin's home to work on cars. One Sunday, she and a friend went to get ice cream and started riding around instead. They ran into Mike and stopped to chat. When they left, she confided in her friend about her crush. Naturally, the next time the friend saw Mike, she told him about Sandra's confidence. The next time Mike was in the neighborhood with Tommy, he went to her home, and they sat on the steps and talked. Sandra considered her parents strict. She wasn't allowed to date until she was sixteen, and at that time, she was only thirteen. Although she and Mike didn't date, this was the dawn of their relationship.

By 1965, Mike was seventeen. He was five feet eight inches tall and slender. He "carried himself pretty well," Archie Slaton said. "He didn't take stuff off anyone."

"He wasn't a big guy, but he was a scrapper," said Larry Hayes.

It was time for Mike to start thinking about military service. The Vietnam War was heating up as Mike joined the military in September 1965.

"As soon as he got to be the age that they could put him in service, his mother immediately did that so he could send money home every month so that he could help her," said Sandra. "Mike didn't want to go into service. He wanted to go to school. She told him no, he had to go into service. While in service, Mike sent her most of his money."

Since he wasn't of draftable age, Mike could select which service to join. He visited all the recruiting offices and chose the Marine Corps.

According to Archie Slaton, "He was very proud of that."

But even more than the idea of wearing the dress blues of the USMC, Mike was interested in the Marine recruiter's promise to send him to helicopter mechanics' school. Perhaps for the first time in his life, the future looked promising for Joseph Michael Watson. He had a cute young girlfriend who adored him. He could serve in an elite branch of service and acquire job skills for the future. Adventure awaited. Mike's future looked bright.

Mike did his Basic Training at Camp Lejeune, North Carolina, then spent time at Camp Garcia, the Marine Corps Air Station in Puerto Rico. Camp Garcia was built in 1960 and used for Marine Amphibious Training. Mike then went back to Camp Lejeune for Food Service Training, then to Camp Pendleton on the West Coast, where he was assigned to Marine Air Group 11 (MAG-11) based in Danang, South Vietnam. He wouldn't be going into helicopter maintenance after all.

The most likely scenario was that the helicopter maintenance school was full. Instead, they sent him to a school where they had an opening, Mess Fundamentals, and Mike became a cook. After this training, Mike received his orders for Vietnam.

While at the airbase in Danang, Mike and Sandra wrote each other constantly. "I received a letter after he got to Vietnam telling of the disappointment that he had been placed in the kitchen to work instead of being with the helicopters," Sandra said. He kept trying to get out of the kitchen. He hated it and said that he wasn't a cook. In his spare time, Mike hung around the chopper crews and asked endless questions about the magnificent machines of his dreams.

The Marine Corps is not always interested in what a Marine wants to do, and they weren't in Mike's case either. So he stayed in the kitchen, cooking and washing pots while he tried to figure out a way to change his MOS.

While in Danang, Mike befriended another young man from

Atlanta, John Doe. Doe was also in food service with MAG-11. John Doe had selected the Marine Corps for many of the same reasons that Mike Watson had—he knew he would be drafted, and John decided he wanted to be part of the best. "I wanted to be a Marine," he said.

The two were the only ones from the Atlanta area in the mess hall.

"He was just a good ole country boy," Doe said. (Obviously, John Doe is a fellow Marine who asked not to be identified. He consented to share his story but also requested that his real name not be mentioned.

"Our Marine Corps training had warned us not to develop close relationships with those we served with due to the rate of casualties experienced during those days in Vietnam," said John Doe. "However, since Mike and I were from Georgia, we bonded immediately. We would talk about things like the Varsity, chili dogs and Frosted Orange drinks, and things like that to bring us back close to home."

John and Mike fell into the same routine with MAG-11, regardless of whether they worked on the day or night watch. "We cooked the chow, then put it out there, cleaned it up, and got ready for the next wave," Doe said.

The pair also served on what was known as "react" squads. At night, they would go outside the air base's barbed wire enclosure and man security posts, also known as listening posts. "He and I both would volunteer for that every chance we got," said Doe. "That way, we could get a little taste of being outside the wire." Sometimes, John and Mike were together outside the wire, sometimes not. Night rocket attacks were constant; they had to keep their heads on a swivel and strain their eyes in the darkness to ensure that communist troops didn't attack the base.

John and Mike also traveled together, arranging their R&R to meet in Bangkok in late 1967 and spending four nights and five days in Thailand's capital. "We had a great time!" Doe said.

"During that time, Mike began talking about extending his tour of duty to allow him to return home to Georgia for thirty days' leave during the Christmas holidays of 1967 and then return to Vietnam for an additional six-month tour of duty," Doe said.

Such extensions happened frequently. In addition to receiving more money, a Marine got a chance to choose what he wanted to do during those six months if he would extend his tour. Mike leaped at the opportunity to finally get into helicopter maintenance. However, these offers were typically informal, and there was rarely anything in writing. There would have been no official training; they would have taken him to the maintenance facility and turned him over to the mechanics to help out. He agreed. He came home on leave still smiling, excited about helicopters and getting the training he wanted so badly.

When Mike returned home, he and Sandra picked up where they had left off, and he and Sandra were together almost daily. Sandra, sixteen, was now old enough to date, and Mike was nineteen. However, she had to be home by 9 p.m. each weeknight. On Friday nights, Sandra and Mike and other couples went to drag races in Fairburn and got to stay out until 11 p.m. He spent more and more time at the Jordan residence, frequently spending the night on the family's couch.

"My family loved him. He was perfect. He just fit," Sandra said. "He came over and ate dinner every night. He enjoyed the family atmosphere that he didn't have at home."

On Thanksgiving, Mike proposed to Sandra at the local drive-in. She said yes immediately. But there was something else that he needed to tell her. "He waited until the night he proposed to me to tell me that he was going back [to Vietnam] and that he was going to get to work in the hangars with the helicopters, and it was only for six months." Sandra begged him not to go back. Still, he told her that he would be safe and that he'd be working on helicopters, not in combat. Mike explained that his mother was living with the truck driver, and she didn't need the money as she had previously. He now had money being deposited into his own bank account, not his mother's. Later, he took Sandra to see a house being built in Senoia and promised her, "When I come back, we're going to buy this house with that money."

"He wanted us to get married then," said Sandra. "So we talked to my parents, though I knew that there was no way at my age that they were going to let me get married, though I was in hopes that they would. They told us that when he came back, that would be my senior year and that I would be graduating, and we could get married then." That would give them time to plan a wedding.

The night they got engaged, they visited the concession stand at the drive-in and heard about Tommy Huddleston.

The day Tommy's body returned to Newnan, Mike was on a trip to Brunswick, Georgia, to find his biological father, John Watson. It's unclear why he went to find his father, but the trip was unsuccessful. When the military tried to contact his father after Mike's death, they noted in their records that he had died. Mike planned to attend Tommy Huddleston's funeral, but his return would cut it close. Sandra was at Oak Hill Cemetery when she felt Mike's arms circle her from behind. He had gotten back in time. In his Marine dress uniform, she said, he "looked so handsome."

After Tommy Huddleston's death, Sandra felt that Mike lost his smile. "He lost his excitement over helicopter training. I look back at everything now, and I feel he knew he wasn't coming back this time. When we took him to the airport for the trip back to Vietnam, there was no smile, no joking around, and no trying to make everyone laugh. Instead of a kiss on the cheek goodbye, he hugged us all and held on silently for a long time."

"Take care of Charles for me," he told Sandra. "Keep him out of trouble."

She told him she would.

He then said, "Love you, gal," and she replied that she loved him. He continued, "Don't worry. Be right back." As he walked off, she saw him wipe his eyes. He never looked back until he went up the steps and reached the airplane door.

"He looked, and he just had this look on his face," Sandra said.

Mike called out, "Love you more than forever," then he was in the plane and gone.

The look on his face bothered Sandra as they got into the car to leave. His mother had noticed it as well. "She mentioned it on the ride back to Newnan," Sandra said. "Even though it was bothering me as well, I said he just didn't want to leave home, you know?"

John Doe was there when Mike got back to Danang. "It is still hard for me to understand why anyone would leave Vietnam and *return*!" Doe said.

Incredibly, instead of working with the helicopters, Mike was sent back to the kitchen to begin the next six months in-country.

Sandra said his letters described how hard his area of Danang was being hit at the end of 1967. "He wrote more about the suffering and death than ever before. Then on New Year's Eve, they were caught off guard. He was also assigned to be a fireman, and the bombing [rockets or mortars] had started many fires. The letter he wrote me in the early-morning hours smelled strongly of smoke. They continued getting hit hard for days."

Official records say that early on the morning of January 8, 1968, there was an explosion in one of the stoves at the Danang Air Base mess hall, and one of the fragments went through Mike Watson's chest, killing him. John, who'd come into the mess hall, had seen Mike working with the portable stoves in the kitchen. These compact stoves had a burner unit that used a combination of air and kerosene to create heat, allowing them to cook.

"At that time," Doe said, "Mike's job was to get those burners fired up and get them in place to prepare the chow. I was about twenty feet from Mike that morning, and I recognized what he was doing. He was bent down, adjusting a burner under a grill. Just as I took a couple more steps, there was a huge explosion. What had happened was the burner had failed and blew off an end cap, and it blew right back into Mike's chest and knocked him backward six to eight feet on his back. Smoke and fire were there, and as it cleared out, we saw Mike lying there, bleeding out of his chest. I took my T-shirt off and tried to compress it [the wound] and stop the bleeding till the medics came in, which was maybe six to eight minutes. As they arrived, they took over treating Mike."

John Doe walked out the back of the mess hall, staggered by what had just occurred. He knew that his friend was dead. As he sat by the back door, the medics brought Mike out on a gurney and loaded him into the medic's wagon. "I walked on over and said my goodbye," John said, choking back the emotion. "Regretfully, I helped load Mike on the transport to the infirmary that morning he was injured, and I never saw him again.

However, I have never forgotten Mike or those memories of our days in Vietnam."

Afterward, Sandra tried almost desperately to find out exactly what had happened. She wrote the commanding officer and contacted some of Mike's friends. Unfortunately, she had little success in her quest for detailed information.

Because Mike Watson had once attended Western School, the spring 1968 Western Yearbook was dedicated to Mike, Jerry Smith, and J.C. Cofield, all killed that school year in Vietnam. Smith had been killed five days before Watson, and their obituaries were both published in the *Newnan Times-Herald* on January 11, 1968. J.C. Cofield died in September of 1967. (See Chapters 5 and 7.)

Though Sandra had promised Mike that she would "take care of Charles," that job turned out to be way more than the teen could handle. Charles spent the next thirty years running from the law or in prison. His story involved theft, running from the police, and killing multiple people. Finally, after a significant stint in prison, he was killed by police in 1996.

"Mike would have been horrified," Sandra said. "Mike's death just did it. His mother didn't want to get him any help. It was just sad."

Sandra received letters from Mike after he died, which was disconcerting. On February 14, a delivery came to the Jordan house—a dozen pink sweetheart roses and a dozen orchids. The card was addressed to Sandra and read, "Happy Valentine's Day-it is almost over. It's February, just a few more months. Do you want matching bands or an engagement ring? Mike." It was like finding out that Mike had died all over again.

Mike's photograph is still on the wall in the Jordan home today.

Mike Watson had always enjoyed the singing of Otis Redding, the "voice of soul." In one of his last letters to Sandra, he mentioned that he had bought a reel-to-reel tape player and wanted Sandra to send him the tape to go in his player or the *Dock of the Bay* album, which had come out in December of 1967. He also noted that "there is a song (by Otis Redding) that you have got to hear from me to you, called 'These Arms of Mine.'"

"I can't tell you how many times I have played that sitting at the cemetery," said Sandra.

She eventually moved on but never forgot Mike. Her current husband was a Marine Corps drill sergeant. "When I met him, I walked into his house, and he had all these pictures and medals on the wall. I'm looking at a group picture, and it was when Mike was in the Marines. I said, 'Oh my God, oh my God. Do you know this guy right here?' He replied, 'Yep, that's old Watson.' So now we have been married for thirty-five years. He was Mike's drill sergeant at Parris Island."

When the Wall That Heals visited Newnan in October 2011, Sandra Jordan Vaughn stood on Bullsboro Drive outside of Oak Hill Cemetery holding a sign that read "Lance Corporal Joseph Michael Watson." As the motorcyclists who escorted the traveling Wall roared by, the woman holding the sign caught their attention, and they commented on the impact that she had on them as they saw her alone outside the cemetery.

"It just made sense to me to be with Mike when they were honoring him, and it was coming right by," Sandra said. "The power of all those motorcycles… I have seen the Wall a lot, and I have never seen a procession like that one, and all of the things that were done that whole time while it was up here [in Newnan], I was drained, but it's like I finally let it go. That week up here, I was able to turn Mike loose and not always say 'What if.' It was magical. It was healing. I felt like that procession brought him home. I felt like it had brought them all home."

**See end notes in the appendix for additional details.*

Born: *February 28, 1948*
Home of record: *Moreland, Georgia*
Died: *January 8, 1968, in Quang Nam province of South Vietnam*
Coweta servicemen who died in the same province: *Daniel Post, Bill Thomas, Larry Pinson, and Jerry Smith*
Unit on death: *MABS-11, MAG-11, 1st Marine Air Wing*
Decorations: *National Defense Service Medal, Vietnam Service Medal with 1 Bronze Service Star, Republic of Vietnam Campaign Medal*
Buried: *Oak Hill Cemetery, Newnan*
Vietnam Memorial, Washington, DC: *Panel 34E Line 2*

Sources
Interview with Larry Hayes, childhood friend
Interview with Judy Proctor, childhood friend
Interview with Archie Slaton, childhood friend
Interview with Sandra Jordan Vaughn, fianceé
Interview with John Doe, Marine Air Group 11
Assistance from Jimmy Davenport, local historian
Assistance from John Boren, USMC and Pam Beavers

References
Coffelt Database, "Joseph Watson." Accessed December 27, 2021. http://coffeltdatabase.org/index.php

Mike Watson and Sandra Vaughn.

CHAPTER NINE

Arthur Hines

Grantville, Georgia

He trusted God. He was at church. He did the things he was supposed to do, whether others were doing them or not.

—Alfred Bohannon

They knew it was coming. They were standing on the track and could feel the train rumbling through that track, but they couldn't move. They were frozen in place, staring at the front of the train as it relentlessly bore down on them. There wasn't anything they could do to circumvent the train and what it meant to their lives. Arthur and Oscar Hines, twins from Grantville, were on that railroad track in early 1967. Figuratively, that train represented the draft, and like many young men of the 1960s, they realized that train had their names on it.

The Hines brothers had managed to avoid the draft for a long time but not illegally. That was happening in many places throughout the country in 1967. In Grantville, Georgia, however, it was Arthur's job that had kept them off that track for so long. Arthur was the main pressman at Bowen Press, a printing company specializing in printing weekly newspapers in the West Georgia region. The shop owner, Leo Bowen, depended on Arthur to keep the presses moving so his company could survive.

"The owner of the shop felt like Arthur Hines was his son. He could not run that place without Arthur, as he had been with him for so long," said Penny Jenkins, who worked part-time at Bowen Press.

"He knew every aspect of the operation. If the press broke down, he could get it going again, and he was just invaluable to him [Bowen]. When it came around to the drafting for the Vietnam War, the owner of the press went before the draft board several times when Arthur's number came up to tell them that he could not operate without him, his business would go under if he was drafted, all these people are going to lose their jobs. He had to have him. So they gave him several deferments, but finally, they wouldn't do that anymore, and they drafted him."

Oscar didn't work at Bowen Press full-time, but Bowen chose him at times on a part-time basis for various jobs.

Leo Bowen appeared before the local draft board, but they weren't as sympathetic as they had been. Shortly afterward, the draft train crashed into the twins, and they both got their notices in the mail. Soon, they were headed to Atlanta to take their US Army physicals. When finished, they were stunned to discover that Arthur had been selected, but the Army had rejected Oscar. The doctors found that Oscar had a heart murmur, probably brought about by the rheumatic fever he had suffered as a child. Oscar was distraught.

"It was the toughest time of my life to see him go," Oscar said. "I wanted to be with him."

Arthur didn't say much. He was probably relieved that Oscar wouldn't have to take this perilous journey into the unknown.

Arthur Hines was twenty-six when he was drafted in early 1967 and would turn twenty-seven a few months later. He couldn't have been any older and been drafted. In 1967, the draft took young men between the ages of eighteen and twenty-six who didn't have a deferment. There was an extensive list of possible deferments recognized by the federal government. The draft lottery system, designed to be fairer to everyone, didn't begin until 1969.

Grantville in the 1960s was a "quiet, peaceful, sleepy little town," according to Johnny Wilson, who grew up there during the 1950s and 1960s. "There was really no crime."

Grantville was a mill town. The Grantville Hosiery Mill provided jobs, and the Mill Foundation provided other amenities. There were at least two grocery stores, a doctor's office, a movie theater, baseball fields, a scout cabin, a terrific in-ground swimming pool, and clay tennis courts reputed to be some of the best in Coweta County. Grantville also had a volunteer fire department that the kids sarcastically called the "Grantville chimney savers" because, by the time they arrived on the scene, the chimney was all that was left of the building. But they always appeared.

Arthur entered the world just before Oscar on May 24, 1941, born to L.D. and Cora Hines of Grantville. L.D. worked at Bonnell Aluminum in Newnan, and Cora worked as a domestic housekeeper in Grantville and Newnan. Cora also cleaned the *Newnan Times-Herald* offices on weekends and worked as something of a personal chauffeur for a woman on Temple Avenue in Newnan. The twins were part of a large family of eight siblings. Eddie Roy was significantly older and out of the house by the time the twins came along. J.D. was the second son, then Arthur and Oscar, followed by Willie Henry, James, Elmer, and Emma Jean, the lone female among the brood.

In addition to working at Bonnell, L.D. worked as a sharecropper on a farm on Blackberry Road and later on Roger Arnold Road, where he and his sons sharecropped for nearly nine years. The children did chores on the farm just as on any other farm in West Georgia. They grew cotton and various vegetables that they could eat themselves or sell in times of plenty. They raised cows and mules and got a bull every two years. The boys loved to play with the animals and trained them to stop and then go. They used scrap lumber to build a go-cart that they initially pulled but then trained the bull to pull instead. The boys taught the bull to stop and go on command while pulling the cart. People passing by would point and stare, as this was such an unusual sight.

"Arthur always wanted to do something," said his brother J.D. Sometimes, Arthur would find a way to make a little money for himself and his brothers. For example, he made brooms from dogwood and sold them for fifteen cents.

The brothers played in the woods all day when they could. They loved the adventure the woods provided. They would often milk a cow, put the milk in a jug, and get some eggs from a chicken. Then they would have their noon meal without returning to the house. The boys dammed up the creek that ran through the property, dodged the snakes, and enjoyed the afternoon swimming. They made bows and arrows and went bird hunting for food. Fishing might also be on the agenda; they cleaned and cooked what they caught right where they hooked it.

Arthur and Oscar were identical twins, and Barham Lundy, a young man who grew up in Grantville during this time, said, "The only way to tell them apart was that you had to know them."

Sometimes, when they got into mischief, their mother had difficulty figuring out which twin was guilty and which was innocent. The only way to reliably tell them apart was a burn mark on Arthur's face; he had tripped near the fireplace as a child, and a little piece of coal had burned him near his right eye. Although they were identical in physical appearance, their personalities differed tremendously.

"Arthur was the leader," Oscar said. "He was a leader to me at school and home. He didn't like [for us] to wear the same clothes, and he didn't like people coming up to us and saying that we were cute. We dressed differently. We were very different people." Oscar also said that if he did something wrong, "Arthur would come to me and tell me not to do that."

Eddie Roy, the oldest brother, remembered that Arthur was a positive leader and very sure of himself. "He wasn't a doubter."

"As long as he is in the group, the group stays together," Oscar said. "Father depended on him. Arthur would listen and do exactly as he said." When the twins visited the hardware store, people knew Arthur and wanted to talk to him. "He was going to talk to people," Oscar said.

Arthur and Oscar attended Grantville Brown Elementary then moved to Central High School in Newnan. Academics were not Arthur's strong suit, and he didn't finish school. Instead, he was good at doing things with his hands, fixing things and becoming the leading "handyman" around the house.

"That young man could take something apart and put it back together. If it was broken, Arthur could fix it," said Eddie Roy Hines (Skinner, Winston. "Small towns once had papers of their own," *Newnan Times-Herald,* August 9, 2015). As Arthur moved into his teenage years, he started cutting his brother's hair as well as that of many of their friends. "I think that he cut everybody's hair in the community," Eddie Roy recalled (Skinner, 2000).

Arthur planned to build a house on a lot given to him by his parents. According to Eddie Roy, "Arthur had that house built in his mind. What would that house have looked like if he had lived to build it?"

Arthur's ability to fix almost anything came into play at Bowen

Press in a building on Railroad Street. While it is hard to determine precisely when Arthur started working for Leo Bowen, it began when Bowen lived on LaGrange Street and his wife, Hortense, ran a florist shop out of their home. The large yard had various shrubs, bushes, and flowers. Bowen cut his hedges straight on top, and Oscar described them as "perfect." Bowen didn't think anyone could trim hedges as well as he could until he gave Arthur Hines a shot at it.

"He was amazed," said Oscar.

Arthur did the pruning as well as, if not better than, Leo Bowen himself. Bowen thought Arthur was interested in doing things the right way, so he hired Arthur to work for him at Bowen Press. He never regretted it.

Grace Jenkins and her daughter, Penny, were employed at Bowen Press. Grace worked full-time creating ads for various newspapers printed by Bowen Press. Penny folded the weekly newspapers by hand, including the *Meriwether Vindicator*, the *Hogansville Herald*, and naturally, the *Grantville Gazette*.

Arthur Hines was the pressman. "Arthur made himself indispensable," Penny said. "He could baby those presses and fix them. Mr. Bowen couldn't run his presses without him. He depended on Arthur."

Oscar said, "Once you showed him, he had it. He had it the next day, no problem at all."

His natural ability as a handyman really stood out at Bowen Press, just as it had on the farm. After Bowen brought Arthur into the printing business, he again needed someone to cut his hedges. He hired Oscar. Oscar trimmed the hedges, and while Leo Bowen didn't complain about the job, Oscar felt he hadn't done as well as Arthur. However, Oscar must not have done too poorly, as Bowen hired him to work at the press when they got swamped. Oscar loved working there and enjoyed working with his brother. Arthur always told Oscar what to do while at work, but Oscar didn't mind; he acknowledged his twin brother as the leader. Penny Jenkins remembers Willie Henry, one of the younger brothers, occasionally worked there too.

Once, Arthur cut his hand on the machinery. He had been working more than fourteen hours and was extremely tired. Penny said Mr. Bowen felt bad about it and paid for the medical treatment since "Arthur was like a son to him."

In Coweta during the 1960s, people could go to the draft board and, if there was a compelling reason, get a temporary deferment, reviewable at a later date. Bowen went to the draft board several times and claimed he couldn't run his business without Arthur Hines. Leo Bowen was sincere and accurate—he really couldn't run his business without Arthur.

"I don't remember Mr. Bowen operating the place without Arthur," said Penny Jenkins. Shortly after Arthur Hines left for military service in 1967, Bowen Press closed for good. Leo Bowen gave away most of his money to folks who needed it.

Regardless of how talented Arthur Hines was with his hands or how good he was with his job on the farm or at Bowen Press, he was still like every other young male during the 1960s. He was interested in cars and girls.

In 1965, he visited a car dealer in Atlanta and came home with a 1957 Chevrolet Bel Air, a two-door hardtop. The car was the talk of Grantville.

"Everyone was talking about it," Oscar said. "I wanted one but couldn't find one just like his." The car was off-white and had a white interior trimmed in black.

"It was in mint condition, and he had fender skirts on it. He was so proud of that car. He had the best-looking car in town," Johnny Wilson said. "It was his pride and joy."

Johnny had a 1960 Chevy Impala two-door hardtop with the same type of motor and transmission as Arthur's Bel Air, but he realized that Arthur was the king of the cars in Grantville. When Johnny saw Arthur go by in this car, he and Arthur waved at each other.

"Everyone that knew him knew that car," said Eddie Roy.

Arthur was interested in a young lady five years his junior, Gabrielle Daniel, and they didn't live far from each other. Arthur was dating another girl when he asked Gabrielle out for the first time, but Gabrielle wasn't playing those games. While thinking he was "real sweet," Gabrielle refused to go out with him until he settled his affairs with the other young lady. She wasn't interested in getting into the middle of anyone's drama. He made a clean break with the other girl. Gabrielle was eighteen at the time, and Arthur was twenty-three.

It was February 1967. Arthur hated to go into the service without Oscar, but he had little choice. He wanted to do his duty.

"When Arthur left, it was his choice," Gabrielle said. "He was thrilled to be a soldier because it was his American duty" (Shanci Jennings, "Saluting a fallen Vietnam Veteran," *Newnan Times-Herald*, May 28, 2000).

"He wanted to contribute, and he loved his country," said Eddie Roy.

Arthur left for Basic Combat Training the last week of February 1967. Fortunately, Arthur didn't have far to go, as he had been assigned to Fort Benning in Columbus, Georgia. Once he completed Basic, he went to Advanced Infantry Training around May 1 at Fort Polk, Louisiana. The Army was grooming him to serve in Vietnam. On completion of AIT, he became an American infantry soldier. He also came home on leave.

In June 1967, Gabrielle worked at a beauty salon in Atlanta called Dames and Dolls. Arthur had just gotten home from Fort Polk and was preparing to go to Vietnam, his next duty station.

"I was hoping they wouldn't send him there, but that was the first thing they did," said Gabrielle. "I felt like they [Arthur and the men who had just completed training] weren't ready."

Arthur proposed to Gabrielle and wanted to get married right away before leaving. She agreed. Oscar decorated the car, and the two lovers traveled to Phenix City, Alabama, to marry then honeymooned in Florida.

"It was just like that," said Gabrielle. She was twenty-one, and Arthur was twenty-six.

On the newlyweds' return to Grantville, they had five days before Arthur was scheduled to leave for Vietnam. They spent that time with each other and with family. On the designated day, Gabrielle took Arthur to the airport in Atlanta, where he would catch his flight to Fort Lewis, Washington, then head to Vietnam. They arrived at the airport late, and the steps had already been pulled back from the plane door. Arthur was told that he would have to return the next day and catch a different flight. However, whether it was for Arthur or for another reason, the steps were pushed back up to the aircraft at the last moment, and as Gabrielle watched, Arthur climbed aboard. That was the last time she ever saw him.

Arthur Hines officially began his year-long tour in Vietnam on July 27, 1967. He became part of C Company, 1st Battalion, 12th Infantry Regiment, 4th Infantry Division, the "Red Warriors" stationed in Kontum Province at the north end of II Corps, the Republic of Vietnam. From July 1967 until January 1968, Hines worked as a "grunt," an infantry soldier in Vietnam. Gabrielle Hines told the *Newnan Times-Herald* what she had learned about Arthur's duties. "During his tour of duty, Hines served as the point man on search and destroy operations, provided perimeter security for his unit, and engaged in assaults of the enemy position. According to his superior officers, Hines adjusted well to the constantly changing situations and dangers inherent in the combat zone" (Jennings, 2000).

Oscar recalled that Arthur's letters home to family never mentioned tough times in Vietnam. This would have been standard practice with the guys there so as not to worry their families. Instead, Arthur always wrote something positive every few days. He even wrote that he was cutting the hair of some soldiers in his unit. Although Arthur's letters never told of any problems or difficult situations, he did tell Oscar what was going on and about the treacherous conditions.

"He would tell me how dangerous it was over there," Oscar said. Once, Arthur wrote to Oscar and wanted him to send him a watch "with nothing shiny on it." Soldiers in Vietnam didn't want anything that glowed or even reflected light as they went into night ambushes or other night operations. Light or reflected light could give their position away and possibly get them and their buddies killed. So Oscar found a watch with a black band and sent it to Arthur.

Gabrielle sent him, at his request, packets of Kool-Aid and chewing gum. Kool-Aid was a standard request for a grunt in Vietnam. The water in their canteens tasted awful, and they dumped packets of Kool-Aid inside to give the water a better flavor, even without the sugar. Kool-Aid packages were also small, light, and easy to ship.

Everyone back in Grantville knew that Arthur was in Vietnam. Arthur's wife, Gabrielle, was now driving the coolest car in town.

When she dented it, it was the talk of Grantville.

At the end of January 1968, the Vietnamese New Year's celebration began. The New Year, or Tet, was the most prominent holiday on the Vietnamese calendar. It was Thanksgiving, Christmas, New Year, and Easter all rolled into one holiday. The word *Tet* is an abbreviation for *Tet Nguyen Dan*, which means Feast of the First Morning, the first morning being the first day of the New Year on the Vietnamese calendar, which is lunar.

The Vietnamese would gather to enjoy fireworks, food, music, and family. Seen as a time for last year's bad luck to be swept away and the good fortune of the New Year to be brought into the home, family reunions and the honoring of ancestors were the most critical holiday customs. The two protagonists worked out a truce for most years during the war so that Tet could be celebrated without interference. As a result, South Vietnamese Army soldiers could go home to be with family, feeling confident they would not be needed. On January 31, 1968, Tet was underway in cities and towns across South Vietnam.

That night, however, the Viet Cong and the North Vietnamese Army, having pre-positioned weapons and supplies at various points across South Vietnam—and in the case of the NVA, having infiltrated thousands of soldiers into positions around South Vietnam—struck. The battle that took place over the next month, known in the United States as the Tet Offensive, would be seen as the turning point of the Vietnam War. Arthur Hines was right in the middle of it.

On January 31 back in Grantville, Gabrielle was preparing to meet Arthur in Hawaii for his long-awaited R&R, which was quickly approaching.

"The day that he was killed, he was walking point, and I always felt guilty that he was walking point and not me," said Robert Valderrama, a squad mate of Arthur. Hines and Valderrama had become buddies over the last seven months. Valderrama was Hispanic, and Hines was Black, so the prejudice that they had both experienced was something that helped them bond.

"Also, we were the same height [five foot six inches], so we were the smallest two guys in the squad. Therefore, we were in the same foxhole together," Valderrama said with a laugh.

Because of his size, Arthur's nickname in Vietnam was "Pee Wee." Another thing that drew him and Valderrama together was C-Rations. Arthur and Robert enjoyed the pound cake and peaches in their C-Rations, as did many other soldiers in Vietnam. If they acquired any pound cake or peaches, they shared. C-rations, c-rats, or just c's were the MREs of the time. Canned meals consisting of a variety of meat, vegetable, and fruit items, they were reasonably easy to carry but not that great to eat.

Hines and Valderrama became tight friends over the months they were together, and Valderrama remembered him as having a very "laid-back" personality. "He accepted whatever life gave him that day and embraced it."

They bivouacked out in the field near Kontum City on February 9, and when they got up the following day, they shared their peaches and pound cake. As they prepared to move out, they discussed whose turn it was to walk point. It was either Hines or Valderrama, but neither could remember who should be up next. Finally, "Pee-Wee" insisted it was his turn, so they saddled up and moved out.

"He got killed about fifteen minutes after our conversation," said Valderrama. "They must have been waiting for us all night."

Charles Lightsey was the radio-telegraph operator (RTO) with the point group as they moved out the morning of February 10, 1968. Mike Morgan of San Francisco was the squad leader, and a soldier they called "Whitey," from Nashville, Tennessee, was behind Arthur. Lightsey recalled "Pee-Wee" walking point and said they hadn't gone more than a hundred yards when they were ambushed. Lightsey said Hines "got it first. They opened up on him with a machine gun and cut him to pieces. We could hear the dadgum bullets fly all around us."

Whitey was shot in the knee. Mike Morgan and Lightsey dove behind nearby trees. Hines was about twenty yards in front of them, but Lightsey knew he was dead. "We had to pull back and leave his body behind," he said.

Lightsey and Morgan grabbed Whitey and, dragging him along, pulled back along the route they had just come, trying to find cover from the bullets still whipping around them.

The American soldiers continued to try to get to Hines's body. No one wanted to leave one of their own behind.

"Soldiers white and black tried to get a hold of him," said Valderrama.

Despite repeated attempts, the soldiers eventually had to withdraw. As a result, they never learned what happened to the body.

Lightsey remembered Hines as "a likable fellow, always had a good sense of humor, cutting up with you."

On being ambushed, he said, "You're always thinking that they are out there. You never know. You always prepare for the worst and hope for the best. That morning, we had no idea that they were waiting for us. We walked right into it."

Whitey was evacuated and never heard from again. He was likely treated and sent home to recover from his wounds. Unfortunately, Arthur Hines's body wouldn't be retrieved until the end of March, and he was declared dead on March 28, 1969, six weeks after the ambush.

Shortly after the February 10 ambush, two soldiers in a green car drove to Gabrielle's mother's home to see Gabrielle. She saw the car pull into the driveway and immediately knew why they were there. She ran to the back of the house and hid until her sister found her a few minutes later.

"These people need to see you," her sister said.

Gabrielle moved toward the front of the house to face the very thing that she had dreaded and that all families with boys in the service feared. This fright was not unique to the Vietnam War but was the same fear that families had felt since the dawn of civilization. She sat in the living room with the soldiers, who explained Arthur's Missing in Action (MIA) status. This status initially gave her hope; at least they weren't there to tell her that he was dead.

The next six weeks were gut-wrenching as Gabrielle waited. The family waited. Grantville waited. The letters she had written him before he was declared missing came back to her mailbox. She was "praying he would be OK. I had just gotten married. I loved this man. I had no time with him. It was rough," she said. "I loved him. Arthur was just a nice guy. He was considerate, liked to joke, and was a leader."

Finally, on March 28, the Army recovered a few remains and sent word to confirm Arthur's death. L.D. and Cora took the news especially hard, which wasn't unexpected.

"He was their son," Gabrielle said.

The news upset the entire town. Leo Bowen passed the word on to Grace Jenkins, who called her daughter. When Penny answered the phone, her mother could barely speak.

The closed-casket funeral was held at Greater Jehovah Baptist Church on Roger Arnold Road. Gabrielle said there was no actual body in the coffin. "I just got a casket and an honor guard," she said. The honor guard gave her Arthur's dog tags.

Penny Jenkins and her mother remembered seeing the large crowd and crying throughout the whole funeral. "They just about had to carry Gabby in and out and the same for Arthur's mother," said Penny.

Leo Bowen came in late and left early, obviously shaken.

"Today, I almost can't talk about it without crying," Penny added. "The military people there in uniform and the folding of the flag and the playing of taps and the twenty-one-guns salute, it's just very, very impressive, a military funeral like that."

Arthur Hines always helped his family financially, whether working on the farm, at Bowen Press, or in the Army. Even in death, he helped his family. The Hines family paid off their house with the money from Arthur's life insurance policy with the military.

"He was a good person. Gabby is a good person. The whole family is a family of good, solid, hardworking people," said Johnny Wilson.

Robert Valderrama always "felt guilty that he got killed and not me. I always wondered if his family knew how brave he was." He pondered who the "lucky ones were, the guys that were killed or the guys that came back."

Whatever the answer, "Pee-Wee is always on my mind," Valderrama said.

"Being a twin brother, you are together all the time. Then you don't see each other again. So you can imagine how that feels," said Oscar.

Gabrielle kept the Bel Air, but it was stolen while she lived in Atlanta.

Gabrielle eventually went to the Vietnam Memorial, the Wall in

Washington, DC, where she realized that it was true; he really was gone. His name was there, engraved on the Wall.

"He was a really, really good person, and everybody loved him," she said. "Arthur was a quiet man, but when he spoke, everyone listened. He loved his family and me."

Gabrielle Hines never remarried.

Born: *May 24, 1941*
Home of record: *Grantville, Georgia*
Died: *February 10, 1968, in Kontum province of South Vietnam*
Coweta servicemen who died in the same province: *Tommy Huddleston, Stevan Pittman*
Unit on death: *1st PLT, C CO, 1st BN, 12th Infantry, 4th Infantry Division*
Decorations: *Purple Heart, Army Commendation Medal, National Defense Service Medal, Vietnam Service Medal, Republic of Vietnam Campaign Medal*
Buried: *Grantville City Cemetery, Grantville*
Vietnam Memorial, Washington, DC: *Panel 38E Line 72*

Sources

Interview with Oscar Hines, twin brother
Interview with J.D. Hines, brother
Interview with Eddie Roy Hines, brother
Interview with Gabrielle Hines, widow
Interview with Johnny and Penny Jenkins Wilson, childhood friends
Interview with Barham Lundy, childhood friend
Interview with Billy Thomasson, *Newnan Times-Herald*
Interview with Robert Valderrama, US Army
Interview with Charles Lightsey, US Army

References

Asia Highlights. "Vietnamese New Year—7 Things You Need to Know." Accessed January 18, 2022. https://www.asiahighlights.com/vietnam/new-year.
Skinner, Winston. "Small towns once had papers of their own," *Newnan Times-Herald,* August 9, 2015. Jennings, Shanci. "Saluting a fallen Vietnam Veteran," *Newnan Times-Herald*, May 28, 2000.
Skinner, Winston. "Fallen Grantville man Remembered," *Newnan Times-Herald*, May 30, 2000.
Coffelt Database, "Arthur Hines." Accessed January 18, 2018. http://coffeltdatabase.org/index.php

Arthur Hines at Bowen Press, Grantville.

CHAPTER TEN

Johnny Curtis. Calhoun

Newnan, Georgia

Greater love hath no man than this, that a man lay down his life for his friends.
—John 15:13

The humidity was oppressive. It encompassed the small six-man team silently waiting in this diminutive piece of jungle near the village of Phu Vinh on the Laotian end of the notorious A Shau valley. The A Shau valley had the reputation of being one of the most lethal places in Vietnam. With little success, American combat units had tried numerous times over the previous three years to run the Viet Cong and North Vietnamese Army out of the valley. This six-man team was not in the valley to run any communist troops out of it. Instead, they were there to observe, monitor, and report their findings to their command, which they had successfully done over the previous few days. Now, they were looking for a way out. This composite Studies and Observations Group team consisted of two Americans and four indigenous soldiers. These highly classified SOG teams were frequently dropped into an area across "the fence" in Laos or Cambodia and carried out their assigned reconnaissance missions. Unfortunately, the designated area usually contained part of the notorious Ho Chi Minh Trail. This infamous trail brought supplies and soldiers around the demilitarized zone (DMZ) and into South Vietnam. This endless aggravation came as part of the 1962 Geneva Conference, which agreed to a Declaration on the Neutrality of Laos. Fourteen countries agreed Laos should not move into the free or communist camps. As part of that agreement, the United

States and the North Vietnamese began to withdraw all military forces, including advisors, from Laos. But the North Vietnamese ignored the treaty, while the Americans tried hard not to break it, at least not visibly.

This SOG team was still in South Vietnam, but the valley served as a conduit for men and material entering South Vietnam from the Ho Chi Minh Trail.

The Studies and Observations Group was an innocuous-sounding name for a highly elite military unit and one of the most secretive to serve during the Vietnam War. SOG team members were drawn from the military's finest volunteers from the Army Green Berets and the Navy SEALS. An American Special Forces soldier led a SOG team and was called a one-zero. He was given a mission, and he planned and directed it. The team was his to run. The second American on the team was dubbed a one-one, and he operated the radio. The radio was critical because it often meant life or death; it was the lifeline that would be used to call in air support and helicopters for extraction of the team. If a third American was on the team, he would be called a one-two. The indigenous soldiers were usually Montagnard tribesmen, who were mountain people or mountaineers. Called "Yards" by the Americans, the Montagnards were a different ethnic group than the lowland Vietnamese. There were thirty different Montagnard tribes in the Vietnamese mountains. They were fierce fighters, and the Special Forces soldiers loved them for their loyalty and aggressiveness in combat.

This particular SOG team was resting at a site near a possible landing zone (LZ) from which they could be whisked away and back to camp. The one-zero of this team was a five-foot-seven, one-hundred-fifty-pound Green Beret, Sergeant Johnny Calhoun of Roanoke, Alabama, and Newnan, Georgia. Calhoun was less than a month from returning home to his wife and new daughter. The one-one was Staff Sergeant Richard Wilson. Between 11 and 11:45 a.m., Calhoun made the radio check with the forward air controller (FAC), call sign *Covey*. Right after he signed off, the silence was shattered by the roar of a CAR-15 from one of the Montagnard soldiers firing at what was later estimated to be a heavily armed company of Viet Cong. The Viet Cong had silently crawled toward the team through the tall grass east of the team's position. The Viet

Cong and the Montagnard soldiers rapidly exchanged fire. Sergeant Calhoun leaped to his feet and moved to a position to view the situation and take command, calling for Wilson to get on the radio for air support and extraction. Suddenly, fire came from the west. The team was now taking fire on two sides. The Montagnards edged away from the fire while the radio in Wilson's hands came apart in a hail of communist bullets.

"We've lost the radio!" Wilson shouted over the clamor of gunfire. "The radio is down!" he screamed, fighting to maintain control. It was March 27, 1968.

Johnny Calhoun was born in Roanoke, Alabama, on July 14, 1945. His mother, Carol, had married a World War II serviceman named Curtis Calhoun when she was fourteen, and Johnny was born when she was sixteen. The couple initially lived in a mill village in Roanoke until they separated. His father moved to Dearborn, Michigan, and Johnny lived with him for a while but eventually returned to live with his mother. Carol moved to Columbus, Georgia, for work when Johnny was in junior high school. Johnny was a mischievous lad, always playfully picking at his mother. Once, when he was little, Carol came out of the house just in time to stop Johnny from pouring a cup of sand into the car's gas tank. According to Carol, he "treated me more like a big sister." Carol moved to Coweta County when Johnny was a teenager because she had family in the area.

As Johnny got old enough to drive, he tested his mother once by not being home at his curfew deadline of 10 p.m. They had previously discussed his curfew, and his mother had emphasized the time. Johnny had left home with a flippant "What are you going to do? I have the car. You don't have any wheels!"

Wheels or not, Carol called the police when Johnny didn't get home on time. A policeman came to the house, and Carol got into the patrol car's back seat and suggested where to look for the tardy youth. Johnny pulled into the drive before Carol and the patrolman could leave. The policeman got out and spoke with Johnny for a moment.

Once Johnny and Carol were alone, he said, "Mother, I can't believe you called the police."

Johnny's excuse was that he'd run out of gas, and his mother replied that she'd heard that one before.

Johnny said, "I can't believe you were sitting in the back of that police car!"

His mother replied, "And you didn't think I had any wheels!"

Johnny didn't attend school in Coweta County, and at some point, he decided to go into the military. Because of his age, his mother had to sign for him to join. She initially resisted, but he persuaded her by saying that he could enlist himself in a year or he would just be drafted. According to Johnny's widow, Faye Hayes, Johnny was patriotic and believed in his country. Johnny joined the military in January of 1963 when he was seventeen years old.

Johnny went through Basic and Advanced Infantry Training. He then volunteered to go to jump school and qualify as a paratrooper. Johnny started jump school in early November of 1965 and exited as a qualified airborne trooper at the end of the month. After jump school, Johnny was stationed at Fort Gordon in Augusta, Georgia. At either Fort Benning or Fort Gordon, Johnny Calhoun volunteered for the Special Forces.

Faye Hayes was born in Hogansville, Georgia, and her family moved to Poplar Road in Newnan when she was in eighth grade. She lived on the dividing line between the two high schools and could have attended either Newnan High School or East Coweta High School. She decided on East Coweta because a friend down the road went there. Carol and Johnny moved into the house directly behind the Hayes home, and Faye occasionally saw Johnny outside with Tommy Huddleston or some of Tommy's brothers. Tommy and brothers Daryl, Bobby, and Danny often went to the Calhoun home to hang out with Johnny.

Faye said she had little contact with Johnny until she was sixteen and he suddenly appeared at her door one day, asking whether she wanted to go on a date with his cousin Daryl.

Faye looked at him. She said later that she thought Johnny was handsome, but that day, she replied, "You tell Daryl to come over and ask me himself!" She eventually went out with Daryl a few times and saw Johnny intermittently after that. They didn't start dating until Johnny began coming home on military leave during her senior year at East Coweta.

Johnny's mother remembered how it started. "I knew Faye before

Johnny even knew her, and I had just fallen in love with her. Johnny had come home on leave, and he said he was going down to see a friend, and I said, 'Have you seen Faye?' He said no. I said, 'She is a pretty girl.' He responded, 'What are you trying to do, get me married'? I said, 'No, I just told you that she is a pretty girl.' So he went on down there. The next morning, I got up and started fixing breakfast. He woke up and said, 'I can't eat right now. Can you iron my shirt? I have to take Faye on a motorcycle ride.' So he went out, took Faye on a motorcycle ride, and then came back to eat."

Faye graduated from East Coweta in late spring of 1965 and dated Johnny steadily whenever he came home from Fort Gordon.

In October 1965, Johnny's grandmother died, and he returned for the funeral. He was picked up at the airport by his uncle, Robert Huddleston, and went to Faye's home upon his arrival in Newnan. About 4 a.m., he knocked on her family's door. Faye's parents worked at night, so Faye was the only one home. Faye got out of bed and peered through the window. Realizing it was Johnny, she opened the door. He proposed to her on the front porch.

They married the next day, October 22, in Phenix City, Alabama. They decided to get rings in Phenix City, but the store they visited was closed. So Johnny temporarily used his mother's ring. Johnny was twenty years old, and Faye was eighteen. That afternoon, they were with Johnny's mother and eating in a restaurant when two policemen walked in. Carol jokingly told them to "put that guy in jail. He just got married!"

Johnny had to have taken a battery of tests to qualify for the Special Forces. Still, according to Andrew Coy, a fellow Green Beret and friend of Johnny during this time, effort and attitude were the most important things to the instructors. When Johnny and Faye married, Johnny had his orders for Special Forces Training and was heading to Fort Bragg, North Carolina. After leaving Newnan, they stopped at Fort Gordon to say goodbye to his numerous friends, who had a wedding gift for the couple.

Faye said the couple had "absolutely nothing" as they moved to North Carolina. They rented a furnished two-bedroom duplex apartment off base, where they began meeting people, including Andrew and his wife, who enjoyed playing cards in the evening.

Johnny invited another couple who had been friends to share the apartment with them until they could find their own place. Don and Janice Ferrell moved in and stayed for six months as Don worked through his training. Johnny would have started in the training group at Fort Bragg. The group's training included modules in planning, unconventional warfare, airborne operations, culture, language, regional analysis, and small-unit tactics. Andrew Coy met Johnny Calhoun during their training and was impressed with Johnny's determination and attitude. According to Coy, even with these personality traits, Johnny still seemed like a happy-go-lucky guy. Once the training group was completed, they moved into their specific job [MOS or Military Occupational Specialty] training. The jobs included medic, communications, demolition, operations, intelligence, and heavy and light weapons. Coy and Calhoun were both trained in the weapons MOS.

Terry Lewis was another Special Forces soldier who knew Johnny Calhoun, but Lewis's relationship with Calhoun was a little different. The two were cousins and had been buddies since the age of ten, when Lewis had lived with the Calhouns in Columbus. Lewis recalled Johnny being good at sports but not obsessed with them. Johnny wasn't the outdoors type either, seldom hunting or fishing. Lewis remembered Johnny being more interested in girls than anything else.

Lewis was drafted about a year after Johnny joined the military and had decided to follow Johnny into the Special Forces. He was at Fort Bragg at the same time as Johnny. Lewis remembered Johnny being a platoon sergeant while Lewis was in the training group. Calhoun gave Lewis guidance whenever they met during this time.

"Johnny was a good person," Lewis said "He didn't back down from nobody. If you had thought anybody would have come back from a scrap like that [Vietnam], you would think he would be the one to come back. Johnny was gung ho. He was a go-getter."

Faye became pregnant, and the Ferrells moved out in September 1966, shortly before a little girl was born. She weighed five and a half pounds at birth, and the proud couple named her Teresa. Soon after the baby was born, a friend of Johnny's sold him all the furniture he had in storage at Fort Bragg, and Johnny and Faye moved into a small house with a little more room for themselves and the baby.

Johnny didn't discuss his training with Faye, but she said "he was a tough guy. He really was. He was a short, stocky guy but strong, very strong." When Johnny graduated from his MOS training, Faye bought him a small statue with his name and date inscribed. It featured a soldier with a gun and wearing a Green Beret.

Within a few months of completing his Special Forces Training, Johnny volunteered to go to Vietnam.

"I got very upset," Faye said. "Why? I knew he was patriotic. I knew he was. I knew his duty was with the service. He put them... I don't want to say first because he loved us, he loved Teresa and me dearly, but he was very patriotic." When Johnny arrived in Vietnam in April of 1967, he was assigned to the 5th Special Forces Group at Phu Bai and later volunteered to join the Studies and Observations Group.

Shortly after Johnny joined the military, Carol had moved to South Carolina for a job. As Johnny prepared to go to Vietnam, he asked his mother to move back to Newnan and take care of Faye and the baby. Johnny didn't want Faye to move to South Carolina with Carol, away from her family and where she didn't know anyone. Faye wanted to be back in the area where she had grown up, but she didn't want to move home, as she didn't always get along with her stepmother.

So Carol moved back to Newnan. She and Faye lived together in a trailer park on the south side of Newnan.

"Faye and I have been close for years. She is my daughter," said Carol.

Faye wrote Johnny every day, and Johnny wrote when he could. The young bride understood. She had picked up on the intense nature of the Special Forces during her time at Fort Bragg and understood Johnny's desire to succeed.

Johnny had been worried about Teresa's lack of hair when he left, so Faye sent pictures of Teresa with a curl. They spoke on the phone once or twice, and about halfway through Johnny's tour, he got his R&R leave and arranged to meet Faye in Hawaii, a typical arrangement for many married guys. Faye left Teresa with Carol and her parents and had her dad drive her to the airport. She and Johnny rendezvoused in early November 1967. The Hawaiian trip was a grand adventure for Faye, and she recalls climbing Diamond Head with Johnny. Faye got tired and stopped about halfway up. Johnny insisted on going all the way to the top. He photographed her from above, sitting there waiting for him. When his mother saw the photo later, she asked about the Vietnamese woman in the photo. Faye explained that the lady was not Vietnamese but very much American!

On Thanksgiving Day of 1967, Faye, Carol, and Teresa were eating Thanksgiving dinner with the Huddleston family when a military car drove into the driveway. Tommy Huddleston, assigned to the 173rd Airborne Brigade, had just died in a fierce battle on Hill 875.

"Well, he got to come home for Tommy's funeral," said Johnny's mother. "The Red Cross girl, when I asked her about it, said she doubted it, very seriously. But he was in the States before they even knew it. He and Tommy were like brothers, you know. You see one, and you see both of them."

Johnny might have had a premonition of his own death while back in Georgia. His mother said, "When Johnny came home for Tommy's funeral, he left dog tags in Teresa's baby bed. He said they could never take him alive because he knew too much."

Those words would soon prove to be prophetic.

In seconds, the morning of March 27, 1968, had exploded into a cacophony of noise and fear. Sergeant Calhoun, seeing the state of the radio and assessing the situation, quickly ordered Wilson to withdraw. Calhoun moved between a withdrawing Wilson and the enemy, now getting extremely close, and laid down highly accurate covering fire, allowing Wilson and the rest of the team to withdraw. The Montagnard that served as the team's interpreter, Ho-Thong, saw blood coming from Calhoun's belly and tried to grab his arm, but Calhoun quickly pulled his arm away and ordered him to "Get out! The team must move!" He left Calhoun and began to move away. Wilson later reported that as he withdrew, he saw Johnny take at least three rounds in the torso. Wilson could do nothing at that point and moved quickly away from the site. He looked back as Calhoun slumped to the ground. Ho-Thong later claimed to have seen Johnny Calhoun produce a grenade and pull the pin while holding it close to his body. He also claimed to hear what he assumed was an explosion shortly after.

The Special Forces and SOG team members would have been a prize capture for the North Vietnamese; it was rumored that there was a price on their heads. In the confusion and the running gun battle with the Viet Cong, the indigenous soldiers separated from Wilson. They stayed on the move, always looking for another spot to hide and get a helicopter in to pick them up. Twenty hours and several skirmishes later, the team was picked up by a "slick," the slang term for a Huey helicopter used for transport work. The slick was covered by a gunship about two hundred meters from the original location. The fire was still intense in the area, and the team had to use a McGuire rig to extract soldiers because of a lack of a landing zone. A McGuire rig was suspended from a helicopter, and soldiers put their leg through the sling loop and their wrist through a wrist loop. The aircraft would have to hover straight up to get the soldiers out of harm's way, as the rope could not be hoisted into the helicopter.

Mike Kessler, a crew chief on the UH-1 Huey that came to extract the team, now lives in California. He vividly remembered the pickup of the team.

> *We were scrambled early the following day to pick up the lone team still in the valley. There was a great sense of urgency to get the mission going, so we ran through the preflight inspection in seconds. The word was that the team was in great peril, and they were about to be overwhelmed. Again, due to the weather, we were without our gunships.*
>
> *Upon reaching clear skies at nearly 10,000', we heard radio transmissions from the American team leader. Here was this big, tough Special Forces trooper, his voice filled with desperation, pleading in a whisper for us to "Hurry! Please hurry!" He said this repeatedly during the next few minutes, and my fear of the impending action turned into a hardened resolve to do everything I could to save that team.*
>
> *We had no trouble locating the team, as Covey* [the forward air controller] *had been with them throughout the early morning and guided us directly to their location.*
>
> *As we rounded a bend to the left, the pilots and I simultaneously spotted purple smoke and a cluster of three*

or four tiger fatigue-clad men. They were in relatively short vegetation, and one guy was waving frantically at us from behind those who were down on one knee in a semi-circle, firing towards the east. They were firing for all they were worth, then reloading and firing again. Guts (Helicopter pilot) immediately spoke on the radio to the team leader, saying, "roger, I have your purple smoke." There was a long second's pause when the American hissed in his desperate voice, "I didn't pop any smoke." He then began saying, "I'm over here. Over here." This was somewhat problematic because we had come to a hover above a team that now might be the enemy dressed in our indigenous personnel's tiger fatigues and firing their CAR-15s. Fortunately, and this was a big clue, they were not firing at us. Also, we had already lowered the ropes, and the team was hurrying to get into the rigs for extraction.

My place was once again on the floor, looking down from the cargo door, giving hovering directions to Guts, as he was unable to look straight down to see where the team needed the ropes delivered to them. Concurrent with this, the American team leader was still trying to get the pilots to locate him, as it was now clear that he had become separated from the other team members. While Guts worked the controls, Mr. Phillips had found the American when the other team members were ready to be lifted out of the jungle. We hovered to his location and picked him up.

The aircraft then did a 180-degree pedal turn, rotating on its axis, as there was no room to maneuver otherwise. We then began as rapid an ascent as we could make, heading east towards safety. It was at just that moment, when the aircraft was the most vulnerable, struggling to gain speed and altitude and heavily laden and with troops hanging on 150' ropes, that the NVA opened up on us. It was just like the day before; a rapid-fire exercise in which we were the target—a cumbersome, slow-moving target. The enemy had withheld their fire until now, knowing we would be more vulnerable while lifting a heavy load. Their goal was to bag the whole lot of us, which seemed like a good bet right then.

Bullets began hitting the aircraft, including one which went through the bulkhead I was holding on to. There was a loud "bang," but I saw nothing and resumed monitoring the troops hanging on the ropes. When we cleared the mouth of the ravine and were no longer receiving direct fire, I took up my M-60 machine gun and commenced firing for all I was worth, back into the enemy in the ravine. While I was blasting away, it became evident that we had suffered some damage, as the pilots could not communicate. I then plugged into a reserve intercom cord and was somewhat annoyed when Covey gave me a direct order to cease firing. I did so grudgingly but was rewarded by seeing jets swooping down on the enemy position, bombing them most effectively.

We began to take stock of our situation as we made our getaway. We had clearly taken some hits, but the aircraft was flying just fine. It was not until this time that I became aware that only five men were beneath the aircraft, not the six we had expected to pick up. We had left one man behind, and it turned out to be an American.

As with the day before, the ropes were somewhat jumbled, and guys were hanging at different levels beneath the aircraft. They were waving for us to set them down, but the pilots were singularly unwilling to land in enemy territory anymore. We kept flying until we reached the east side of the mountains, where we found an American artillery base. The guys on the ropes were oscillating back and forth like a pendulum, and there was some concern that we would drag them to death trying to put them on the ground. The pilots decided that we could break their oscillations best by having them hit some tree branches. We did this, and they did get onto the ground. There was, of course, some dismay from those who had broken legs and arms with this maneuver, but they were at least safe from the enemy.

To this day, I have a vivid recollection of jumping from the aircraft after we landed, crying my eyes out as we ran to the jumble of guys lying all over the ground.

It was at that moment that we learned that we had lost the official team leader, Johnny C. Calhoun, who had been wounded the day before and had ordered the others to leave him behind. He had sacrificed himself to hold off the enemy and gain a head start for his teammates. In 2008, I met SOG author John "Tilt" Meyer, author of Across the Fence *and* On the Ground. *He steered me to internet sources and personal friends who filled in some of the blanks. Johnny was assigned to FOB-3* [Forward Operating Base] *in Khe Sanh, and he was sent to FOB-1 to lead a "composite team" when FOB-1 ran out of operational teams, as the show had to go on.*

The team had no chance to go back and recover Calhoun's body because of the enemy activity in the area and the risk to their own lives. For the same reason, a reconnaissance team to be inserted into the area was canceled two days later. Instead, American aircraft conducted visual surveillance and made broadcasts in the hope that Calhoun had survived, avoided capture, and was looking for a way out. The survey produced nothing but gunfire, which in and of itself was something.

On March 29, 1968, four months after the death of Tommy Huddleston, the family took another blow. The dreaded sight for any military wife appeared outside Faye and Carol's door. An Army car rolled up, and in it were a few men in uniform along with Faye's father. Instantly, Faye knew what was happening and assumed Johnny had been killed. The Missing in Action label was much more difficult.

"The days after were a torment," Faye recalled. "They kept telling us that they had no more information. I kept thinking they would be able to tell me something in a few days, but they never had more information. This went on and on and on."

The family held out hope that perhaps Johnny had escaped his predicament. The military had an officer who kept in touch with Faye monthly, keeping her up to date on anything new regarding Johnny and ensuring she was doing all right.

"They were good about that," Faye said.

In 1974, Johnny Calhoun was awarded the Distinguished Service Cross for his actions on March 27, 1968. The only medal higher is the Medal of Honor.

"Johnny gave the ultimate sacrifice, and anyone who does that deserves every honor they can get, whatever the situation. We got our freedom because of people like Johnny," said Terry Lewis.

Johnny Calhoun was also declared dead in 1974.

"It was sad for all of us, but we knew that it was the best thing to do at the time, but it didn't make it any easier," Faye said. "I was hoping that it would give us some closure because those last six years were rough on all of us. Those years were very long and hard."

In 1975, Faye remarried a fellow from her class at East Coweta High School.

While in school, she didn't know Charles Bassett, but they met at a local skating rink where Faye took Teresa to skate. When Faye remarried, the military stopped contacting her and began contacting her daughter, Teresa, though not as frequently. In the mid-1990s, someone got in touch with Teresa with a videotape of an interrogation of a possible POW and wanted to know if it might be Johnny. Faye and Carol reviewed the tape and thought it looked like Johnny, but there were a couple of things that just weren't right; the most obvious to Faye and her mother-in-law were his arms.

Johnny was short and stocky with short arms. The guy in the video had much longer arms.

"It did look like Johnny," said Faye, "but I knew it wasn't him, and so did his mother."

They had to send the video back. "The man on the video looked like he had been brainwashed," said Faye. "It was a pretty sad video to watch." Shortly after this incident, the government asked the family for a sample of their DNA.

The Vietnam War brought a focus on the POW/MIA issue more than any previous conflict had. During the 1970s, POW/MIA activists began pushing the US government to account for all military personnel listed as MIA or originally reported as POWs. Over time, the POW/MIA issue took on a life of its own. The idea that a conspiracy had left POWs in Vietnamese hands was featured in popular films. During the 1990s, relations were normalized between the United States and Vietnam; the Vietnamese agreed to cooperate in the search for Americans classified as Missing in Action. The Joint Task Force—Full Accounting was established to take advantage of this cooperation and determine what had happened to those listed as missing, bring home the remains of service members left in Vietnam, and bring closure to the families. Regardless of claims that the government was not trying to account for these men, it appears that they had gone to great lengths over many years to investigate even the most ludicrous of tales.

From government documents regarding MIA Staff Sergeant Johnny Calhoun:

> *January 1997: The US Ambassador to Cambodia reported that he had been contacted by several Cambodian officials who claimed to have access to a live American POW. Two POW/MIA activists speculated the POW could be SSG Calhoun, based on the source's story of his loss incident. An analyst from DIA interviewed the alleged American, who was in fact, a tall, ethnic minority tribesman from Vietnam; he was not SSG Calhoun. His name was Y Rak, and he claimed that since he was so old, he must have been born in 1930. He could not remember his American name or being American, but people kept telling him he must be American due to his height (6'2") so he had decided that he was American. Y Rak explained his lack of memory concerning the English language and his American background by saying that the Vietnamese drained all his American blood and replaced it with Montagnard blood. This had taken his English language capability and had left him speaking only Vietnamese (with a Montagnard accent). The alleged American was very obviously not an American. The story is a fabrication.*
>
> *January 1997: A Lao source in Cambodia provided three photos and two pieces of paper with alleged biographical information about US POWs. One photo showed two men, and on the back was written "Johnny Calhoun," "1930," and "Strung Treng." The second photo showed the same two men in a jeep with six other people. The third photo showed one Caucasian with one Asian man. Written on the back were the words "Larry Stevens." On one of the papers was information relating to Larry Stevens. The second paper mentioned Mark Smith, a POW/MIA activist, and was*

reportedly written by Kenneth Stonebraker. The first two photos showed Y Rak, including the one with "Calhoun" written on the back. The third photo showed a man who is reported to be an American tourist from Seattle. The individual in the photo was not SSG Calhoun. The source's story is not credible.

January/February 1997: A source, an American citizen, reported that during a trip to Cambodia, some Cambodian men let him interview a US POW. DPMO [Defense Prisoner of War/Missing Personnel] interviewed the source on two separate occasions. During the first interview, the source said the name of the POW was "Robertson Calhoun" and that he could not speak English. During the second interview, the source said the POW's name was John Leaver, and that he was fluent in English. Due to the source contradicting himself on these and additional details, his story was assessed to be a fabrication.

The most promising leads involved local Vietnamese men, one in the village of Hong Thuong near the Laotian border and not far from the village of Phu Vinh. In July 1993, a joint team visited the village and interviewed Mr. Nguyen Xuan Toan. Mr. Toan described an engagement with a small Special Forces team in late 1967 that involved the death of a Black US soldier. Mr. Toan claimed that his unit recovered several items from the slain American, but they left the body. The joint team visited the site but found nothing. In December 1993, the team visited Phu Vinh village to interview Mr. Con Nieng and Mr. Nguyen Xuan Mai. Both were members of the same Viet Cong unit as Mr. Toan. They recalled a team consisting of five ARVN and one US soldier around June 1968. According to the two men, one US soldier was killed, putting the ARVN soldiers to flight. The soldier that died was white. The weapon and rucksack of the dead American were scavenged, but the body was left in the field. Mr. Nieng believed it to be in the vicinity of a stream at least three meters underwater at that time because it was the rainy season. The team returned in May of 1994, and Mr. Mai led them to the site that had been discussed earlier. The team found several fighting positions but no remains or personal effects.

In 2008, the team returned and interviewed Mr. Mai again. His story remained unchanged, though now he thought the soldier was Black. The team revisited the site and used metal detectors but again found nothing.

In 2012, a team returned to Hong Thuong's village and interviewed Mr. Toan for a second time. He gave some additional details. He described how his unit had found signs that a Special Forces unit was in the area and had organized to kill or capture the team. He claimed that he discovered the unit in the previously mentioned location, which Mr. Nieng and Mr. Mai had corroborated. He had deployed his unit to try to capture the team but was discovered attempting to surprise them. A firefight broke out, and Mr. Toan shot and killed the American. The ARVN soldiers tried to evade and were picked up by a helicopter using a rope ladder.

While the details given by the Vietnamese men were not exactly what the Americans believed to have happened in March of 1968, the discrepancies could be a result of the passage of time. Mr. Toan could not recall what happened to the body.

Take care of him Dear God wherever he may be
And do bring him home so we all may see
The one we all love so true and so dear
And hope and pray that soon he will be here

Thank you again Dear God for all you have done
For you know that he is "Our Husband, Father, and Son"[1]

—Faye Hayes Calhoun (Bassett)

** *See end notes in the appendix for the full poem by Faye.*

Born: *July 14, 1945*
Died: *March 27, 1968, in Thua Thien province of South Vietnam*
Coweta servicemen who died in the same province: *Charles Walthall, Robert Webb, Eddy Couch, Wayne Vessell, and John Dozier*
Unit on death: *FOB 3, CCN, MACV-SOG, 5th Special Forces*

Group
Decorations: *Distinguished Service Cross, Purple Heart, National Defense Service Medal, Vietnam Service Medal, Republic of Vietnam Campaign Medal, Georgia Military Hall of Fame*
Buried: There is no gravesite or family memorial for Johnny Calhoun until he returns home.
Vietnam Memorial, Washington, DC: Panel 46-E, Line 45

Sources
Interview with Carol Leseur, mother
Interview with Faye Hayes Bassett, widow
Interview with Andrew Coy, US Army
Interview with Terry Lewis, US Army
Email interview with Mike Kessler, US Army, Huey crew member
Assistance from John Stryker Meyer, US Army, SOG One-Zero

References
Documents from the Joint Task Force—Full Accounting, Case 1106-0-01.

Johnny and Carol.

Johnny Calhoun, 2nd from left.

Johnny in Vietnam.

Faye, Johnny, and Teresa

Photos courtesy of Faye Bassett and Carol Leseur.

CHAPTER ELEVEN

Charles Edward Walthall

Palmetto, Georgia

Airborne: Trust me, it's not a club. It's a brotherhood that few understand and even fewer are a part of.
—Anonymous

Tuesday, February 10, 1948, was the quintessential winter day in the western part of Georgia—cold, gray, and windy. The temperature wouldn't break 38 degrees. This area of Georgia was in the first stages of drought; it hadn't rained in January and wouldn't rain again until June. In the small town of Palmetto, Miss Dorothy Amos was forced to ignore the weather and focus instead on the hungry infant who had entered her family's life that day. His father, Charles Frank Walthall, lived in Palmetto and drove a school bus in Fayette County. Even though they weren't married, Dorothy decided to name him after his father, and he was christened Charles Edward Walthall. Charles would grow up in this rural town outside of Atlanta, immersed in a family of women.

There's no evidence that Charles regretted his lack of a full-time father. His grandmother, mother, and her sisters, Charles's aunts, looked after him. He spent much of his childhood at his grandmother's farm on Palmetto-Cascade Road. Charles's uncle, John Jeffry, lived on the farm and provided most of the physical labor. He was the "man of the house" and would have been Charles's most significant male influence. His grandmother's farm produced cotton and sugar cane and syrup. In addition, they canned vegetables every year. Charles helped in this work as he grew up.

One of Charles's cousins, William Walthall, said Charles enjoyed playing baseball and football out in the yard. Another cousin, Ralph Brown, came to the farm to ride bikes and play ball with Charles. Four children frequently played together on the farm: Charles, Ralph, Leavy Solomon, and one other whose name is unknown. (Leavy Solomon was killed in Vietnam seven and a half months after Charles. See Chapter 18.)

Charles and Leavy attended Palmetto Elementary. Charles was taken down the long dirt road from the farmhouse to the road to catch the bus every morning. His mother always made sure he had a nice lunch. All the kids wanted to see Charles's lunch, hoping he would share some of it with them.

Loving superhero comic books, Charles often took what money he had to buy two or three at a time.

"He is the only Black guy that could go to the drug store in Palmetto and sit on the floor and read them books just like a white guy," said Ralph Brown. "They never said anything to him."

Charles entered Fairburn High School in 1962. He was noted for two things there. First, he played offensive tackle for the Fairburn High football team, which wasn't known for being very good but was reasonably successful while Charles was involved.

"He was a big guy," said Brown.

Charles was also known as an excellent student who enjoyed science. In his senior year, he won first prize for his science fair project. He graduated from Fairburn High School in 1966.

After graduating, Walthall enrolled at Morris Brown College in Atlanta and also worked at the Greyhound bus station in Atlanta. Charles did not, however, return for his sophomore year. Instead, he attended the International Business Machines (IBM) training school before the draft finally caught up with him.

At the end of August 1968, Walthall started Basic Combat Training at Fort Benning, Georgia. After completing Basic Training, he moved on to Fort Gordon. Near Augusta, Georgia, this military base was typically the training home for the Signal Corps and the Military Police, not the infantry. At this time, however, Fort Gordon had been ordered to begin a combination course of Advanced Infantry Training (AIT) plus Airborne Training. The Airborne Infantry Training course graduates would head directly to jump school at Fort Benning or go north to Fort Bragg and Special Forces Training.

The recently opened part of the post that conducted this nine-week training course had been dubbed Camp Crocket. The soldiers lived in Quonset huts erected on the site by the Army. There was a mockup of a Vietnamese village for training purposes. The food and water were appalling and the heat oppressive. The camp, placed as far away from the main post as possible, was in heavily forested land.

"The idea was to keep the grunts out of sight and isolated from the main post population," George Hoffman said on vietvet.org. "We grunts only saw Fort Gordon once coming in and once going out, and the same was true of Augusta. The training was nonstop and very physical. Constant cycling of troops through the camp graduated one company (approx 176 men) each week. After eight weeks of advanced airborne infantry training, the entire company was bussed to Fort Benning, Georgia for jump school."

Any soldier who opted out of jump school and wasn't already headed to Special Forces or Long-Range Reconnaissance Team Training was slated for Vietnam. While Charles Walthall had no idea he would end up in this hellhole, it can be assumed that he volunteered to try this new method of preparing soldiers to jump from military aircraft.

Walthall got on the bus at the end of the eight weeks and watched as the driver turned south, back to Fort Benning. He had successfully passed the physical qualifications for Airborne. Now, Walthall wanted to prove he could actually become airborne qualified. Upon arrival at Fort Benning, he began the three-week course that would make him an airborne trooper.

Week one was ground week. Soldiers started every day with a five-mile run before breakfast. They spent the week learning and practicing how to crash into the ground when coming down in their parachutes. They jumped off platforms to learn how to "hit, shift, and rotate" to land without hurting themselves. The week was dedicated to physical training and landing practice.

Week two was tower week. In addition to the constant physical training, Walthall was introduced to the Swing Landing Trainer, a device that would swing the soldier back and forth in his parachute harness about three to four feet off the ground then drop him to the ground to practice landing. Next, the instructors introduced the trainees to a 250-foot tower. They were pulled up this crane-like structure in their parachute harness, with their parachutes already deployed, and then dropped, again practicing the landing. The instructors called it the PLF—the parachute landing fall.

Week three was jump week. Every Airborne student had to make five jumps to qualify as a paratrooper. The instructors got students on the plane and taught them how to prepare for their jump. Each planeload of paratroopers was called a "stick." The soldiers boarded the aircraft with a parachute on their back and a reserve chute on their chest.

Just before they got over the drop zone, the jumpmaster yelled and signaled for the "stick" to "Stand up!"

They immediately complied.

The jumpmaster roared, "Hook up!"

They took the hook connected to their parachute and hooked it over the cable running along the middle of the aircraft's roof.

The jumpmaster again shouted to the paratroopers to make himself heard over the noise of the engines. "Check equipment!"

Everyone checked the equipment of the soldier in front of them.

Then the jumpmaster was back again. "Sound off for equipment check!"

From the back to the front of the aircraft came a series of yells of "OK," and each paratrooper slapped the butt or shoulder of the paratrooper in front of him. The first paratrooper of the stick got ready at the door. When the jumpmaster saw the green light, he slapped the soldier and shouted again, "Go!"

The paratrooper launched out into the sky. He tucked as the parachute was automatically pulled out of the bag by the hook attached to the cable. He counted one thousand, two thousand, three thousand then looked up and checked his parachute to make sure there were no problems. If there was a problem, he had a reserve chute to fall back on. If all was well, "There wasn't anything to do but prepare for the landing," said David Brown of the 173rd Airborne Brigade. The same procedure was repeated back in the plane until the entire stick was out the door.

Once Charles Walthall completed his five jumps, they pinned his wings on his chest, and he was given a thirty-day leave. Afterward, Charles was sent straight to his assigned unit, the 101st Airborne, already in Vietnam. (The three other Airborne-qualified Coweta soldiers in this book—Johnny Calhoun, Chapter 10, Tommy Huddleston, Chapter 6, and Robert Webb, Chapter 24—would have gone through the same training.)

Ralph Brown said he remembers Charles coming home on leave because of an unusual incident. Brown saw his father, Charles's uncle, give Charles a shot of whiskey. Ralph had never seen Charles drink before.

"He's a grown man now. He's in the Army," Ralph's father said.

That was the last time Ralph ever saw Charles Walthall.

Leonard Lipscomb also remembers Charles being home on that same leave. Leonard was heading to a dance at Fairburn High School, and Charles wanted to accompany him. "He wanted to stop by and buy some beer. I didn't drink, and I thought that was odd, him drinking beer, you know. At my age, I thought drinking beer was bad." Lipscomb laughed. "He said that he knew he wasn't coming back from Vietnam, and he was going to go ahead and drink." So Leonard took him to the dance, and that was the last time he saw Charles Walthall.

Walthall flew from Atlanta to Oakland, California. After he left California on a civilian airliner, his next stop would have been the Hawaiian Islands, where the plane would refuel and he would spend the night. From there, the soldiers flew directly into Vietnam. Charles Walthall arrived in Vietnam on February 27, 1968. As Walthall exited the aircraft, he was likely struck by the suffocating heat and the overwhelming smell of burning human waste.

Walthall arrived at the tail end of the first phase of the infamous Tet Offensive, which had begun during the early morning hours of January 31. The Viet Cong and the North Vietnamese Army had simultaneously struck US Army installations and provincial capitals all over South Vietnam. Using 85,000 troops and prepositioned weapons, the communist forces attacked over one hundred major cities and towns across South Vietnam. As Walthall stepped off the plane in Vietnam, fighting still raged in areas across the country, most notably at Khe Sanh and Hue, as the American military systematically destroyed the exposed communist forces.

Assigned to B Company, 2nd Battalion, 502nd Infantry Regiment of the 101st Airborne Division, Walthall was stationed at

Camp Eagle in Thua Thien province, not far from the ancient Vietnamese capital city of Hue. Camp Eagle had been established only a few months but quickly became a 101st Airborne post "in the middle of the jungle," according to Sergeant Herb McCool.

"Camp Eagle was situated in a hilly, jungle area. There were a lot of very tall trees in the area. Only our camp was cleared of the jungle. Everything else was forest," he said.

In the I Corps part of South Vietnam, this province stretched from the South China Sea coastline on the east to Laos and the Ho Chi Minh Trail on the west. Camp Eagle was open to attack and had been assaulted numerous times since the Tet Offensive began, but the communists had yet to break through the defenses.

The first phase of the Tet Offensive had begun to subside when Walthall arrived at Camp Eagle. During March and April 1968, combat soldiers throughout Vietnam were learning how to survive in this harsh and dangerous environment. Ralph Brown said Charles became ill while in Vietnam but is unsure about the particular ailment, though he mentioned malaria as a possibility. He remembers seeing a photograph of Charles in pajamas on a beach. Charles would have been out of action for at least two weeks if he had been along the coast and recuperating from malaria. Then it was back to patrolling and setting up ambushes.

Phase two of the Tet Offensive kicked off in May 1968. Frequently called the May Offensive or mini-Tet, this phase again saw communist forces assaulting targets throughout South Vietnam. Statistics for this offensive reported even more American casualties than in phase one.

On Tuesday, May 21, 1968, Camp Eagle was attacked with an estimated three hundred 82mm motor rounds and 122mm rockets. This barrage was immediately followed by an attack launched by the North Vietnamese Army. Fifty-four North Vietnamese soldiers were killed during the attack. Sixty-eight Americans were wounded, thirteen Americans were killed, and several of the replacements happened to be in the wrong place at the wrong time. One of those killed in the initial volley of shells was Charles Walthall.

Charles's body was returned to Palmetto, taken to his mother's home, and guarded twenty-four hours a day by two soldiers. Dorothy Amos wanted desperately to open the casket and make sure it was her son, but the guards refused to allow it. The casket remained closed throughout the funeral and burial. Ralph Brown remembers the flag being draped over the coffin. In less than a year, he would see another flag on a coffin of a family member. William Walthall got a letter about Charles's death, but his family didn't want him to come home for this funeral; he had already been home recently for the death of an uncle.

On Wednesday, June 5, the funeral for Charles Walthall was held at Ramah Baptist Church in Palmetto. He rests today in Palmetto Cemetery.

Ralph Brown characterized Charles Walthall as a "good-hearted person," and William Walthall said he was a "jolly kind of guy." Both remembered that he liked to laugh and loved to have fun.

On September 6, 1968, the US Army presented Dorothy Amos with a Bronze Star for her son's service and bravery.

Born: *February 10, 1948*
Home of record: *Palmetto, Georgia*
Died: *May 21, 1968, in Thua Thien province of South Vietnam*
Coweta servicemen who died in the same province: *Robert Webb, Eddy Couch, Wayne Vessell, John Dozier, and Johnny Calhoun*
Unit on death: *B CO, 2nd BN, 502nd Infantry, 101st ABN Division*
Decorations: *Bronze Star, Purple Heart, Good Conduct Medal, National Defense Service Medal, Vietnam Service Medal, Republic of Vietnam Campaign Medal*
Buried: *Palmetto Cemetery, Palmetto*
Vietnam Memorial, Washington, DC: *Panel 65E Line 3*

Sources

Interview with Ralph Brown, cousin
Interview with William Walthall, uncle
Interview with Leonard Lipscomb, childhood friend
Assistance from David Brown, US Army

References

Coffelt Database, "Charles Walthall." Accessed March 3, 2022. http://coffeltdatabase.org/index.php
"Remembering Camp Crockett." Accessed March 4, 2022. http://campcrockett.blogspot.com/
Taipei Signal Army. "A Camp within a Fort: Camp Crocket, Georgia." http://taipeisignalarmy.blogspot.com/2014/11/a-camp-within-fort-camp-crocket-georgia.html
War Tales. "Former Sgt. Herb McCool Escaped without a Scratch during 3 tours in Vietnam." https://donmooreswartales.com/2013/08/30/herb-mc-cool/

Charles Walthall, left, date unknown, and his graduation picture, 1966.

CHAPTER TWELVE

Terry Allen

Newnan, Georgia

"There is a thin line that separates laughter and pain, comedy and tragedy, humor and hurt."
—Erma Bombeck

"I remember the night Terry and his friend left for Vietnam. He had a friend from Chicago, and they had come to Newnan," said Ronald Smith. "I was living in Atlanta [and had come down to Newnan], and we had spent that whole day together. Not just me but everyone around Fairmount was with Terry because he was leaving that night. So after we had fun that day and as we have said, he was funny as hell, he had a good sense of humor, he said we [Terry and his friend] have to be at the airport at about 7:00 p.m. So I said, OK, I am going back to Atlanta so I can drop you at the airport. So I dropped Terry and his friend at the airport. We hugged and said our goodbyes. We were very close."

"One month later, I got a call. My mom called me, and she said, 'Terry was killed in Vietnam.' I said don't tell me that! That hit me hard."

Terry Allen was born on King Street (now Ball Street) in Newnan to Ed and Virginia Allen on January 5, 1948. He was the only child born to the couple; they divorced shortly after his birth, with Ed moving to Philadelphia. Over the next few years, Virginia had three other children: Gloria, Lonnie, and Vivian. Despite his move, Ed Allen stayed in contact with Terry as he was growing up, often sending him clothes, shoes, and other gifts. In 1955, Virginia met and married Rawson Thompson, who was raising five children of his own.

"It was *The Brady Bunch*," Gloria said with a laugh.

Terry was in elementary school and living at his grandmother's house with his family when his mother remarried. Terry's grandmother, Mary Stevenson, had nine sons and four daughters, "an entire baseball team and the cheerleaders to go with it," according to Edward Stevenson, one of Mary's sons.

Virginia was one of Mary's oldest children, so Edward, only nine months older than Terry, was his uncle. Everyone assumed they were brothers as they grew up and went to school together.

"You aren't going to get no better uncle and nephew than Edward and Terry," said Jerry Walton, a friend of the two.

"They were just like brothers," said George Hart, another childhood friend.

Rawson and Virginia moved into a house on Mary Ann Street, less than a mile away from Virginia's mother and her siblings on King (Ball) Street. Gloria, Lonnie, and Vivian went to the new home with their mother, stepfather, and new stepbrothers and sisters; Terry was allowed to stay with his grandmother and his uncles.

"There were so many other boys in the house that my grandmother said he could stay there," said Gloria. From his grandmother's house on King Street to Mary Ann Street, a path allowed everyone to go back and forth between the two homes.

Evelyn Thompson, one of Terry's stepsisters, was three years younger and already knew Terry from school when suddenly, they became family. She got along well with Terry. She described him as intelligent, articulate, kind, and gentle. "He was so patient and loving with us," Evelyn said.

Terry enjoyed playing with his closest sister, Gloria, who was only two years younger. They would often swing from the vines and play in the woods. Gloria remembered that he liked hominy, a type of canned corn. He often heated a can of it on a stove to eat for a snack while relishing the fact that he was aggravating Gloria, who hated the concoction.

"He was the only person I have ever known to eat that stuff, but he loved it," Gloria said.

The close-knit neighborhood where Terry Allen grew up during the 1950s and 1960s was known as London Hill. It was located off McIntosh Street, which has since been renamed Martin Luther King Boulevard, and between the Chalk Level and Fairmount neighborhoods. Robinson Park was located at the end of Ball Street close to East Broad Street, the present location of Highland Apartments.

George Hart lived "up the hill" from Terry Allen and his uncle, Edward Stevenson, on Mitchell Street in the Chalk Level neighborhood. "We had to go down the hill, then across a little creek to get to the park. We were called the Mountain Men, and we called them the London Hill Eagles," Hart said. "We swung on a vine across that creek, like Tarzan. The kids from this area used to play sports together at the park."The boys seemed always involved in sports unless there was a girl around, according to Edward Stevenson, Alfred Ragland, Ronald Smith, Jerry Walton, Frank Wynn, and George Hart. Terry's reputation as a ladies' man started at a young age.

The youngsters played football, basketball, and baseball, depending on the season. "There was not too much to do in Newnan, not for the Blacks. Not much to do in Newnan except go to school and play sports," Stevenson said.

Robinson Park was also used for practice by the Howard Warner football team.

"As a kid, I used to run down the bottom of the hill to watch those guys hustle over there to practice. They used to do that just about every evening," said George Hart.

"The team had to run a couple of miles to get to Robinson Park to practice and then run back to Howard Warner afterward," said Edward Stevenson.

The Howard Warner team got hand-me-down uniforms and equipment from Newnan High School, and sometimes, when they had received a new batch of clothing or equipment, they threw away their old equipment or uniforms in the park trash cans. The younger kids scrounged the items out of the trash can, so the clothing and equipment enjoyed a remarkably long life.

The school situation for Black students was unquestionably more complicated than for white students. When these African American students grew up, there was an elementary school on Pinson Street, and when they completed elementary school, they moved on to Howard Warner High School. Howard Warner wasn't a large facility, and often the students were required to attend school in shifts, from 8 a.m. until noon and from 1-5 p.m., or they were bused to Westside or Ruth Hill, both of which can be accessed off Belk Road. Central High School for African American students opened for the 1955-1956 school year, while Howard Warner became an elementary school.[1]

"They [the Coweta County School System] did the best they could do with the money they were dealing with," said Edward Stevenson. "We did what we had to do and had a good time doing it."

Terry Allen, Edward Stevenson, Alfred Ragland, Ronald Smith, Frank Wynn, and George Hart all attended these schools from an early age.

Jerry Walton met Terry in second grade. "He didn't care anything about school," Walton said. "He was a guy to tell jokes. But he and Edward [Stevenson], if you didn't know it, you would think they were brothers."

"No one would know he [Edward] was the uncle unless you told them," said Ronald Smith.

Everybody walked to school unless they were being bused to the Belk Road area. Terry, Uncle Edward, and Terry's sister Gloria walked every morning from the London Hill neighborhood to Howard Warner and back again in the afternoon, a total of one and a half miles.

"That was a long walk," Gloria said. "I was two years younger than Terry and three years younger than Edward, and sometimes my socks wouldn't stay up, and I had to stop and fix that. You know, we had to carry all our books. We had no lockers. It was cold in the winter. I would be crying because I couldn't keep up, and Edward would always stop and come back and get me, but Terry would leave me."

Terry might have been annoyed with his little sister on the walks to Howard Warner, but that didn't keep him from being protective of her when Gloria became a freshman at Central High School and Terry entered his junior year. Terry wouldn't let his friends say anything to his sister, and he told Gloria not to say anything to them.

"When Terry was in twelfth grade, Mother would give Terry a dollar. Now, we didn't have a lot of money, so he would make change after he paid for his lunch, and he would give me thirty-five cents for my lunch," Gloria said. She would go into the gym where Terry had homeroom to get her lunch money. She needed to get back into her class as soon as possible because "when the bell rang, you had to be in your seat. All his buddies would be in the bleachers to the left as I walked in. Not one guy in there thought I was cute, but they would say stuff to aggravate him. They would say, 'Woohoo, where is she going?' Now, I'm just looking for Terry. I just want my thirty-five cents. I didn't know who was hollering and talking, but Terry would get an instant attitude. He would get mad. 'Don't say anything to my sister. Don't say nothing to her,' he would say."

As Terry Allen and his friends entered Central High School, they were maturing and developing. Gloria remembers Terry and Edward learning to shave with some shaving cream that smelled like rotten eggs. Terry was putting on some muscle and had developed into a rather good-looking young man. But like his physical body, Terry's personality continued to develop. An extrovert, he always joked with people even though the joking sometimes wasn't appreciated.

Alfred Ragland lived across Mary Ann Street from Terry's mother. Terry and Edward were frequently at the house and got to know Ragland and later attended Central High School with him.

"He was joking all the time," Ragland said. "Our friendship wasn't that great because he picked too much." Frequently, Edward told Terry to back off, saying he was going too far.

"Whatever you did, you were not going to get the last word. Terry got the last word," Frank Wynn said.

"You would be very mad at him, but you would be laughing at the end of the fuss. He definitely was a comedian," said Ronald Smith.

"He wasn't doing it in a hostile way," added Jerry Walton. "It was just the way he was."

Once, while attending Central High School, Terry got some wire-rimmed spectacles and wore them around the school. This caused much merriment among his friends, who started calling him "Charley Weaver" after actor Cliff Arquette's television character, who wore wire-rimmed spectacles.[2] At Central High School, Terry

Allen was bigger than life.

Even while Terry lived on King Street with his grandmother, he walked to his mother's house for breakfast every morning.

"It didn't matter how cold it was," said Gloria. "My mother was a great cook. Every morning, we would hear that knock on the door. He would come in and eat breakfast."

His stepfather was usually there as well. He worked the third shift at Bonnell, came home, ate breakfast, then drove a school bus route for the Coweta County School System. After breakfast, Terry's mother gave him money for lunch, and he got dressed for school. Virginia had his shirts starched and ironed.

"He was neat and clean all the time," said George Hart. "His blue jeans would be so sharp with that crease. You could cut butter with that crease." Terry always liked having his shoes shined too. When Terry Allen went to school, he looked good. Real good.

Naturally, the girls at school noticed how smooth Terry looked, and he enjoyed their attention. His friends believed that he not only enjoyed being around females but was also obsessed with them. Terry would play ball with the guys at any location, but when a girl appeared, he moved on and paid attention to the young lady.

"He loved the ladies, and the ladies loved him," said Evelyn Rosser.

Gloria pointed out that Terry could also be arrogant with the young ladies. He told one young lady that she wouldn't be popular if she didn't know him, Jerry Walton said. In high school, they would call Terry at home, and he wouldn't speak to them. But he was especially close to Katie Almon and Alice Hayes.

Katie met him at Central High. "He chased me," said Katie. "He was a fun, very nice guy." She had several classes with him, including history, physical education, and music. They continued to date even after they graduated. He also dated and was close to Alice Hayes. Terry Allen's family stayed in contact with both girls for years after Terry's death.

Looking good at school didn't necessarily help Terry with academics at Central High.

"When he went to his classes [at Central], he treated them all the same. He didn't like any of them," said Frank Wynn, though Gloria thought Terry didn't mind attending Shop class, where he could work with his hands. However, he always made it from one grade to the next. Terry did what he had to do, as Edward had said. He wasn't involved in sports at Central, though he did go out for football once. Coach Henry Seldon, the highly respected coach of the Central High School Panthers, was tough. Terry tried out for the team for one day but never returned. He decided football wasn't for him.

Central High School played football games at Pickett Field near downtown Newnan. Newnan High School played there as well but on different nights since Drake Stadium wasn't built until 1966. Central had a home game while Newnan played away from home and vice versa. In the corner of the field were bleachers where white fans could sit.

"A lot of whites would come down to the game and sit in that corner bleacher," said Ronald Smith.

"Everywhere I went, he [Terry] went," said Edward Stevenson. Except for one place.

"There was one thing he wouldn't do with us. Skip school. He wouldn't do it," Jerry Walton said. "Me and Clarence [another friend] would just leave, but he wouldn't do that."

Edward agreed. "We would skip school and enjoy ourselves, but not Terry."

"We never had any trouble back then," said George Hart. "Most of our parents didn't bring us up like that. We had to be home at a certain time. Television didn't go any longer than eleven or eleven thirty, and it would end with someone saying, 'Do you know where your children are?' The parents knew where you were. You were at home."

As Terry grew up, he worked a few jobs to bring in extra money. During the summer, he picked peaches and used the money he earned for school clothes. In high school, he worked at Douglas and Lomason, the company that made aluminum trim for cars, which was located on Highway 16 West across the street from Playtex.[3] This money helped Terry and Edward buy a car while in high school. However, the engine died a few weeks after the purchase. After a neighbor looked at it, the boys told the guy who had sold it to them to come get the car and bring their money. He complied.

One night, after some event at Central High School, Terry and a group of friends were walking home in the dark down McIntosh

Street when a car plowed into them. No one remembers for sure, but there were at least four students, and every one of them was injured. The impact knocked Terry out of his shoes and bruised him severely, but fortunately, he had no broken bones.

"I can remember this," said Katie Almon. "We had a talent show, and he said he wasn't going. I was the mistress of ceremonies, so I went."

Terry ended up going too.

"When we left the talent show," Katie said, "he was walking down the street with some other girl, and that's when the accident occurred. 'If you had come with me,' I told him, 'you wouldn't have been hit by that car.'"

Terry ended up in the hospital that evening and into the next day. "All the women that loved him came to the hospital to see him," Katie said with a laugh. Even more significantly, he missed school the next day.

Terry Allen had never missed school, ever. He was now a senior. The Central administration was sympathetic and didn't count the day against Terry on his attendance record.

In the spring of 1966, Terry Allen graduated with 159 of his classmates. He and Hattie Thurman were the only students with perfect attendance.[4]

After graduation, Edward and Terry headed to Dayton, Ohio, and spent six weeks with family there. They returned home that summer, and shortly after that, Edward was drafted, entering service in September of 1966. Terry continued to work at Douglas and Lomason and bought a green 1957 Chevy. It wasn't pristine; it didn't even have a headliner. But it ran and got him where he wanted to go.

"I remember the Chevy. He tried to teach me to drive a shift," said Katie Almon. "He finally decided, 'You aren't going to drive my car no more.' I never learned how to drive a shift."

Alfred Ragland had been drafted in the spring of 1967. Before he went to Vietnam, Terry found him and wanted him to take a ride in his car. Ragland resisted; he thought Terry was picking at him. Instead, Terry shook his hand and told him, "I just wanted to let you know that we will miss you, and I wanted to spend a little time with you before you left."

Terry Allen was drafted during the summer or early fall of 1967 and went to Basic Combat Training in November.

"My mother, she cried, and she cried, and she cried. She didn't want him to go to the military," said Gloria. "It was just terrible back then."

"I don't really think anybody wanted to be drafted, but if you are drafted, just have to take it in stride and move on, and that is what he did," said Evelyn Thompson.

Fortunately, Terry's Basic Combat Training was at Fort Benning. While this was as close as the training could get, it still seemed quite a distance to all of Terry's family. However, the proximity of the training allowed Terry to go home for a few weekends and take some friends to Newnan with him. In January 1968, he continued at Fort Benning with his Advanced Infantry Training, completing it in March as an infantry soldier. The Tet Offensive, occurring in Vietnam during this training cycle, would have been a predominant topic of conversation. By the end of April, Terry Allen was on his way to Vietnam.

"Before he went off to Vietnam, his uncle Edward told him that you can't have fun there. This is serious," said Katie Almon. "He was just a fun guy, you know? So, we were dating, and when he got ready to go, he said, 'Baby, when I come back, I think I am coming home in a box.' I responded immediately, 'Don't say that! Stop saying that!' 'I'm scared,' he replied. So, I told him you have to be positive. He kept saying he wasn't coming back. I guess he had a premonition. I don't know. So we went to church that Sunday before he went off to Vietnam."

On May 10, 1968, Terry Allen was located with his new unit, Company B, 1st Battalion, 46th Infantry Regiment, 198th Infantry Brigade of the Americal Division. The 1st Battalion was known as "the Professionals" and had been in-country only seven months when Terry got his assignment. The "Professionals" had arrived by ship in October 1967 and deployed around the town of Chu Lai, Quang Tin Province of I Corps, South Vietnam. October and November saw the battalion getting organized, oriented, and trained to conduct operations in Vietnam. The first combat operations that the 1st Battalion engaged in began in December 1967 and continued through April 1968. These operations consisted of Search and

Destroy missions in the Chu Lai region. May 1968 saw the beginning of the Professionals' involvement in their first major operation, code-named Burlington Trail.

The 1/46 was already involved in Operation Burlington Trail when Terry Allen arrived and joined the unit. The Burlington Trail Area of Operations (A-O) was dominated by a dirt road dubbed Route 533. It ran between Tam Ky, the capital of Quang Nam Province, and Tien Phuoc, a Special Forces Camp in Quang Tin Province. One of the goals of Burlington Trail was to ensure that this road stayed open. Another objective was to clear an area known as Base Area 117 in the mountains to the south of Route 533, which intelligence indicated was the site of large-scale NVA base camps. Since late March and early April, there appeared to be increased enemy activity in these areas, and the American military was determined to eliminate that activity.

Burlington Trail involved the First Battalion, 46th Infantry—Terry Allen's unit—the First Battalion, 6th Infantry, parts of the 1st Cavalry Division, and the 6th ARVN Regiment (South Vietnamese Army). Units from the 1/6 occupied a hill in enemy territory and quickly converted it into a firebase. Dubbed LZ Bowman, it was soon occupied by the artillery that virtually all firebases in Vietnam contained. In addition, headquarters and communication units and medical personnel all established themselves quickly at LZ Bowman.

May found these units in sporadic engagements with communist forces. They had some success uncovering arms caches and even found a weapons repair shop but no large body of VC or NVA soldiers. The American units were frequently hit with mortars in the evening, so the American soldiers knew the enemy was there. They just needed to get them out in the open to engage and defeat them. Terry Allen joined the unit on May 10 and was soon involved in the hunt for the enemy.

Terry frequently wrote letters home. When he wrote Edward, he addressed the letters to "Uncle Edward," which he had never done before. Edward believes Terry was under fire and realized that things had gotten serious. Gloria said that like other soldiers who wanted to improve the taste of the water in their canteens, Terry asked for Kool-Aid, so they sent the powder packets in their letters to him. Years later, when she examined those letters that had been returned, they still smelled of Kool-Aid. In addition, Terry wrote about his homesickness and the food, which he despised. Occasionally, the family recorded cassette tapes to communicate with Terry.

In June, the operational tempo picked up. Engagements with the enemy occurred almost daily. Patrols from LZ Bowman continued to make contact with communist troops; helicopters were shot down. On June 12, Company C, 1/46, was attacked by more than 100 NVA troops who employed several automatic weapons, tear gas, and a flamethrower. On June 13, C Company was attacked again. This time, B Company, Terry Allen's company, was also attacked. June 16 and 17 saw B Company again in heavy contact with enemy forces.

Then there was a short lull in the fighting. The tension mounted on all the units involved.

At 11:16 a.m. on June 23, two 81mm mortar rounds fired from an American mortar team from LZ Bowman landed in B Company's night defensive position. The after-action report described it this way, with clarifications by the author.

> *At 1100 hours, B/1-46 [B Company, First Battalion, 46th Infantry Regiment] received 2 81mm rounds in their NDP [night defensive position] at BT134076 [map coordinate], resulting in 4 KHA and 17 WHA [Killed Hostile Action/Wounded Hostile Action]. Further investigation revealed that C/1-46 [C Company] had fired the rounds from BT142074. Co B was approximately 800 meters from the location they called in. [Company B was 800 meters from where the shells were supposed to land.] Investigation was conducted, and disciplinary action recommended.*

Four soldiers were killed by friendly fire that day. James Richardson of Pennsylvania, an assistant machine gunner with Company B, had written home from Vietnam shortly before his death that he had been in combat for twenty-seven days and had only three more days to go before getting a break. Neither he nor Terry Allen ever made it to the break.

It is unclear why the shells were fired, how they had gotten so grossly off course, and what disciplinary action was recommended. Terry Allen was the second of two young men from Coweta County killed by friendly fire in Vietnam, the first being Tommy Huddleston, (Chapter 6).

By the end of Operation Burlington Trail, which continued until November 1968, 129 Americans had been killed. The operation had not successfully cleared the area of communist troops.

Katie Almon had been at a picnic Saturday, June 22, when she started "feeling funny." When she went to bed that evening, "I dreamed we were at this church that had all these flowers. The flowers were arranged across the front like on a horseshoe. I dreamt that."

Katie worked as a tutor with Edwina Stevenson, Edward's sister and Terry's aunt, at Ruth Hill Elementary School. That Monday, June 24, a couple of Newnan police officers went to the school and asked Edwina to go with them. They needed to speak with her mother and wanted her there. Katie wondered what was going on. She discovered what happened when Edwina called her later that afternoon. "It was sad. It was a hard knock. It really was," she said.

In Gloria's last letter from Terry, he had gotten paid and planned to go to Saigon, where he said he would buy her a present. However, he would never have the opportunity to bring her a gift from Vietnam.

"He just left so early," said his mother, Virginia.

Edward Stevenson left his base at Colorado Springs, TDY (temporary duty), boarded a military aircraft, and met Terry's body at Dover Air Force Base in Delaware. He escorted the body to Chicago and then to Atlanta, where Sellers-Smith Funeral Home had a hearse waiting.

"I didn't think I could make it through," Stevenson said. "I knew who was in that casket." But looking back, Stevenson said, "I think that was my job. My shoulders were big enough to carry it. Faith brought me through" *(Newnan Times-Herald,* May 30, 2006*)*.

Edward said an odd thing happened with the casket. In Chicago, the casket went onto the plane last. When they arrived in Atlanta, Edward expected it to come off the plane first. Instead, the casket came off the plane last. "His body wasn't there," Edward said.

"Then it was the last thing that came off the flight." For the past fifty years, Edward has tried to figure out how that could have happened.

The body returned to Newnan and went straight to the funeral home. The body couldn't be moved unless Edward was there, and he took his job seriously since it was his nephew and buddy, Terry. "When I got here, I knew what I had to do. It hurt me worse than anything in the world," he said. Edward stayed with Terry's body as his honor guard, virtually around the clock for the next few days. Edward said this was the only time in his life that he considered suicide. "I had eight brothers, and that hurt me worse than anything. We grew up like twins."

"He remembered being alone with the casket at Newnan Chapel United Methodist Church, sharing a conversation as he felt the presence of his nephew and friend" (*Newnan-Times Herald,* May 2006*)*.

Gloria went to the funeral home with her mother, and Edward was in the room. There was glass on the top of the casket, so they could see the body. A sticker on the glass indicated that the Army had performed reconstruction work on Terry's head so that he would be presentable at the funeral. Edward ripped the sticker off before Virginia could see it. Gloria thought it looked like him; it did look like work had been done on a small area of his head. However, when she spotted the small scar near his mouth, she knew it was her brother. The scar was from the pedestrian accident that Terry had been involved in a few years before.

"It looked like him, but I knew that was my brother when I saw that little scar," Gloria said.

"I came down the street to the funeral home, and Edward had just walked out," said George Hart. "He said it's tough in there, so I went on in there and saw Terry's body and everything… that was one of the worst days of my life."

"I thought he was still running around with the girls," said Alfred Ragland. "While I was in Vietnam, I got a letter from his mother saying Terry died. Died? What? How? What do you mean? Vietnam? Last time I saw him was over around Fairmount!" Ragland, a helicopter door gunner during the war, believes that Terry's death contributed to his own problems with PTSD, post-traumatic stress disorder. He could never get over the guilt about how he hadn't handled the teasing well when they were together and hadn't spent time with Terry before they left for Vietnam.

The funeral was held at Newnan Chapel United Methodist Church on Robinson Street on July 12, 1968. Katie Almon served as one of the six flower ladies, young women classmates of Terry at Central High School, who carried flowers out of the church when the funeral was over. "The funeral was at the church, and it was set up just the way I dreamt it," Katie said.

"He took pride in going and protecting his country. I think that he was proud of that," said Evelyn Thompson.

Edward was supposed to report back to Colorado Springs after the funeral. Instead, he stayed in Newnan for the next three weeks. As a result, he was considered AWOL or Absent Without Official Leave. One of his sisters begged him to return, but he refused to listen. He was despondent over Terry's death and was apathetic about what might happen to him. But when his mother lectured him about returning, he finally relented.

"I went back, and I got busted," he said.

On May 29, 2006, approximately four hundred people gathered for the annual Memorial Day Service at Temple Avenue and Jackson Street, now known as Veterans Memorial Park. The Coweta Veterans Club always hosts and plans the Memorial Day event. Since 1994, the Club has memorialized men from Coweta County who have died in service of their country by highlighting one of them during the Memorial Day Service. The program is called "Honor All by Remembering One." In 2006, that man was Terry Allen.

The Central High School Class of 1966 happened to be having their fortieth class reunion that weekend, and many of them attended the ceremony. Gloria Crook, Edward Stevenson, and Alfred Ragland shared memories of Terry with the crowd. Katie Almon sang. It was a moving moment for Terry's family and friends as they reflected on his life, cut short by an accident of war. In the early 1990s, Terry Allen's brother Lonnie was killed in a tragic accident. Virginia Thompson buried two of her children.

Edward Stevenson would leave military service in September 1968 and move to Detroit, Michigan. While there, he was the driving force in the chartering of the Colin Powell American Veterans Post

(AMVETS). On March 17, 2007, the Terry Allen Buffalo Soldiers AMVETS Post 910 was chartered to honor his nephew. Stevenson was instrumental in starting this post, just as he had been in Detroit. The Terry Allen Post in Newnan still exists today.

"I never saw a frown on that guy's face," said George Hart. "He was smiling. His eyes just lit up all the time. His eyes were almost squinched up because he was smiling all the time."

"He was a fun guy. Everybody loved him," reflected Katie Almon. "It was never a dull moment when he was in the room. It was always lively."

In the program for Terry Allen's funeral was a sonnet by John Donne.

"Death, be not proud, though some have called thee mighty and dreadful, for thou art not so... one short sleep past, we wake eternally
And Death shall be no more..."

**See end notes in the appendix for additional details.*

***Born**: January 5, 1948, in Newnan, Georgia*
***Home of record:** Newnan, Georgia*
***Died**: June 23, 1968, in Quang Tin province of South Vietnam*
***Coweta servicemen who died in the same province**: Tim Cole and Warner Hughie*
***Unit on death**: B CO, 1st BN, 46th Infantry, 198th Infantry BDE, Americal Division*
***Decorations:** Bronze Star, Purple Heart, Good Conduct Medal, National Defense Service Medal, Vietnam Service Medal, Republic of Vietnam Gallantry Cross with Palm, Republic of Vietnam Campaign Medal*
***Buried:** Eastgate Cemetery, Newnan*
***Vietnam Memorial, Washington, DC:** Panel 55W Line 20*

Sources
Interview with Virginia Thompson, mother
Interview with Gloria Stevenson Crook, sister
Interview with Evelyn Thompson Rosser, stepsister

Interview with Edward Stevenson, uncle
Interview with Willie (Jerry) Walton, childhood friend
Interview with George (BoBo) Hart, childhood friend
Interview with Frank (Coon) Wynn, childhood friend
Interview with Ronald (Snake) Smith, childhood friend
Interview with Alfred (Rag) Ragland, childhood friend
Interview with Katie Almon, childhood friend
Interview with Leslie Hines, Americal Division Veterans Association Vietnam Historian

References

Coffelt Database, "Terry Allen." Accessed March 21, 2019. http://coffeltdatabase.org/index.php
Sarah Fay Campbell, "AMVETS Post named for Terry Allen Jr., Vietnam Soldier." *Newnan Times-Herald*, February 24, 2021.
"Terry Allen Honored." *Newnan Times-Herald*, May 30, 2006.

Terry Allen, 1965 and graduation picture, 1966.

Photos courtesy of Gloria Crook.

CHAPTER THIRTEEN

Wayne Jackson Vessell

Haralson/Senoia, Georgia

Some people spend an entire lifetime wondering if they made a difference in the world. But the Marines don't have that problem.
—Ronald Reagan

"He was a sweet guy."

But on the morning of Tuesday, July 9, 1968, that "sweet guy" was looking and feeling anything but sweet. Wayne Vessell was loaded with more than fifty pounds of gear and standing on the flight deck of the *USS Tripoli* (LPH-10), shifting his feet back and forth, trying to find a comfortable stance to balance the weight. The things he had on were standard-issue Marine Corps, nothing unusual. The USMC equipment load was designed to keep Wayne in the field and fighting for two to three days. He wore a flak jacket designed to protect him against shrapnel. Almost everything else was attached to his web gear or in a rucksack—ammunition, grenades, c-rations, a canteen, a first aid kit, a flashlight, and an entrenching tool. He also carried an M-16 rifle. Every piece of equipment was important, but each piece added weight.

It was early in the morning, but the sun was already glistening off the South China Sea near the coast of South Vietnam. Unfortunately, the temperature and humidity always ruined the beauty of the sun in this land. Both weather indicators were steadily climbing as Vessell and the Marines of his unit waited to board the choppers that would lift them off the ship's deck and take them into combat. He longed to board a UH-1 Huey helicopter. There, he could sit at the door with his legs hanging out and the wind blowing over him. However, he wouldn't board the Huey this morning; instead, he would board a

Marine CH-46 Sea Knight helicopter. The Sea Knight is a Marine chopper that looks very similar to the Army's Chinook, though smaller and less powerful.

The Sea Knight helicopters of HMM-265 could each carry an entire squad of Marines—twelve to thirteen Marines at full strength—with one lift. (The acronym HMM stands for Helicopter Marine Medium.) It took four Sea Knights to deliver a platoon into the waiting landing zones. The cargo and passenger area, where the Marines stood holding on, was noisy and smelly because the engine was directly above it. The helicopter shook violently throughout its flight, and that, combined with the smell, frequently caused vomiting on the way to the LZ. It was unpleasant, and the Marines were anxious to get off. Twelve Sea Knights in HMM-265 were stationed on the *USS Tripoli.* If all the birds were flying, which would be extremely unlikely, the Marines could hit an LZ with three platoons on every lift. The other Marines would be forced to wait back on the *USS Tripoli* for the choppers to shuttle them into the landing zone. That day's combat assault likely took four lifts to get the two companies of Marines into their assigned LZ.

Finally, it was Vessell's turn. He took a deep breath and climbed aboard the Sea Knight. The helicopter slowly lifted off the ship's deck and gradually turned toward the shore. The nose dipped, the rotor's speed increased, and the aircraft roared off to find the landing zone and Wayne Vessell to find his destiny.

Vessell had been on and off an LPH—or Landing Platform Helicopter, a type of US Navy ship—for the past three weeks. On June 16, Wayne and Company G of the 2nd Battalion of the 7th Marines boarded the *USS Valley Forge* (LPH-8) in Danang Harbor and traveled for two days to Subic Bay in the Philippine Islands. The operation they planned to conduct on their return, Operation Eager Yankee, involved an amphibious landing like the one on D-Day, the specialty of the USMC. The 7th Marines had not undertaken an amphibious landing recently, so they felt some practice was in order.

Practice landings were designed to imitate the actual operation as closely as possible. One company landed on a beach, and two companies were ferried to landing zones inland by chopper. The command chronology (HQ Battalion Landing Team 2/7, July 1-31, 1968) characterized the training as "invaluable," and the commander said that "overall, the landing exercise was characterized by a high degree of enthusiasm and cooperation by all to make the training as beneficial and realistic as possible."

On July 5, the Marines transferred to the USS *Tripoli* (LPH-10) and returned to Vietnam. They arrived on July 8 and wasted no time beginning Operation Eager Yankee. Fortunately for the operation planners, the area they targeted wasn't far from Danang. The target was the Phu Thu and Phu Vang districts in the Thua Thien Province. These districts were on a peninsula parallel to the coastline, not far from the city of Phu Bai, and look very similar to the Outer Banks in North Carolina.

The mission objective, according to the command chronology of the 2nd Battalion of the 7th Marines, "was to conduct an amphibious assault in the area of operations (A-O) to find, fix, destroy enemy forces, and capture and destroy enemy material and fortifications, and to conduct such other operations as assigned."

Company G (Golf), which included Wayne Vessell, was assigned to be transported by helicopter that morning. Company E (Echo) had been selected to make the amphibious landing, which they had done before daylight. It had proceeded without a hitch. Now, Companies G and H (Hotel) were flying into the area, heading toward two landing zones that had been preselected and code-named LZ Pine and LZ Cedar. Although Reconnaissance units had gotten into the area earlier that morning and given the all-clear signal, the Marines on those helicopters were tense. It was impossible to fly into any LZ in Vietnam and not be apprehensive. Golf and Hotel quickly dropped into their assigned landing zones. The Sea Knight squadron flared, landed, and dropped the back ramp. The door gunners sprayed the tree line with bullets. The Marines came out of the helicopters, peeled to both sides of the bird, and went prone. As soon as the last Marine bailed out, the helicopters pulled away. A few seconds earlier, the landing zone was a cacophony of noise, but now it was almost silent. The Marines were fortunate this time; they had landed without incident.

The plan was the classic Hammer and Anvil tactic. Golf and Hotel Companies, inserted via helicopter, would sweep down the peninsula and drive any enemy forces in front of them into the blocking force. The blocking force was Echo Company, which landed amphibiously at the other end of the peninsula. If all went as planned, there would be no escape for the communist forces.

Now that Wayne Vessell and the rest of Golf Company were on the ground, the extreme heat returned. Even the command chronology commented on it. "Intense heat and humidity," it stated, "slowed the speed of the movement of troops."

Regardless of the heat, the Marines had little contact with the enemy forces in the area. July 9 and 10 saw no significant engagements. They did deal with booby traps and harassment fire, mostly at night when the companies set up camp. Local civilians were surprisingly willing to provide information on the local Viet Cong. There were even a few "Chieu hoi" enemy soldiers.

The term "Chieu hoi" is translated "open arms." As part of the propaganda war, Americans dropped leaflets offering good treatment of any communist soldier who turned himself in to Allied forces. VC or NVA soldiers would sometimes surrender to American forces waving these leaflets. The term eventually became a verb.

Between July 9 and July 11, the Marines captured fourteen Viet Cong and had two Viet Cong "Chieu hoi." On July 11, Vessell's company was led to a Viet Cong hospital by a Chieu hoi, set up in an old schoolhouse. The Marines were astounded. The hospital was 150 feet long and 30 feet wide. It was large enough for 100 beds, and the Marines recovered two sandbags full of medical supplies.

On Saturday, July 13, a Huey on a resupply mission to the recently inserted Company F (Foxtrot) was shot down. F Company immediately set up a perimeter around the chopper to provide security. Unfortunately, Foxtrot took rocket fire early that afternoon, setting the helicopter ablaze. After getting the fire under control, a Navy heavy-lift helicopter picked up the Huey and removed it from the area. That left the members of Fox Company in a precarious situation.

Sunday, July 14, dawned hot and humid—again. Helicopters were on the move to extract F Company. Alas, one of the Hueys tasked with picking up the company had a fuel line burst, and it set down in the landing zone. A platoon from Golf Company, including Wayne Vessell, was sent to reinforce Foxtrot and provide security along with the members of Foxtrot still on the ground. The mechanics worked feverishly to repair the damaged helicopter.

Everything was quiet, or as quiet as it could get. There was still the whine of insects that the Marines had become accustomed to hearing. The mechanics talked softly then swore loudly. The security team constantly scanned the terrain around them, cursing the heat to themselves and hoping they could get out of there soon.

Then a Marine screamed the word they all dreaded. "Incoming!"

They scrambled to "get small" and find some cover. Then the stillness was swept away by a roar of modern weapons. Mortars and RPG rockets struck the ground, causing dirt and rock to fly around the landing zone. Rifle fire exploded around the Marines, who quickly returned fire as they had been trained to do.

Almost as soon as it started, it was over. Silence returned to the landing zone. The Marines cautiously looked around. Then they scrambled for their buddies. The cry of "medic" soon filled the air. A few hours later, the Marines were lifted out after the helicopter had been repaired. On one of the helicopters was a body.

The Vessell family was originally from the area of southeastern Coweta County and northern Meriwether County, with the town of Haralson the focal point, but the family moved to Gilmer, Texas, in 1929. Clinton Vessell was a child when his family traveled to Texas. He grew up and married a young lady named Elizabeth there, and they had three children before their fourth and last child, Wayne, was born on May 6, 1944. Wayne's three older siblings were William, Margaret, and Laverne. Unfortunately for the entire family, Wayne's mother, Elizabeth, died of pneumonia in November 1945 at Fort Smith, Arkansas, where she was buried. Although the oldest son, William, was eleven, Wayne was only eighteen months old when his mother died.

In 1950, Clinton Vessell moved his family back to Georgia, and they settled in Haralson, the area of Coweta and Meriwether Counties where his family had originated twenty-one years earlier. He farmed and continued to raise his family on his own.

Gwen Horne was born in Haralson and moved to Senoia when she was five. She remembers the local police knocking on her door in 1944 to tell her family that her uncle had died on a European battlefield. The same year the Vessells moved back to Georgia, Gwen suffered her own trauma—her mother died in their home.

Gwen's mother had a severe problem with high blood pressure, and doctors weren't optimistic about her long-term survival. One afternoon, she lay down to nap, had a cerebral hemorrhage, and never woke up. Gwen found her when she returned home from school. Gwen said, "It was pretty rough."

Gwen's father remarried in 1952. Her new stepmother attended Pleasant Hill Baptist Church south of Senoia, and Gwen and her father attended church with her. One evening, William Vessell, Wayne's older brother, showed up at the church.

"I just thought he was the most handsome thing I had ever seen," Gwen said with a laugh. She was twelve years old.

In time, William became a driver for the church, picking up people who didn't have transportation so they could attend, so Gwen continued to see him. She thought he was tired of trying to help his father farm, and William decided he needed a drastic change in his life.

In 1954, he joined the United States Marine Corps. The next year, he married sixteen-year-old Gwen Horne.

In 1957, William and Gwen were sent to Albany, Georgia, to work at the Marine Corps Logistics Base.[1] They were accompanied by William's father, sister Laverne, and twelve-year-old Wayne. Then in 1958, Clinton, Laverne, and Wayne all moved to Oklahoma, where Clinton's sister lived. Wayne's sister, Margaret, who had two little girls, also lived in the area. William was sent to California to a three-month school, so Gwen went to Oklahoma to be with the family. While there, Laverne married, and she stayed in Oklahoma on the family's return to Georgia. Wayne was the only child left at home.

Around 1960, Clinton and Wayne moved back to Haralson. Gwen left Oklahoma and rejoined William. Wayne attended East Coweta for a short time but never completed school.

In 1963, Wayne Vessell, eighteen, followed his siblings in matrimony by marrying a fifteen-year-old girl from LaGrange named Lina Blakely. The couple lived with Wayne's father in Haralson, and they had two daughters, Elizabeth (Beth), born in 1963, and Pam, born in 1965. Wayne worked at a textile mill in LaGrange. Regrettably, the couple separated and eventually divorced. Lina kept custody and raised the two girls. She eventually remarried and continued to live in LaGrange. The divorce was tough. Wayne didn't have any money, so child support for his two girls was virtually nonexistent.

After his divorce in 1965, Wayne and his father went south to live with William and Gwen, now stationed in Jacksonville, Florida. Wayne landed a job with North American Van Lines. William and Gwen had two little girls who adored their uncle Wayne. Every time they saw a Van Lines truck, they would sing out, "There goes Wayne!"

That November, Wayne, Gwen, and the girls took William to California. He had orders for Vietnam. The troop buildup in Vietnam was shifting into high gear. They enjoyed Thanksgiving Day with William then began the drive back across the country the following day. Wayne and Gwen shared the driving and the job of keeping the children entertained. When they finally got to Jacksonville, Clinton had returned to Georgia, but Wayne stayed for a time to help his sister-in-law.

Wayne drove a Volkswagen Beetle. Gwen's girls frequently rode in the VW, which they loved. If he went someplace, he took his nieces with him. He picked them up at day care when Gwen was working. He stayed with his sister-in-law until the early summer of 1966 then returned to Haralson.

Two noteworthy things happened in Wayne's life that summer and fall of 1966. First, he met a young lady named Elaine Hunnicutt. Elaine had been born in Haralson in 1950 and had a twin brother. Her parents, Luke and Lena Hunnicutt, had five boys and five girls. Elaine's father had passed away, and the family lived in Senoia. Wayne's father dated Elaine's mother, and it is assumed that was how they met. Also that fall, Wayne decided to join the Marine Corps. Gwen thinks he "got tired of here and there. He just decided to do something with himself."

When he enlisted in the Marine Corps, he listed Senoia as his home.

Like all East Coast Marines, Vessell headed to Parris Island for one of the most intense experiences of his life, Basic Combat Training. It was October 1967, and the Vietnam War was constantly in the news. His brother, William, was already in Vietnam, and William's service evidently influenced Wayne to join the Marine

Corps. Wayne got through the grueling Basic Training and in December was assigned to Camp Lejeune for Advanced Infantry Training. He graduated from AIT in mid-February 1968. The Tet Offensive was still raging at the time of his graduation. William had returned home and managed to see his brother in January 1968 to encourage him. Wayne Vessell was headed to Vietnam.

In February, Elaine Hunnicutt told Wayne that she was pregnant.

During the first week of March, Wayne was sent to Marine Corp base El Toro and left for Vietnam on March 8, 1968. He arrived in Okinawa on March 10, and three days later, he was flown from Okinawa to Danang, South Vietnam. Once in the combat zone, he was assigned as a replacement to G Company 2nd Battalion, 7th Marines, 1st Marine Division. The 7th Marines were assigned to I Corps, the northernmost part of South Vietnam. During the Tet Offensive, the 7th Marines had fought bravely in and around Danang, causing considerable casualties to the Viet Cong and the North Vietnamese Army. However, the Marines had also suffered and were desperate to rebuild their troop numbers to full strength.

In March and April of 1968, Wayne would have been fully engaged with learning how things were done in Vietnam to stay alive. While the Tet Offensive had wound down, the war had not ended. His unit continued to engage in various patrols and ambushes typical of this conflict. He corresponded with his family via the US Postal Service, as did almost every American serviceman. In May, Vessell would likely have participated in Operation Allen Brook to clear Go Noi Island of communist forces. Intelligence had determined that the island was one of the places where the communists had felt secure enough to build up their forces and supplies for the recent Tet Offensive. The American military believed they needed to take that security away.

In June came Operation Eager Yankee. The commanding officer summarized this operation as one of poor intelligence and insignificant enemy contact, and he noted that medical evacuation was sometimes unsatisfactory. The operation, while largely unsuccessful, still cost the Marines fifteen killed in action and fifty-eight wounded in action. One of those fifteen killed was Wayne Vessell, who was shot and killed three months and one day after arriving in Vietnam.

The family got the news within the next couple of days.

"We lived in Sneads Ferry, North Carolina [near Camp Lejeune] at that time, so we packed up the next day and came to Georgia," Gwen said. "We met the plane when his body came in [to Atlanta]. His ribbons had gotten shifted, I guess, in transit. So my husband got upset about that, and they opened the casket up, you know, the glass part, and he fixed everything."

The funeral was held at Hillcrest Chapel, and Gwen was horrified when "the makeup started wearing off, and you could see pieces of metal coming out of his head." If accurate, this would indicate that Vessell had also taken shrapnel from a rocket or mortar that day.

When the twenty-one-gun salute began, Vessell's daughter, Elizabeth, exclaimed loudly, "They just shot my daddy!" At that moment, everyone in the room was in tears.

"He was a sweet guy," Gwen said. "He was like my little brother. He was a good kid."

Three months later, in October 1968, a baby boy would be born to Elaine Hunnicutt. She named him Wayne Jackson Vessell.

** See end notes in the appendix for additional details.*

***Born**: May 6, 1944*
***Home of record**: Senoia, Georgia*
***Died**: July 14, 1968, in Thua Thien province of South Vietnam*
***Coweta servicemen who died in the same province**: Charles Walthall, Robert Webb, Eddy Couch, John Dozier, and Johnny Calhoun*
***Unit on death**: G CO, 2nd BN, 7th Marines, 1st Marine Division*
***Decorations:** Purple Heart, National Defense Service Medal, Vietnam Service Medal with 1 Bronze Service Star, Republic of Vietnam Campaign Medal*
***Buried:** Pleasant Hill Baptist Church, Senoia*
***Vietnam Memorial, Washington, DC:** Panel 52W Line 32*

Sources

Interview with Gwen Vessell, sister-in-law
Assistance from John Boren, USMC
Assistance from Al Mark, military historian
Assistance from Jeff Sexton, USMC HMM-261 and HMM 265 CH-46 crew member

References

Coffelt Database, "Wayne Vessell." Accessed February 4, 2022. http://coffeltdatabase.org/index.php
Texas Tech University Records of War. "US Marines in Vietnam." Accessed February 23, 2022. http://www.recordsofwar.com/vietnam/usmc/USMC_Rvn.htm

Wayne Vessell, date unknown. Elaine Hunnicutt and Wayne Vessell, 1967.

Photos courtesy of Kim Welborn.

CHAPTER FOURTEEN

Bobby Freeman

Grantville, Georgia

Bobby was the most adventurous of all of us when it comes to taking chances and doing things where there is a possibility that you could be either hurt or killed or caught.
—Barham Lundy

The 9th Infantry Division was first created and activated during the Great War of 1914-1918. Since the United States entered the war late (1917) and the war ended so quickly after it got involved (1918), the division was never deployed to Europe and thus never saw combat. Despite their sputtering start, they saw action during World War II, when the 9th Infantry went ashore in North Africa and Sicily and engaged the German Wehrmacht. On June 6, 1944, the 9th landed at Utah Beach as part of Operation Overlord, also known as D-Day. Over the next eleven months, the "Old Reliables," as they were called, fought their way into the heart of Nazi Germany, serving heroically and capably until the end of the European war. After serving in the German occupation force and the beginning of the Cold War, the 9th Infantry Division was deactivated in 1962.

But the 9th Infantry wasn't destined to be relegated to a World War II history book; instead, it would be reactivated and rebuilt and transferred to Vietnam in late 1966 and early 1967. The 9th was assigned to a unique area, the Mekong Delta in the southernmost part of South Vietnam. The division's second brigade became the "Riverine force" and learned to work with Navy units in and out of the rivers and canals stretching across much of southern Vietnam's IV Corps region. The Mobile Riverine Force consisted of a wide variety of vessels adapted by the Navy to help control traffic on the canals and rivers of the Mekong Delta. The soldiers often slept aboard Navy vessels, and depending on the mission, the Navy would transport or support the soldiers. Army troops could also be transported and supported by Army helicopters or even armored personnel carriers. *(*See Jessie Cofield, Chapter 5.)

The two military branches worked well together in IV Corps; they had little choice.

October 1967 found Bobby Freeman of Grantville, Georgia, living and fighting in the Mekong Delta of South Vietnam. This trip to the Delta was the first time Freeman had been out of the state of Georgia.

Bobby Freeman was born on November 20, 1945. World War II had concluded a few months earlier, and the United States was beginning one of its greatest economic and baby booms. Bobby, born in Grantville, was the second child of Frank and Virginia Freeman. His brother Frank was born in 1944, his younger brother, Hayward, in 1949, and the youngest child and only girl, Brenda Nell, in 1952.

Frank Freeman was a World War II veteran. He had driven trucks for the Army and served in the Pacific. Frank Freeman was in school for cooks and bakers at Fort Benning when the war ended. Upon his discharge and return to Grantville, he worked at the Grantville Mill, eventually moving on to the William L. Bonnell Company in Newnan, where he later retired. Virginia, Bobby's mother, worked as a housekeeper in various homes and occasionally took in washing and ironing.

"She was a wonderful cook," said her daughter, Brenda Nell.

The family purchased a house on Edmund Lee Circle from the owners of the Grantville Mill.

Bobby looked just like his father and acted exactly like him as well, according to Barham Lundy, a childhood friend. Bobby had a powerful personality and always behaved like the oldest sibling.

"If Mom and Dad wanted something done, he would always run out and do it first," said his sister, Brenda Nell. "He would give you the shirt off his back. He was my favorite brother. I could talk to him about anything."

Bobby attended Grantville Brown School through the eighth grade. While in second grade, he met classmates who would become his closest companions for the next ten years. Bobby was the oldest of the group; others were Barham Lundy, Robert Jackson, Francis Young, Jim Strozier, and Jerry Heard. This group of boys stayed together throughout the 1950s and 1960s, graduating from high school in 1964.

"In this little town, if you saw one of us, you saw all of us," Lundy said. He called the group "the posse." Though mischievous, the "posse" avoided trouble because of their parents' rules and guidance. Virtually all of them went on to live productive lives. Bobby, Jim, and Francis lived on one side of Grantville, while Lundy lived on the other. He rode his bike over or walked to where his buddies lived.

"Those guys were like my brothers," Lundy said. As youngsters, they shot marbles, played baseball, rode bikes, roller-skated, and later, chased girls. They had fun together and never argued or got into fights. There was no leader in the group, and everyone was equal except in school, where Jerry excelled. Lundy said the "posse" would get a honey bun almost daily at a Grantville store. "Those were the good times."

Bobby loved playing ball and building go-carts out of wood and old bike parts. As he grew older, he enjoyed fishing and racing cars.

The "posse" also rode the school bus together. Some guys sat in front with the girls, while others shot spitballs and rubber bands in the back. "It was just good-natured fun," Lundy said. "Bobby would rag you, make jokes on you, but never make you want to fight. He was just funny."

As Bobby and his friends entered Central High School in Newnan, the fun seemed to be… a little more fun.

"They used to have a little 'meetup' at our house to sit and talk about girls and going to little parties," Brenda Nell said. The boys were in the same grade but never in the same classes since teachers made sure to keep them apart. Bobby never played any school sports. He never seemed interested, though he was pretty good at playground basketball.

"Bobby was never scared of nothing," Lundy said. "He'd try anything." He said Bobby was always the first to go, whether sledding on cardboard when it snowed or swinging on kudzu vines.

Occasionally, he got hurt. One time, a cherry bomb went off in his hand, and he got tar on his arm while working on a roof.

Regardless, Bobby didn't complain; he just moved on with life.

In the fall, Bobby and Barham hung around after school, talking to girls until their friends Francis Young and Jim Strozier finished football practice. Then the four hitchhiked back to Grantville, as none of them had a car.

Bobby grew considerably while in high school. By the time he graduated from Central High School in 1964, he was approximately six three. He was a good-looking kid with a great smile. His grin showed a small gap between his front teeth, making him even more charming. Despite his height, he was often described as keeping a low profile. He wasn't loud or boisterous. He dressed well, as did many young men of the day. He kept his shoes shined so much that he could see himself in the reflection.

While at Central High School, Bobby met and dated Brenda Lundy, Barham's cousin. They continued to date after graduation and married in 1968.

Three days after graduation, Barham Lundy and Jerry Heard were in the US Army. Bobby wasn't drafted until late 1966. He was excited about his upcoming military service, but his family wasn't as enthusiastic.

"We didn't want to talk about it much," Brenda Nell said.

Freeman went to Basic Training in February 1967 down the road at Fort Benning. This was the first time any Freeman children had been away from home. From Fort Benning, he went north for Advanced Infantry Training to Fort Gordon, near Augusta, Georgia. This military base was typically the training home for the Signal Corps and the Military Police, not the infantry. However, Fort Gordon had been ordered to begin a combination course of Advanced Infantry Training (AIT) plus Airborne Training. The Airborne Infantry Training course graduates would head directly to jump school at Fort Benning or go north to Fort Bragg and Special Forces Training.

The recently opened part of the post that conducted this nine-week training course had been dubbed Camp Crocket. The soldiers lived in Quonset huts erected on the site by the Army. There was a mockup of a Vietnamese village for training purposes. The food and water were appalling and the heat oppressive. The camp, placed as far away from the main post as possible, was in an area of heavily forested land.

"The idea was to keep the grunts out of sight and isolated from the main post population," George Hoffman wrote on vietvet.org. "We grunts only saw Fort Gordon once coming in and once going out, and the same was true of Augusta. The training was nonstop and very physical. Constant cycling of troops through the camp graduated one company (approximately 176 men) each week. After eight weeks of advanced airborne infantry training, the entire company was bused to Fort Benning, Georgia for jump school."

Any soldier who opted out of jump school and wasn't already headed to Special Forces or Long-Range Reconnaissance Team Training was slated for Vietnam. Bobby Freeman didn't opt for any of this specialized training, and shortly after the end of AIT, he was on his way to Vietnam. His MOS was an indirect fire crewman, a mortarman. (Camp Crockett was closed by 1970, and all airborne training reverted to Fort Benning.)

Bobby's family hoped he would stay in the states for a while after completing his training, but instead, he was sent to Vietnam after a month's leave. "We were shocked" at how quickly he left for Vietnam, Brenda Nell said.

Freeman arrived in Vietnam the first week of October 1967 and was assigned to C Company, 4th Battalion, 47th Infantry Regiment of the 9th Infantry Division. He was in IV Corps, the area dominated by the Mekong Delta, the central geographic feature of this region. The Mekong River is one of the longest rivers in the world, moving through China, Myanmar, Thailand, Laos, Cambodia, and into the southern part of Vietnam. Canals were dug, primarily during the French occupation of Vietnam, to connect many of the Mekong tributaries in the Delta. As a result, this is one of Vietnam's most extensive rice-growing regions.

While the information on Bobby Freeman's combat time in Vietnam is scarce, we can reference some of the activities he was involved in based on the nature of his assignment in the Mekong Delta with the 9th Infantry Division. For example, a September 1, 1968, newsletter sent home from River Assault Flotilla One—the flotilla to which Bobby's unit was attached—described a joint Navy-Army mission in the Mekong Delta. Freeman would have been involved in these types of operations during the ten months he spent in-country. Captain R. S. Salzer, Commander, River Assault Flotilla One, wrote in the newsletter:

> *We select the area for each of our many operations on the basis of the latest intelligence information regarding current locations of enemy forces, in coordination with appropriate Army commands and Vietnamese authorities.*
>
> *Our planners then go to work to draw up the details of the operation. Some of the things that they must consider are the number of friendly troops and assault craft required to do the job, how many boats of each type will be required, what waterways can and cannot be used due to depth, width, or other factors such as vegetation growing in the water, and what the tidal situation is in the target area. The tides are very severe in this part of the world and have a great bearing on our operations. Frequently, we must plan our transits so that we cross shallow areas at high tide or pass beneath low bridges at low tide. Once, down south of Can Tho, we even jacked up a bridge a few feet so that the boats could pass beneath. It is imperative that all such matters be carefully planned in advance, but we must be careful to ensure that the planners do not compromise the security of an operation by too much coordination or identifiable reconnaissance.*
>
> *Many of our operations feature dawn or predawn landings. Thus, the troops often board the boats for the transit to the operational area between midnight and four o'clock in the morning. Regardless of the early hour, we always have a hot breakfast ready for both the boat crewman and the infantrymen before they go.*
>
> *Three assault boats at a time come alongside the pontoons beside each barracks ship to embark the Army troops. Although we operate at darkened ship conditions in the Delta, we do use a few red lights of low candlepower, covered on the sides and focused downward on the pontoons, to provide the small amount of visibility required for the infantrymen to assemble their packs and safely climb aboard the ATCs (Armored Troop Carriers).*
>
> *Once the ATCs are loaded, the boats form into a column*

and begin the trip to the op area. Leading the formation are two or four ASPB (Assault Support Patrol Boat) minesweepers followed by a Monitor and then a group of ATCs. [Monitors were the largest boats with the largest weapons of all Riverine craft. They were named after the USS Monitor *of Civil War fame.] Other Monitors and flame-throwing ATCs are interspersed among the ATCs to protect the troop-laden convoy. The Squadron Commander controls the actions of his boat from aboard a CCD (Command and Communications Boat) which is usually near the middle of the column. The Army artillery barges, escorted by other Navy assault craft, will have left earlier so that they will be in place and ready to fire prior to the time the troop convoy begins moving into the dangerously narrow waterways near the operational area.*

Enroute to the landing site, many of the soldiers will be catching a few final hours of sleep. The first part of the journey will be along one of the larger rivers, where the boat crewmen will be able to relax somewhat, although all gun mounts will be manned and ready for action should the column be attacked.

As the boats near their objective area and turn in to one of the hundreds of small streams, everyone becomes more alert. Most areas of the Delta are heavily populated, and therefore, we do not open fire unless first fired upon. In some unpopulated VC-dominated regions where we have every reason to expect enemy ambushes, we may "recon by fire" while going through such areas. By firing at suspicious spots and bunkers with cannons and grenades, we can sometimes surprise the enemy into opening fire prematurely. At the least, it tends to spoil his aim.

Finally, we reach the area where the landing is to be made. We may have "softened" the beach for the ground assault with jet air strikes, helicopter gunship ordnance, artillery fire, or fire from the boats. We always stand ready to provide supporting fire to the troops prior to, during, and after the landing. The Monitors, CCDs, and ASPBs, continue to cruise in mid-stream with every weapon at the ready as

> *the ATCs are beached to debark the troops. After the Army has gone ashore, the boats will frequently take up blocking stations to prevent the escape of the Viet Cong by sampan.*
>
> *The troops will normally stay ashore for two to three days, although we may move them by boat to many different locations during that period of time. By the end of three days, every sailor and soldier is ready to return to the ships for a warm shower, hot meal, and clean bed.*

"When he went, we waited and waited for letters, and we didn't get very many," said Brenda Nell.

Bobby was busy. He wrote Brenda Lundy first, then his mother and father, followed by his siblings. Brenda Nell said she and her parents constantly went back and forth to the post office and repeatedly asked Brenda Lundy, "Have you heard from him?" If Brenda Nell discovered a letter when she went to the post office, she ran home whooping, and the family gathered to read it.

Bobby enjoyed flying on the Huey helicopters, Brenda Nell said. There were probably many reasons for Bobby's attraction to them. First, he had probably seen a helicopter only a few times before getting into the military and certainly had never ridden in one. Second, riding in a Huey was one of the few ways a soldier could get some relief from the unrelenting heat and humidity in Vietnam. Third, Bobby had a knack for mechanics and working with his hands; this intricate machine must have been an endless source of fascination. Ironically, it was a Huey helicopter that would kill Bobby Freeman.

When Bobby got his opportunity to go on R&R sometime in the spring of 1968, he met Brenda Lundy in Hawaii, where they married and honeymooned.

In July 1968, Bobby's unit conducted operations with the South Vietnamese Army (ARVN). The 9th Infantry Division inserted "almost 3,000 Allied soldiers into an area where no Allied and few Vietnamese soldiers had ever dared venture before; the wide stretch of marshland zigzagging southwest of Can Tho to the notorious, legendary U Minh Forest, for centuries a haven for pirates, smugglers, bandits, and recently the Viet Cong" (MRF Association, "U Minh Forest").

On August 3, Bobby Freeman's 4th Battalion conducted multiple airmobile insertions, leading to some successes. From August 4 to August 6, the 4th Battalion served as a reaction force, which stands by in case the units in combat need reinforcement quickly and managed to get some rest. On August 7 and 8, the 4th Battalion rejoined the fight and penetrated the notorious U Minh Forest of Kien Hoa Province. (The U Minh Forest was thirty square miles of communist territory. In 1968, it was known to be a VC base camp. Today, it's a national park.) The operation's goal was to establish a land base in this province.

"Airmobile insertions, beach assaults, and air cavalry recon were conducted for five days," according to the 9th Division's August operational report. The enemy losses involved sixty-four Viet Cong killed, 130 bunkers destroyed, and a large amount of equipment seized. August saw twenty-three American soldiers killed in action, including Bobby Freeman from Grantville. The report said:

> *On August 12th, 1968, a U.S. Army Helicopter UH-1D (#66-00820) from the 191st Assault Helicopter Company, call sign "White 5," was returning to Bearcat Base in a flight of five aircraft following the completion of a combat operation for the 9th Infantry Division when it suffered a tail rotor failure and crashed one nautical mile northwest of Rach Kien. The flight was at 1500 feet in a diamond formation with White 5 in the slot. Approximately 10 minutes out of Dong Tam, White 5 transmitted, "White 5 going down, tail rotor failure." The aircraft was observed to descend in a relatively level attitude, with the main rotor turning very slowly. The number two aircraft in the formation, flown by aircraft commander CW2 Wiegman, broke from the formation and followed the aircraft down. The aircraft struck the ground in a slightly nose-low attitude in a rice paddy with apparently very little forward motion. The aircraft commander and the pilot were pinned in the wreckage by the instrument panel. A fire ignited in the passenger compartment. An attempt was made to extract the*

> *personnel from the burning wreckage, and one passenger was removed but had apparently died on impact. A total of four crew members and six passengers perished in the crash. The four lost crew members were pilot CPT Arnold W. Luke, co-pilot WO1 Terry R. Jens Jr., crew chief SP5 Gerald A. Wilson, and gunner SP4 Arturo D. Montion. The lost passengers were SGT Thaddeus Durrett, SP4 Bobby Freeman, SFC Merlin H. Bergan, SSGT Lonnie J. Tullier, SGT Thomas E. Mortice III, and a Vietnamese national.*

According to the Annual Supplement History of the 191st Assault Helicopter Company, "The present mission assigned to the 191st Assault Helicopter Company, although unstated in a mission statement, is the direct support of the operations of the 9th Infantry Division. Approximately 98% of the operations at the present time are combat assault operations in support of 9th Division units." The 191st was considered a top-notch unit, but something went wrong on August 12. Bobby Freeman's death was considered "non-hostile"—in other words, an accident. If a helicopter loses its tail rotor, the aircraft can go into an uncontrollable spin. The pilot needs to get the aircraft on the ground as quickly as possible, which usually entails an autorotation, which involves using the wind to power the main rotor instead of the engine. The pilot would have looked for an open area to land the aircraft in a nose-up configuration. The pilot did land in a rice paddy, an open space. However, rice paddies are separated by berms of earth, making landing much more complex and possibly explaining hitting the ground in a nose-down configuration. What is difficult to understand is why the main rotor was turning so slowly that the other choppers on the flight noted it in their reports on the accident.

Brenda Nell Freeman was at her sister-in-law's home when the soldiers pulled up in a government automobile. When they got out, the women began screaming with the anguish that came with realization. They knew what that car and those soldiers meant to their families. Then in a perfect example of a fight-or-flight response, Bobby's wife burst out of the back door and ran away. Brenda Nell and the soldiers caught her. The women held each other and sobbed. They couldn't believe it. Bobby was missing.

Brenda Nell worried about her parents. Did they already know? Suddenly, she felt that she had to get home right away. But when she arrived home, she found the same heartache she had just left. "That is a day that I will never forget in my whole life," she said. She kept asking, "Why? Why at twenty-two years old did he have to die? It just tore my heart out."

On September 8, 1968, the military returned to change Bobby's Missing in Action status to Killed in Action.

Bobby Freeman's body returned home sealed. There would be no viewing of the body, unquestionably due to the fire resulting from the crash. As a result, the Freeman family "never had the chance to see him at all. It was very hard," said Brenda Nell. "All we got was his dog tags."

When it was time for the funeral at John Wesley United Methodist Church in Grantville, "It was hard to get dressed because we still didn't want to believe it," Brenda Nell remembered. She didn't want to go to the funeral, "but we had to in honor of him. We knew that was something he wanted to do. He wanted to serve his country, so we had to respect his wishes."

Her grandmother kept saying, "He is not in there. He just got angry and decided not to come back to Georgia."

Brenda said, "When she died, she believed he was still in Vietnam, that he had married, had a new family, and didn't want to return to Georgia. For years, I waited to see if he would come back like my grandma said."

Bobby's death took a toll on the entire family, especially his mother. Shortly after Bobby's death, she experienced what was later described as a nervous breakdown.

Brenda Nell was in high school when her brother died. She had been excited about learning to play the clarinet and being in the band, and Bobby had been so proud of her. After her brother's death, she looked at her clarinet and decided she could never play it again.

"The news of Bobby Freeman's death came to all of us at the same time," said Barham Lundy. Only three of the "posse" were left at Bobby's funeral. Robert Jackson had died of an accident while the group was in high school. Jerry Heard had died shortly before Bobby in a car accident in Atlanta. Bobby's death left just Lundy, Francis Young, and Jim Strozier. It "pushed us closer together," Lundy said.

Young went on to college and worked for the State of Georgia for many years. Strozier served in the Army, worked at the Atlanta Police Department, and became an investigator for the Atlanta District Attorney's office. Lundy served in the Army, went into business, and served on the Grantville City Council.

"I believe if he hadn't gotten killed, Bobby would have stayed in the military for twenty years," Lundy said. "He had that mind. I promise you that he would have retired from the military. With his mindset and his personality, Bobby probably would have retired as an E-8 or E-9 because Bobby was a leader. He wasn't a follower. He liked to get out front. An officer? No telling how high he could have gone. He was a go-getter."

"You won't find a nicer person than Bobby," Lundy said. "He was good as gold." Barham Lundy has not eaten a honey bun since Bobby's death.

Bobby's sister Brenda Nell has never forgotten her brother and attempts to ensure that others don't either. "Bobby was always a hero," she said. "He taught us how to love, continue being a family, never give up, and be strong. He was an inspiration." Eventually, she picked up her clarinet again and played the instrument to honor her brother.

Brenda Nell Freeman was apprehensive but excited when the Wall That Heals came to Newnan in October 2011. Until that time, she said, she had "closed off so much of it because it was so painful," but by the time the Wall arrived in Newnan, she couldn't wait to touch it.

After the Wall That Heals left Newnan, Brenda Nell said she was grateful to all of those "who made it possible for me to be able to face forty-three years ago. The things that I could not face, I locked in a closet that had been locked for years. I was able to accept my brother's death and feel a sense of peace now. I have so much respect for the veterans now, and I can feel so much love for them."

***Born**: November 20, 1945*

***Home of record**: Grantville, Georgia*
***Died**: August 12, 1968, in Long An province of South Vietnam*
***Coweta servicemen who died in the same province**: None*
***Unit on Death**: C CO, 4th Battalion, 47th Infantry, 9th Infantry Division*
***Decorations:** Bronze Star with Oak Leaf Cluster, Purple Heart, Air Medal, Good Conduct Medal, National Defense Service Medal, Vietnam Service Medal, Vietnam Campaign Medal*
***Buried:** Grantville City Cemetery, Grantville*
***Vietnam Memorial, Washington, DC:** Panel 49W Line 53*

Sources
Interview with Brenda Freeman, sister
Interview with Barham Lundy, childhood friend
Assistance from William Killian, researcher

References
Coffelt Database, "Bobby Freeman." Accessed June 17, 2019. http://coffeltdatabase.org/index.php
Find a Grave. "Bobby Freeman." Accessed April 23, 2020. https://www.findagrave.com/memorial/65522310/bobby-freeman
The Vietnam Center & Sam Johnson Vietnam Archive. "Newsletter from R.S. Salzer, Commander River Assault Flotilla One. Accessed April 19, 2022. https://vva.vietnam.ttu.edu/repositories/2/digital_objects/71311
The Vietnam Center & Sam Johnson Vietnam Archive. "Army 1968 191st Assault Hel Co Jul-Dec." Accessed April 20, 2022. https://vva.vietnam.ttu.edu/repositories/2/digital_objects/329988
The Vietnam Center & Sam Johnson Vietnam Archive. "Report, U.S. Army- 9th Infantry Division Operational Report, Lesson Learned, 1 August 1968 through 31 October 1968." Accessed April 20, 2022. https://vva.vietnam.ttu.edu/repositories/2/digital_objects/536063
The Mobile Riverine Force. "U-Minh Forest." Accessed April 20, 2022. https://www.mrfa.org/us-army/9th-infantry-division-index/u-minh-forest/

CHAPTER FIFTEEN

Timothy Cole Jr.

Newnan, Georgia

But when you lose someone killed in action...There are no words for it. Your world is forever changed.
—Carolese Cole Gullatt

Timothy Cole Jr.'s entire world was his family, their dairy cattle, and the Madras community.

By 1962, Tim Sr. and Louise Cole owned 1,800 acres in the rural Madras area of Coweta County. Their dairy farm had fifty-sixty milk cows, numerous sheep, and additional cows for beef. The Coles went "high-tech" for the time and installed the first automated dairy in Coweta County. The Coles took the quality of their dairy products very seriously; everything was scrubbed down after every milking. They didn't allow anyone who didn't need to be there in the barn with the cows, and they attempted to limit loud noises. "Do not disturb the cows" was their mantra. Tim Sr. called the cows his "ladies," and they were "ladies in waiting" when they were ready to be milked.

"We had excellent milk," said Carolese Cole.

"Skip could do anything," recalled Phillip Smith, who was about the same age as Tim Jr., commonly known as Skip. Phillip's father started a dairy farm about the same time as the Coles, and the two families grew extremely close.

"When Skip was ten years old, he could get on a tractor, whatever kind of tractor it was, hook it to a plow, fertilizer, spreader, hay bailer, he could go do it all. When he was ten years old, he could do it!" Smith said.

Carolese confirmed that Skip could drive a tractor and farm equipment from the time he was small. Tim Sr. once needed to bail some hay for someone south of Newnan. Skip, who had to stand when he drove to reach the pedals, piloted the tractor into Newnan via Jackson Street, headed through downtown, and went on to Moreland.

Sheriff Lamar Potts was sitting with a group of older gentlemen playing checkers outside the courthouse when he looked over and saw the youngster on the tractor. He jumped to his feet, looked at the guys, and asked, "Who is that kid on the tractor?"

One of the guys glanced up, looked down at the checkerboard, and made his move. He finally replied, "That's just Tim Cole's son."

Sheriff Potts studied the tractor as it went out of sight, nodded imperceptibly, looked at his friends, said "Oh," and sat back down.

On Tuesday, November 13, 1962, Skip Cole was a sixteen-year-old junior at Newnan High School. His mother was pregnant with the family's third child. Skip was awake early and doing his chores around the farm before he returned to the house to prepare for school. As he started to leave the house, he hugged his father. They likely started wrestling, which frequently happened as Skip left for school. His father was fifty-one and seemed full of life.

Usually, when Skip arrived home from school, his father was at the barn, preparing for the four o'clock milking. But his father wasn't there that Tuesday when Skip arrived at the barn. None of the tasks to prepare for the afternoon milking had been completed. That was unusual since Tim Cole Sr. was a hardworking, conscientious man who cared deeply for his cows. Finally, a farmhand walked into the barn, and Skip asked about his father. The farmhand told him that Tim Cole Sr. had been taken away in an ambulance.

After Skip discovered what had happened, he turned and headed to the barn. The cows had to be milked. He got to work.

McKoon's Funeral Home had sent a hearse that contained a stretcher and an oxygen tank that would get Tim Cole Sr. to the hospital and hopefully keep him alive. But Skip's father had a massive heart attack and died that afternoon.

After she learned of her husband's death, Louise called Joan Cox, Skip's half sister, and her husband, Joel, and told them about Tim Sr. She asked Joel to speak with Skip about his father. When Joel and Joan arrived, Skip was already in the barn, milking the cows. Joel quickly determined that Skip was unaware of his father's status and explained what had happened. Skip nodded and, without speaking, kept milking cows. As Joel stood there wondering what to do, he thought he heard some sniffling from the area where Skip was working.

Timothy "Skip" Cole Jr. was born on December 19, 1946, outside Luthersville, Georgia. Skip's father, Tim Sr., and his mother, Louise, had married in 1943. Tim Sr. had enlisted in the US Navy in 1945, although he was in his thirties at the time. In 1945, Tim Sr. was sent to the Pacific Theater, where he served on board the Destroyer Escort *USS Jesse Rutherford*. He returned home in 1946, and his son was born soon afterward. When Skip was born, Tim Sr. managed a farm between Moreland and Luthersville that was owned by three brothers: Young, Rhodes, and Lester Trammell. (Young Trammell was the grandfather of Winston, Rhodes, and Robert Skinner, all of whom would become prominent members of the Newnan/Coweta community.)

Skip was the oldest child of the family, which would include two younger sisters, Carolese and Angela. Carolese was the first female child, born in 1954, causing one of Tim's young friends to ask, "Miss Louise, is he really a girl?"

Tim Sr. was well versed in using heavy construction equipment, which was what he was hired to do for Coweta County. He was so good with the equipment that he trained people on its use. The Coles moved from the Moreland-Luthersville area to Roscoe Road to join other family members who lived there.[1]

While Tim Sr. enjoyed the job with heavy equipment, he also had a passion for farming and working with dairy cows. He found a farm for sale in the Madras community, purchased it, and turned it into a dairy. The Cole family became an integral part of the Madras community and members of Macedonia Baptist Church. Tim Sr. became a community leader within a large local dairy co-op and taught farming at West Georgia College.

"They were well known and very loved" in the community, according to their niece, Annie Joe Horn.

Tim Sr. enjoyed picking up extended family members after Sunday church for a picnic and swimming at his family's farm. Skip worshipped his father and couldn't help inheriting his passion for his family and community.

Skip was still young when the family settled in Madras. During her early teenage years, Annie Joe was his occasional babysitter. She took care of him when needed while the Coles lived in Luthersville and even after they moved to Madras. Annie Joe said Louise was a nurturing caregiver and called her aunt "Ise" (pronounced "Eeze"), which was short for "Louise."

Another cousin, Robert Cole, remembered playing with his brother Billy and Skip when they were young. Robert said they were just "country boys" and fondly recalled the weekend family get-togethers where they climbed young pine trees. The boys would shimmy up the tree and see how far the tree would bend with their weight before it broke. They caught snakes, and they fished and hunted behind Dunaway Gardens. They climbed trees and swung on vines. They built fires in the winter, busted the ice covering a pond, and jumped into the icy water. They warmed themselves by the fire when they got out. One time, they challenged five friends to this contest. Three jumped into the pond, and two refused. The two who refused to jump were the ones who got sick!

Scotty Scott was another friend of Skip Cole, and his family also had a farm in the Madras area. He said the families had an unofficial reciprocal arrangement and came to each other's aid when needed. Scotty recalled helping get the cows up, baling hay, and performing seasonal farm chores. The Coles had tractors that Scotty's family didn't own, so Scotty learned how to drive these machines from Skip. The two got along well, and Scotty remembers having spend-the-night parties at Skip's home when they were kids.

Pat Gillespie, another friend, lived on Buddy West Road, still out in the country but not far from Skip's home on Happy Valley Circle or Macedonia Baptist Church, where their families attended church. Skip was one year younger than Pat, but they both participated in the youth group at Macedonia Baptist on Sunday evenings. Pat's family attended church on Sunday morning, and the Coles graciously picked her up for evening church, as they did for several youngsters over the years, whether for evening church, Vacation Bible School, or various youth functions. For a few years as children, Pat and Skip called each other boyfriend and girlfriend. They even sat together during services. Of course, they were never old enough to date. Tim Sr. and Louise taught Sunday school at the church, and Pat said they had fun-filled Sunday school parties at the

Cole farm. The yard was large and had a stream nearby. Tim Sr. built bonfires, and the kids roasted hot dogs on a stick. It was idyllic.

There were several little boys in the Madras area, and all of them seemed to attend Macedonia Baptist. Skip's primary circle of friends came from there—brothers Riley and Brandt Shelnutt, Willis Potts, Tommy Hyde, and Phillip Smith. These kids remained involved in the church through their teenage years.

"Tim had a lovely tenor voice and sang regularly in our church choir," said Carolese. Several years later, he sang with the Glee Club and the Baptist Student Union Men's Choir while attending Georgia Tech.

Skip's family became close to the Smith family, who lived "next door," but "next door" was two miles away. With both families in the dairy business, Lamar and Sophia Smith had a great deal in common with Tim and Louise Cole.

Skip met Phillip Smith in second grade at Madras Elementary School, and the two became instant pals. The two families shared countless meals in addition to Thanksgiving and Christmas. Phillip recalled Skip being a good student and enjoying the backyard sports the boys used to play in the neighborhood or at church. As a teenager, Skip played touch football on Sunday afternoon and had his friend Willis Potts's tooth mark on his head to prove it. Skip and Phillip enjoyed fishing and hunting, and Phillip said Skip was an excellent shot. Despite all these activities, Skip was interested primarily in motors and farm work.

Thanksgiving was an important holiday for the Smiths and the Coles. The meal was usually served at the Smith home, and they prepared the turkey for dinner. Louise Cole made dressing, biscuits, and pie to complement the turkey. One Thanksgiving Day at the Smith home, the weather was frigid. Skip and Phillip had gone outside and down to the creek. Skip decided to see if he could swing across the stream on a vine. Unfortunately, the vine broke, and Skip splashed into the ice-cold water. Naturally, he had to head home and change.

On Christmas Day, the Smiths visited the Cole home while Louise took care of the meat, and Sophia added vegetables and dessert. Louise even hosted a dinner when Phillip announced his engagement to Susan Powers. Louise prepared steak, mashed potatoes and gravy, and various other sides. The Coles enjoyed entertaining; it would have been rare not to have someone, whether family or friends, at Sunday dinner.

When it was time to go to school, most Madras kids already knew each other. All the children from this part of Coweta County attended Madras Elementary School for first through eighth grades.

When Skip and Phillip were in elementary school, they were with a group who walked from school to the Cole home. They played ball and had games for the students and teachers upon arrival. Then they walked back to Madras Elementary at the end of an exhausting but enjoyable day. Smith estimated it to be two or three miles each way.[2]

The boys also participated in the "field night" held for all county schools at Pickett Field in Newnan. Competitions included the one-hundred-yard dash, the sack race, and the three-legged race. Skip ran in the potato race. In this race, teams of four students ran, one at a time, to a designated spot, picked up a can containing a rock, and ran back. The following student ran to a can a little farther away than the last and ran back until all four students had made the run.[3]

As their eighth-grade year wound down, students at Madras Elementary knew that change was around the corner. They would be moving on to Newnan High, a school of more than eight hundred students. These new high school students were picked up by the elementary school bus and taken to Madras Elementary. Then they boarded another bus for the trip to Newnan High School on LaGrange Street. Skip was remembered as always being polite on the bus and using the time to prepare for his classes.

When they first arrived at Newnan High, the Madras students found it overwhelming. The massive main building and the vast gym were intimidating, especially compared to the small Madras school. The Madras students were separated and in class with many students they didn't know, who lived in different parts of the county and shared different experiences than these country kids.

As he got older, Skip had his own bedroom and bathroom. Carolese remembered him listening to the radio as he got ready for school. They could always tune in to an AM station with all the pop hits. The country was only three to four years away from the Beatles and the British invasion.

Randy Sewell was a high school friend of Skip. He said the

school "was strict, but I don't remember it as an unpleasant or unhappy place, not for me. It was really a secure, kind of comfortable place."

"No surprises," said Jere Hall, another high school friend. "If you stepped out of line, Mr. Evans would put you back in line." O. P. Evans was the principal of Newnan High School.

Skip and many other students from Madras couldn't participate in many extracurricular activities at Newnan High since the distance between the school and the Madras community was too great. Skip did join the Future Farmers of America (FFA), a popular club for students from farming families. Robert Cole, also a member, recalled attending competitions with other school FFA chapters and competing in events like log cutting. Skip was also a member of the Beta Club, another service club. He didn't attempt to play sports at school; he had too many responsibilities at the farm. Skip eventually lost his Beta Club membership because he couldn't participate in any activities due to his responsibilities on the farm.

Skip had an active social life during high school, especially after he became old enough to drive. He dated many young ladies in the local area.

"He loved girls, and they loved him," Carolese said with a smile. "But he treated the girls with respect." He never got serious with any young women in his teens; he was just looking to have fun.

One female student who attended Newnan High School with Skip, Patsy Cochran, said "he was dreamy." Everyone seemed to like Skip Cole. He was quiet, but he got along well with everyone and always seemed to be smiling.

"He always liked to help people," said Robert Cole.

"Skip was a typical boy, but he was smart," said friend Bobby Jacobs.

Joel and Joan Cox were at the Cole residence when Tim Sr. and Skip went to the barn to deliver a calf. They decided to tag along. Skip was helping his father with the delivery, but the calf was stillborn.

"I remember Skippy working so hard to make sure the cow didn't see the calf and how compassionate he was," said Joan.

At seventeen, Skip got his own automobile, a black 1957 Chevrolet with a black roll-and-tuck interior. Skip and his friends nicknamed it Black Beauty.

"It was beautiful," said Bobby Jacobs.

Skip and his cousins Robert and Billy rebuilt the engine. Billy owned a 1956 Ford, and he and Skip often met up on Highway 29 and raced to town.

"That '57, you couldn't hold a candle to it," Robert said. "That was one of the fastest cars I have ever seen."

Skip got a kit to convert the shift from the steering column to the floor and installed it himself.

"He could really drive that car," Phillip Smith said. Once, Skip and Phillip drove to Atlanta to see a NASCAR race. On the way there, "he passed every car we came across." Phillip told Skip, "The race is going to have to be pretty good to beat this."

Skip Cole was more responsible than most boys his age, but he was still a male. And a teenager. One evening, Skip, John Davis, and John Modrak had Modrak's mother's car out for a spin and decided to see which one could take the curve on Macedonia Road the fastest. The curve was in front of a church with a brick wall along the roadway. Skip was the first to attempt to set the record. Unfortunately, he skidded into the brick wall and damaged the car so severely that it could only be driven in reverse. The boys backed down the road until they got to Roscoe Road, where they ran the car into a ditch. They told everyone that they had been run off the road. (None of the sources mentioned how John Modrak's mother took the news.)

Skip was in his junior year at Newnan High School that November when his father died. People from Macedonia Baptist jumped in to help the family, but Skip was now responsible for the farm and the family. His sister Carolese, seven years younger, was in third grade, and his mother, Louise, was pregnant. Dropping out of school was not an option for Skip, so he went to school and spoke with the principal, Mr. O. P. Evans. They worked out a "work-based learning" scenario. Skip would rise about 4 a.m., do his farm chores, and arrive at school by 11 a.m. Then he would start his classes.

"He was smart and had good grades," remembered Pat Gillespie. "He was a responsible kid. He would help other kids with their math, including me."

Skip took arduous academic classes while running the dairy farm and successfully navigated his last two years at Newnan High School.

"He really became a man and the leader of the family at that time," said Joan Cox.

Skip's sister Angela was born in February 1963. Carolese remembered the time that Skip was carrying Angela and a woman approached him. She thought he was the father. The woman needed help, so after handing Angela to another family member, he walked with the woman and helped her with her problem. He didn't explain his circumstances, probably not wanting to embarrass her.

As Skip prepared to graduate from Newnan High in 1964, a tremendous change had already begun. President Kennedy had been assassinated, and the Beatles had arrived in America. Newnan High School, however, remained unchanged; it remained no-nonsense and conservative. It was much smaller than it is today, and it was segregated. During the Cuban Missile Crisis of October 1962, students practiced getting under their desks in case of nuclear war. Although the Vietnam War had not started in earnest, the draft still pulled young men into the military. At Newnan High, though, students couldn't go out of the front door until dismissal. On the last school day of 1964, the seniors challenged Mr. Evans's authority by going to school with their shirttails untucked. As a result, they were all sent home.

As graduation neared, Skip and his mother had a momentous decision to make. Deciding to auction the dairy cows and equipment couldn't have been easy for Skip or his mother; he loved the animals, and farming was a connection to his father. However, Skip was going to college. Three boys from Macedonia Baptist Church would graduate from Newnan High School and attend Georgia Tech that fall: Skip Cole, Willis Potts, and Riley Shelnutt.

Jim Lawson and John Cureton rode around with Skip one night around graduation. Once again, three teenage boys were in a car.

"Show me what this thing will do," said Jim.

Skip hit the gas so forcefully that when he shifted from first gear to second gear, the knobs on the radio came off.

The 1964-1965 academic year saw Skip living in Atlanta and attending Georgia Tech as a textile engineering major. Skip had gotten into a co-op program that involved him working at Georgia

Power so that the company paid his tuition. His cousin and babysitter, Annie Joe, was married and living in Atlanta. Skip visited with her and her baby daughter every Wednesday afternoon. Annie Joe took pleasure in making foods that Skip enjoyed eating. One of his favorite treats was cinnamon rolls, which she made on many occasions specifically for him.

While at Georgia Tech, Skip met and befriended many people through the Baptist Student Union, where he was an active member. One of those people was Gil Gibson, originally from Pennsylvania. Gil had joined the Navy and, in the fall of 1964, had started working with a Naval Reserve Seabee unit on the Georgia Tech campus, where he was a construction electrician. In 1966, Skip helped Gil rewire the house that the Baptist Student Union was moving into that summer. Gil noted that Skip could do almost anything and was willing to help with nearly everything.

"He was Mr. Cool," said Gibson. "I never saw him get excited, never saw him get upset. He was always laid-back."

Gil Gibson described Skip as having a "sly, dry wit" and being a great singer. Once a month, Skip visited the Georgia Baptist Hospital School of Nursing. Some BSU guys and student nurses would walk outside the rooms and sing to patients. "He was everywhere, doing everything," Gibson said. "He always had a side to him that he would do whatever he needed to do, whatever it took, regardless of what it was, school, his mother, or the farm."

In 1967, during Gil's junior year, money was short, and he was tired of school. He went to the Navy Reserve center and asked about getting a couple of years of active duty. Unsurprisingly, they agreed. Three weeks later, Gil Gibson was on his way to a Seabee Battalion in Vietnam. Three months later, the battalion was home. (Even during the Vietnam War, Seabee units deployed as battalions.) The battalion integrated their replacements, retrained, and returned in January 1968. The next time Gil Gibson would see Skip Cole would be in Vietnam.

During the summer of 1966, Skip and fourteen members from Baptist Student Unions across the University System of Georgia signed up for a summer-long mission trip to the Native-American reservation in Cherokee, North Carolina. Students from Georgia Tech, West Georgia College, Tift College, Georgia Southern

University, Mercer, the University of Georgia, and Valdosta State College came together to build a Baptist church for area locals who had lost their church in a fire. After the mishap, the members of Bethabara Baptist had moved to an old church building that the local Methodist church had generously allowed them to use. They acquired property and took out a $10,000 loan to build a new church. That money enabled them to purchase the materials but wasn't enough to hire the people to erect the structure. The church leadership contacted the Southern Baptist Convention, and soon the Baptist Student Unions were recruiting students across Georgia, culminating in the team that descended on Cherokee that summer.

When the team arrived in Cherokee, they lodged in a local elementary school in Big Cove, a community about ten miles from where they would work. The school had a gymnasium and was equipped with a kitchen. Beds were brought into the classrooms, and the students were put up dormitory-style. Since Big Cove was on the Cherokee reservation, the students interacted with the local tribe.

"We really enjoyed getting to know the people," said Bobby Childree, one of the team members.

The church provided a carpenter and brick mason for the work, and the students did all the manual labor.

"We were pretty much on a deadline to get that church built. It turned out to be a big project," said Childree. "With sixteen of us, it was a doable project, and we had a very good leader, Walter Porter. He knew what he was doing. The Porters did a really good job of balancing work with fun."

When they arrived at the construction site, they found a flat property where little had been done. That changed quickly. The road grader sitting there was put to work. The church foundation had already been poured, though the team later poured an additional foundation for the building dubbed "the annex," which would contain Sunday school rooms and church offices.

Skip oversaw the electrical work, using skills that he had learned growing up on the farm.

"He was so knowledgeable about electricity," said Lambert.

"The young men looked up to him for his skills and basic construction knowledge," said Cheryl Smith, one of the females on that mission team.

At the end of the day, the team enjoyed stopping at one of the many creeks in the area, cooling off and cutting up.

The girls took turns preparing lunch to carry to the work site, and dinner was often prepared in the evenings at the school. They ate a lot of hamburgers, lasagna, salads, scrambled eggs, and bacon. They drank gallons of iced tea and lemonade.

These fourteen students and their adult sponsors, Mr. and Mrs. Walter Porter, hit it off and became terrific friends. In some cases, they became more than just friends.

A female student from Valdosta State caught Skip's eye as they worked together that summer. Peggy Calhoun from Quitman, Georgia, was a soft-spoken Southern girl who played the organ at her home church and was an outstanding pianist. She played the piano for the church services at Bethabara on Sundays and when the mission group gathered to sing after the evening meal. To many, it appeared that the two fell in love almost "at first sight."

"You could see the attraction between them," said Walter Lambert.

Peggy was a junior at Valdosta State and active in the Baptist Student Union, where the Porters were directors. She was majoring in Sociology and minoring in Music. Peggy had been involved in church music since she was twelve, and everyone in Cherokee recognized her ability.

"I don't know when Tim noticed me, but I know when I noticed him. That was the first week out," she said. "He was a natural leader, and he was one of those people that are gifted with the ability to make things happen, to be able to figure things out."

The two grew closer as the summer progressed. "Tim was fun. Oh Lord, he was fun," Peggy said. "We laughed a lot. A lot. He was the kind of person you felt like you could trust. And you could."

The Cherokee mission trip was a cultural awakening for Peggy and many on the team. The Porters pushed them to look outside themselves and see the world around them. They learned to eat bean bread, and they learned about other ways to worship. They discovered that people lived differently than they did.

"We did a lot of growing and stretching in that time that we had not anticipated and that we didn't truly appreciate until years later," Peggy said.

By August, the project was completed.

"We moved into it and started using it the week before they left," Lambert said. While there was great joy in the new building, there was also a tinge of regret that their new friends were leaving. "They had just become a part of us," he said. "I worked with Tim a lot. He was just a friend I took up with. He was one of the nicest people I ever met or worked with. When I heard that he got killed, it was heartbreaking. There is something in the Bible about people that do something, and it continues," said Lambert. "Every time I come into this sanctuary and turn the lights on, he comes to mind. I think of Tim."

Bethabara Baptist Church is still in existence and has a plaque in the church lobby listing all the students who gave up the summer of 1966 to help those in need. While the building has expanded over the years, the original building still stands and looks great today.

Skip Cole was at a critical point in his life during the summer of 1966. During his freshman and sophomore years at Georgia Tech, he had come home most weekends. His friend and fellow Georgia Tech student Jere Hall frequently caught a ride back to Newnan with him. Hall described Skip as struggling with his academic workload and concerned over his grades. Gil Gibson had noted the same thing. Skip knew he would lose his draft exemption if he left school. It was possible that since he was the sole surviving son, he might be deferred from being drafted. However, his cousins Robert and Billy had already been conscripted, and Skip didn't think it was fitting that he could avoid military service but they couldn't.

Skip wanted to serve and help other people. He had known that was his destiny since he was young. Skip had spoken with a pastor at the Baptist Student Union about military service and his desire to serve others. The pastor had suggested he serve on an Army Air Ambulance unit.

That fall, Skip returned to Georgia Tech as a junior. He spoke with the Army recruiter about becoming a Dust-Off pilot. While Skip and Peggy were still dating, they corresponded by mail, as long-distance phone calls were prohibitively expensive. She wasn't involved in his decision to enter the military.

On January 4, 1967, after completing the fall semester, Timothy "Skip" Cole was sworn in at the Military Entrance Processing

Station on Ponce de Leon Boulevard in Atlanta. Many of his friends in Newnan were stunned; it seemed so sudden. But Skip's life had gradually been heading in that direction. He sold his much-loved Black Beauty and bought a car for Peggy. He was on his way to Basic Combat Training at Fort Polk, Louisiana.

Many of the young men whose stories are recorded in this book went to Advanced Infantry Training at Fort Polk, Louisiana. Their next stop would be Vietnam. Skip Cole went to Basic Combat Training at Fort Polk because he was on track to becoming a helicopter pilot, and all helicopter pilot (Warrant Officer) candidates did Basic Training at Fort Polk. His next stop would be Fort Wolters, Texas. Even in Basic Combat Training, Skip Cole helped others; he helped recruits with lower education levels read and write letters to and from their family.

In March, he traveled to Fort Wolters in Mineral Wells, Texas, for Flight School (Basic and Primary Flight Training). Skip had befriended Al Michaels, another soldier at Fort Polk who was on track to become a helicopter pilot. They reunited at Fort Wolters and were together for about a month before being divided alphabetically into flights. Their friendship would affect Al Michaels's life in profound ways.

Skip and Peggy Calhoun had not given up on their relationship, even with Skip's entrance into the military. Skip managed to get leave, and on Sunday, October 1, 1967, Timothy "Skip" Cole and Peggy Calhoun were united in marriage at Pauline Baptist Church, Peggy's home church in South Georgia. Peggy's sister Gail, Carolese Cole, and two girls from the North Carolina mission team served as bridesmaids. Hill Hammock of College Park, a friend of Skip from Georgia Tech, served as best man. Skip's four-year-old sister, Angela, was the flower girl. When it came time to walk down the aisle, Angela froze. Skip went down the aisle and encouraged her to join him at the front of the church, which she finally agreed to do. Louise Cole wore pink with a pillbox hat.

"Very Jackie Kennedy," said Carolese.

Skip could have worn his military uniform but chose to wear a tuxedo instead. Unfortunately, Skip's military training kept them from a honeymoon, as the couple went straight to Fort Rucker, Alabama.

Skip would have learned the basics of flying at Fort Wolters with various training helicopters. After completing training there, he was sent to Fort Rucker in August to learn to fly US Army helicopters.

There were several Army helicopters that servicemen might learn to fly, but the most common and most recognizable was the Utility Helicopter-1 (UH-1), commonly called the Huey. The Huey helicopter became iconic during the Vietnam War, not only to the soldiers in Vietnam but also to the public in the United States and worldwide on nightly television broadcasts. To the soldier in Vietnam, it was the machine that took you into the intensity of combat, but it was also the machine that brought you supplies and got you out of the muck, whether you were finished with the mission, you were wounded, or even if you were dead. At Fort Rucker, soldiers learned to fly this symbol of America.

From August until December 1967, Skip learned to fly using only instruments, formation flying, emergency procedures, and the combat tactics he would later use in Vietnam. There was no question that the warrant officer candidates would soon be in-country. Skip Cole graduated near the top of his class. Louise, Carolese, Angela, and Peggy attended his graduation from flight school, with Peggy pinning his rank and Skip receiving his wings.

After Skip and Al Michaels completed flight training in December, they headed to Fort Sam Houston for six weeks of medical training. Upon completion, Skip and Al enjoyed a month's leave; in late February 1968, they were on the way to the air ambulance service in Vietnam. In the book *Dead Men Flying*, MOH recipient Patrick Brady said:

> *At the center of the humanitarian efforts were the air ambulance operations—the most dangerous aviation operations. About one-third of all air ambulance crew members became casualties, and the loss of air ambulances was 3.3 times that of all other types of helicopter missions. The air ambulance crew members, who made up a small percentage of the helicopter crewmen who served in Viet Nam, suffered a disproportionately high percentage of the deaths.*

Skip Cole would have likely agreed with that statement, but as he once said, "I'm not asking for a place of safety. I am asking for a place of service."

As Skip left for Vietnam, Peggy returned to school in Valdosta. She remembers a classmate whose husband had been shot down but wasn't listed as missing in action. "That kind of reality was all around," she said.

Upon arrival in Southeast Asia, Skip and Al were assigned to the 45th Medical Company. Skip was sent to the 1st Platoon stationed in Long Binh; Al was assigned to the 4th Platoon stationed at Lai Khe. Once they arrived, they had a couple of days to settle in with their units and get over the jet lag. Then they were assigned as co-pilots and flew "ash and trash" missions for the next week. "Ash and Trash" were non-combative flights. The initiation period ended shortly afterward, and two weeks after being introduced to their unit, they were flying as co-pilots on combat missions.

Once these pilots began flying combat missions, the intensity increased exponentially. The operations office posted a duty roster that attempted to fairly assign pilots to the vital work they were there to perform. Those in the crew listed as "first-up" didn't change clothes for twenty-four hours because they needed to get into the air as soon as possible once the call came in. The pilots accepted every mission they possibly could. The mission went to the "second-up" crew only if they got overloaded. Once pilots caught up, they resumed taking every mission. If a crew was "third-up," they might be called on to run missions if things got super intense, or they might be asked to perform routine tasks like patient transfers.

Crews never turned down a mission. That was the job; they knew the "grunts" were counting on them. Crews never talked about missions or tried to outdo each other. It wasn't a game but a life-or-death task. When the call came in, the aircraft commander (AC) sprinted to the operations room to get the necessary information. The rest of the crew got the helicopter started and ready to go. Once the AC got to the aircraft, they took off. Everything else could be figured out during the flight. Their goal was to leave the base in five minutes or less. They might not be able to accomplish the mission due to weather, but they always tried. Dust-Off was one of the few Huey units that flew at night.

Sometimes there were a lot of missions, and sometimes there weren't. While waiting for a call, pilots might do other things like playing sports, dealing cards, writing letters home, or working on their suntans.

There were no days off since every crew was always in standby mode. If a pilot had flown over one hundred hours in a month, which was against regulations, they might be given a couple of days completely work-free, but that didn't happen often.

The Dust-Off units were spread out geographically so effectively that they could get anywhere in Vietnam within thirty minutes. While these choppers were unarmed and clearly marked with a red cross, they were targeted by the communist forces as if they were the most dangerous weapon controlled by the United States.

Willie Boyd had been in-country and stationed at Long Binh since November 1967 when he climbed into a Dust-Off chopper next to Skip Cole in March of 1968. Willie was the aircraft commander on this flight.

"We didn't talk that much because initially, in Vietnam, unless you went on a mission and then had time to sit down and wait to fly another mission, then you might strike up some conversation about where you were from and what have you. That day, we focused on flying the mission," he said. Willie described Skip on that flight as "not an aggressive guy to come out and strike up a conversation. But still, I could tell he was very attentive to what was going on" and "he showed no signs of being afraid."

After three months, Skip Cole became an aircraft commander, call sign *Dust-Off 19*. Typically, it took approximately five months to earn that status.

"He was young to be an aircraft commander," said Carolese. "But he had a knack, a gift for flying."

"That is one of those prime positions. Any aviator wants to be in that position," said Boyd.

The aircraft commander was responsible for everything. He planned how the mission would be flown after they took off. He was responsible for finding the patient, dodging other aircraft and friendly artillery, and making an approach that might give the helicopter the least exposure to enemy fire. According to the Standard Operating Procedures for the 45th Med Detachment, "The aircraft commander is in command of the aircraft, crew, and passengers. He is responsible for all that happens and does not happen aboard the aircraft. He is responsible for the successful completion of all missions.

It was a lot of authority for a twenty-one-year-old. Skip Cole managed it with skill and aplomb.

The following are excerpts from missions for which the US Army recognized Skip's courage and flying ability.

Tim Cole's original Distinguished Flying Cross citation.
May 5, 1968.

During a nighttime field standby, an urgent request was received to evacuate numerous casualties that resulted from a Viet Cong assault on the village of My Tho. Upon arrival at the battle site, Tim Cole saw that the Viet Cong had the village surrounded. Ignoring heavy hostile fire, he expertly maneuvered his helicopter without landing lights to the first two pick-up points and successfully evacuated the wounded to medical facilities. Upon returning, he was informed that the final evacuation landing point was a small area surrounded by tall obstacles. He maneuvered through a difficult 100-foot descent into the evacuation point and loaded the final casualties.

Distinguished Flying Cross citation, First Oak Leaf Cluster.
May 8, 1968.

While answering an urgent request to rescue several Vietnamese soldiers near Can Giouc, making a low-level, high-speed approach to the pick-up site, his helicopter came under intense fire from the enemy positions less than 100 meters away. Despite the murderous fusillade, he held his position until all the casualties were safely aboard. After transporting them to a nearby medical facility, he returned and expertly accomplished another extraction while armor-piercing bullets slashed his helicopter. He then returned to the same area and made two more extractions in a flooded rice paddy in full view of the enemy forces.

Distinguished Flying Cross citation, Second Oak Leaf Cluster. May 9, 1968.

Within minutes after he received an urgent request to evacuate a Vietnamese soldier, Mister Cole was circling about the battle site. The ground commander informed him that sporadic fire was being received from nearby Viet Cong positions. Unhesitatingly, he flew the unarmed aircraft into the pick-up site. Suddenly the enemy unleashed a tremendous volume of fire at the ship, and the ground commander radioed instructions for the helicopter to pull out. Disregarding the warning and his safety, Mister Cole chose to complete the approach. Despite the deadly accurate fire which ripped through the cockpit, he maintained his position while the crew loaded the injured man aboard. He departed only when he was certain that the patient and both crew members had reboarded the helicopter.

Distinguished Flying Cross citation, Third Oak Leaf Cluster. July 30, 1968.

Mister Cole received an emergency request to evacuate a number of wounded Vietnamese and American soldiers from a battlefield in the Mekong Delta. Swiftly directing his aircraft to the pick-up area, he established radio contact with the ground force and learned that it was under intense Viet Cong small arms and automatic weapons fire. After requesting a smoke marker to pinpoint the location of the landing zone, he noticed not one but two areas being marked and was informed that one marker was released by the enemy forces in an attempt to draw his ship into an ambush. Realizing that the Viet Cong positions were extremely close to the landing site, Warrant Officer Cole directed his craft onto a low-level, high-speed tactical approach only to be met with a withering fusillade which struck his helicopter time and time again. Seeing that the ground unit was pinned down and unable to load the casualties, he broke off his approach and rose to orbit while the wounded were removed to a new location. Although critically low on fuel, Warrant Officer Cole again directed his aircraft to the pick-up site. When all of the wounded were aboard, the unarmed ship rose to safety and sped to medical facilities.

Distinguished Flying Cross citation, Fourth Oak Leaf Cluster. June 18, 1968.

Informed that a troop lift helicopter had crashed in the rugged, mountainous terrain, Mister Cole quickly prepared the ship for flight and within minutes was over the crash site. Disregarding the existence of known hostile units in the area, as well as the danger from the burning and exploding ammunition and fuel of the downed ship, he smoothly and expertly guided his craft down over the site. Despite the constantly shifting weight in the cargo compartment and gusty winds from nearby mountain ridgelines, he maintained a precision hover above the crashed helicopter as a medical aidman (the medic) was lowered to help the survivors. After two injured crewmen and the aidman were hoisted up to the ship, he sped to the nearest medical facilities.

Despite his hectic schedule, Skip corresponded regularly with his family in Newnan. Before he departed for Vietnam, he purchased reel-to-reel tape recorders from the Army Post Exchange (PX). Skip recorded messages for his mother and sisters while in Vietnam, and the family would gather around and listen to them upon their arrival in Georgia. He sent separate tapes and letters to his wife. The family then recorded a message and sent the tape back to Vietnam. He frequently wrote letters to family members and friends as well. Skip had been in Vietnam for about two months when he wrote to Annie Joe on April 21, 1968.

Thank you for the lovely Easter card and letter. It was so good to hear from you. I'm sorry Geran [Annie Joe's daughter] *was sick, and I do hope she's over it by now.*

Since I got your letter, I've been a little bit busier (thank goodness). I've flown quite a bit—just a day or 2 off for rest. I really do like it that way—makes the time pass much faster. "Charlie" has been quite active this past week as a result we've had a lot of business. We have 5 crews on "ready" here at Long Binh. 1st and 2nd up crews fly emergency field pick-ups, 3rd up flys routine transfers from hospital to hospital, 4th up is V.I.P., and 5th up is used to replace a ship if one gets shot down. After a crew flys 8-9 hrs in a day they quit—it's dangerous to continue really. Then the whole schedule shifts up and 3rd or 4th up may move up to 1st or 2nd. When things get active like they were this week, everybody ends up flying. We have a platoon (6 ships and crews) at Lai Khe (northwest of here almost 30 miles). They all flew 10-11 hours on Friday, so I (flying 4th up here) went up there to help them. That's the way it's been—everybody busy. It's quieted down now tho—Charlie has eased off.

I'm afraid I can't get enthused over peace talks. VC are too well dug in in this country. I feel the only way to win is the extensive, damaging bombing of all of North VN. It doesn't sound nice—but this whole mess isn't nice. I am located about 20 miles northeast of Saigon and I'm aware of all the wounded hauled out in a 75 mile radius of Saigon. The number is quite high—too many for the advances made.

I'm glad Ed is back at Devin's. I do hope he'll be happy, whatever he finds himself doing. Is your daddy still having his kidney trouble? I just wish all your folks could be well.

Tell Geran I said "hi" and give her a hug for me. I sure do miss all my folks at home. I don't think too much in terms of going home—that's too far off. Thinking about it would only make it worse.

You asked about cows in VN. Over here they have water buffalo in all the rice paddies. When we're flying, we either fly at 2,000' or higher or down on the deck. Anywhere in between makes it too easy for the VC to shoot you. When flying "low level" (down in the trees at 120-140 MPH), it's always fun to fly across a rice paddy and scatter the buffalo by flying right across their backs. The flying over here teaches you to have complete control of the ship and fly it at its maximum limits. It's experience I'll use from now on.

Write when you can. I think of you often and pray you'll all be well to enjoy the beautiful spring.

God bless you always.

Love,
Skip

Macedonia Baptist Church members were doing their best to support the service people in Vietnam, especially those from the local area. Once, Skip was named the Soldier of the Week, and everyone was asked to write a letter to the Cole boy. They listed his address in the church bulletin. Many people wrote letters, and some even wrote postcards. Many church members had known him since he was a child, so they used his childhood nickname when they wrote: Skippy. When these letters arrived in Vietnam, they caused some confusion in the detachment; everyone in the unit knew him as Tim. The fun began once the guys realized the letters were intended for him. It started one day when Skip was on the way back to base after flying a mission. Suddenly, the radio crackled as the transmitter button was held down. The pilot's ears perked up to determine what was happening and if more patients needed to be picked up. Instead, they heard the dispatcher at the base ask, "Where's Skippy? We're looking for Skippy. Does anyone know where Skippy might be?" It's unclear whether Skip responded to the call amid the laughter.

Meanwhile, Al Michaels was doing the same things as Skip, only at Lai Khe. The two would occasionally be in touch via radio or, from time to time, see each other at the 93rd Evac Hospital when they flew patient transfer missions. Finally, five months into their tour, Al was transferred to the 1st Platoon at Long Binh. Skip and his roommate, Hank Miller, built a bunk bed so Al could berth in their hooch. Skip was thrilled to be reunited with his buddy, but Al Michaels was even more excited to be back in the same unit as Skip.

"He had his Bible but didn't force religion on anyone," Al said. "He wrote his mother faithfully, occasionally doing recordings. He was just an outstanding, even exceptional young man."

Skip and Al decided to take their R&R together in October 1968. They planned the leave to coincide with Skip and Peggy's first wedding anniversary. Al Michaels was four years older than Skip. He was married, and his wife, Nancy, had given birth shortly before he left for Vietnam. The two wives arranged to meet their husbands in Hawaii, with Nancy leaving their six-month-old baby with family. Skip and Al stayed together until they reunited with their wives and went their separate ways for the week.

While Skip and Peggy had fun in Hawaii, Peggy didn't consider it a honeymoon. The fact that her husband would return to Vietnam "was always hanging over our head," she said.

Peggy also noticed a difference in Skip, who she thought seemed a little disillusioned. He enjoyed the work, "but I think he hated the fact that it was necessary." That week, Peggy perceived things in Skip that he might never have realized. "There was a sense that what Tim was seeing was something that I would never see and never be able to know, and he didn't want me to see it and be able to know it. There was a sadness about him that was really hard for me to bear. There was a sense that he had really grown up hard in the time that he had been gone and we had been separated."

At the end of the week, Skip and Al headed back to Vietnam while the wives left for home. The men had five and a half months left in their tours.

Gil Gibson knew Skip was in Vietnam; he just didn't know where he was stationed. Gil worked as a combat engineer for the 3rd Marine Division and was stationed in Chu Lai. One day, he was surprised to receive a letter from Skip, and they began to correspond. In early October, Gil received a note from Skip that said he had just met Peggy on R&R and was being transferred to Chu Lai to join the 54th Med Detachment. As it happened, Gil could see the 54th Med Detachment area from where he was located.

Skip had returned from Hawaii on October 7. On October 9, he was transferred to the 54th Med Detachment, which was short of aircraft commanders and needed assistance. Al Michaels still doesn't know why Skip was selected to go. Other pilots could have been sent, including himself. Instead, Skip got his gear together, said some hurried goodbyes to his buddies, and departed.

On October 17, Skip invited Gil to dinner at the Officers' Club at the 54th Med Detachment. Gil was headed home from Vietnam on October 18, so he was glad to meet up with his friend before leaving. Gil went to his lieutenant and asked to borrow a jeep to drive to the neighboring base. He told the officer about Skip. The lieutenant agreed he could use a jeep but noted that Gil, a petty officer second class, wasn't an officer and therefore wouldn't be allowed to eat at the Med Detachment's Officers' Club. Gil was stumped; perhaps he and Skip hadn't thought this through. As Gil pondered how to solve his dilemma, the lieutenant reached into his desk and produced the insignia indicating that the wearer was a lieutenant. He handed it to Gibson.

Skip was waiting for Gil when "Lieutenant" Gibson pulled up in front of the Officers' Club. He looked at him quizzically. "I thought you were a petty officer," Skip said.

"Well, tonight…" Gil responded before explaining his temporary promotion. Gil Gibson boarded the "freedom bird" and returned home the next day.

On October 18, Skip Cole and his crew were first-up, and the medical business was booming. Skip was on his way back from a patient transfer mission when the call came. Skip could have let the next crew take it, but he was already in the air, so he replied that he would divert. No gunships were available to help cover the pickup, but Skip went in as he had many times before. The pickup involved two dog handlers with their dogs. Skip started to lift off after securing the soldiers and their companions. Suddenly, the Huey was riddled with automatic weapons fire. It hit the ground immediately and burst into flame. The two dog handlers and their dogs were thrown out of the helicopter. The wreckage was still aflame when the dog handlers and the one surviving dog were picked up by a follow-up helicopter. The chopper also picked up one crew member, who died on the flight to the hospital.

The pilot, Gary Doolittle, Aircraft Commander Timothy "Skip" Cole, and the two crew members were dead.[4]

Timothy Cole Jr. was awarded the Silver Star, the nation's third-highest award for valor, for his actions that day. His citation reads:

Award of the Silver Star

General Orders 2 January 1970

Cole, Timothy JR Warrant Officer W1 United States Army

54th Medical Detachment, 67 Medical Group, 44th Medical Brigade

Reason: For gallantry in action while engaged in military operations involving conflict with an armed hostile force in

> *the Republic of Vietnam: Warrant Officer Cole distinguished himself on 18 October 1968 while serving as commander of a helicopter ambulance during a rescue mission west of Tam Ky in the Republic of Vietnam. Warrant Officer Cole was returning his helicopter to Chu Lai after completing a routine patient transfer to DaNang when he monitored an urgent radio message from elements of the Americal Division requesting the evacuation of two soldiers seriously wounded in fighting with enemy troops. Without the support of helicopter gunships or tactical fighter aircraft, Warrant Officer Cole diverted his aircraft to the position of the friendly unit, which only moments before had been receiving heavy enemy fire. Although subjected to sporadic small arms fire in his approach of the friendly unit's position, Warrant Officer Cole skillfully maneuvered his helicopter into the landing zone and received the wounded Americans. With the two casualties safely on board, he then lifted off and the evacuation helicopter came under heavy automatic weapons fire. The aircraft spun out of control and crashed almost immediately. Warrant Officer Cole was killed in the crash along with the three members of the crew. The two wounded soldiers, for whom he had risked and given his life, were thrown from the wreckage, and miraculously spared serious injury. Warrant Officer Cole's gallantry in action, at the cost of his life, was in keeping with the highest traditions of the military service and reflects great credit upon himself, his unit, and the United States Army.*

The day before Skip had left for Vietnam, he had pinned a set of his pilot's wings on Annie Joe's daughter's outfit. On October 18, she went to get her daughter dressed, and when she picked up the wings, they fell apart. She later realized they had disintegrated the day Skip died.

Sophia Smith had just returned home from a visit with Louise Cole when she got an urgent call saying that she needed to return to the Cole home as soon as possible (no one knows who called Sophia that day). Louise didn't understand why Sophia had returned, though she was unconcerned. Then the phone rang.

Skip was initially listed as Missing in Action, but that changed to Killed in Action within the week. Peggy, who was in Valdosta, was notified of her husband's death by the military. She left for Newnan almost immediately.

Robert Cole was in Vietnam when he received a letter from his mother about Skip's death. Robert didn't even know that Skip was in Vietnam until he got the letter from his mother. She told him that the only way they had been able to identify Skip was by his ring. His wallet was also found in the wreckage.

"He was the only person I knew personally who had been killed," said Jim Lawson. "Even though he had been one of thousands, he was important to me. I had known him, had gone to school with him, and he had gone to Vietnam, and now he was dead. So that really brought the big picture to a small picture for me."

Gil Gibson had processed out of the military in Rhode Island, visited his parents in Pennsylvania, and was back at Georgia Tech. He strolled into the Baptist Student Union, and someone there asked if he had seen Skip in Vietnam. After Gibson answered yes, the student replied, "His funeral is tomorrow."

"It still feels like a kick in the gut," Gibson said. "I would have traded places with him gladly."

Once Skip Cole's body was identified and prepared, Al Michaels was assigned to escort the body home. Al believes Peggy requested him for the escort mission.

Al flew home and met up with the body in Dover, Delaware. They flew from there to Philadelphia then to Atlanta. McKoon Funeral Home met the plane in Atlanta with a hearse and took Skip Cole home.

Al Michaels stayed at the Cole home before the funeral. The survivor assistance officer, Major Sam Hudson, stayed elsewhere, even though Louise Cole soon came to view Hudson as one of the family, but the house was packed.

Al Michaels recalled Lamar Smith coming by one evening before the funeral and taking him for a ride in his pickup truck. They stopped at a little country store, where Al expected they might get a beer. Instead, Smith bought them bottles of Coca-Cola out of the vending machine, and the two of them sat down with their feet dangling off the side porch, drank the "soda pops," and contemplated life—and death.

Wednesday, October 30, 1968, was a beautiful day. The funeral service for Skip was that afternoon at Macedonia Baptist Church, which was full of family and friends. One side of the church was filled with students from the Georgia Tech BSU, including the mission team that had grown so close in Cherokee, North Carolina. The casket was closed.

Rev. Searcy Jackson conducted the service. Al Michaels and Major Hudson practiced folding the flag beforehand then performed the action successfully during the funeral before presenting the flag to Peggy. This was the only military aspect of the funeral. Neither man remembered much more about the service. It was held in the church, then everyone moved outside to the cemetery near the sanctuary, where Timothy "Skip" Cole rests today.

Gil Gibson also made it to the funeral that day but had no recollection of it for forty-three years. Then in mid-October 2011, he drove back to Newnan to visit the Traveling Wall and honor his friend. Gil met Carolese at Macedonia Baptist Church to visit Skip's grave. As soon as he drove into the parking lot and looked at the church, the memories flooded into his consciousness. He walked into the church and found where he had sat during the service. Gil retraced his steps from the church to the cemetery and Skip's grave.

"I am very glad those memories came back," he said.

Louise, characteristically, was more concerned about others during this time. She thought Al Michaels needed to see his family while in the country. So she asked Major Hudson how long she could keep Al with her. Hudson allowed her to keep him as long as she needed him—within reason. Soon, Al Michaels was on a flight to Pittsburgh to spend a day with his family. He returned to Newnan for a day, then it was back to Dover to catch a flight and eventually rejoin his unit in Vietnam.

Louise Cole always impressed the Michaels family. "She always treated us like that. We were family from the first time we met her," said Al. In the years following Skip's death, Louise enjoyed having the Michaels family visit. She especially enjoyed rocking Al and Nancy's children when they were young.

"In some ways, Tim was outstanding. In other ways, he was just an ordinary guy, but when the opportunity came, he did extraordinary things," said Gil Gibson. "The guys that have so much to live for are the guys that seem always to get killed."

Peggy's family adored their son-in-law, and "when he was killed, you would have thought that they had lost a son," said Carolese.

Peggy agreed, saying that her father always felt guilty about his failure to talk Skip out of going into the military. However, Peggy wanted to forget her personal tragedy. She returned to Newnan for one of Skip's medal presentations, "but I just couldn't bear to do it anymore." She described it as "running away" when she started over and entered seminary. Eventually, she remarried, to a ministerial student, and she now lives in North Carolina.

After Skip's death, Major Hudson stayed in contact with Al Michaels and the Cole family. Hudson lost a son in the bombing of the Marine Corps barracks in Beirut, Lebanon, in 1983.

Al Michaels returned from Vietnam and became an instructor pilot at Fort Rucker. He stopped in Newnan frequently to visit the Cole family until Louise's death in 2010. The Cole family was so appreciative of Al and Nancy.

"The Lord gave me another big brother and a sister," Carolese said with a smile.

Following Skip's death, Louise Cole was presented with medals that he had earned in Vietnam. Often, the awards were presented at Macedonia Baptist. Louise continued to work in her church, especially with the Women's Missionary Union (WMU). She frequently traveled to other churches in the area to help them start a WMU program. Winston Skinner recalled her coming to his little church to help them with a WMU program.

"She was very sweet and gracious," he said.

Today, Madras Middle School gives a highly coveted Citizenship Award in Timothy Cole's name to a deserving eighth grader each year. In 1975, a group of alumni from the Georgia Tech Baptist Student Union (now the Baptist Campus Ministry or BCM) set up a scholarship fund in Skip's name, which became the Timothy Cole Jr. Memorial Fund. The alums who attended the meeting kicked in $3,500, which would equal almost $19,000 today. This money is used at the discretion of the director and is designed to meet the short-term needs of BCM students and operates as a no-interest loan. In its forty years of existence, no one has ever failed to repay a loan.

Angela Cole was born after her father's death, so she never knew him. She was just five when her sibling was killed in Vietnam, so she has few memories of her brother. Carolese, however, was fourteen when her brother died on a foreign battlefield. She has many memories of Skip and the trauma that her family experienced. As the Vietnam War ended in the 1970s, most Americans wanted to forget and get on with their lives. Carolese couldn't forget about the war and the brother she had lost. It wasn't until 1999 that she finally got the closure she desperately needed.

On Memorial Day 1999, the Newnan Veterans of Foreign Wars Post 2667 held a memorial service with the theme of "Honor All by Remembering One." That year, the one who represented the young men from Coweta who had been killed in all the twentieth-century wars was Timothy "Skip" Cole. Searcy Jackson had already honored Skip at Macedonia Baptist the day before. Now, he gave the invocation and shared a few comments about Skip to those gathered in Veterans Memorial Park. Major Hudson and Al Michaels returned to honor Skip.

Three hundred fifty people attended that Memorial Day service. The VFW folded a flag and presented it to Louise Cole to replace the one from Skip's coffin. That flag had been lost in a house fire.

The ceremony "was incredibly special," said Carolese. "You have confirmed my memories and given me some new ones to cherish," she said in a *Newnan-Times Herald* article. "You have allowed me to have the release I have desperately needed for the past thirty-one years."

Carolese later visited the Vietnam Memorial, the "Wall" in Washington, DC, with her mother and sister.

"The emotion is so overpowering," she said. "I would just stare at that panel and wonder, who died with you? Where are they?"

The crew who died with Skip Cole included Gary Doolittle, co-pilot; Victor Hernandez, crew chief; and Robert Dieffenbach, the medic. As Carolese pulled the story together and discovered the names of the crew, she realized that the names were right there next to Skip's on the black panel. The "Wall" lists the service people who were together when they died, so the young men and women are often beside the very people with whom they served.

"They were always there, but I never knew," Carolese said.

Carolese had first experienced death from the Vietnam War when Donald Lowery was killed in 1967; she had known the Lowery family in Madras. When they dedicated the Madras gymnasium in Donald's honor, Carolese was in eighth grade. She sang *America the Beautiful* solo; she possessed an incredible voice like her brother. She was friends with Teresa Bowen, Warner Hughie's girlfriend, and visited the funeral home when he was killed in 1970. "When you lose someone that is killed in action…" She paused. "There are no words for it. Your world is forever changed."

In 2008, Al Michaels nominated Skip Cole to the Dust-Off Hall of Fame in San Antonio, Texas. Carolese and her daughter attended Skip's induction and were moved by the outpouring of love, support, and appreciation, not only for her brother but for her as well. Carolese and her daughter also visited with Harry Miller, Skip's roommate with the 45th Med Detachment, who came from California for the ceremonies. Colonel Robert Romines, also elected to the Hall of Fame in 2008, referred to Tim Cole as "one of the best pilots I ever knew."

Carolese met a crew member on her brother's aircraft who was up next and would have taken the flight if Skip had declined the mission. His roommate had been a member of Skip's crew. The man she met had suffered from survivor's guilt ever since that day. This is where she finally saw the names of the crew members who died along with her brother.

When Willie Boyd left Vietnam, he "tried to forget the people who had been killed. I didn't want to remember," he said. He went on to spend twenty-four years in military service. In 1990, he was stationed in Washington, DC, when he and his wife, Virginia, decided to drive to her hometown in Alabama. They traveled down Interstate 85 and decided to cut over to Alabama through Newnan. Virginia was impressed by the quaint downtown and the people she met.

Four years later, Boyd retired from the military. When he asked his wife where she wanted to live, she said Newnan, Georgia. So they proceeded to buy a house that was being built on Water's Edge Lane, near the B. T. Brown reservoir, and moved there in December 1994. The neighborhood was still under construction. Virginia decided to have a party and meet the neighbors, but Willie wasn't sure how many might come. As it turned out, everyone in the neighborhood showed up at the Boyd home that evening.

Willie Boyd was on the deck meeting and greeting people when he ran into neighbor Hank Berkowitz, a fellow Vietnam veteran. Willie was wearing a combat medic T-shirt. Hank immediately struck up a conversation with him about their shared experiences, eventually mentioning his wife's cousin, who had also been a Dust-Off pilot in Vietnam. "Do you remember or did you hear the name Skip Cole while in Vietnam?" Hank asked.

"No, I don't remember a Skip Cole," Willie replied. "But I did know a Timothy Cole."

Hank's wife, Annie Joe, who had been listening, jumped out of her chair and joined the conversation. Annie Joe and Willie spent some time talking about Skip. Eventually, she proclaimed that Willie had to talk to Skip's mother. Within a few weeks, Boyd met Louise Cole and soon became a member of the extended Cole family. When the VFW honored Skip Cole on Memorial Day 1999, Boyd wasn't on the program. However, Louise insisted that Willie speak, and Willie Boyd was at the podium before the ceremony ended.

There have been five Timothy Coles in the family. Robert Cole's great-uncle was a Timothy Cole, Skip's father was a Timothy, Skip was a Timothy, Robert Cole's son was named Timothy, and his grandson was named Timothy as well. In addition, both John Davis and Willis Potts named children after Tim.

Tommy Askew, Daryl Wiggins, and Andy Evans also served in Vietnam after the Cherokee mission trip. Peggy related something that Andy Evans told her later.

"I remember thinking if Tim Cole couldn't make it through, then I might as well kiss it goodbye because I was going to be dead in the first two weeks," he said.

The mission team from 1966 still has reunions today. Askew and Evans both named children after Tim.

Peggy Calhoun Hester took her children to the Vietnam Memorial in Washington, DC, and told them the story of Timothy "Skip" Cole so he wouldn't be forgotten.

"One of the curses of dying young is that you are always remembered in your youth, with all your potential laid out in front of you," said Peggy. It is not like when you have lived awhile, and what you have done speaks for who you are. Tim never had a chance to do that."

In the *Sonnet from Senior Tigers, Newnan High School Empyrean, 1964,* the last line reads, "We hope the legacy we left is great!"[5] If Timothy "Skip" Cole serves as an example of the Newnan High School Class of 1964, then their legacy is more than great. It is meaningful. It is significant. It is extraordinary. Timothy "Skip" Cole left a legacy that can never be forgotten.[6]

**See end notes in the appendix for additional details.*

***Born**: December 19, 1946, in Newnan, Georgia*
***Died**: October 18, 1968, in Quang Tin province of South Vietnam*
Coweta servicemen who died in the same province: *Terry Allen and Warner Hughie*
***Unit on death**: 54th Med Det, 498th Med CO, 67th Med Group, 44th Med BDE*
***Decorations:** Distinguished Flying Cross with 1st Oak Leaf Cluster, Purple Heart, Air Medal, National Defense Service Medal, Vietnam Service Medal, Vietnam Campaign Medal, Dust-Off Hall of Fame, Georgia Military Hall of Fame*
***Buried:** Macedonia Baptist Church, Newnan*
***Vietnam Memorial, Washington, DC:** Panel 41W Line 72*

Sources
Interview with Bobby Jacobs, childhood friend
Interview with Scotty Scott, childhood friend
Interview with David Brown, childhood friend
Interview with Ronald Brown, childhood friend
Interview with Pat Gillespie, childhood friend
Interview with Phillip Smith, childhood friend
Interview with Jim Lawson, childhood friend
Interview with Jere Hall, childhood friend
Interview with Randy Sewell, childhood friend
Interview with Annie Jo Horn Berkowitz, cousin
Interview with Rob Cole, cousin
Interview with Al Michaels, US Army

Interview with Tony Armstrong, US Army
Interview with Gil Gibson, US Navy
Interview with Bobby Childree, member of Cherokee Mission Trip
Interview with Peggy Calhoun Hester, widow
Interview with Carolese Cole Gullatt, sister
Interview with Joan Cox, half sister, and her husband, Joel
Interview with Winston Skinner, *Newnan Times-Herald*
Assistance from Patsy Cochran and Cheryl Smith Coffman

References

Coffelt Database, "Timothy Cole." Accessed July 2016. http://coffeltdatabase.org/index.php
Winston Skinner. "Vietnam veteran recalled as hero by family, friends." *Newnan Times-Herald*, June 1, 1999.
Winston Skinner. "Dustoff Hall of Fame honors fallen Coweta veteran of Vietnam." *Newnan Times-Herald*, March 1, 2009.
"Timothy Cole Jr." Dustoff Hall of Fame, accessed May 14, 2022. https://dustoff.org/hall-of-fame/
"Timothy Cole Jr." Georgia Military Hall of Fame, accessed May 14, 2022. https://gmvhof.org/inductees/

Tim Cole, 1964.

Tim with his mother, Louise, Carolese and Angela.

Tim Cole

Peggy and Tim.

Wedding Day, October 1967

Tim Cole in Vietnam.

Tim Cole in Vietnam.

Photos courtesy of Carolese Gullatt and Joan Cox.

CHAPTER SIXTEEN

James Clayton Kerr

Palmetto, Georgia

Pleasure of love lasts but a moment.
Pain of love lasts a lifetime.
—Bette Davis

It was early morning on December 26, 1961. As in many communities across the country, Christmas had been an exciting time for children in this Palmetto neighborhood. Christmas Day had come and gone in the Kerr household. Unique gifts had been opened, and appetizing foods had been eaten. A Christmas glow still encompassed the home. The Kerrs had finally sent the children to bed, and soon, Earl and Frances Kerr followed.

Palmetto, Georgia, was and still is a small rural town. The town's seeming safety made it an excellent environment in which to grow up. However, at approximately 6 a.m., the household's feeling of security was shattered when one of the family's kerosene heaters caught fire. On his way to work at Del-Mar Cabinets in Villa Rica, Earl raised the alarm when he went back into the house, having forgotten his keys. The family scrambled out as quickly as possible, trying to avoid the flames and smoke that threatened to engulf the home before they could escape. Most of the family exited through the front door and assembled on the front lawn to watch their home burn. When Frances looked around and counted children, she was horrified to realize she was missing a child. Her second child, Donald, wasn't with the others. Everyone looked around for Donald, thinking he might still be in the house but not wanting to voice that thought. Relief swept through the group as Donald appeared; he had exited through the back door. Neighbors assembled with the family in the front yard and watched the beautiful house on Cobb Street with the large front porch as it burned.

Earl and Frances Kerr had five children—Doug, Donald, Evelyn, James, and Judy.

According to James's childhood friend Carl Watson, "His mama could cook. Boy, could she cook."

Earl had placed a basketball goal in the driveway, so the Kerr home was a hub of neighborhood activity. Jimmy Hines recalled daily looking down the street to see if anything was going on that he might want to join. He woke with a start the morning of December 26, looked down the street, and saw the Kerr house in flames.

"I remember my mother waking me up that morning, and she was kind of frantic," he recalled. "She said Bubba's house was on fire. I remember walking out on our porch, and there was just this huge glow in the darkness, so I just stood there and watched."

The local Methodist church had an empty parsonage, and they temporarily sheltered the family. The community brought clothes for the household to the church. According to Hines, the family later rented a home on Toombs Street with a good football playing field. The Kerr family lived there for the next ten years.

James, Earl and Frances's fourth child and third son, was a typical youngster. If something was going on, he wanted to be associated with it. James enjoyed scaring trick-or-treating kids during the Halloween festivities, but he knew that if he did something unruly, everyone would know in five minutes. In a small town like Palmetto, everyone knew everyone else's business!

Jimmy Hines described Palmetto as a place where parents didn't worry about where kids were until it got dark, and he said the "whole town was your playground." Those who went anywhere hitchhiked. All the boys had BB guns. James and Jimmy also learned to build and fly line-controlled airplanes. A neighbor helped them, and they used a nearby field as an airstrip for the planes.

Mike Smith moved to Palmetto as a shy nine-year-old. James came around, quickly became his friend, played, and introduced him to other local kids. Mike always appreciated James for his acceptance. He became good friends with James and Donald. "We all started hanging around together, doing things together and being kids. We all got along so well. We never had a fight between any of us that I can remember. I spent more time at his house than mine."

When Mike went home with the Kerr boys, he recalled, their mom frequently said, "Damn, here comes that little ole Smith boy," though Donald or James would reply, "Well, he followed me home again."

James's younger sister, Judy, remembers James as "my protector. No one bothered me." But when Judy was a toddler, she had difficulty pronouncing "brother," and instead, it came out as Bubba. That was what everyone in Palmetto called him until he went into the military. His mother, Frances, described him as a "quiet person. He never gave us any problems growing up. He was a very good person to know."

James's biggest passion growing up was playing ball. According to Jimmy Hines, even in elementary school, James was always chosen first for a softball game; his reputation as a hitter overshadowed everyone else's.

"He was the strongest guy," Hines said. "He could hit the ball farther than anyone else. Our playground didn't have fencing, and there was a road that came in down there. When Bubba hit the ball over your head, it was going across the street and into that neighbor's yard. Nobody else could do that. He had a strength about him with a bat in his hand that the rest of us just didn't have."

James was always known as an excellent ballplayer, as were his brothers. James and his brother Doug often played together around the Palmetto area. Since Doug was five years older, when James tagged along to play, the older boys usually used him as a "fill-in" if they needed another player. While not as organized as today's Little League, local baseball teams formed and played teams from Union City and Fairburn. Teams became known by their color, and James was the catcher on the "green" team from Palmetto. Eventually, they got uniforms.

John Harris of Fairburn characterized James and his ability on a ball field.

> *Bubba was special in so many ways. Everybody liked Bubba. He was from Palmetto, and I was from Fairburn, and the kids from those areas were brought together by baseball. Sometimes we played against each other, and sometimes we*

> *played together. It was a good way to get to know other people from different communities. There was Duncan Park in Fairburn, and there was a city park in Palmetto right off Highway 29. We also played some games at Madras occasionally.*
>
> *Bubba could hit! When we played Fairburn vs. Palmetto, I usually pitched, and he would more than likely put the bat on the ball. He was the most consistent hitter they had. When teams were cobbled together, he would catch, and I would pitch, and he was the best catcher I ever threw to. He had an instinct for the game, and when he caught, he was aware of everything happening in the game. Also, nobody ran on Bubba. He was the first catcher I ever played with that threw behind a runner at first and picked him off. He also had a great demeanor. Whenever I might get a little rattled, he would come out to the mound and calm things down. Not everybody can do that. As a person, he had that gift of putting people at ease. In the early sixties, among a bunch of young teenagers, that wasn't the easiest thing to do.*

James also enjoyed hunting rabbits and, on occasion, fishing with his father. Earl was a good fisherman, though James didn't seem to take to it as he did to hunting and playing ball. Many of James's friends decided to make a swimming hole near some of the guys' homes, so they and James dammed up a creek using burlap sacks that once held food. They called it Froggy Pond. The swimming hole was ten to fifteen feet deep and originally had a swing across it. Later, they got a guidewire and created a zip line. Jimmy Hines remembers having mud ball fights and getting hit by one mud ball that James threw so hard it knocked him to the ground. According to Mike Smith, the boys had built the dam so well that they later used dynamite to open the creek back up.

Mike Smith, Jimmy Hines, Carl Watson, Donald, and James were all in Boy Scout Troop 154. The Baptist church originally sponsored the troop, but later, sponsorship was moved to the Methodist church. Eventually, the childhood friends grew up and grew apart. As the guys moved into their high school years, they became more interested in money, cars, and girls. It took money to get a vehicle and have a girlfriend, so they searched for odd jobs in and around Palmetto. James cut grass and helped at a local service station, changing tires and doing other jobs. He moved on and worked for an electrical company during his sophomore and junior year in high school, which may have played a role in his MOS when he got into the military. Some of the money he earned went to the Roosevelt Drive-In Theater on Route 29 in College Park. The Roosevelt was the place to be on a Friday night. Kids would often sneak their friends into the theater by hiding them in the trunk, or they might park in the back row and their friends would come out of the woods and get into the car with them. Sometimes they got caught, and sometimes they didn't.

Judy recalled James standing up for the little guy. Once when she was in eighth grade and James was in tenth, several of her friends told her that James was in the principal's office. She scrambled to find out what had happened. She discovered that a student had been bullying a smaller kid, and somebody had given James five dollars to "take care of it." James found the student, walked up to him, and asked him if he was that boy. When the lad answered yes, James struck him so hard that the boy was knocked unconscious.

James attended Campbell High School in Fairburn and met the love of his life in ninth grade, a young lady named Shelia Terry.

"I was in the eighth grade, and he had a girlfriend, but I just thought he was the cutest looking, most handsome guy," Shelia said. "He noticed me and eventually just started walking me to my classes. It just evolved from there."

James was fifteen, and Shelia was fourteen. They enjoyed going to the Roosevelt Drive-In together, frequently on a double date since James wasn't old enough to drive. "We often went Friday, Saturday, and Sunday. We just had a good time," Shelia said.

Occasionally, James and a friend would hide two friends in the trunk when they got to Shelia's house. "It appeared to my parents that it was just John [the driver], James, and me. When we got to the end of the driveway, he would open the trunk, and they would all get in, and we would ride around. Once, we even rode through Peachtree City before it was developed."

James and Shelia also spent many hours at the softball field. "We didn't care what we did as long as we were together. We were young and in love. We would talk on the phone for hours. I can remember talking on the phone about silly things, but all we lived for was just to be together. It was definitely love at first sight. We were very happy just to be together."

There was an area on Highway 29 back then that boys from the Palmetto-Fairburn area used to visit during the evening to drag race or watch the races. James didn't own a car but ran his father's Ford Rambler down the strip once and got a medal. According to Shelia, it was a big joke. He was the only car in that class. "He had a great sense of humor!" she said.

The two of them never had a class together at Campbell, but they stood out as a couple there. "He would always walk me to my classes. Because I was so short and he was so tall, we were an item at school because we drew attention. He was six one or six two, and I was four ten. So there was quite a bit of difference in our sizes."

Carl Watson recalled that James "was very possessive of what he had. I remember some guy was trying to put a hit on his girl, on Shelia, at school, and he just walked up to him at school one day and just cleaned his plow. James was very possessive of her. He was very possessive of most of the friends that he had. He would do a lot for his friends that he wouldn't do for other people."

At the end of his junior year, James decided to enter military service. Carl Watson recalled the two of them talking about the draft and joining the service because they both knew they didn't have the income to go to college. James's brothers, Doug and Donald, were already in the Navy. In 1966, James left school after completing his eleventh-grade year and joined the Army.

"I didn't like it, but he had made up his mind that he was going to do it," Shelia said. "There really wasn't any talking him out of it. I think his parents really wanted him to join the military if he wasn't going to be in school so that he could get some training, to have something to fall back on."

James went south to Fort Benning in 1966, where he did Basic Training, then headed to Fort Huachuca in Arizona, where he finished his Advanced Training with a Military Occupational Specialty (MOS) as a tactical wire operations specialist. While at Fort Huachuca, he wrote home, "The time sure is passing fast here. I just hope I don't get sent to Vietnam. They are sending a lot of men to Vietnam from here."

James wasn't assigned to Vietnam when his training ended but instead went to Germany. James and Shelia tried to wed before he left, but their attempts to overcome their youth were doomed to failure. Shelia's parents wouldn't sign the papers. James and Shelia traveled to Ringgold, Georgia, and attempted to get a judge to marry them but were refused. Admitting defeat, James left Shelia in Georgia and traveled to Germany in 1967 as part of the force shielding the Western Europeans from the Soviet Union and the Warsaw Pact. James didn't like Germany very much. Shelia said he told her in one letter that he "didn't have a refrigerator in the room, but it didn't matter because it was so cold outside, he didn't really need one."

While in Germany, he did the unimaginable. "James volunteered for Vietnam… He felt guilty for being in Germany while other people were fighting a war," Shelia said.

Carl Watson confirmed that "he decided that he was playing war while everyone else was in the war. That is why he decided he would volunteer for Vietnam."

Shelia desperately needed to speak with him directly. "I called him in Germany, and back then, that was just unheard of. I mean, we didn't have any money. But I called him and did get to talk to him, and I begged him not to go to Vietnam. He told me it was too late. He had already put in the paperwork. That was all I knew. I did not know he was coming home. I didn't know anything."

A few weeks later, Shelia was watching the popular *Lawrence Welk Show* on television at her parents' house. Suddenly, the family's dogs began frantically barking. Her mother turned on the floodlights, and Shelia saw James coming up the walkway. "Needless to say, I was beside myself with joy. It was wonderful. I could not believe he was home. I will never forget how I felt," she said.

James and Shelia had been writing back and forth for a year while he was in Germany, and her parents realized they were serious. "I didn't even ask them. They just suggested that we get married before he went to Vietnam," she said.

Shelia's sister worked at the Fulton County Courthouse in Atlanta and arranged for Shelia and James to marry there four days later, on February 1, 1968. Shelia wore a white two-piece suit and a white hat on the happiest day of her life. They rode a bus to Atlanta, got married, rode the bus back to Shelia's house, and borrowed her mother's car. Their honeymoon consisted of a two-night stay in a hotel in Forest Park. When they returned to Palmetto, they lived in the Terrys' basement, which had a small kitchen.

James was nineteen. Shelia was eighteen and a senior at Campbell High School. They lived there for a month, deeply in love, and enjoyed their time together. Then a friend was killed in a car accident. Shelia said the funeral was their first time in church together, and it was difficult because James was facing duty in Vietnam. Suddenly, they were aware of their mortality. Then the month vanished; the time had come for James to ship out for Vietnam. James flew from Atlanta to California, where he called Shelia one last time.

"I remember the day he left very well. I cried so much," she said.

After graduating high school, Shelia got a job at Rich's in Atlanta while living at home. She eventually bought a mobile home from her sister, placed it on her father's property, and fixed it up for when James came home. Even when he left for Vietnam, Shelia knew she would see him again. She worried yet still had a sense of peace. She felt that things would be well. Then, in the fall of 1968, James was granted an R&R leave. Many married men went to Hawaii to meet their wives when given leave, and James was no exception. Shelia almost didn't travel to Hawaii because of the expense, but she met James there from November 4 to 11, 1968.

Once she arrived in Hawaii, she stayed at the airport, waiting for James, who was arriving later.[1] The R&R was bliss for the couple. They walked on the beach, swam in the hotel pool, and relished being together. They had tickets to see Aretha Franklin, but she'd had an accident and had to cancel. James's friend Carl Watson was also in Hawaii at that point in his military career.

"I just recently found out that I was stationed in Hawaii when he was on R&R in Hawaii, with Shelia," Watson said. "I was at Pearl Harbor. Our paths just never crossed."

There were sad moments in Hawaii as well. James kept assuring Shelia it was very safe where he was based. But he also told her he had two fears—he didn't want to return home paralyzed, and he didn't want his body lying in camp for a long time.

Sheila remembered the fear vividly. "I would go to bed and just get up sick, just throw up because I was so worried," she said. When she got on the plane home from Hawaii, she "knew that I would not see him again. It is hard to believe that I knew, but I knew." She was with three girls who had also traveled to see their husbands. They had become friends and even hung out together in Hawaii. Bob Hope was on her flight home. James had hoped to see one of his shows while in Vietnam, but instead, Shelia saw him on the airplane. The girls got photographs and sent them to each other after returning home. One of the girls later lived in the mobile home with Shelia for a short time.

On December 6, a month after her rendezvous with James in Hawaii, Shelia attended a Christmas party at the Rich's where she worked. When they played the famous Bing Crosby Christmas ballad "I'll Be Home for Christmas," Shelia unexplainably became highly emotional. She found out later that James had died that day.

James went to Vietnam in March of 1968 as a tactical wire operations specialist shortly after the infamous Tet Offensive. He was assigned to Battery A, 5th Battalion, 77th Artillery in the 9th Infantry Division in the Mekong Delta. A tactical wire operations specialist worked with communications; the soldiers in Vietnam were cross-trained to handle all communications requirements. They laid cable for the artillery units, which involved communication wire between gun sections and the fire direction center (FDC), usually involving a switchboard hookup. In some cases, tactical cable was laid for a few miles to connect unit locations and primary radio communications backup. A good communication guy was critical to the mission, especially in artillery units whose motto was "Shoot, Move, and Communicate."

The 9th Infantry Division worked closely with the Navy Riverine Forces to root out the Viet Cong in the Delta region of South Vietnam. James wrote letters home during his tour, and every note was shared with the family. (James was called Clay while in Vietnam, from his middle name of Clayton.) In each letter, he kept a countdown of the days. He would use the word "short" and the number of days on each correspondence. The term "short" had special meaning to the young men and women who served in

Vietnam. All service people went to Vietnam expecting to spend twelve months in the war zone; Marines spent thirteen months. Being in Vietnam was measured in days, and someone "short" usually had less than ninety-nine days to go on his Vietnam tour. It was cause for celebration and time to count the days until only a "wake up" remained. Being "short" was a measure of status to his peers. When James returned to camp after his R&R in Hawaii, he had only a little more than three months to go on his year-long Vietnam tour.

"The memory and the night we lost your brother will always stick in my mind and my heart. We didn't really know what happened and didn't find out until after the ground attack was ended. He had been with us, sharing a gift box from home. He was running to the mess tent to get bread when the attack happened," Staff Sergeant Thomas Turner of A Battery wrote to Judy Kerr. "I'm sorry to say that I didn't know James that well, but trust me when I say this, we were all brothers."

The Army car arrived at Shelia's house on a Sunday morning, escorted by the local police to help them find the rural family home. Shelia's brother was also serving in Vietnam, and when she walked into the living room with her family gathered around, she didn't know if it was about her brother Benny or her husband. She just knew that the news was going to be dreadful. Shelia was devastated to learn that James had been killed. The Army didn't tell her exactly what happened. Later, she got the story of the attack on the artillery base via letters from guys there, including the chaplain. The medic who treated James contacted her to tell her that James hadn't suffered. "We didn't even get a letter from James after he returned to Vietnam from Hawaii," Shelia said. Six letters she had mailed to James in Vietnam found their way back into her mailbox.

Judy had just had a baby when James left for Vietnam. When James said goodbye, he told Judy to share the baby with Shelia because he and Shelia wouldn't have one of their own. Judy took that as a premonition of his death. Nevertheless, Judy insisted he would be back.

James's mother, Frances, was in Washington State when the news came of her son's death. She had to make a long journey home, which had now become even longer. About a week after she got the news that James had been killed in action, she received a letter from him, mailed before the attack on his base. He wanted to let her know that he was back in camp from the Hawaiian R&R and that everything was OK.

"She never got over it," said Shelia.

Carl Watson was part of a Marine detachment on a Navy vessel in the Caribbean and couldn't return for the funeral. Mike Smith was in the Army in Alaska and couldn't return either.

"That was the worst thing that ever happened to me. I think that I cried like a baby for a month. He was my best friend," said Smith.

Doug and Donald, who had joined the Navy in 1963, had finished their enlistments. So Shelia requested that her brother Benny escort James's body home from Vietnam. When the body came home, one of Doug's friends at Delta called and told him which flight James would arrive on.

The family needed to see the body to ensure it was James.

"I was just so relieved that we could see him and know it was him," Shelia said. "Stories were going around about people finding rocks in the caskets instead of bodies, things like that, so I was just very relieved that we could look and see that it was him."

James was buried on December 17, 1968, and the passing years have not dimmed the pain for the Kerr family.

"I think it is hard to talk about it. It is hard to relive it, but at the same time, you never get over it, so you might just as well face it and talk about it," said Shelia.

She said she gets along great with James's brothers and sisters, who still treat her like family and include her in their gatherings. "We have a great relationship," she said. "I love them."

Shelia eventually remarried, to a kind and caring man who also knew James when he was growing up. Twenty-nine years after James's death, Shelia visited the Vietnam Memorial in Washington, DC, and found James's name on the Wall.

"My children didn't know what to think," Shelia said as she recalled that visit for a reporter in the 1990s. "When I saw James's name there, I just fell apart. I didn't think I would, but I did. It was the realization of seeing that Wall. The way it's built is just so moving. To stand there so far from home and see his name on that Wall was an honor for me."

Carl Watson said James will never be forgotten. “He was one of the few people that were willing to give everything he had for what he believed in.” On his leg, Carl has a fallen warrior memorial tattoo of James’s initials and the date he died. “He will be memorialized till the day I die.”

“I wouldn’t take nothing for the days that me and Bubba had together,” said Mike Smith. “So many good memories and so many bad memories. But I think that the good outweighs the bad. I’m thinking of all the good times we had and the good times we could have had if he had lived, and I’m assuming that we would still be friends because we were just that close when we were young. Right now, I know where he is, and I can go see him anytime that I want to, and that is peaceful.” Smith visits James’s grave twice a year. “That is my tribute to him.”

In 1997, Frances Kerr got a phone call from an editor of a small newspaper in Pottstown, Pennsylvania, James W. Kerr. He had visited the Wall in Washington, DC, and, not knowing anyone whose name was on the memorial, decided to see if anyone on the Wall shared his name. He found James C. Kerr from Palmetto. Frances was elderly and hesitant to talk about her son with this stranger. Judy finally contacted Mr. Kerr, and as a result, he wrote a moving Memorial Day tribute in honor of James C. Kerr in the Pottstown *Mercury*. Frances, Judy, and Shelia were all interviewed for the article. Jim Kerr sent them a copy. They have stayed in touch, and Judy visited him in Pennsylvania in August of 1997.

Friend Janice Burdette wrote this for Sheila Terry Kerr on December 6, 1968.[2]

God has a purpose in all that he does;
Though his will is not to cause pain:
Who are we ---to question God?
Acceptance is all that remains.
But in God you’ll find the courage and strength to face this trial and loss.
And remember, James died for the lives of men; Such as Jesus died on the cross.

One little drop in the fountain of life
If lost, is surely missed,
For without that drop and its contribution the pond will never exist.

One small life in this world of men
If lost, most surely is missed,
For the lives of men have made this world and without them a world wouldn't exist.

**See end notes in the appendix for additional details.*

***Born**: July 16, 1948*
***Home of record**: Palmetto, Georgia*
***Died**: December 6, 1968, in Kien Phong province of South Vietnam*
***Coweta servicemen who died in the same province**: None*
***Unit on death**: A BTRY, 6th BN, 77th Artillery, 9th Infantry Division*
***Decorations:** Bronze Star, Purple Heart, Good Conduct Medal, National Defense Service Medal, Vietnam Service Medal, Republic of Vietnam Campaign Medal with attached Device*
***Buried:** Holly Hill Cemetery, Fairburn*
***Vietnam Memorial, Washington, DC:** Panel 37W Row 51*

Sources
Interview with Doug Kerr, brother
Interview with Judy Kerr Thompson, sister
Interview with Shelia Terry Entrenkin, widow
Interview with Carl Watson, childhood friend
Interview with Mike Smith, childhood friend
Interview with Jimmy Hines, childhood friend
Email interview with John Harris, childhood friend
Email interview with Thomas Turner, US Army
Assistance from Lee Harper, US Army

References
Coffelt Database, "James Kerr." Accessed May 3, 2017.
http://coffeltdatabase.org/index.p

James and Shelia

James Kerr (right) in Vietnam.

James Kerr in Vietnam

The Kerr Family receiving James' Bronze Star.

Photos courtesy of Shelia Entrenkin & Judy Thompson.

CHAPTER SEVENTEEN

Robert Edward Couch

Senoia, Georgia

Quick wit, quicker smile, quickest to defend that in which he truly believes... ebony-black hair accentuates deeply mysterious eyes that sparkle with mischief or shine with understanding... efficient treasurer, competent student, excellent friend... our Sir Galahad... "The Pure in Heart..."

***—1967 East Coweta Yearbook, the* Kowetian**

Eddy Couch needed to make a decision.

Eddy had graduated from East Coweta High School in the spring of 1967. He had hoped to get a job at Westinghouse or possibly the Ford Motor Company in Hapeville, where his father worked. Unfortunately, neither place would consider hiring him because of his uncertain draft status. Companies weren't interested in hiring and training a young man who might be taken by the draft soon afterward, and this was a common problem for young men during the 1960s and eventually led to the draft lottery.

His brother Barry had already been in the Army for several months. Eddy knew he was likely to be drafted at some point. He could wait and see in order to delay the inevitable or just go ahead and get it done. Eddy decided to face the problem instead of running from it; he joined the US Army.

Eddy Couch started his Basic Combat Training in October 1967 at Fort Benning. Once it was completed, he took leave before moving to Advanced Infantry Training at Fort McClellan, Alabama. Eddy's uncle, Ronald "Ronny" Whitlock, spent time with Eddy during his leave. Whitlock and Eddy's mother drove him to Alabama for his AIT, and the three stopped for lunch in Carrollton on the way.

After completing AIT, Couch volunteered to attend non-commissioned officer (NCO) school (primarily the rank of sergeant) and then volunteered to go to Vietnam. While in AIT and NCO school, he corresponded with his high school buddy Ray McKnight. Ray was never clear on why Eddy volunteered for Vietnam. Perhaps he was facing a problem instead of avoiding it, just as he had done before.

Eddy stayed at Fort McClellan for almost six months. When he finished his training during the summer of 1968, he called some of his pals to come pick him up and take him back to Senoia. His brother Barry, Ray, and another friend from East Coweta, Charles Williams, headed to the base to pick him up. On the drive home, Barry and Eddy got into an argument. Barry stopped the vehicle, and the brothers leaped out and started fighting along the side of the road. Ray and Charles followed them out of the car and broke it up, and everyone got back in the car. Off they went. By the time they got to Senoia, the disagreement was forgotten.

Today, Ray McKnight can't remember the reason for the fight.

Eddy Couch had a thirty-day leave before going to Vietnam, and he packed as much as possible into that month. He lounged on the beach at Panama City with buddies Carl Williams and Pete Wilson. He visited Stone Mountain. He returned to College Park, where he had grown up, and unsuccessfully attempted to visit his family's old house. It had already been torn down due to the expansion of the Atlanta airport. He and Ray went to Riverdale for hot Krispy Kreme doughnuts, and of course, Eddy spent time with family and friends in Senoia before saying his goodbyes.

When it was time for him to catch the flight to Vietnam, the same bunch who had picked him up at Fort McClellan took him to the Atlanta airport. He told his parents goodbye that morning at home. Now he could relax and have a little fun on the way to the airport. Ray, Carl, Barry, and Eddy laughed and cut up all the way to the airport.

When they got there, the laughing stopped. Now it was real.

Somberly, the three friends walked Eddy onto the Delta flight and to his seat. According to McKnight, walking a serviceman to his seat on the plane was a common practice at that time. Eddy said goodbye to Charles and hugged Barry. Ray was standing in the aircraft aisle, waiting to tell his best friend goodbye. Eddy finally turned to Ray and gripped his hand as it lay on the back of Eddy's seat. He stared intently into Ray McKnight's eyes. He spoke deliberately and said, "Ray, I will never see you again."

Ray was taken aback. What did Eddy mean? Ray finally sputtered, "Eddy, don't say that. Don't even think that. You'll be back in no time."

Eddy stopped him. "No, I really mean it. I don't think that I'll ever see you again." The emotion was tangible. The two young men stared at each other. They hugged and cried.

Then it was time to get off the plane. Ray slowly left Eddy in his seat, stealing a last glance as he disembarked.

The drive home was sober. Gone was the boisterousness of the trip to the airport. The young men were primarily left with their own thoughts and worry for their friend. Eddy's words were on Ray's mind all the way to Senoia. He told Barry what had occurred, and neither knew what to make of it.

Eddy called Ray upon his arrival in Oakland and told him everything was all right and said he felt better. He asked Ray to write him and gave him the address. It was the last time Ray McKnight would ever speak with Eddy.

Eddy Couch was born on July 22, 1949. He was the younger of two boys, with Barry being born in 1947. According to childhood friend Tommy Harris, Eddy looked like his mother, and Barry looked like his father.

Eddy and Barry were tight, and "if you saw one, you saw the other," said Robin Horne, who later married Barry Couch.

Like Siamese twins, they were inseparable. They defended each other and loved each other. The brothers attended Maple Street Elementary and Clayton Middle School, both in College Park.

Eddy's father, Vance Couch, was originally from Senoia and served as an Army medic in the Pacific during World War II. Upon his return to Senoia, he worked at Southern Mills. When Ford Motor Company opened and started hiring, he and a couple of other veterans hitchhiked to Hapeville, got in line, and landed a job. The family eventually moved to College Park to be closer to the Ford plant. His wife, Eleanor "Elna" Whitlock Couch, grew up in the

Aberdeen/ Line Creek community, now part of Peachtree City, where her family owned a farm. The family went to church on the spot where Best Buy in Peachtree City is currently located. She worked primarily in the home, caring for their two boys, Marcus Barry and Robert Edward.

Eddy's parents "were two very, very good people," said Robin Horne Couch, their daughter-in-law. "You could not have found anyone better than Vance and Eleanor."

As a World War II veteran, Vance Couch had seen combat and returned home with PTSD. People couldn't make any sudden noise around him, recalled Ronny Whitlock. Whitlock called him "Pa Couch." When Ronny was at their home, if he got up in the middle of the night to use the bathroom, he called out, "Pa Couch, I'm going to the bathroom!" to ensure that Vance wasn't startled.

With Eddy on the verge of entering high school, Vance and Elna moved back to Senoia. The first house they moved into had no electricity or indoor plumbing. Vance continued to work at Ford while Elna, with the boys in high school, picked up the odd job here and there to help out. She worked with a local florist as well as at Southern Mills. In addition, Vance was elected to the Senoia City Council. Senoia was a small town; everyone knew everyone and their business. Regardless, according to their daughter-in-law, the Couch family "stood out." Senoia native Robin Horne married Barry in 1992 and was already familiar with the Couch family.

Ronald Whitlock's father died when Ronny was two. Elna Couch was his older sister. There were five boys after Elna, with Ronny the youngest. Vance and Elna, along with some of the other sisters, helped raise the boys. Ronny was older than the Couch boys but still close to them. Ronny considered the two to be his brothers, so Vance became his surrogate father. While Ronny lived with the Couches and attended high school in College Park, Vance took him to buy his first car. Vance picked out a 1957 Chevrolet because even though it wasn't a Ford, it was the best car on the lot.

Of course, Barry and Eddy weren't perfect. They fought, and at times, they could drive their mother crazy.

Ronny said that one time, Elna took the boys to a doctor in Fayetteville to get their vaccinations. Barry and Eddy weren't interested in getting their shots. The doctor's office was in an old house with a front porch railing. When the boys got out of the car, they ran from one side of the vehicle to the other. Elna chased them and was embarrassed as people watched, undoubtedly with great amusement. Finally, Elna got them to the front porch, where they broke free again. Barry went one way, and Eddy went the other. Elna went after them again, much to the delight of the onlookers. Eventually, she wrestled both boys into the doctor's office, where they finally received their shots.

Another such trip found the family at a country store on Highway 54. The watermelons were coming in. The owner thought the boys were cute and told them if they could get a melon in the car on their own, they could have it. Barry and Eddy picked out the most enormous melon they could find and rolled it to the car. They struggled to pick it up and get it into the car, but they finally succeeded. The owner was amazed but kept his word and let them return home with his best melon.

As an elementary school student, Eddy once got into a big fight at a neighbor's house. Ronny Whitlock heard Eddy call "time out," and the boy complied. Unfortunately, Eddy proceeded to knock his tooth out. Eddy got into trouble for that. Peers never messed with one of the Couch boys at school. To do so was to have both of them after you.[1]

When Whitlock graduated from high school in 1963, Vance, Elna, and the boys were moving back to Senoia. Ronny joined the Air Force and eventually was assigned to work on B-52 bombers. He was stationed at Robins Air Force Base and often traveled to Senoia to spend the weekend with either the Couch family or a sister in Haralson. He would be discharged from the Air Force in 1967, just as the Couch boys were finishing high school and facing military service themselves.

In 1963, Barry and Eddy Couch started at East Coweta High School on Highway 16, the present-day site of East Coweta Middle School. Barry was a junior while Eddy was a freshman. East Coweta had a student population of only four hundred students, so just as in the town of Senoia, everyone in the school knew everybody else and their business. Eddy fit right into this environment. A good student, he was sincere and fun-loving.

"Everyone loved Eddy. He was such a nice fellow, and he was so cute," said Vicki Hill.

"He was raised proper," said Tommy Harris, another friend. "Everybody liked Eddy Couch. He was always cutting up, grinning, and smiling."

When Eddy was a sophomore, he met Ray McKnight, and they became instant friends. He also befriended several other boys: Jerry Thompson, John Bidney, Bill Canada, Jodie Cox, Dennis Dean, and Steve Hubbard. These eight young men collectively became known as "the group." They did everything together.

"Everything that they did was cool," Vicki Hill said.

Eddy Couch parlayed his ability to connect with his classmates into politics and was elected class treasurer his senior year. He also participated in the senior play and played left field on the East Coweta baseball team. His friend Ray McKnight played shortstop, and because of their proximity on the field, they kept up a constant banter.[2]

Eddy and Ray also enjoyed double-dating.

"Eddy didn't have a problem getting a date," Ray said, "and it always seemed to be with a different girl." Ray dated Julianne, who later became his wife. Occasionally, Eddy went along with Ray and Julianne. "It wasn't awkward at all. We just enjoyed having Eddy with us," Ray said.

Most teenagers within twenty miles of Senoia flocked to "teen club" on the weekends, including Eddy Couch and "the group." The club was held at the Freeman Sasser American Legion Post 174 in Senoia in a large room where more than a hundred teens could gather. The post provided chaperones, who maintained a tight grip on behavior. No alcohol was tolerated, and there was no hanging around in the parking lot. The chaperones likely knew the teens' parents, which helped keep them from mischief. Regardless, the kids loved to get a soft drink and socialize. If they were lucky, they listened to a live band and danced. Eddy loved those nights at teen club since he enjoyed the music and loved to dance.

After the teen club closed for the evening, the kids often went to Reagan's Dairy Spot and Grill on Highway 85 outside Senoia. The building used to be a gas station but now served hamburgers, hot dogs, corn dogs, chicken, and ice cream. Reagan's also had a jukebox, pinball machines, and picnic tables. The parking lot was full of automobiles on Friday and Saturday nights. Teenagers sat on their cars, and the socializing continued. Informal car judging also went on. Kids would judge the looks and try to guess the speed of the autos on display. This often led to racing on the long, straight stretch of Highway 85 near Reagan's.

During the summer, when a teenager wasn't working at home or a job, they went to the local pool, teen club, and Reagan's. There was little else to do unless they went to Newnan or headed to Atlanta.

Eddy Couch was preoccupied with school and an active teenage social life, and he also worked a job. In 1963, Bobby Hatchett purchased the Gulf Service Station on State Route 16, near the intersection of Luther Bailey and Broad Street, across from Crook's Store. Eddy began working for Hatchett around 1965. He pumped gas, fixed flat tires, and did whatever was asked of him well and with a good attitude. Hatchett had known the family for several years and knew they supported Eddy.

"He'd beat me over there in the morning. He'd be waiting for me to open up," Hatchett said with a laugh. Occasionally, Eddy opened the station for Hatchett at 7 a.m. Ronny Whitlock always got his gas there so he could visit with Eddy.

During the 1960s, there was a lot of pulp wooding, logging, and farming around Senoia. Many of the big trucks involved in these occupations parked at the Gulf Station on Friday to get serviced over the weekend. They would have the truck filled with gas, the air pressure in the tires checked, the oil changed, and other maintenance completed. The drivers all got along well with Eddy, who often did the work himself.

"He was real dependable, and everybody liked him," said Bobby Hatchett.

Tommy Harris worked at the Gulf Station during the same period, and he and Eddy made sure that one of them covered each shift and that all the work was completed. Ray McKnight said he believes Barry Couch also worked there for a time. Eddy Couch continued to work at the service station until he joined the military in the fall of 1967. While the Gulf Station is no longer there, the building, painted green and serving as a bargain store, survives.

In June 1967, the "group" graduated from East Coweta High School. Ray McKnight was accepted into West Georgia College, now the University of West Georgia. Though a good student, Eddy wasn't interested in returning to school. Instead, he kept working at the Gulf Station.

During the first half of 1967, Eddy's brother, Barry, who had graduated in 1965, and his friend Jerry Thompson were drafted. "When that happened," said Tommy Harris, "Eddy said he was going to join." Tommy joined about the same time, and in October 1967, both were in Basic Combat Training at Fort Benning. That year, Tommy Harris rode home for Christmas with Eddy and Barry. It was the last time he saw Eddy Couch; the military took them in different directions.

When Eddy joined the military that summer, he owned a four-door Falcon. His father purchased a gold-and-bronze two-door Ford Fairlane 500 for Eddy that fall.

"It looked like Eddy," said Vicki Hill.

Eddy proceeded to Fort McClellan for Advanced Infantry Training and was at Fort Benning for the first phase of NCO Training in February. Phase two took him to Fort McClellan, where he finished in early September of 1968, was picked up by his friends, and brought back to Coweta County. A few days later, he was on his way to Vietnam.

In April of 1968, Tommy Harris was posted in the III Corps section of Vietnam. Eddy Couch arrived in mid-September and was sent to Bien Hoa in I Corps. His assignment was to Headquarters and Headquarters Company, 2nd Battalion, 506th Infantry Regiment of the 101st Airborne Division. It took Tommy and Eddy about a month to make contact, but they started writing to each other regularly. Most letters received from home in Vietnam were destroyed after being read and possibly passed around for buddies to read. No one wanted to take the chance that communist troops might find them.

Upon arrival in Vietnam, Eddy Couch would have kept his mouth shut and tried to learn what was going on and how his unit did things. That was the only way to survive, and Eddy would undoubtedly have known that and acted accordingly.

"When you get there is when you learn," said Tommy Harris.

Later, Harris ran into a few soldiers who served with Eddy and was told he was well-liked, even as a new guy. In due course, Eddy was given the command of a squad and the nickname "Sofa" because his last name was Couch.

Tommy was hoping to get to I Corps and see Eddy at some point, but Eddy Couch would be there for only four months.

During those four months, Eddy wrote two letters home that still survive.

September 18, 1968. Sent from Vietnam to Elna Couch. Entire letter.

Hello Ma,

Thought I drop you a few lines to let you [know] I'm doing fine. Just got back off of a 4 day operation. Beating out the Rice paddies and checking villages. My feet are sore and my arms are scratched up a little but other than that I'm fine. Well I finally found out how it feels to be shot at. It's a weird feeling. Tell Barry I was walking point Monday and the VC opened up with two automatic weapons. We lost one man the whole time we were gone.I've received two letters from you and one from Aunt Nez. Really was glad to get them. Sometime next week I want you to fix me up a package and sent it. Not very big though. Some Kool-Aid pre-sweetened, some paper and a couple of pens. 2 pk Marlboro. Thats about all I run short on.Hope Margene is better. Tell her I think about her a lot and hope Mr. Wade gets off the second shift.Tell Grady, Margaret and Martha Ann I send my love. I hope Martha Ann received the picture I sent her. Tell Pa not to work to hard and to behave himself. It's getting dark so I'll close for now.Love Always Forever,Eddy

December 21, 1968. Sent from Vietnam to unknown recipient. Entire letter.

Hello,

Thought I would drop you a few lines to let you know I'm doing okay. Received the package with cigarettes, candy and film. Thank you very much.We're still in Camp Evans, pulling bunker guard and details. It's better to be in the field than back here. You have to put up with too much bull---- !Received a package from Aunt Mary today. Cigarettes, cake and candy. Well I see that Barry got his leave. Tell him I said to go to work and make me and him some money! HAHA! Well it just doesn't seem like X-mas over here. My squad had to check the wire on the perimeter today. And when we got there I was soaking wet with sweat. It has been real nice. Sunshine without rain. Well that's about all I know. Tell everyone hello for me. Take care of yourself. Love always, Eddy

Shortly after Christmas, Tommy Harris was out on a firebase. A Chinook flew in and unloaded a jeep and a trailer. They had started unfolding a large antenna from the trailer when Harris learned some good news—the antenna would allow them to call home. Tommy made an appointment to call then returned at the specified time. He called home and got his mother on the line. Toward the end of Tommy's allotted time, his mother asked him if he knew about Eddy. He didn't. His mother said she had to go but would write and explain everything to him. At that point, the letter wasn't necessary. Tommy already knew. A few days later, a letter he had written to Eddy was returned to him. On the envelope was the word "Deceased."

Even though Eddy was the squad leader, he liked to walk point on patrol. This was unusual, as most squad leaders walked toward the middle of the patrol column. On this particular patrol, the NVA allowed Eddy to walk through the ambush while waiting for the middle part of the patrol, where the squad leader and the radio-telephone operator, or RTO, would typically be walking. When the middle part arrived in the kill zone, the ambush was sprung. Eddy heard the fire and realized what had happened. He rushed back into the kill zone. His medal citation describes the action that Eddy Couch took that fateful day.

Sgt. Robert E. Couch distinguished himself while serving as a Squad Leader during combat operations in the vicinity of Thon Dieu, Republic of Vietnam. While moving through densely wooded thickets, the platoon in which Sgt. Couch was moving came under heavy fire from an estimated platoon-sized enemy force. He immediately maneuvered his men on a line, and while under heavy hostile fire, he personally placed his men in strategic positions. Sergeant Couch moved among his men, directing their line of fire and inspiring them through his courage. As the battle continued, the enemy began to withdraw. Sgt. Couch then led his men in pursuit, but as they closed in on the enemy force, an anti-personnel mine exploded, wounding several members of the squad to the left flank. Sgt. Couch instructed his men to take positions and return fire as he and another man moved into the booby-trapped area to recover the wounded members of the beleaguered squad. Sgt. Couch moved one man to safety, but as he again moved into the contested area, a second mine exploded, mortally wounding the courageous young leader.

The explosion blew Eddy's legs off. He died either instantly or shortly after the explosion.

In Senoia, the word arrived that Eddy Couch was Missing in Action (MIA). Though worried, Ronny Whitlock and Ray McKnight waited for some word and continued to be optimistic

"I just knew it would be all right, that they would find him," said Ronny.

At Reagan's that weekend, Ray saw someone who had just returned from Vietnam. He told Ray bluntly that MIA meant KIA. Two days later, the veteran was proven correct when word came that Eddy had been killed. Whitlock was at the Couch home when the military pulled up, and two officers got out of the car. Elna asked Ronny and Vance's brother, Grady Couch, to go to the Ford plant and tell Vance. Vance and Grady had served in World War II together.

"That was a sad journey home," said Ronny.

"That tore the whole town up," said Vicki Hill. "I felt so bad for his momma and daddy."

When Eddy died, people were at the Couch home for days. Many young people came to the house to be "close" to Eddy and support the family. The community support seemed to help Barry, who struggled with feelings of guilt. He was still at Fort Benning, not in Vietnam. Ironically, Barry had completed the paperwork to send his brother overseas. He often went to Ronny's house in Fayetteville during this time just to get away.

When Ronny Whitlock went to the funeral home, he had convinced himself that it wouldn't be Eddy's body in the casket. However, when he opened the coffin, he recognized Eddy at once. His anguished cries of grief that followed, he later felt, embarrassed his family.

"I was so angry when Eddy died that I decided never to believe in God again," said Ronny. God had taken his father, and now he had taken Eddy. How could a loving God explain these things? Ronny shook his fist at God in the parking lot of Hillcrest Funeral Home in Newnan and told him he hated him. Nonetheless, in 1970, Ronny started college and graduated with a major in theology, moving on to a career as a minister.

As Eddy's funeral approached, Ray McKnight got a call from the Couch home. Elna wanted to see him. Apprehensively, Ray went to the house. The "group" thought they might be asked to serve as pallbearers. Ray was embarrassed to face Elna because Eddy was gone and he was still here. Whether Elna had ever entertained those thoughts, she graciously welcomed Ray. Elna told him that she planned to ask her brothers to be the pallbearers. Elna wanted Ray and the friends that made up the "group" to hear it from her. So five Whitlocks took care of Eddy during the funeral—Ronny, Winston, Mark, Larry, and Bobby—along with Jimmy Young.

On January 8, 1969, the funeral took place at the Methodist church in Senoia. The "group" went to the casket in front of the church to see Eddy one last time, though the guys had to steel themselves to make the walk. They wanted to remember him the way he had always been—quick with the wit, the smile, and the laugh. Ray said it was emotional, but when he saw Eddy, he looked normal. The "group" eventually retreated and sat on the front row of the upstairs balcony during the service. Six of the seven young men there that day would subsequently go to Vietnam. Ray McKnight was next to go and was assigned to an area near the spot where Eddy had died. All six returned home, but the "group" has gotten together only once in the more than fifty years since Eddy's death.

Vicki Hill received a few letters from Eddy after he was declared Missing in Action. A couple of her letters to Eddy were returned as undeliverable.

In April, an Army officer from Fort McPherson visited Senoia to present Vance and Elna with the medals Eddy had earned while serving his country. One of those medals was the Silver Star, the third-highest award for heroism that the United States military can bestow.

After Eddy's death, Vance and Elna closed off the living room in their home and made it a museum to Eddy, filling it with photographs and memorabilia of their son. Then they seemed to remember that Barry was still in their lives and added Barry's photos and memorabilia. Barry and his first wife, Sandra, had their first child and the Couches' first grandchild in 1970, and they named him Marcus Edward.

"He was the apple of everyone's eye," said Ronny Whitlock.

In July of 1976, at age six, Marcus was killed in an accident at Senoia Park. Photographs and memorabilia about Marcus joined those of Eddy and Barry in his grandparents' museum shortly afterward.

In 1997, the old wooden bridge connecting Senoia with Fayette County was replaced by a newer, safer bridge. In 2001, the Senoia City Council, led by Mayor Joan Trammell, voted unanimously to dedicate the new bridge to Eddy Couch.When the bridge was dedicated on Veterans Day 2001, the whole family attended. Vance was ill but still went and was excited about the honor for his son. Vance had rarely spoken about Eddy, though after many years, Elna finally talked to people about her son. The ceremony took place in Senoia's Veterans Park. It included the East Coweta Marine ROTC Color Guard, the 101st Airborne Division Honor Guard, the East Coweta Middle School Band, and students from Eastside Elementary. Ronny Whitlock spoke for the family, and Ray McKnight spoke on behalf of Eddy's many friends. Elna talked to a reporter from the *Atlanta Journal-Constitution* about the honor being paid to her son.

"When I think about how much love I have missed by not having him..." she said. "But you have to be strong, and I've had to be strong for Vance and my other son, Barry. It took some time to get my tongue loosened about talking about Eddy, but it's kind of a release to let go of some of the hurt." Elna continued, "It's been thirty-two years, and now he won't be forgotten thanks to the naming of the bridge, but I think he's sitting up there looking down and grinning."

Vance Couch died in 2005 at eighty-eight. Barry Couch died of a heart attack in March 2009 at sixty-two. Six months later, in September of 2009, Elna Couch passed away after a fight with cancer. She was eighty-two.

Ten years later, on Memorial Day 2011, the Senoia Area Historical Society spearheaded another effort to honor Eddy Couch by dedicating a flagpole in his honor in the Senoia City Cemetery.

Ronny Whitlock returned to the Senoia area in 1977 as a pastor. He served as Vance and Elna's pastor for the last twenty years of their lives. Today, he and his wife live on Stallings Road on property given to them by Vance Couch. Stallings Road is the same road where the Senoia cemetery is located, so Ronny Whitlock passes Eddy Couch and his family daily and never fails to think about them.

"You don't think about it when it first happens," Ronny said, "because you're hurting yourself, but this whole community hurt for those guys."

**See end notes in the appendix for additional details.*

**To see the catalog of original letters to and from Eddy Couch, visit www.bettermencoweta.com.

***Born**: July 22, 1949*
***Home of record**: Senoia, Georgia*
***Died**: December 30, 1968, in Thua Thien province of South Vietnam*
***Coweta servicemen who died in the same province**: Charles Walthall, Robert Webb, John Dozier, Wayne Vessell, and Johnny Calhoun*
***Unit on death**: HHC, 2nd BN, 506th Infantry, 101st ABN Division*
***Decorations:** Silver Star, Bronze Star, Purple Heart, Air Medal, Good Conduct Medal, National Defense Service Medal, Republic of Vietnam Military Merit Medal, Vietnam Service Medal with 4*

Bronze Star Devices, Republic of Vietnam Gallantry Cross with unit Palm, Republic of Vietnam Campaign Medal
Buried: *Senoia City Cemetery, Senoia*
Vietnam Memorial, Washington, DC: *Panel 35W Line 8*

Sources
Interview with Robin Couch, sister-in-law
Interview with Ron Whitlock, uncle
Interview with Vicki Hill Whitlock, childhood friend
Interview with Bobby Hatchett, employer
Interview with Thomas McKoon, childhood friend
Interview with Tommy Harris, childhood friend
Interview with Ray McKnight, childhood friend

References
Coffelt Database, "Edward Couch." Accessed November 29, 2020. http://coffeltdatabase.org/index.php
"Silver Star and Other Medals Are Presented to Hero's Mother." *Newnan Times-Herald,* April 17, 1969.
Abby Brunks. "32 Years later, Senoia salutes his memory." *Atlanta Journal-Constitution*, July 19, 2001.
Abby Brunks. "Senoia salutes Sgt. Eddy Couch." *Atlanta Journal-Constitution,* November 15, 2001.

Barry and Eddy.

Eddy's Senior picture, 1967.

Eddy Couch in Vietnam

Photos courtesy of Ronald Whitlock.

CHAPTER EIGHTEEN

Leavy Carlton Solomon

Palmetto, Georgia

There is no glamour in being a battlefield company aidman. What we did mostly was under fire and in the shaking throes of fear.

—Keith Kreitman, Company Medic, World War II

US Army Vietnam Veteran Arnold Krause was in Vietnam in January 1969, and in 2014, he recalled the scene.

> *We were continuing our foot patrols along Six Alpha. By now, the VC had started to place booby traps with tripwires along the routes we were patrolling. We never tried to walk on the same route (you don't ever walk on paths), so we would vary our distance from the road. This did not help. I stopped one day to rest only to notice a tripwire at my feet running to a grenade. It is now January 11th, and we are on road security once again. By this time, we have almost made trails along the sides of the road. Moving away from the perimeter of Fire Support Base Pershing, I yell out to "lock and load," and everyone chambers a round and flips the safety on their M-16s. Today, Doc Solomon joins our merry band of brothers for a stroll in the country. The first part of the patrol is fairly easy as the terrain is open and uncluttered. But out a little further, we begin to maneuver our way through the rubble of once stately brick and mortar dwellings. When they were first built, these homes must have been a sight to see.*

> *Now you can't visualize how this country must have looked before all the wars and destruction. My squad (fourth squad) and the first squad are moving along the east side of the road toward Trang Bang near an old schoolhouse. The second and third squads and Lieutenant Michael Sheehan make up the rest of the patrol. They are across the road on the west side, moving in parallel. We are out ahead of the 65th Engineers sweeping the road for mines. Along the way, Doc Solomon is doing some medcap* [Medical Civic Action Programs] *work with the local villagers. My squad has the point, and we are several hundred meters ahead of the sweep team. It is slow going, walking then waiting for the engineers to complete their mine sweeping along each section of the red dirt road. We pause to wait when there is a loud explosion to our rear. We see a column of black and red smoke from the blast quickly rise into the sky. I turned and yelled, "What just happened? What just happened?"*

Leavy Solomon was born to Willie Gus and Maggie Ruth Williams Solomon on October 3, 1946, in Palmetto, Georgia.

By all accounts, Willie and Maggie were hard workers and good people. Willie had a body shop where he worked on local vehicles. Maggie worked at Palmetto Elementary School. When Leavy was old enough, he went to school with his mother at Palmetto Elementary through eighth grade. Leavy's relatives described him as a quiet but fun-loving child. He wasn't very good at or interested in sports, though he participated with family and friends and "was kind of a loner," according to Leonard Lipscomb, who grew up with Solomon.

Leavy's cousin, Ralph Brown, said Leavy was nicknamed "Candy" for an obvious reason—he really liked candy.

His cousin Alice Reese said that Leavy "liked to pick at you" and recalled him being superstitious. He would tell her, "Don't touch my feet with that broom, or I'll go to jail." Where he picked that up is unknown. Alice went to Raymond Baptist Church with the Solomon family and remembered Leavy's crush on the pastor's daughter. Another cousin who Leavy liked to play with was Charles Walthall. (See Charles Walthall, Chapter 11.)

Leavy Solomon left Palmetto Elementary School in 1961 and started ninth grade at Fairburn High School, graduating four years later in 1965. He went to work for Southern Airways at a small airport adjacent to Atlanta Municipal Airport (now Hartsfield-Jackson International Airport). Leavy had a relative who worked there. He made enough money to purchase a nice car. Cousin Ralph Brown thought it was a 1963 Chevrolet, while Alice Reese said Leavy owned a 1956 Chevrolet that was blue and white. Regardless of the year of the car, Leavy seemed to be doing well.

In 1968, Leavy was either drafted or joined the US Army. He was sworn into the service on March 21, 1968, and headed to Fort Benning to begin his Basic Combat Training.

"Basic training is a process of strength building, character-shaping, drilling by marching in formations, and learning the basics of military discipline and how to become proficient in firing weapons," said Arnold Krause, who served with Leavy in Vietnam. "The training lasts for a period of eight weeks. Over those weeks, Leavy and other members of his Platoon and Company would be molded or forged into a unit that would begin to think as one rather than act independently."

Usually, at the beginning of Basic Combat Training, recruits were evaluated with aptitude and psychology tests. These tests helped the Army determine the job most appropriate for the young man's abilities. As a result, Leavy Solomon was given an MOS of 91A, medic.

Advanced Training for Leavy Solomon was held at Fort Sam Houston, outside San Antonio, Texas, where he learned to be a combat medic. The training was extensive and intensive. The soldiers learned to give shots, draw blood, start an IV, and splint a broken bone. They learned to treat gunshot wounds, perform amputations, and avoid shock. They also studied stretcher usage, correct procedures for moving and carrying patients, techniques for approaching and treating patients in combat situations, and other medical techniques and methods.

After graduating from advanced training, Leavy was granted a thirty-day leave and headed home for relaxation and goodbyes before reporting for duty in California. Alice Reese recalled him saying, "I'm going to California."

She said, "Next thing we knew, he was in Vietnam, and then he was gone."

If Leavy's experience was like that of many men who went to Vietnam, he traveled to Oakland Army Base in California, a deportation depot that arranged his transportation to his next duty station, the Republic of Vietnam.

Arnold Krause picked up the story.

> *Upon arriving in Oakland and reporting in, it takes only a day or two for Leavy to be placed on a manifest which assigns him to an aircraft (in this case, a commercial Boeing 707) which will depart from Travis AFB, a short 30 minutes away by bus in the nearby town of Fairfield. The flight takes about 15 hours, stopping to refuel in Honolulu and again at Clark AFB in the Philippines. Leavy lands at Tan Son Nhut AFB and, upon the door to the aircraft opening, gets his first introduction to Vietnam by the smell of the air that penetrates the cabin interior. After debarking from the plane, he climbs aboard a bus or deuce and a half truck [a two and a half-ton Army truck] and is transported over to Camp Alpha, the 90th Replacement Center at Bien Hoa. It is September 2, 1968, and Leavy is starting his tour of duty in Vietnam.*
>
> *At the 90th Replacement Center are many barracks to house the incoming replacements. It is here that each Battalion or Brigade in the field sends in their requests for new recruits. It will only take a few days for Leavy to receive the orders that will send him to his next destination and what unit he will be assigned to for the next year. Leavy C. Solomon is told to report to HHC* [Headquarters, Headquarters Company] *2nd Battalion, 12th Infantry, 3rd Brigade, 25th Division, known as the Tropic Lightning Division. Their nickname came from the fact that they were formed in the Hawaiian Islands and the Taro leaf is the emblem of their unit patch. The time must be around the 4th or 5th of September now. Before Leavy can report to his new unit, he is required to fly to Cu Chi, the 25th Division base camp using a C-123 or C7A Caribou as*

transportation. Here, he will spend three days in orientation school, explaining to him his surroundings, who the enemy is, and what to be careful of. It is mandatory training for all division personnel.
September 9 or somewhere around this date, Leavy climbs aboard a Huey slick, UH1D Iroquois helicopter, or maybe a CH-47 Chinook and is transported down to a laager site in the middle of a rice paddy near Hoc Mon, about five miles west of Saigon where he now joins up with his new unit, the 2/12th "Warriors." Reporting in to the head Battalion medical officer, Leavy is told that he will be attached to Charlie Co, and his Platoon is the 3rd Platoon. Medics, like journalists, are embedded into a unit. They live there and work there but are really part of another command, HHC, in this case. After six months in the field, if a medic is still functional and not all shot up, he will move back out of the field and report to the Battalion Aid Station, where he will spend the rest of his tour in relative safety.

Leavy reports to his new Platoon and gets introduced around to some of the guys. For Leavy, it was too soon to know or for anyone to have an opinion of him. He was not overly big or tall, somewhat slim of stature like the rest of us because that is what the country did to you. Most men dropped 20 or more pounds during the year they were in combat. Leavy wore a pair of heavy framed glasses and kept to himself initially.

During this time, Charlie Company and the rest of the Battalion were about to be relocated from Hoc Mon, where they had been bivouacked since the first week of July. The Brigade receives orders to move, and our Battalion is sent to Trang Bang, about twelve miles west of Cu Chi, to Fire Support Base Stuart. Charlie Company remains here from Sept 22nd until October 3rd when it joins up with the rest of the Battalion at Fire Support Base (FSB) Pershing, six clicks (six thousand meters) north of Trang Bang. The two fire support bases are connected by a road called TL-6A or Six Alpha. This road, over time, will cause a lot of grief to the

Battalion and to Charlie Company. An FSB normally has a battery of artillery guns collocated along with an infantry unit, company-sized or larger, for protection. In this case, FSB Pershing was home to the 2/12th, the whole Battalion, about 500 men.

During the next three months, from October through December, the Battalion launches numerous combat aerial assaults, search and destroy missions to our north and east. It is a hotbed of activity, and enemy engagements are frequent. During one spell, Charlie Company makes contact with the enemy for twenty-two straight days. Medics have to go out with the Platoon both day and night. Sometimes they pull double duty, having patrolled with the company during the daytime, then having to go out at night on ambush patrol. We all griped about what we had to do, but we followed orders. In between our patrols to the east, each company takes turns providing road security along Six Alpha. This road is the main supply road which we use to bring in food and ammo from Cu Chi by truck.

One of the favorite missions that Medics performed was doing a MEDCAP. This was a trip out to a local village where we did some public relations, and while doing that, the medics would tend to the medical needs of the villagers, mostly young and older women and many kids. They would get their shots, sores, or wounds attended to and usually a good dosing of some type of powder for lice or other bugs that lived on humans. Generally, it was a good day for everyone.

Doc Solomon did his duties faithfully while he was with the company. I know he did not talk a lot and did not mix it up much. We did not have any issues with race in Vietnam. I had plenty of black, Hispanic, and white buddies there. The different races tended to hang out with each other, but beyond that, we were one big family trying to survive this war. You knew you could count on Leavy to do his job just as you could count on guys in your squad to "have your back" and protect you.

The Battalion gets into both major and minor firefights

all the way through Christmas. December was especially bad for Charlie Company. A booby trap killed five guys in 1st Platoon on December 3. A week later, we lost our company commander Lt. R.W. McDaniel (severely wounded) and killed are his RTO and a platoon Sgt in one firefight. Two days later, out on Six Alpha, our platoon leader Lt. James Merrett, SP4 Ron Stepsie, and SP4 Robert Beltran are overrun by a group of VC and are killed. On December 14th, we land into a hot LZ, and Sgt Richard Conlin is killed. We have eleven KIA's in the month.

While located at FSB Pershing, our movements and what we were doing started taking on a pattern. A series of roads connected FSB Pershing, 6 Alpha from Pershing to Trang Bang, then QL-1, which ran southeast to Cu Chi, where the 25th Division base camp was located, and on to Saigon. We got supplies at first by helicopter, and then someone decided to start sending supplies via truck out of Cu Chi. When the VC saw what we were doing, they started to mine the roads. After a few trucks got blown up, we had to escort the 65th Engineering Battalion every day to sweep the entire length of the road. Every day some platoon got assigned road security as their mission.

On the section between Trang Bang and FSB Pershing, we would send patrols out to escort the 65th Battalion engineers, and we would walk off and away from the road, usually a distance of 25 to 50 meters. They (VC) saw the pattern we were using, and we started getting sniper fire, and on occasion, they would try to ambush us. We usually sent out a platoon (25 men) to cover this assignment. We tried a really brilliant strategy where we had checkpoints along the route between Pershing and TB (about 3 miles) and were ordered to set up outposts manned by three men. We had an outpost at the far end near Trang Bang, one in the middle and one closer to Pershing. We then swung two-foot patrols that would loop between the far end to the middle and return, and the other patrol would start near Pershing, look to the center, and return. Unfortunately, the VC jumped our far outpost on December 12th, killing our platoon leader and two of my friends.

Then came January 11.

I turned and yelled, "What just happened? What just happened?"

The reply confirmed the sergeant's fear. "Doc Solomon stepped on a mine. He's dead."

Lieutenant Sheehan recalled that day.

> *The guy that I knew as Solomon was in the road on a medcap, serving the Vietnamese who came to the road as the Engineer's support vehicles followed behind the mine sweep team. After he stepped on a mine, I went to the road with my RTO and a few others. There was a large crater in the red earth from a sandbag mine intended for a vehicle, probably similar to the one that got me several months later. Those sandbag mines were often triggered by a homemade "little bamboo box" made from a couple of opposing segments of bamboo wrapped with bare wire. I don't think that there was a lot of quality control. The device required a large bag of ammonium nitrate fertilizer, a little C4 plastered around an electrical blasting cap buried in the middle of the fertilizer, and a D-sized battery or a couple of cells of an AN-PRC-25 battery. It seemed to me that there was a disabled jeep on the south side of the crater, but I can't be sure of that, as my mind apparently focused on the image of Solomon's body.*

"Most of the guys loved the medics (docs) because they are unarmed, and they will put their lives on the line anytime," said Sergeant Krause. "We lost LOTS of medics while I was there. Leavy was even-tempered, polite, and easy to get along with. He was only with us for about four months. Then, just like that, death strikes out. It's quick and merciless this time but painful nonetheless. He was a good kid who did his job without fear and reservation. Like all the good Joes, he will be missed by us."

Leavy Solomon's funeral was held on January 26, 1969, at Ramah Baptist in Palmetto.

"We had never been to a funeral where they shot the guns," said Alice Reese. "We had never been through anything like that. My brother, he couldn't take it. He left the cemetery."

Leavy's father, Willie, had agreed to keep his son's car for him until he returned. Now he had a reminder of his lost son in the driveway every day.

***Born**: October 3, 1946*
***Home of record**: Palmetto, Georgia*
***Died**: January 11, 1969, in Hau Nghia province of South Vietnam*
***Coweta servicemen who died in the same province**: Donald Lowery*
***Unit on death**: HHC, 2nd Battalion, 12th Infantry, 25th Infantry Division*
***Decorations:** Bronze Star, Purple Heart, Good Conduct Medal, National Defense Service Medal, Vietnam Service Medal, Vietnam Campaign Medal*
***Buried:** Palmetto Cemetery, Palmetto*
***Vietnam Memorial, Washington, DC:** Panel 35W Line 73*

Sources
Interview with Alice Reese, cousin
Interview with Ralph Brown, cousin
Interview with Leonard Lipscomb, childhood friend
Email interview with Arnold Krause, US Army

References
Coffelt Database, "Leavy Solomon." Accessed March 17, 2022. http://coffeltdatabase.org/index.php

CHAPTER NINETEEN

Edgar Stevan Pittman

Moreland, Georgia

It was like a big hole. He was missing. He was more like my brother than my nephew. After he passed away, I would have dreams about him. We all missed him. Mom and Dad and his mom, it was really hard for them.

Linda Carroll Fleming

Stevan Pittman was excited but anxious. He walked slowly around the block to the local 7-Eleven store directly behind the home in College Park, a place he had become so familiar with over the past few years. His cousin, Aubrey Boswell, walked silently alongside him. He and Aubrey had become buddies over these past few years, and Stevan would miss him. Aubrey's parents, Harold and Alice Boswell, walked a little ahead, holding hands. They had been extraordinarily generous with their nephew, and they were preparing to say farewell. They had signed the papers to allow their Stevan to join the Army at age seventeen, but it didn't mean they liked it.

The Vietnam War had raged since 1965, yet Stevan had talked about joining the Army for the past year, virtually nonstop. Three of his uncles had joined the Navy, and it was his turn to enlist. He wouldn't be joining the Navy, however. He had joined the US Army in September 1966 instead of being drafted. Now it was March 1967, and it was time to go. The bus to Fort Benning stopped at this particular 7-Eleven. It was so convenient that it appeared to be Stevan's destiny. Finally, the bus pulled up, and everyone hugged Stevan. A tear streamed down Alice's face. Stevan stepped up and into the bus, and with a quick wave, he was gone.

Edgar Stevan Pittman was born to Raymond Pittman and nineteen-year-old Myrtle Carroll of Moreland, Georgia. Myrtle had married Raymond Pittman in the fall of 1948 and moved from Moreland to Newnan. Three months later, Myrtle left Raymond and returned home to her parents. However, she took something home with her from that marriage—a pregnancy that resulted in the birth of Edgar Stevan Pittman, named Edgar after his grandfather, in September of 1949.

In the fall of 1940, Edgar Carroll and his brother, Auvie Harvie Carroll, went to Newnan to register for the draft. In 1940, draft registration was required of all men between twenty-one and forty-five. Auvie was registered without incident; his draft card was dated November 14, 1940. However, when the draft board spoke with Edgar, they discovered he had five children. The man registering the brothers told Edgar to go home and said he already had a war to fight!

Auvie, however, was called up and served in the Army during World War II; Edgar never heard from the draft board again. Congress had passed the first peacetime draft in American history on September 16, 1940, and draft registration began shortly afterward. The first draftees entered service in mid-November 1940.

When Stevan finally made his appearance in the Carroll home nine months after the return of Myrtle, it was already crowded. Several children of various ages were already clamoring for attention. Myrtle's father, Edgar Lee Carroll, was a sharecropper when Stevan was born but started working as a carpenter shortly afterward.

"We didn't think of it as sharecropping. We just thought of it as living on so-and-so's place and farming," said Eddie Carroll, Stevan's uncle, who was five years younger than Stevan. "He (Stevan) wanted to help before he was big enough to help with the farming. Stevan wasn't big enough to hold the hoe up, but he said, 'If you get me a little hoe, I'll help cop [chop].'"

Myrtle's mother, Lessie Pearl, managed the home. Eventually, she and Edgar would produce nine children: Myrtle, Amy, Betty, Benny, Bobby, Millard (Dicky), Linda, Grace, and Eddie. Stevan was born between Grace and Eddie, so while Eddie was five years younger, he was actually Stevan's uncle.

The family loved Stevan. His grandfather Edgar and his aunt Amy teased him by calling him Riddles Barlow, a goofy character in the Snuffy Smith comic strip. They often referred to him as "Barlow Man." The other children had fun with him in different ways. They repeatedly tried to get him to say "butter biscuit" as he was learning to talk, but it would come out as "bum bididly," which would send them into paroxysms of laughter. His favorite food was cornbread and syrup, which seemed ridiculous to the other children.[1] The kids loved to play tricks on him by "putting sugar on the most awful things," said Linda, and then watching him eat it.

Occasionally, though, there were some scares. When Stevan was nine months old, some of the family headed to Hogansville to see their grandmother, Stevan's great-grandmother. Edgar drove, Lessie Pearl and Edgar's sister Alice (Stevan's aunt Alice) sat in the middle and passenger seats, and Grace sat in her mother's lap. There were no laws about child seats or seat belts in those days, and few cars had them. Amy, Betty, Linda, and Stevan all sat in the back seat. Linda climbed up the back of the front seat, trying to look over it at Grace. Amy snatched her back and fussed at her. As the family went through Grantville, the car was struck by a drunk driver. Without restraints of any kind, the results were devastating. Three-year-old Grace had a broken back. Linda couldn't use her arms for a few days but gradually recovered. Stevan had a broken collarbone. Lessie's leg was severely broken, and doctors on the scene thought it might have to be amputated. Instead, they sent her to Piedmont Atlanta, where they saved her leg.

Lessie had an extended hospital stay. Linda said she remembers seeing her mother in Atlanta and was amazed by all the bright lights in the city. Lessie finally returned home with a cast on her leg, and Grace ended up in a full-body cast. Linda had to see the doctor in Newnan a week later, and it was the first time she had ever been to a doctor's office. She was five years old.

Stevan was raised as a typical country boy. His life consisted of chores, play, and mischief. He liked fishing and guns.

Eddie Carroll and Stevan played with a BB gun in the yard. Eddie would hold up a piece of linoleum, and Stevan would shoot it with his BB gun. "He was a pretty good shot," said Eddie. So Stevan hit it then hit it again and again as it got smaller. "He was a little older than me, so he talked me into holding it, and it was really tiny. The last time he hit me on the fingernail, it turned all black, something I think about and laugh about today. He wasn't being mean or anything. He just thought he could hit it."

One of Stevan's aunts, Linda, was four and a half when he was born. "He grew up like my brother, and he was the first person that I ever lost," she said. "It was very hard. He enjoyed making people proud of him. He would always work hard."

Stevan didn't appear to have much of a relationship with his father, and when Stevan was still very young, his mother remarried. When Stevan was ten, the family moved to a home between Grantville and Moreland. The house had three rooms and few amenities, though his grandfather added a bathroom. Myrtle and her new husband, Johnny Landrum, moved to Moreland after the family set up shop in the new house, living with them then moving to First Avenue in Newnan. Their first child, Stevan's half sister, Carol, was born there.

Stevan's new stepfather, Johnny Landrum, was described by family members as a funny guy who laughed a lot. Johnny worked with Myrtle's dad in his carpentry business. Stevan bounced around between the Carroll family's home in Moreland and his mother and stepfather's home in Newnan. He attended Atkinson Elementary School, not far from his parents' home on First Avenue.

When he visited Moreland, he liked to sit on the porch with his aunts and uncles and wave at cars as they whizzed by. Bobby, Dicky, Linda, Grace, and Eddie were all there. He enjoyed going on dates with Linda and her boyfriend but eventually wore out his welcome with the boyfriend, Pete. Linda recalled the time she and Pete took Steven along to a local mill with a waterfall and stunning scenery. The next time they went, Pete didn't want to take Stevan. She said Stevan stood on the porch when they left, looking melancholy. Stevan didn't lessen Pete's attraction to Linda, however, as she and Pete would marry in due course.

When Stevan was a young teen, his life took a peculiar turn. He went to live with his aunt Alice and uncle Harold in a two-story Victorian-style home in College Park. His parents were struggling, his grandparents were overwhelmed, and he still visited Moreland a great deal. Alice had always loved her nieces and nephews and enjoyed spoiling them. They returned her affection. Harold worked with his oldest son, Jimmy, as a contractor. Alice worked at Autolite Battery. Jimmy was already married and had a little girl. Harold and Alice's younger son, Aubrey, was about Stevan's age. The two would become fast friends, but it didn't start that way.

Aubrey admitted that he was initially jealous of his parents' attention to Stevan. His older brother was gone, and Aubrey was the only child in the house until Stevan arrived. He had to share his room with Stevan, which he resented. It took him about six months to accept the new situation.

Nevertheless, once Aubrey got over his jealousy, he relates that he and Stevan did everything together. They rode bikes. They loved to play with little toy soldiers. "I think that was one reason he may have joined the Army," explained Aubrey. They wrestled nonstop and fought like brothers.

"I have nothing but fond memories," Aubrey said. "We were just really close. You saw one of us, and you saw both of us. He was not a single bit of trouble as a child. He was always so grateful for my parents taking him in that he was always respectful and never gave us any trouble."

Except once. Aubrey's brother Jimmy and his wife, Gloria, lived with them off and on during these years. Suddenly, there was a baby stroller in the house. Aubrey and Stevan's bedroom window opened onto the home's roof. Stevan dared Aubrey to push the baby carriage off the top of the house. Aubrey's mother, Alice, was the home's disciplinarian and was unhappy about the baby carriage.

"That was the first whipping I ever got," Aubrey said.

Cathy Boswell was Jimmy's daughter, and Alice and Harold were Cathy's grandparents. She was about ten years younger than Aubrey and Stevan. "I just remember feeling like I had two older brothers," she said. Of course, the two older brothers loved to harass the younger girl. There was a huge oak tree in the Boswells' front yard, and the boys thought it was funny to climb the tree and leave Cathy crying at the bottom. Cathy got some payback when her mom invariably came out and yelled at them to get out of the tree.

Cathy also remembered Stevan and Aubrey using shovels to dig a storm shelter in the backyard. The Boswells might have believed that the sanctuary could double as a fallout shelter in case of nuclear war with the USSR. Consequently, the family canned a lot of food and kept it in that location.

The two boys walked to school about two blocks away. Stevan was never fond of school and didn't do particularly well. After attending Russell High School for a year and a half, he left during his sophomore year and never returned. His obituary claims that he also attended Newnan High School, although there is no evidence of that.

By the time Stevan turned seventeen, he had grown into a tall, slender, lanky young man with slightly blond hair and a contagious smile. He stood five eleven and weighed 155 pounds.

"He was always skinny as a beanpole and never gained an ounce," Aubrey said. "It used to make me so mad he could eat whatever he wanted, and it didn't affect him. I could look at a candy bar and gain weight."

According to his obituary, Stevan worked at Coweta General Hospital on Hospital Road during this time. Despite his hospital work, Stevan had started smoking by the time he was seventeen, which was not uncommon in 1966; smoking was portrayed in advertisements and movies as something that made a person cool, popular with the young ladies, and invincible. Eventually, the health risks of smoking would become more commonly known, but the government didn't place warnings on cigarette packs until 1969. When Stevan Pittman walked to the 7-Eleven to meet the bus that day in 1966, he probably wanted a cigarette very badly. He might have also had something else weighing on him—a neighborhood girl he had met while living with the Boswells.

While the young lady's name remains a mystery, Cathy Boswell insisted that he asked this woman to marry him after entering the military and while he was home on leave.

Stevan went to Fort Benning for his Basic Training. Once finished, he was sent to Fort Polk, Louisiana, for Advanced Infantry Training. This was the standard route for an infantryman on the path to Vietnam. Stevan Pittman was not trained as an infantryman at Fort Polk but rather had the MOS of a tactical wire operations specialist. He would run communication wire for his assigned unit.

"We hoped it would give him a good start. He loved the Army," said Linda Carroll.

According to his military records, he got orders to Germany as part of the NATO forces instead of going to Vietnam. NATO was the dream assignment of every soldier during this time. It's unclear whether Stevan was promised a duty slot in Germany if he joined or if he just ended up there. He was stationed at Nellingen Kaserne, a World War II Luftwaffe base near Stuttgart, converted by American forces stationed in Germany. Assigned to the Headquarters Company of the 94th Engineering Battalion, he worked in communications for the company. He arrived in Germany in August of 1967 and stayed there for the next sixteen months. While there, he finished his schooling and was awarded his GED in 1968.

Stevan made a momentous decision at Nellingen. Aubrey Boswell pointed out that Stevan liked Germany and wrote that he was planning to reenlist—early. "He felt like he needed to go back in and help," Aubrey said.

At the end of April 1968, Stevan reenlisted in the Army for three years and would be eligible to get out in April 1971. Why he enlisted then instead of later is a mystery. Some of his family thought he got leave during Christmas because he reenlisted. Perhaps that was the case, as he signed his name and returned home in December. He thought he would return to Nellingen, but he would never see that base again.[2]

Exactly when Stevan Pittman realized that he wouldn't be going back to Germany after his leave is unclear. At some point, he received his orders for Vietnam. This may have been when Stevan asked the young lady to marry him. It is also probable that this was when he began visiting a church. Aubrey Boswell said that Stevan wasn't real religious as a teenager. He didn't go to church and wasn't interested in the Bible. Despite this, Eddie Carroll believes that Stevan started thinking he might not make it home from Vietnam, started going to church, and eventually accepted Jesus as his Savior. Stevan's obituary says, "He was a member of the New Hope Baptist Church," which is still in Coweta County.

"He wanted to be a chaplain but didn't have the education for that," said Linda Carroll. "While he was in Vietnam, he sent a big family Bible to his church, and that just made us happy that he was living a good life."

In January 1969, Stevan arrived and started his one-year tour in

South Vietnam. He was assigned to A Company of the 20th Engineer Battalion, 937th Engineering Group, located along the coast of South Vietnam in the city of Qui Nhon. The Vietnam War was at the dawn of a change in strategy. Richard Nixon's inauguration that month as the nation's thirty-seventh president brought a plan to get American boys out of Vietnam. Nixon called it "Vietnamization," which involved the gradual movement of American troops out of the country while turning over the responsibilities for the defense of the country to the military forces of South Vietnam, the Army of the Republic of Vietnam or ARVN. Stevan Pittman had no idea that he would become one of the early American victims of this new strategy.

In his book *The Phantom of Ben Het*, the author, Sergeant James Lamerson, said he didn't believe Vietnamization would work. He quoted the Military Assistance Command Vietnam (MACV) as having predicted in a report to President Nixon that the ARVN "could not now, or in the foreseeable future, handle both VC and sizable NVA forces without US combat support." Nixon, however, facing an increasingly hostile Congress and population, chose to ignore the report and plunge ahead with his plan to extricate the United States from Vietnam.

It is unclear when Stevan Pittman arrived at the Special Forces Camp called Ben Het, not far from Dak To. Ben Het was near the convergence of South Vietnam, Laos, and Cambodia and not far from the notorious Ho Chi Minh Trail. It sat astride a route for the North Vietnamese Army to enter South Vietnam from the Ho Chi Minh Trail. Initially, the camp consisted of twelve US Army Green Berets, a twelve-man ARVN Special Forces team, and a five-hundred-man Civilian Irregular Defense Group (CIDG) of Montagnard mercenaries. During the first few months of 1969, the camp could count on being reinforced by American soldiers if necessary. In April, however, responsibility for the base was passed to the ARVN as part of the Vietnamization program. American artillery was still in range if needed. Dak To held the largest group of artillery pieces and had five hundred American combat engineers stationed there.

In May and June of 1969, the most likely time of Stevan's move to this area, the North Vietnamese had begun massing and menacing both Dak To and Ben Het. The South Vietnamese forces designated to keep the road open between the two bases and assist when needed gradually abandoned the Americans in both places, leaving them to the mercy of the North Vietnamese. By mid June, Ben Het had been surrounded by the North Vietnamese, who had code-named it Dien Bien Phu and proceeded to make sure everyone knew that they had done so by putting it out on loudspeakers near the camp. (The battle of Dien Bien Phu, 1954, was fought between French and Viet Minh forces, the forerunner to the North Vietnamese Army. The French were surrounded and forced to surrender. France withdrew from Vietnam a few months later.)

The 937th Engineering Group hauled construction materials and airfield matting, which was used to construct airfield runways, from Dak To to Ben Het. Stevan might have been involved with this work but certainly ran communication wire wherever needed. He likely worked with the artillery batteries stationed there as well. Larry Thomas was an artilleryman in one of the three artillery batteries assigned to Ben Het and said:

> *As I recall, there were approximately three different artillery batteries at Ben Het, so we were not all together or from the same unit and spread apart as well. There were some Green Berets and some Montagnard forces as well. We spent most days in a bunker or different shelters where we slept. We were even gassed, sent in, I assume by mortars.* [That was CS gas, also known as Tear Gas.] *Phantom jets provided support by dropping bombs outside the perimeter, as well as Cobra gunship helicopters providing fire support. Some days we scrounged for something to eat and we collected water by digging a hole to insert our rubber ponchos to catch water from rain or moisture so we could wash and brush our teeth. We laughed, told jokes or stories about home or just bitched about our predicament. We caught a nap when we could.*

The Carroll family received mail from Stevan about what he was doing and the friends he'd made. He sent pictures of himself exercising and talked about building up his muscles.

"He just wanted us to be proud of him, and we were," said Linda. "He was working hard and trying hard."

The family wrote to him as well and passed along their love. If he mentioned anything to his family about his predicament at Ben Het, they don't recall it. His aunt Amy recalled getting a letter from him suggesting that he might stop to see her and her husband in Reno, Nevada, when he got home from Vietnam. Amy's husband worked for the National Forest Service there. She immediately wrote back to encourage him to visit and sent a package of goodies. Unfortunately, he would never make it to Reno.

June 23 dawned, and the camp was shrouded in fog. There was little drinking water available; the men drank beer for breakfast. There were an estimated 1,500 to 2,000 North Vietnamese troops outside the camp. They dug tunnels and trenches on the north hill of the camp and had gotten close to the bunkers. The artillery, mortar, and rocket fire were constant. There was even danger from the dud shells that buried themselves in the soil of the camp. It could be catastrophic if something or someone hit them the wrong way. The bunker that Larry Thomas had been assigned to had been attacked and destroyed early that morning. A convoy had successfully broken through the roadblock to the camp and had delivered ammunition and other supplies. The Army told the family that Stevan was running communication wire that day.

The MACV summary of that day reads:

> *Kontum Province. The I FFV [1st Field Force-Vietnam] fire support base collocated with the Republic of Vietnam Civilian Irregular Defense Group (CIDG) camp at Ben Het (280 miles NNE of Saigon) received 195 rounds of 85mm artillery, 120mm, 50mm, and 82mm mortar and recoilless rifle fire. Less than 3 of the 82mm mortar rounds contained a CS-type riot control agent. Light casualties, no damage.*

The "light casualties" on June 23, 1969, meant Edgar Stevan Pittman. He was the only one killed at Ben Het that day. There may have been "no damage" to Ben Het, but the damage reverberates to this day in Pittman's family.

Alice and Harold Boswell were the first family members to see the Army sedan pull up in their drive. Cathy Boswell said her parents, Jimmy and Gloria, were devastated, and her mother fainted. "She had always referred to Steve and Aubrey as her boys," said Cathy.

When her mother regained consciousness, she kept repeating, "My boy, my boy."

The car left and took the chilling news to Moreland and the Carroll family. The vehicle then proceeded to find Stevan's father. According to Bo Brown, Stevan's nephew, his grandfather remembered two cars rolling up to the home. Raymond Pittman had served in Korea and knew immediately that this wasn't a social visit. However, while aware that Stevan was in the Army, Pittman hadn't been aware that Stevan was in Vietnam. Initially, he thought there had been a training accident and that Stevan might have been injured. The men from the US Army quickly dispelled that notion, and Raymond headed over to see Myrtle. He was the first one to reach her with the news. When Raymond told her, she fainted, and he caught her before she hit the floor.

"It was like a big hole," said Linda. "He was missing. After he passed away, I would have dreams about him. We all missed him. Mom and Dad and his mom, it was really hard for them." She said most of the family went to her sister's house, and Myrtle was in shock. Family members from his father's side came, which was hard because they hadn't been in his life up to that point.

It took a few weeks for Stevan's body to return to Moreland. The body eventually went to the Carroll residence, where a soldier stayed with it.[3] Stevan was almost unrecognizable. The explosion and the mortar shrapnel had severely damaged his body. A wig hid the shrapnel wounds on his head. Instead of a closed casket funeral, the Army put plexiglass atop the casket so that no one could reach out and touch the body but could still see it. The first time Linda went up to the casket, she collapsed. Her husband, Pete, caught her before she landed on the floor.

As a child, Stevan had cut his lip in an accident, leaving a scar. That was how the family could distinguish that it was him. For younger family members, however, seeing him was terrifying.

Cathy Boswell can still recall the casket in the home and the church. "I couldn't understand what was in the casket," she said. "It didn't look like Steve, and there was glass over the casket." Her most vivid memory is of constantly being told, "Don't lean on the glass."

A full military funeral was held at First Baptist Church in Moreland. It was heart-wrenching. The military gave the flag to his half sister, Carol. He was buried in Southview Cemetery in Moreland, and his mother, Myrtle, had a photograph put on the tombstone. Inexplicably, someone later tore it off, cutting the families like a knife, although the photograph was later replaced.

"He was a guy, he was a regular guy, but he was a tender person, and we loved him a lot," Linda said.

Edgar Carroll had lost his first grandchild in December of 1968 in a gun accident. Benny's son was target shooting when a bullet ricocheted and killed him. Tragedy struck the family again six months later when they lost a second grandson, Stevan.

"It was not a good year for us," said Linda. But it didn't end there. Stevan had given Linda's daughter, Kelly, a cross necklace when she was a baby, and it was stolen ten years later in a burglary. "That hurt because it was precious to us."

"My grandfather never got over his death. It broke his heart to the end of his life," said Stevan's nephew, Bo Brown.

Linda has visited the Vietnam Memorial in Washington, DC. "It is kind of an overwhelming thing. You have a lot of emotions. But I felt pride that he had been willing to give his life for our country because that is why we are here now, because of men like him."

When Edgar Stevan Pittman was killed at Ben Het, he was nineteen years old.

**See end notes in the appendix for additional details.*

***Born**: September 28, 1949*
***Home of record**: Moreland, Georgia*
***Died**: June 23, 1969, in Kontum province of South Vietnam*
***Coweta servicemen who died in the same province**: Tommy Huddleston and Arthur Hines*
***Unit on Death**: A CO, 20th ENG BN, 937th ENG Group, 18th ENG BDE*

Decorations: *Purple Heart, National Defense Service Medal, Vietnam Service Medal, Vietnam Campaign Medal*
Buried: *Southview Cemetery, Moreland*
Vietnam Memorial, Washington, DC: *Panel 21W Line 1*

Sources
Interview with Aubrey Boswell, cousin
Interview with Cathy Boswell Craven, second cousin
Interview with Eddie Carroll, uncle
Interview with Linda Carroll Fleming, aunt
Interview with Bo Brown, nephew
Email interview with Larry Thomas, 3rd Battalion, 6th Artillery, 52nd Artillery Group
Correspondence with Amy Carroll Schoneskeck, aunt
Assistance from Tim Carroll, second cousin

References
Lamerson, John D. *The Phantom of Ben Het.* Lamerson Publishing, 2001
SOFREP. "Battle for Ben Het Special Forces A-Camp June 23, 1969." Accessed November 30, 2021.
The 1/92nd Field Artillery Association-Vietnam. "Ben Het/Dak To. May-July 1969." Accessed November 30, 2021. http://www.bravecannons.org/History/hist_benhet.html
HistoryNet. "Paving the Way for American's Fighting Forces." Accessed November 30, 2021. https://www.historynet.com/paving-way-americas-fighting-forces.htm
Coffelt Database, "Edgar Pittman." Accessed December 2, 2021. http://coffeltdatabase.org/index.php

Stevan Pittman, dates unknown.

Photos courtesy of Linda Fleming.

CHAPTER TWENTY

Larry Gunnel Pinson

Grantville, Georgia

Larry G. Pinson, he was from Georgia. Grantville, Georgia. Wow. I will never forget that. He used to love that place.

—Peace Foxx

It was a Friday night in the fall of 1966. The Central High School team in Newnan played football that evening in Rome, Georgia. The defensive end for the Panthers was an eleventh-grade lad whose pals called him by his middle name, Gunnel. He had just gone out for football that year, and this was his first season on the gridiron. What he lacked in experience, he made up for in hustle and determination.

"He listened to what the coach told him to do," said teammate Rayford Patterson. "He hustled all the time. He was a good football player."

The legendary Henry Seldon coached the Central High School Panthers.

"He tried to treat everyone fairly," Patterson recalled. "He didn't do a lot of hollering. If you made a mistake, he would just take you out and let you watch. Sometimes you can learn more just by watching than by being in the mix. That is the way he coached."

Seldon had seen something he liked in Gunnel Pinson, so the young man was on the field that Friday evening in Rome. Until he wasn't.

"He got clipped from behind," said Patterson.

Gunnel went down, and the coaches rushed onto the field. It was instantly apparent that he was in terrible pain. Once the coaches examined the injury, they were horrified to find his leg broken. Gunnel was rushed to the hospital and stayed the weekend in Rome.

"I didn't think he would come back," Patterson said, but Gunnel Pinson did come back.

Barham Lundy's eyes flashed as he spoke. "The males in his family were men," said the Grantville native. "He had an uncle who could pick up the back of a car, back then when cars were cars! They were a family of giants. There were no wimps in that family. You understand what I'm saying?"

Born on January 27, 1950, Larry Gunnel Pinson of Grantville was the oldest child of Jimmy and Geraldine Pinson. Both his grandfather and his father worked on the railroad. Lundy recalled them as men who "worked, drank, and partied hard. After they had a few drinks, the 'this is what I can do' challenges began, and they often involved picking up a car."

Gunnel was followed by five other children, four sisters and one brother: Joyce, Johnny, Brenda, Linda, and Walline. As the oldest child, Gunnel was the role model for his siblings and was often responsible for them while their parents worked.

"He was a great mentor. He watched over us so well," his sister Brenda said. "Even when he was young, he had great responsibilities because he was the oldest. So all of us knew we had a brother we could depend on."

Family members took their Christianity seriously. As everyone gathered around the dinner table, with their father at the head and Gunnel at the other end, they blessed the food as a family, one of the "precious moments" that Brenda recalled. All of the children had to quote a Bible verse. And being the oldest had its perks, as Gunnel always got to choose the piece of chicken he desired.

Brenda described Gunnel as loving, tenderhearted, watchful, and quiet, with great character and integrity. One day, Geraldine had made cornbread but needed to go to the store before it finished baking. She told Gunnel to make sure it didn't burn. He reassured her that the cornbread was in good hands, but everyone got busy doing their own thing, and the cornbread burned. Gunnel took the cornbread out of the oven, and the top was completely black.

"He started scraping the top, but that didn't work," Brenda said. Finally, he stopped and thought a moment, desperately trying to find a solution before their mother returned home. He turned and looked at his siblings. "Y'all, everybody pray."

They stared at him. He prayed. They all prayed.

He was terrified of getting in trouble, Brenda said, and when Geraldine returned, she smelled the burned cornbread. Gunnel was honest and told her what had happened. To Geraldine's credit, though annoyed, she didn't physically punish Gunnel or put him on restriction but simply lectured him about responsibility.

As Gunnel moved into his teenage years, he was a "go-getter," according to both Barham Lundy and Gunnel's sister Brenda. "There was nothing he didn't think he could do," Brenda said.

As a teen, Gunnel was tall and good-looking. He cut quite a figure at Central High School but was also a good student, and all his teachers seemed to like him. He made certain that the young men treated his teenage sister correctly as she matured. Brenda said he treated his girlfriend, Miss Joan Strickland, like he expected his sister to be treated, and they dated throughout high school.

"He was head over heels about Joan," she said. The couple planned to marry after his stint in the military. Brenda still considers Joan to be her sister-in-law even though she and Gunnel never married.

Gunnel recovered from the compound fracture he suffered in Rome in the fall of 1966. He returned in the fall of 1967 to his defensive end spot and was again a solid football player for Coach Seldon and the Central High School Panthers. The 1967 season was the best that Central had ever put together; they went undefeated during the regular season and made it to the state semifinals. The Panthers hosted the game at Drake Stadium, losing to Spencer High School of Columbus 25-14. It was the only blemish on their record.

Gunnel's parents set rules that all the children had to abide by, regardless of age. There were a few exceptions. When Gunnel went to his senior prom, he got home late. He knocked on the window of the bedroom that he and Johnny shared, hoping to get his brother's attention so Johnny would open the window. His mother, a light sleeper, heard the commotion and got up to see what was happening. When she realized the situation, she helped her son through the window so he could avoid his father's anger. Brenda remembered how happy he was the following day and how he told everyone about his great time the evening before. Fortunately, Jimmy Pinson never found out about the nighttime shenanigans.

When Gunnel graduated from Central High School in 1968, he didn't have money to go to college, and his football career was behind him. Facing the draft and after talking to recruiters who visited Central, he joined the Marine Corps along with his cousin, Willie James Pinson, and the quarterback on the 1967 team, Sammy Davis. Gunnel left immediately after graduation and was at Parris Island and in Basic Training by the first week of June 1968. From Parris Island, he moved to Advanced Training at Camp Lejeune. Gunnel was trained with an MOS of 0351, antitank assault man, today called an infantry assault man. The assault man was a regular infantryman but was also trained to use rockets and explosives to destroy tanks and bunkers. Gunnel's weapons training wrapped up toward the end of October 1968, and he received his thirty-day leave. The day he left Grantville for Vietnam was an emotional one for the Pinson family.

"We all cried," said Brenda. Gunnel hugged and reassured everyone that he would be back and would stay in touch while he was gone. Their parents "shed a few tears that day," Brenda said.

By the first week of December, Gunnel was in Vietnam, assigned to H&S Company, 3rd Battalion, 1st Marines in Quang Nam Province of I Corps. He had little in-country training or downtime. According to his military records, he started his tour on December 9, 1968, and on December 10, he "participated in combat operations against insurgent communist forces in RVN (Republic of Vietnam; South Vietnam)." This was likely during the early stages of Operation Taylor Common he also participated in the operation's final phase, from January 27 until February 14, 1969. Operation Taylor Common was an extensive search and destroy mission undertaken by the First Marine Division. Their goal was to clear the An Hoa area of I Corps of enemy combatants and develop a series of fire support bases, making it difficult for the North Vietnamese Army to infiltrate South Vietnam from the Ho Chi Minh Trail in Laos.

Gunnel's military records showed that he was also involved in Operation Oklahoma Hills from March 31 until May 11. Similar to Taylor Common, this operation was in a different part of the Quang Nam province. The Marines destroyed two base camps of North Vietnamese Army troops without significant fighting. Forty-four

Marines were killed, and more than nine hundred Marines suffered combat or non-combat-related injuries.

From the end of May until mid-September, Pinson was a part of Operation Pipestone Canyon. This operation included South Korean and ARVN troops and was designed to clear Go Noi Island, south of Danang, of communist insurgents. The island had been nicknamed Dodge City because of trouble found there. By November, the enemy forces had been eliminated from the island.

During September, the 3rd Battalion continued to conduct assigned combat operations in Quang Nam Province.

"He came in young, naive, ready to kick some butt. Typical. I was the same way," said Peace Foxx, Marine buddy of Gunnel Pinson. The antitank MOS gave the officers in the field flexibility as far as where they might use him; it gave them a variety of choices, including one that brought him and Foxx together.

> *It's been a long time since I met a brother straight from the world that fell into this "Hell's Paradise" with the heaviness of a true brother. All you needed was someone to bring this light closer to the surface for you. I guess "Bro Foxx" was the chosen one.*
> —*Anonymous, from Gunnel Pinson's* The View of Vietnam *photograph album*

Peace Foxx had arrived in Vietnam in late August 1968, approximately three months before Pinson. He had become proficient with an M-60 machine gun. Foxx and Pinson were from different backgrounds yet meshed almost immediately. Gunnel was from a large family and a rural setting; Peace was from the city and had been homeless and on the street since he was fourteen.

"Gunnel kept me going for a long time because he constantly wanted information from me. I was the street kid, and he was the country bumpkin. He wanted to be cool, just like me. Like I was cool or something," Foxx said with a hint of sarcasm. Pinson and Foxx followed similar paths through the Marine Corps. Gunnel had become an antitank assault man then was moved to the M-60 machine gun. Peace had been trained in mortars then moved to the M-60.

Foxx remembered the day his platoon sergeant came to see him with Pinson in tow. The sergeant told him, "I got a new assistant gunner for you." In Vietnam, a machine gun crew consisted of a gunner, an assistant gunner, and typically at least one or two ammo bearers. Gunnel fed the ammunition into the weapon as an assistant gunner while Foxx fired it. Because of his responsibility, he would always be nearby if the gun was needed in a hurry. Foxx was also responsible for teaching the assistant gunner how to use the gun so that the assistant could take it over at any time and in any situation. For example, Foxx taught Pinson to find where the most fire was coming from, dump a load into that area, then move before the enemy could concentrate their fire on the gun. Foxx found that Gunnel absorbed these lessons quickly. During the next six weeks, the two bonded.

> *He was always trying to keep us up, you know? He was always trying to crack some kind of joke, some stupid joke, we'd all start laughing, and he had this big body shake laugh, you know. He was well-trusted and well-liked. We were told before we went there that we couldn't get too close to people, but in fact, you had to in order to help you survive what we were going through. We had to have a camaraderie that went beyond anything... I couldn't find that here if I tried. We were brothers.*

That was how soldiers in war had described themselves since the beginning of time. That ideal undeniably held true in Vietnam when soldiers were in combat, but they were frequently separated by race once the shooting stopped. With the Civil Rights Movement dividing the country back home, African American soldiers in Vietnam felt that the other Blacks in their unit were really their brothers. The Black Marines in Pinson's unit called each other by a shortened version of that word; they just called each other "Bro."

In Gunnel's *The View of Vietnam* photograph album, which he had with him in Vietnam and finally made its way back to his family, other Black Marines wrote messages to him like high school students write in each other's yearbook. Even though these young Marines weren't far from high school age, their comments reflected a more mature, almost visceral message that would never be found in a high school yearbook. The Civil Rights Movement was at its height and had been rocked six months before the start of Gunnel's tour in Vietnam by the assassination of Martin Luther King. African Americans were fighting to end segregation, voter suppression, and discrimination in virtually all areas of American society. Yet here they were, half a world away, fighting for someone else's freedom from oppression.

> *The time that we have been over here together, look back upon it, Bro, every once in a while. You never thought of a relationship like this outside of your family. We've learned how to appreciate more, how important our life is, and how the lives of your loved ones are so much a part of your life. It's a shame that you have to experience a war before you finally realize how important your life is... you learned a lot from me, and I definitely learned some things from you. When you first got here, you can almost say that you were taken under my wing. When I first got here, I was taken under some heavy brother's wing. Now Bro, now you can say to yourself, I'm one of the heaviest black brothers in the Nam. And when you slide to the world in a way, it won't be as much of a hassle as it was when you left the world. If I could, I would rap all through this book. But I'm going to be the good black brother that I am and draw this to a close...*
> *—Peace Foxx, from Gunnel Pinson's* The View of Vietnam *photograph album*

In due course, another squad lost a gunner, and the platoon sergeant went to Foxx to see if he thought Pinson was ready to step into this position. While Foxx hated to see Pinson go to another squad, he gave him a ringing endorsement. Gunnel had learned fast and knew how to use the gun; he wasn't just pulling the trigger as a kid might do with a video game. A gunner had to think about what they were doing, and Gunnel was the man for the job. Later that day, Gunnel ran to see Foxx, excited about getting his own gun.

Shortly afterward, the platoon was assigned security for five bridges, with Peace Foxx's squad on one of the bridges and

Gunnel's squad on the next one over. One afternoon, Foxx saw a group of enemy soldiers moving through the field between the two bridges. He was dumbfounded. They were in the open, making noise.

"They were worse than we were," Foxx said. Peace was so stunned that he froze. "It was like we weren't even there," he said. "Do you see what I am seeing?" he whispered over the radio to Gunnel.

Gunnel didn't even bother to answer. He just opened up with the M-60. Gunnel finally responded, "Just follow my tracers!"

Peace Foxx did as he was told.

This was Pinson's first action on the M-60, and he had proven that he was up to the job. A couple of tanks followed up in the field and along the wood line. They found blood trails and took maps from a couple of bodies. Typically after combat, Pinson and Foxx got together to talk—about home, family, girls, and other topics, but they didn't talk about the action itself. They allowed time for the adrenaline to bleed off.

Our time is growing short for us to get away from Charlie Cong (but it don't mean nothing), but we'll be going back to the free world on that shiny bird, you just keep the faith and spirit, and you'll overcome so until we meet again be smooth and keep the power. {Remember wherever you go, there you are.}
— Grant, from Gunnel Pinson's The View of Vietnam *photograph album*

Peace Foxx's last day in Vietnam is still seared into his memory. Although he was discouraged from going, he went down to Gunnel's bunker. Why take the chance? But he entered the bunker and greeted Gunnel. Soon, a "howling" began. They didn't know what it was and didn't want to deal with it. The Marines braced themselves. Soon, the "howling" source emerged from the tree line—three Vietnamese women talking loudly in their native tongue. The woman in the middle carried a sack that appeared heavy. The Marines came out of the bunker and demanded that the women stop. What was in the sack? Whatever was in there, it couldn't be good. Finally, the woman began to dump the bag's contents onto the ground. The Marines pulled their weapons up and trained them on the three women. Three dead infants, two to three months old, fell out onto the ground. They were full of shrapnel holes. The women wanted money as compensation for their deaths.

"That was the last thing I saw of the war," said Foxx.

Gunnel would have to deal with this now, Foxx thought as he turned to leave.

He has no recollection of getting home.

Back in Grantville, as the months dragged on, Gunnel's family waited and worried. He wrote letters to everyone, though he expressed his feelings to his mother the most. Regardless of the "brothers" he had made in Vietnam, he was desperately homesick. He told his mother how much he wanted to go home. By early September 1969, he was getting "short." He was three months away from returning home and looked forward to it.

September found Gunnel still on bridge security. Foxx had rotated home the month before. The bridges were on Highway 1, an east-to-west road that ran from Danang to Laos. The supplies that ran over these bridges—supplies headed to Marines and soldiers out on firebases and landing zones closer to the Ho Chi Minh Trail in Laos—caused the bridges to be invaluable. So one squad of twelve Marines kept watch at each of the five bridges.

The Marines set up their night security with two Marines on each end of the bridge. Marines weren't set up in a roadblock configuration but rather as a checkpoint. Two to three Marines in a jeep sped back and forth over the bridge. The three Marines in the jeep were the driver, a rifleman in a passenger seat, and a machine gunner. They were there to respond to anything at either end of the bridge. They also kept an eye on the river for floaters or swimmers trying to approach the bridge with explosives. The rest of the squad that wasn't on duty hung out under the bridge, talking, drinking coffee, or sleeping. Pinson would have tried to sleep during the day, as he would be up all night.

"He was one of the guys. He fit in well, and he did his job," said Bob Millison, who was in Pinson's squad. "When we went on patrol, he held up his end, you know. He was a Marine."

On September 19, 1969, the bridge that Gunnel's squad was responsible for guarding—Tango Bridge in Marine parlance—was attacked with mortars and rifle fire. Initially, confusion reigned. Then the Marines' training kicked in. Everything happened quickly, yet it seemed as if everything moved in slow motion. Marines ran for cover as the shells and gunfire converged on the area around the bridge. While it is unclear what position Gunnel was in at the time of the attack, it appears that he dove into the river, hoping to escape the fire. He had many pounds of equipment on him. The river had a powerful current and was swollen from recent rainfall. Gunnel Pinson, the country boy from Grantville, Georgia, disappeared into the water.

After the communist soldiers withdrew, the Marines took stock of who was injured and realized Gunnel wasn't there. The search for Gunnel began, and the Marines eventually requested a diving team from the Reconnaissance Battalion. As the next day dawned, the diving team finally arrived and started the search. An unattributed post on Find-a-Grave states, "On the evening of September 19th, a drowning was reported to have occurred at a bridge near the village of My An two kilometers northeast of Hill 37. A search was immediately initiated for the missing Marine. LCpl Larry Pinson's remains were found on September 22nd downriver from where he had gone missing." His military records confirm this information.

Gunnel Pinson's last letter home was on a reel-to-reel tape. He had a player, as did his family. Brenda saw the letter as a farewell. He encouraged his family to do right in life. She wondered why he said those things since he would be home soon. Did Gunnel have some sort of premonition? (The tape is still in the family's hands, in the reel-to-reel player they had in the 1960s. They can no longer get it to play.)

When the Marine Corps representatives and chaplain came to the Pinson home in Grantville, everyone rushed to the door. They were told their son and brother, Gunnel, was missing in action. Geraldine sent the children to their rooms. About a week later, the Marine Corps notified the family of Gunnel's death. Geraldine was in shock and couldn't believe that her son wouldn't be coming home. Gunnel's cousin, Willie Pinson, also in Vietnam, escorted the body home. However, the casket was to remain closed. Though Geraldine wanted to verify that it was her son, the Marine Corps denied her request to open the coffin.

Larry Gunnel Pinson's funeral was held at St. Paul's Christian Methodist Church in Lone Oak. Many of his classmates from Central High School attended. The family had an explanation from the military about what had happened, but they couldn't verify that it was Gunnel. Why wouldn't the Marines allow them to open the casket? Had a mortar round exploded in the water? Were there others in the water as well who caused identification complications? Gunnel was laid to rest in the cemetery at the church, where he rests today.[1]

"I used to ask why I am still here and Gunnel is not," said Foxx. He had resisted going to the Wall in Washington, DC, but his brother finally talked him into it. "I went to the Wall for the first time in 1984. I'll never forget it. I went there. I was hungover. That is the only way I could have gone." Foxx sighed. "I couldn't even open the book [that lists the location of the name being sought]. I looked at it, and I collapsed. I knew a lot of guys on that Wall, you know." All of Peace Foxx's frustration and pain bubbled to the surface. He asked his brother to look up Gunnel. "Larry G. Pinson, I said, 1969. He was from Georgia. Grantville, Georgia. Wow. I will never forget that. He used to love that place."

His brother found the name and assisted Foxx to Panel 18W Line 114. Foxx was disheveled, eyes full of tears and his nose running. He knelt on the ground near that panel. The memories washed over him.

After the funeral, Peace Foxx called Gunnel's sister Brenda to express his grief at Gunnel's tragic death. Brenda asked him a question that he did not anticipate: "What kind of person was my brother?"

Peace considered the question for a moment, and his emotions following Gunnel's loss and the year in Vietnam slowly bubbled to the surface, feelings that he had desperately tried to suppress. He began to cry.

**See end notes in the appendix for additional details.*

***Born**: January 27, 1950*
***Home of record**: Grantville, Georgia*
***Died**: September 19, 1969, in Quang Nam province of South*

Vietnam
Coweta servicemen who died in the same province*: Daniel Post, Bill Thomas, Mike Watson, and Jerry Smith*
Unit on death*: H & S CO, 3rd BN, 1st Marines, 1st Marine Division*
Decorations: *Purple Heart, National Defense Service Medal, Vietnam Service Medal, Republic of Vietnam Cross of Gallantry with Unit Palm, Vietnam Campaign Medal*
Buried: *St. Paul AME Church Cemetery, Meriwether County*
Vietnam Memorial, Washington, DC: *Panel 18W Line 114*

Sources
Interview with Barham Lundy, childhood friend
Interview with Brenda Pinson Clark, sister
Interview with Rayford Patterson, childhood friend
Interview with Bob Millison, USMC
Interview with Peace Foxx, USMC

References
Military History Fandom. "Operation Taylor Common." Accessed November 12, 2020. https://military-history.fandom.com/wiki/Operation_Taylor_Common
Military History Fandom. "Operation Oklahoma Hills." Accessed November 12, 2020. https://military-history.fandom.com/wiki/Operation_Oklahoma_Hills
Historica. "Operation Pipestone Canyon." Accessed November 12, 2020. https://historica.fandom.com/wiki/Operation_Pipestone_Canyon
Find-a-Grave. "Larry Gunnell Pinson." Accessed November 12, 2020. https://www.findagrave.com/memorial/154393089/larry-gunnell-pinson
Coffelt Database, "Larry Pinson." Accessed November 3, 2021. http://coffeltdatabase.org/index

Gunnel's parents and sisters.

Graduation, 1968

Gunnel Pinson in Vietnam

Photos courtesy of Brenda Clark.

CHAPTER TWENTY-ONE

Warner Prater Hughie

Newnan, Georgia

I was so in love with you. I was planning to start my life with you as soon as you returned from Vietnam. But God had other plans. Even after all these years, I have never forgotten you and know I will see you in Heaven one sweet day. Thank you for loving me, and the time we had together. Thank you for your sacrifice to our great country!

— Teresa Bowen McDonald

Bruce Howard was exhausted and a long way from his home in Georgia. He was part of Delta Company, 229th Aviation Battalion of the 1st Cavalry Division, and his job was to help keep the Cobra gunships flying in his part of Vietnam. He worked twelve-hour shifts seven days a week at Dau Tieng, a base camp severely downsized throughout 1969 as part of the Vietnamization process. Now it was early 1970, and even though the base camp wasn't as large as it had once been, Dau Tieng was still a hive of activity for the Cobra unit stationed there. This particular night appeared to be no different than the many others Howard had endured over the past three months. He looked forward to getting some sleep.

Howard returned to his bunker, a below-ground protective room as deep into the Vietnamese soil as possible, fortified with sandbags and a tin roof with more sandbags on top. The camp at Dau Tieng was a frequent victim of rocket and mortar attacks, and even though he and his comrades lived in a "hooch" above ground, they often slept in the protection of the bunker. That night, Bruce came in alone and got a strange sensation as he lay down in his bunk. Initially,

Bruce couldn't put his finger on what was bothering him. He strained to see and hear what might be happening outside the bunker. Nothing. Suddenly, he realized with a start that it felt as if he was being watched. He felt a presence. But he was alone, wasn't he? He fumbled for his flashlight and clicked the light on. He slowly shined the light around the bunker, looking for someone or something. Nothing. He checked the corners for a rat or even a cobra snake, both of which had a reputation for climbing into bunkers for shelter regardless of who was there. Again, he saw nothing. He shook his head and thought about home. He thought about his buddy, Warner.

Bruce Howard had met Warner Hughie at Newnan Junior High their first week of seventh grade. They were in a second-floor classroom with a large window looking out over Temple Avenue, close to where it intersects with Jackson Street.[1] The teacher had stepped out of the room, and the boys in the classroom moved into action. They wadded up paper and tried to shoot it out the window into the trash can on the sidewalk. Finally, someone warned, "The teacher's coming!" and everyone scrambled for their seats. Everyone made it except Tommy Wright. He was hustled to the principal's office, where, under duress, he proceeded to give up the names of everyone involved. Bruce, Alan Boyd, and Warner Hughie were all marched to the office and given five "licks" apiece. Those five licks cemented a bond between these youngsters, who became the best of friends throughout their childhood.

Bruce had gone to Basic Training at Fort Benning with Warner Hughie; they had been in the same company but different platoons. After Basic, the Army sent them in different directions for Advanced Infantry Training. Bruce Howard went to Fort Eustis, Virginia, for transportation school, where he was trained as a helicopter electrician. Warner went to Fort Polk, Louisiana, to prepare for Vietnam. They arrived in Vietnam at about the same time but in different parts of the country.

After the feeling in the bunker that night, "the foremost thought in my head was that he (Warner) had been killed," Howard said. That thought dogged him for the next five days before he finally shook it.

A few months later, Howard took his R&R leave, and he went to Hawaii to meet his wife, Martha. He put the war aside and enjoyed spending time with his spouse and enjoying the sights. On his last night on R&R, his wife began crying since Howard was headed to Vietnam the next day. He tried to console her and assured her everything would be OK and that he would be home soon. Finally, she looked at him, and the look in her eyes told him there was something more.

"You don't know, do you?" she choked out.

He stared at her. Howard knew. "Yeah, Warner's dead, isn't he?"

She nodded as sobs wracked her body. He pulled her close, and they held each other. Howard thought back to that night in the bunker.

Eighteen years later, Bruce Howard was in his home alone, reading, when he heard a still, small voice. It seemed to say, "That presence that you felt back in your bunker in Vietnam was an angel trying to tell you that Warner was with the angels now."

On January 4, 1949, Warner Hughie was born to James and Grace Hughie of Newnan. He was the second of five children. Jimmy was the oldest, followed by Warner, Oscar, Bob, and Lisa, with an average of four years between them. James Hughie worked for the railroad and was good with his hands, so when he and Grace bought the small house on a dirt road on the south side of Newnan, Gordon Road, he performed all of the additions and remodeling to adapt to the family's growth. While they never had much money, James never had much use for credit and preferred to pay for things upfront. So all the children were born in and grew up in this home.

Warner was a soft-spoken child in a small, quiet, rural town. When Warner spoke, he spoke slowly and deliberately, almost mimicking the pace of life in Newnan, Georgia, during the 1950s and 1960s. Warner attended Atkinson Elementary on Nimmons Street, only a few miles from his home, and got involved in Boy Scouts in his early teens. He joined the troop based at East Newnan Methodist Church, where Bruce Howard and Alan Boyd were members. Thomas McKoon, another troop member, said that he and Warner attended the Methodist Youth Fellowship meeting on Monday then attended Boy Scouts at the same church on Thursday. The troop went on campouts and visited Camp Thunder, the Boy Scout Camp in Thomaston, Georgia. Warner moved from Atkinson Elementary to Newnan Junior High then Newnan High School.

Thomas McKoon rode the same bus with Warner during their first few years of high school; McKoon got on the bus first, then it picked up Warner and his older brother, Jimmy. Warner loved to get attention on the bus by pulling his eyelids out, blinking, and pulling them back, causing them to stay up.[2] McKoon recalled that Warner did that every Friday afternoon without fail on the way home from school. The students on the bus looked forward to it.

When the bus pulled up in front of Warner and Jimmy's house, Warner would disembark and call out, "Thank God it's Friday."

Rick Melville also remembers Warner from Newnan High School. "He was a humble, quiet person, never in trouble," he said.

According to Bruce Howard, the thing that might get you into trouble would be running off with your parents' cigarettes so that you and your buddies could experiment. The guys used to do that on occasion. At Newnan High School, Warner was part of the Future Farmers of America club and worked in the lunchroom to pay for his lunch.

Warner spent a lot of time playing ball and visiting Alan Boyd and Tim Wilson on East Newnan Road. Whatever they were doing, "Warner was in the middle of it all," said Tim Wilson. Tim and Warner played a joke on the lady who worked in Tim's family's home. They told her that Warner had a twin brother named Robert. One day, Warner would be Warner. The next day, Warner would be Robert. The "twins" were never together at the same time. The poor lady never figured it out.

Before Warner could drive, his father would come pick him up, but since he didn't know which house Warner might be in at that moment, he rode down the street, blowing his horn in short, rapid bursts. *Toot. Toot. Toot. Toot.* Warner would recognize the horn and be out of whatever house he was in and on the road in a flash.

As Warner began high school, the attractions of most teenage boys began to surface—socialization, girls, and cars. While generally quiet, Warner participated in many of the things that teenagers in Newnan engaged in during this time. The drive-in and Alamo theaters. The skating rink. The Dairy Bar (Big John's) to Brazier Burger to Burger Chef car cruise.

Warner, Bruce Howard, Alan Boyd, and Tommy Wright occasionally skipped school and drove to the Krystal at East Point to see who could eat the most Krystal hamburgers. Afterward, they would go to Hogansville to an old rock quarry called the "Rock Hole," where they competed to climb the quarry wall.

"If anyone has ever seen the movie *Stand by Me*, that could have been a chapter out of our lives," Howard said. "We definitely had a lot of good times."

At the end of Warner's sophomore year at Newnan High School, he, Bruce Howard, and Alan Boyd decided to attend East Coweta High School, starting with their junior year. At that time, if you furnished your transportation, you could go to whatever school you chose. If you had to ride a bus, you had to attend the closest school. Alan Boyd lived on East Newnan Road near the area known as Five Points, not far from Warner's home on Gordon Road. On their way to East Coweta every day, he and Bruce took turns picking up Warner.[3] The boys thought they would have a better chance of graduating from high school if they attended East Coweta since they believed it wasn't as tough academically as Newnan. So the 1966-1967 school year saw them in Senoia.

Then there were girls. Warner was a good-looking guy with piercing eyes and a California surfer look, which certainly must have attracted his fair share of female company. Deberah Williams was at East Coweta at the same time as Warner.

"I remember him very well because he was so funny. We were in World History together," Williams said. "What was his friend's name? Alan Boyd. Warner and Alan were like best buddies. They kind of played off of each other. They were always funny and always making us laugh, cracking up the class, interrupting the class. They kept the staff at the school on their toes." One day during science class, she heard somebody say that Warner was in the boys' bathroom and had put a cherry bomb in the commode and flushed it.

"All of a sudden, we heard a boom," Williams said. "That was Warner and Alan, and they would do such funny things."

One young lady jumped to the front of the line during Warner's junior and senior high school years. At the time, Alan Boyd was dating a girl named Debbie Cammons, and the two decided to set Warner up on a blind date. But the night the four were supposed to go out, Alan and Debbie couldn't go, so they asked another couple to cover for them. This couple got Warner then went to pick up his date.

"When he walked to the door, and I saw him, and he saw me, it was love at first sight," Teresa Bowen said. "I met him for the first time when he came to the door that night. He had a great smile and was so handsome, and we just fell in love right then. He was always such a gentleman and made me feel like a princess." Warner and Teresa were a couple from that point on.

"They really fell in love as young sweethearts in high school," said Debbie Cammons.

Warner Hughie got a job at a business across from the Playtex plant, Douglas and Lomason, which made chrome-plated bumpers.[4] Warner worked the second shift after school and saved money to buy a 1956 Chevy Bel-Air. When he bought the car, it didn't have a motor, but he soon acquired one and got the car running.

"It was a dark-turquoise-and-white car. That is the car we dated in, and I loved it," said Teresa. "I would sit right next to him and ride there all the time."

That wasn't the only car in Warner's life. Warner and friend Eddie Jones worked on a Camaro they liked to race. According to Warner's brother Oscar, the car could do a quarter mile in eleven seconds.

While Warner worked on automobiles and dated Teresa, he also developed a sense of humor. When his younger brother Bob rode in his car, on seeing a stop sign, Warner would reach over and grab Bob's head, "stopping" him.

"You know, just kid stuff," Bob said.

David Segrest, an East Coweta High School graduate, was a freshman when Warner was a senior. The freshmen and seniors were big rivals at East Coweta, and the competition between classes was fierce. Segrest said a group of freshman boys would run into the gym at the end of Warner's physical education class and pile on him. He would sling them off, and they would keep jumping on him.

"It was the best time," Segrest said. "I don't even know that he knew who we were other than we were kids, you know. We always called Warner 'Mr. Spock' because of his haircut. That is a great memory for me. We were just kids like we all were back then."

But the fun and games were nearing the end for Warner and the

Class of 1969. While Richard Nixon took office in January with a pledge to get American boys out of Vietnam, the draft continued plucking young men from their homes. Unfortunately, the Hughies didn't have the money to avoid the draft by sending Warner to college, and Warner was drafted in the spring of 1969 while still a senior at East Coweta High School.

When Warner got his draft notice, "won't nobody happy," his brother Oscar recalled.

Regardless, Warner left for Basic Training before participating in his high school graduation. He departed for Fort Benning the last week of classes, along with Bruce Howard and another Coweta native, George Massey. George's father, Aaron Massey, had just been elected sheriff of Coweta County and served from 1969-1984.

The boys spent June, July, and the better part of August at Fort Benning during the hottest part of the year. After the first month, they could get weekend passes, and either the Howards or the Masseys would pick up the three boys so they could spend the weekend back home.

"He was a very likable young man, full of laughter, a bit shy, but fun to be around," said George Massey. "We would drop him off on Highway 29, coming back to Newnan, and pick him up on the way back to the base."

At the end of Basic Training, Warner's family and Teresa picked him up and took him home for a well-deserved leave. After the break, Howard and Massey moved on to Advanced Training in different parts of the country. Warner, meanwhile, flew to Fort Polk for Advanced Infantry Training, the first time he had ever been on an airplane. Fort Polk was the infantry school for Vietnam-bound soldiers.

Warner returned home from Fort Polk at the end of October 1969 for a thirty-day leave before shipping out to Vietnam. Warner needed to take care of a few personal things before he left to go overseas. First, he gave Oscar temporary custody of his car to drive, maintain, and shuttle Momma wherever she might need to go, as she didn't drive. Second, he got engaged to his girlfriend, Teresa.

"He proposed right before he left for Vietnam," Teresa said. "He bought me an engagement ring and told me he would get me a bigger one when he got home." Teresa, eighteen, was a senior in high school.

Warner left home in November and made a stopover in Washington State, probably at Fort Lewis. There he thought of Teresa again.

She said, "The Supremes singing group were popular at that time, so he bought and sent me the record 'Someday We'll Be Together!' I will never forget that."[5]

Warner Hughie arrived in Vietnam in December of 1969 and was assigned to the Americal Division upon arrival.[6] He was in D Company, 4th Battalion, 31st Infantry, 196th Infantry Brigade. D Company was assigned to protect a village called Hiep Duc, which was at the base of a mountain. Hiep Duc was a village set up for refugees from the communist forces in the area. There were two Landing Zones in the vicinity, LZ Siberia and LZ West. LZ Siberia sat above the village of Hiep Duc, while LZ West contained all the large artillery pieces to support American servicemen in that area. American soldiers conducting "sweeps" of that area never got outside artillery range.

Warner quickly picked up a nickname in his squad.

"Everyone had a nickname," said Ron Ward, Warner's squad leader. Because Warner's last name was Hughie, the guys in his squad called him Dewey *and* Louie, after the Donald Duck cartoon characters. "He took his nickname and went with it and came with a smile no matter what he was called," Ward said with a laugh.

"He was just a Southern gentleman. I mean, he was a kid like us, but he was just a real nice guy," said Bob Delzell, Warner's platoon sergeant. When the squad conducted sweeps, they might be out for several days. Then they would "laager" or have an overnight encampment in a defensible spot in the evening. They would pair up and put their ponchos together, creating a shelter for the evening when they were not on watch. Warner's poncho buddy was Dan McCann from Chicago.

Warner wrote his family letters diligently. He and Teresa corresponded nonstop. Oscar recalls that Warner wrote about getting "jungle rot." This skin abrasion was caused by heat, sweat, and friction, and it can also be acquired by bacteria, common in the tropics. Bob Hughie remembers getting frequent letters from Warner. Unfortunately, the letters disappeared after one too many moves. Warner's family believed that he carried an M-60 machine gun, but the guys in his squad corrected that misconception. It is more likely that he was a machine gun ammo bearer. In Vietnam, a machine gun crew consisted of a gunner, an assistant gunner, and typically one or two ammo bearers. The ammo bearer carried two to four belts, each with 400 rounds for the M-60 machine gun, when the squad was on patrol.

The first three months of 1970 saw this area of Vietnam comparatively quiet. "He was there in a relatively calm period. We hadn't had contact since, I want to say, December," said Ron Ward, Warner's squad leader. On March 12, 1970, the squad moved out to sweep an area they had never traversed. "Sweeps were almost a daily thing. This one was memorable only because of the way it ended," Ward said.

The mission that day was to go to a spot where they might laager the next night to see if it was suitable. They made it to the location they were looking for without incident and headed back. It was a bright, clear day, but the heat, as usual, was oppressive. Jim Savering was walking point, Warner Hughie was second, and Ron Ward was third, with the rest of the squad following.

"In retrospect, I should have had him walk further back. It was just one of those idyllic days. Everything was just as easy as can be, but when you relax, this is what happens," Ward said.

Typically, the squad leader would walk fifth or sixth in the patrol, but Ward was closer to the front, as Savering was walking point for the first time and wanted to be close. Ron Ward had walked point many times before being made squad leader, and he wanted to ensure Savering was all right. They were almost back to their camp.

There was a sudden flash, and an explosion ripped through the late afternoon. Bob Delzell's head jerked up in surprise. He wasn't that far away, and the sound penetrated through him and his squad. "What the hell? This area was quiet!" Once Delzell and his squad got their bearings, they crashed through the thick jungle toward the noise. Delzell was frantic. He remembers thinking, "What's going on? Is everyone all right?" Could they get a medevac helicopter in? Ward's squad was close enough to the camp that the guys there heard the explosion and saw smoke rising from the vegetation.

Ron Ward was on his back on the trail. He felt that things were moving in slow motion. Ron wasn't in pain; that would come later. Ron was worried about the guys around him, whom he was responsible for getting home. He struggled to get up and managed to get to his knees. He couldn't hear. The explosion had taken that away, but he could see, and what he saw wasn't good.

The soldiers from camp headed toward the smoke, so Bob Delzell, confident that they would need to get a medical evacuation chopper in, started looking for an LZ. The vegetation was thick, and he didn't see a conspicuous place for the helicopter to land. With their machetes, the squad began to cut a Landing Zone through a wide area of bamboo growth. Even though they hadn't yet seen any of the victims of the explosion, the urgency was palpable. "The guys knew that the helicopter had to get in to save people, so they were working so hard they were almost killing themselves. In combat, it's different than any other job. You basically will kill yourself to save somebody else," said Delzell.

They cut the LZ in a matter of minutes, with a young Black soldier from Macon named Willie Coleman leading the way. Ron Ward and Coleman were buddies, and there was nothing that Willie wouldn't do for Ron. Delzell posted about Warner Hughie and the March 12, 1970, incident on the VVMF Wall of Faces site on April 26, 2021.

> *I remember how kind and gentle you were; you were in my company in the field. Your platoon hit a booby trap, killing you and wounding several others. We cut out a small landing zone with machetes in a bamboo grove to get you and the others out. It was so hot some of us started dropping from heatstroke, but that did not matter. We would have died trying to save you all. Big Willie cut most of the bamboo away like Paul Bunyan. He was a gentle, soft-spoken, huge black kid from Macon, Georgia, your home state. For a time, I was your platoon leader at 19. You will never be forgotten; you are in my prayers every single night.*

Ron Ward had passed out, but before losing consciousness, he saw Hughie and Savering lying in the trail in front of him. Savering was severely wounded, but he would recover. What follows is his account of what happened, posted on Facebook on March 12, 2017.

Today's date, March 12, has a special significance for me, for it was on this day 47 years ago that I walked into a booby trap in Viet Nam. One man from the state of Georgia, Warner Hughie, was killed and another brother-in-arms, Ron Ward, was injured in the same explosion. Here is the short story of how the events of that day unfolded.

It was early in the morning that our platoon lieutenant informed us that captain Lynch wanted our squad to hike to a spot circled on his map several clicks distant from our camp (one click equals 1000 meters). Our mission was to assess whether that new location was sufficiently defendable to serve as a new base of operations. The company never spent more than a few days at any one location as it would leave us more vulnerable for sniper fire, booby traps, mortar fire or possibly a night assault. The lieutenant pointed to a dotted line on the map indicating a trail that we were to follow to the other side of the mountain to the proposed new base. The vegetation was so dense that in order to hike that distance without traveling on a trail was nearly impossible. The trek could have been made only by chopping a path with the help of a machete and would have taken at least a day to complete. For missions of this type, we would travel light, taking only our M16s, extra ammo and water. Our food, poncho covers, backpack and personal items were left behind.

I was point man so I started off with the rest of the squad following one behind the other spaced a few yards apart as was the standard operating procedure. The vegetation lower on the mountain was less dense so I was able to find the trail after a short distance. As we proceeded up the mountain, the bamboo and elephant grass became much thicker making it very hard to stay on course. After a while I lost the trail but continued to push forward hoping to find it again but without success. I felt a leech on my leg so I stopped and unbloused my pants and boot to pull it off. Hughie, who was walking backup, pushed forward and found a dried creek bed. The

> *creek's path was in the general direction that we wanted to go and since walking in the creek bed was easier than pushing through the jungle, Hughie continued to lead the way around the side of the mountain.*
>
> *Eventually, after an hour or so of walking and on the other side of the ridge, we came across the lost trail and followed it the rest of the way to our destination. We stayed only a short time to confirm that the location was an acceptable campsite then headed back on the path toward our company. I once again took the point. As we went higher up the mountain, the path became harder to follow. The only way I could stay on the trail was to put my M16 vertically in front of me and use it like a wedge as I looked at the ground so as not to get off of the path. As we neared the top of the ridge, I must have tripped the booby trap. The device had a delayed firing pin since the explosion went off after I had passed but right beside Hughie who was walking second. Hughie took most of the blast. I remember being blown forward and having the wind knocked out of me. I remember rising to my knees with my head on the ground and blood running off of my shoulders. Ron Ward, who was third in line, was hit in the front. At least one and probably more guys who were behind Ron were also wounded. I recall calling out Hughie's name asking him if he were alright and I think I recall him making a moaning response. I'm pretty sure he died soon after that. I didn't lose consciousness but have little memory of much else. I do recall two sounds which stick out in my mind: the sound of guys chopping away the vegetation to create a place for the dust-off helicopter to land and the familiar wop-wop sound of a helicopter coming to pick us up.*

When the medics arrived, they started to work. Seven of the eleven guys in the squad had taken shrapnel, with Warner Hughie killed outright. Ward and Savering were severely injured. Nevertheless, they got the two and Warner to the medevac helicopter that arrived in Delzell's landing zone. The chopper got into the LZ without problem but couldn't get out without Delzell's squad cutting additional bamboo. With that completed, the helicopter slowly lifted off. Ward regained consciousness in flight but was in a daze. He dimly remembers the chopper landing at LZ West and Warner Hughie being lifted from the helicopter. The helicopter headed to a hospital, but it was clear that Warner didn't need the medical treatment that the hospital could provide. Ward and Savering eventually were sent to the hospital in Japan and later returned to the United States to recover from their wounds.

Warner Hughie's military records state that Warner "was killed while on a combat operation when a booby trap detonated." Although undoubtedly true, it is lacking in detail. While Jim Savering is convinced that he triggered the device, neither he nor Ron Ward are even sure what type of device was touched off that day. A tripwire connected to a grenade was one of Vietnam's most common booby traps, but Savering doesn't mention a tripwire. Ward believed it was more powerful than a grenade, so perhaps it was a device like a dud American mortar shell rigged to be stepped on, similar to a land mine. In that case, Savering could have triggered the device as he described, or Hughie might have triggered it himself by stepping on it.

"The area they were in had not been traveled for a long time, and it may have been an old booby trap," said Bob Delzell.

Whatever the case, Warner Hughie took the brunt of the explosion.

According to Oscar Hughie, who was sixteen, the US Army visited their house a few days later, around 4 a.m. The two Army men knocking at his door told them that Warner's death was instantaneous. Bob Hughie, twelve, after learning about the day and time of his brother's death, recalled the cold chill that had run down his back at that very same time. He became convinced that he had the chill at the exact moment Warner died.

"I remember my mama, it tore her up bad," said Bob. "She never got over it."

"I was spending the weekend with some relatives in LaGrange and was still asleep that Saturday morning," Teresa said. "The doorbell rang, and my mom and dad had come from Newnan to get me and tell me. I remember I wanted to get to his mom, and at that time, all I could think of was that my life was over."

Hillcrest Chapel handled the arrangements for the funeral, held at Mills Chapel Baptist Church on Friday, March 20. One of the military escorts allegedly said something to some of Warner's friends about him possibly living through his wounds. Alan Boyd got angry and reportedly snapped at the escort, "We don't care anything about you! Shut up!"

"I knew when I saw him in the casket that all of him wasn't there," said Oscar.

The casket had glass over it, and someone paying their respects could see only half of the body. Warner wore white gloves. The glove on the left looked empty, Oscar said, but otherwise, "they had him fixed up pretty good."

The funeral filled the church. Oscar said it rained the whole time he was at the funeral home, but the weather cleared for the funeral. James Hughie insisted on driving himself alone to the church.

"It was at the old Mills Chapel that had a balcony, and it was packed with people," said Teresa. "I remember standing at the casket in front of the church with a light-blue dress on. He was sealed in glass. I couldn't touch him, and it didn't look like him. They had his hair brushed back, and he always wore his hair down, like, with bangs, I guess you'd say."

The pallbearers included Alan Boyd, Tim Wilson, Rader Bowen, Chester McClain, Pat McNeill, Curtis Mote, and Eddie Jones. Bruce Howard and Tommy Wright were in Vietnam. Warner was buried in Oak Hill Cemetery.

"I was a senior in high school when this happened," Teresa said. When he got killed, his mom went to the jewelry store, got the matching wedding band he had bought, and gave it to me. It wasn't a great set, but I loved it. I also received a letter after the fact from him. I remember it said, 'We are supposed to be going up on the mountain, but I doubt we will make it.' We had already buried him then. I wish I could find those letters."

"He was one of the sweetest guys from the whole bunch of boys from East Coweta that I knew," said Debbie Cammons. "He was so, so sweet. I know that our hearts got broken when he was drafted, and when he died, it was a terrible, terrible day for us."

"Warner's mom and dad were good people," said Bruce Howard. "On Veterans Day, his mom was really proud of her son."

"He's a hero to me," said Rick Melville. "Growing up with him, I would never have picked him as that kind of person. He was just so quiet. It was a pleasure to know him and the other people in his family. They were good people. I will always carry a part of his memory with me."

The Hughie family felt the pain of Warner's loss. Warner's oldest brother, Jimmy, won't talk about Warner even today. James and Grace divorced after their children moved on and out of the house.

According to Tim Wilson, who attended Unity Baptist Church with Grace Hughie, Grace suffered for years after Warner's death. "She told me one day that she had gone to see one of those fortune tellers, and they told her that Warner was not killed in the war but that he had been captured, was a prisoner, and would be coming home. She took that for the gospel. She was looking forward to him coming home." Tim paused. "She mourned him, and she never got over it. We talked about it all the time at church. I thought, how cruel. Why would they say something like that?"

Gordon Road, where the Hughie family had grown up, is now paved and dedicated to Warner Hughie and his service during the Vietnam War.

The 1956 Chevy Bel-Air that Warner had put together and driven while in high school was inherited by Oscar. He drove it and worked on it for a couple of years after Warner died. Unfortunately, the car was rear-ended, and the accident bent the frame. The insurance company totaled the car, and Oscar traded it in.

"I often wonder how my life would have turned out if Warner had not been killed," said Teresa. "It was only [by] the grace of God that I have survived. Warner was killed on March 12, 1970. He was buried on March 20. I married in 1971 and was married for a little over twenty-five years to a wonderful guy named David Thompson, who died from an accident on March 10, 1996. He was buried on March 12, the exact date that Warner died, so March hasn't been so good to me. I am remarried to another wonderful guy, God has blessed my life, but Warner and I were so in love. I just never got the chance to share a life with him."

"He used to say that he was going to have so many children that he was going to need a school bus to haul them around in," said Oscar Hughie.

When she was interviewed for this book, Teresa Bowen McDonald drove a school bus.

**See end notes in the appendix for additional details.*

***Born**: January 4, 1949*
***Home of record**: Newnan, Georgia*
***Died**: March 12, 1970, in Quang Tin province of South Vietnam*
***Coweta servicemen who died in the same province**: Tim Cole and Terry Allen*
***Unit on death**: D CO, 4th BN, 31st Infantry, 196th Infantry Brigade, Americal Division*
***Decorations:** Bronze Star, Purple Heart, Good Conduct Medal, National Defense Service Medal, Vietnam Military Merit Medal, Vietnam Service Medal with one bronze service star, Republic of Vietnam Gallantry Cross with Palm, Republic of Vietnam Campaign Medal*
***Buried:** Oak Hill Cemetery, Newnan*
***Vietnam Memorial, Washington, DC:** Panel 13W Line 118*

Sources

Interview with Oscar Hughie, brother
Interview with Bob Hughie, brother
Interview with Bruce Howard, childhood friend
Interview with Archie Slaton, childhood friend
Interview with David Segrest, childhood friend
Interview with Thomas McKoon, childhood friend
Interview with Rick Melville, childhood friend
Interview with Deberah Williams, childhood friend
Interview with Fred Cox, childhood friend
Interview with Pat McNeill, childhood friend
Interview with Debbie Cammons Olmstead, childhood friend
Interview with Tim Wilson, childhood friend
Email interview with Teresa Bowen McDonald, fianceé
Email interview with George Massey, US Army
Interview with Bob Delzell, US Army
Interview with Ron Ward, US Army
Email interview with Jim Savering, US Army

Assistance from Jimmy Davenport

References

Vietnam Veterans Memorial Fund. "Wall of Faces." Accessed January 10, 2022. https://www.vvmf.org/Wall-of-Faces/24670/WARNER-P-HUGHIE/
Coffelt Database, "Warner Hughie." Accessed July 3, 2018. http://coffeltdatabase.org/index.php

Warner Hughie in Vietnam.

CHAPTER TWENTY-TWO

William Henry Thomas

Senoia, Georgia

I am not going to live very long. I am going to die young. I feel it.

—Bill Thomas, as related to his sister, Barbara Thomas Jenkerson

Three former Marines, all of whom served in Vietnam, stay in contact after all these years. Mike Clayton lives near West Point, Bailey Eames lives in North Carolina, and Bob Balogh is in Massachusetts. Nearly every time they communicate, Bill Thomas's name comes up. Bob Balogh told why that is.

> *We were all Field Radio Operators (MOS 2531, code for military occupation specialty) with Second Battalion, First Marine Regiment, First Marine Division stationed by the village of Nui Kim Son near China Beach, maybe 7 miles south of Danang. It was 1969-1970. Bill Thomas from Georgia came in-country after the three of us in late 1969. One of the many jobs the radio operators performed was Rat Patrol, riding in a Jeep from sunset to sunrise, back and forth on the dirt road from Nui Kim Son to the Tu Cau Bridge. In the Jeep was a driver, a radioman in the front passenger seat, and an M-60 machine gun operator in back. The Jeep was stripped down, meaning no windshield, no doors, nothing covering the back, headlights remained off.*
>
> *Think about it.*
>
> *Up and down the road in the middle of the night.*
>
> *We were sitting ducks for the Viet Cong lurking in the*

dark, sometimes literally mocking us.

One night in early 1970, I was too burned out from too many Rat Patrols, and I needed a night off. Bill Thomas was overanxious to see more action than taking another shift on radio watch in a safe bunker in our rear area.

I asked him to switch for one night.

He was gung ho.

I remember sharing a warm beer with him before he went out that night...

Bill Thomas was born in Rome, Georgia, and named for his father, Sergeant William H. Thomas Sr., a veteran of World War II and, in the early 1950s, still a member of the US Army. Bill's mother, Clara, worked at Battery State Hospital in Rome. Initially, Battery State was an Army hospital that treated wounded service members during World War II. In 1946, the state took over the hospital from the federal government and turned it into a tuberculosis sanatorium. Clara's mother had died of tuberculosis when Clara was five years old, so she was determined to assist people who suffered from the fatal disease. Bill had three older sisters: Patricia, who was called by her middle name, Gayle; Barbara, who was known as Bobbie; and Paulette. Bobbie had been born two years before Bill, on July 9, 1949. Bill was born on June 10, 1951, and their mother consistently seemed to get confused about their birthdays. As a result, they became known as "Billy and Bobbie" throughout their childhood.

One of Bill's cousins, Ronnie Duke, lived in Rome during this time. Six years older than Bill, he treated Bill like his little brother. Bill and Ronnie lived in a rural setting where they saw cows, horses, and other farm animals daily. They built forts and played cowboys and Indians. Their grandfather ran a sawmill and a little general store, and according to Ronnie, "we always had something to do." They swept sawdust, carried goods, and helped themselves to candy at the store. Once, when Bill was just three, he walked up behind a man cutting wood and was struck by an ax. This incident seemed to set a pattern of danger for the rest of Bill's life, and it also left him with a lifelong scar between his eyes.

In 1954, Clara filed for divorce and moved with her children to

Orlando, Florida, to be closer to her sister, Mary. The four children kept their father's surname, even though he was no longer involved in their lives, but Clara did not. While working at a local restaurant in Orlando, she met Waldemar Zimmerman, stationed at McCoy Air Force Base just south of Orlando, and remarried. Because Bill was so young when he left Rome, he had no recollection of his biological father and always accepted Zimmerman as his real father. The girls embraced "Zimm" as well, and their mother had one last child, Michael Zimmerman, their half brother and the youngest of the clan. Gayle had to look out for all the younger siblings, and she had a challenging job with Bill.

The sisters said that as a child, Bill was accident-prone. Danger seemed to find him.

"He could walk across the yard, and if there was a hole in it, he was going to fall in and break his arm," said Gayle.

When Bill was six and living in Orlando, he was walking on an old water heater lying in a nearby vacant lot when lightning struck him. Several children played on or near the water heater, but Bill was on it when lightning struck nearby, knocking him off the appliance and out of his shoes and burning the bottoms of his feet. Unconscious, Bill was rushed to the hospital, where he spent the following week.

Bill also had a problem sleeping. He could talk like he was awake and walk almost anywhere but still be asleep. Once, he sleepwalked a couple of blocks to his aunt Mary's screened porch, where he lay down and went back to sleep.

After Clara and Waldemar Zimmerman were married, the family began moving from Air Force base to Air Force base. The sisters can't remember all the places where they lived. They know they were in Washington State in 1965 and Illinois in 1966. One place they do recall is Albany, Georgia. They lived in a small cinder block home not far from the Air Force base. Gayle graduated high school in Albany, married, and had her first child there. When Bill was fourteen, his stepfather left for the Pacific. Zimmerman spent time on Guam, and as a flight engineer, he flew into Vietnam, which he didn't much care for; he noted they were shooting at you there! Zimmerman was eventually assigned to Okinawa, but no housing for the family was available. So he put his name on the list, and his family back in the States had to make do until base housing became available.

Bobbie returned to Rome and lived with her father's sister, her aunt Maddie Thomas Edwards. Bobbie attended Pepperell High School during her junior year. Bill wanted to stay with his mother, so he landed in Senoia, Georgia, with his mother, his sister Gayle, and his half brother, Mike. Gayle was with them since her husband, whom she met in Albany, was in the Air Force and was stationed in Guam then. Bill's family moved in with his aunt and uncle, another of his mom's sisters and her husband, Carmen and Charles Atkins. He would spend the next eight months in Coweta County.

Bill Thomas was due to enter high school when he moved, so in the fall of 1966, he entered ninth grade at East Coweta High School as a member of the class of 1970. East Coweta was a much smaller and more intimate place in 1966 than it is today. Unsurprisingly, Bill had little problem adapting and finding friends.

"He was likable and right away popular, and he was cute," said classmate Deberah Williams. Bill had even been voted a class officer.

Bill was very athletic as well. In Physical Education class, "he could hit the hound out of the ball," said Betty Banks, another classmate.

Deberah and Betty saw him at the dances at the teen club sponsored by the Senoia Lions Club on Saturday nights. The Senoia Teen Club was the "happening" place for Senoia teens during the 1960s.

"We thought it was so big," said Vicki Hill, a friend of Bill's at East Coweta. "You didn't live in Senoia and not go to teen club. It was open on Saturday night from 7 p.m. until 11 p.m., though it wasn't cool to get there until 8 p.m." They danced and occasionally had a live band. A Coke machine was available, and snacks were sold from a window toward the back of the building. The other place for teens to go in this part of the county was Reagan's Dairy Spot and Grill on Highway 85. Reagan's was a great place to get a hamburger and ice cream and listen to popular music.

Vicki Hill rode the school bus with Bill and considered him a good friend and a nice guy. She also thought he was cute and had pretty eyes and a "Beatles" haircut. "We had a good time on the bus," she remembered. "We talked and laughed, and I'm sure we made fun of everything."

Fred Cox met Bill at East Coweta. Bill was a year older than Fred, but they bonded over cigarettes. They used to talk on the smoke breaks by the gym. This was a fairly common practice around the country up through the 1970s and even into the 1980s. East Coweta had a smoke break in the morning and afternoon for students who wanted to partake.

Cox said that Bill reminded him of the Kevin Bacon character in the movie *Footloose*. "I mentioned this to another girl I went to school with, and she agreed with me," Cox said with a laugh. "He came to the school from somewhere else. He wasn't wild. Kevin Bacon wasn't really wild, he was just different. But he [Bill] was just different, and I think he brought a lot of things to the school. When he came here, he just had a whole lot more knowledge about the world than what we had."

"He was not the type of person that walked into a room and sucked the air out of it. He was not loud, look at me, I need some attention. Nothing, nothing like that," Vicki said. "He was more of a type of person that walked into a room, and he didn't want you to notice him, and after he got comfortable with you, he would talk and carry on. I don't think that Bill was here long enough to ever really, you know, have a good strong relationship with anybody. He probably had not had that anywhere else either, with him being in a military family."

Bill did have one consistently strong relationship during the years before his time in Senoia, and that was with his cousin Ronnie Duke, whom he had been close to as a child growing up in Rome. By the time Bill was living in Senoia, Ronnie was twenty and had joined the Marine Corps a few years earlier. He had been wounded in Vietnam, and Bill's family was on hand to see him when he arrived at the hospital in Illinois. It was the first time they had seen Ronnie in a couple of years. When Ronnie recovered, he moved back to Georgia. Ronnie was from a family of builders and contractors, and Bill worked with them during his summers, learning carpentry and running errands. He also worked on various houses in Atlanta with his uncle's company. Bill had continued to stay close to Ronnie and his family and saw them often. Ronnie saw Bill as positive and friendly, and he believed that Bill enjoyed life. Bill was also a pretty good artist. He was even allowed to paint a mural in Ronnie's basement. Ronnie said he believes it was because of his own service that Bill became fascinated with the Marine Corps.

During the summer of 1967, the Thomas family got their vaccinations at Fort McClellan, packed their bags, and headed to Okinawa. Zimmerman had finally secured base housing for the family. Bill spent the next two years on this island, famously fought over during World War II. He went back to school at Kubasaki High School, the school for American military dependents, where the students thought he and Bobbie were twins.

"He looked out for me," Bobbie said. She adjusted to Okinawa quickly. She enjoyed the airman's pool, bowled, and did well in school. She also learned to develop black-and-white photographs in a darkroom. Bobbie said everyone liked Bill, who was often called "sweet William" or "sweet Billy." He had a girlfriend, Amy, who was the same age as Bobbie.

The move to Okinawa seems to have affected Bill more than it did the other siblings. He struggled and didn't like the school. He missed his friends back in the States. Bill began to do things just to get in trouble. He skipped school and got Bobbie to write an excuse for him. Bill could frequently be found on the beach; he enjoyed the water and was a good swimmer. Once, he took off for a few days with a friend after stealing some beer. The Military Police (MP) found them. Bill's stepfather went to his commanding officer and attempted to explain.

While on Okinawa, Bill also grew more adventurous. Instead of danger finding him, he began to look for it. He nearly fell from a cliff. He hunted and killed snakes. He explored the Okinawa caves, which could be especially dangerous. Only twenty years earlier, the Japanese had used these caves to fight the Americans at the end of the Second World War. Live ordnance and booby traps might still be in those caves. He had several close calls.

Once, Bill and his buddies were spotted throwing apples and tomatoes at incoming planes. Military policemen went to the house and told Bill's mother that Bill was the fastest kid they had ever had to chase. He had beaten them back to the house, but they knew where to look for him.

"I don't know why he would do that," Bobbie said. "He knew later that it was crazy. I talked to him after he had been in Basic Training and everything. He said the Marines were the best thing that could have ever happened to him. He wasn't a bad kid. Billy didn't really like school, but Billy wasn't dumb. He was smart. But he just did not like school."

The grammar and spelling, copied verbatim from Bill's letters, reflect the writer's youth and the rush in which they were frequently written.

On October 25, 1968, Bill wrote to Vicki Hill in Senoia: Entire letter.

> *Dear Vicki,*
>
> *Surprize, you probably don't even remember me, well its Bill Thomas. Please don't hate me for not writing, there is so much to do over here that I don't even have enough time to sleep (not really). I am really sorry Vicki, so please write back.*
>
> *I will be back in Senoia by January 10, 1969. My family is going to Texas, but I am going to stay with my Aunt in Senoia.*
>
> *The reason I haven't been writing is because I fell in love with this girl, her name is Amy Rohrback. Well anyway we were getting along just fine for about 7 months and she went back to the states to go to college, and I haven't heard from her since and Vicki it just about kill me. I was feeling sorry for myself but I snap out of that mood in about a month. And anyway that's why I haven't been writing. I can't wait till I get back to Senoia. This place is a groove but I am getting into to much trouble. That's enough of my problems.*
>
> *Well, how have you been, fine I hope, you're probably married are you? I sure hope everybody has not forgot me. How is Betty Joe? Be sure to tell everybody I said hi, that is if everybody is still around. Ever since Amy left me, it just dawned on me that I haven't written anybody in months, so please forgive me. I know I said it earlier in this letter, but I feel so bad about not writing. How is Jody and Perry? Vicki please write me as soon as you can because I don't want to*

come back to Senoia and find out everybody is gone. I bet everybody has forgot me. I really don't know what to say, except please write me and fill me in on whats going on, so I can write more, so please write soon that is if you still remember. Write if you don't remember to. I hate to close this letter like this but I don't know what to write so be sweet and please write because I want to hear from you real bad.
Love always,
Bill or B.T.

Zimmerman continued to get in trouble with his commanding officer because of Bill's misbehavior. Bobbie had graduated from high school and returned to Rome, Georgia. Bill had finished tenth grade but didn't want to go back to school. His stepfather just wasn't sure what to do with him. Bill wouldn't return to school and wanted to join the military. He wanted to be like his cousin Ronnie and join the Marines, but he was seventeen and needed a parent to sign the paper. His mother refused, so Waldemar Zimmerman signed it. Zimmerman felt like the Marines would force Bill to grow up.

"If I had still been there, I would have talked him out of it," said Bobbie. However, she later realized that he really wanted to be in the military and a combination of things had led him there. When it came time to fill in the hometown of record, Bill listed the last town he had lived in before coming to Okinawa: Senoia, Georgia.

Fred Cox remembered Bill had told him he wanted to go into the Marines, even back at East Coweta High School. Bill got his wish, and in December 1968, two months after he had written Vicki Hill that he would visit Senoia in January, he was sworn in to the Marine Corps in Honolulu, Hawaii.

"I told him not to do it," said Ronnie Duke. "He did it anyway." Bill went into Basic Training at the Recruit Training Depot in San Diego.

Bill sent this undated letter to Vicki Hill in Senoia and wrote it from boot camp, likely in January or February of 1969.

Hi Sweetie it's me B.T.
Dear Vicki,
How are you? Fine I hope. Well I told you I would write you when I got in Boot Camp. Sorry I didn't write sooner but

> *I lost your address so I wrote my Aunt and she called your mom and got your address for me, that goes to show you that I was thinking of you.*
>
> *I sure was sorry to hear about Eddie, damn I can't imagine how his parents feel. [Eddy Couch died in Vietnam on December 31, 1968. See Chapter 17.]*
>
> *This boot camp is hell but I am struggling along. Well sweetie, how is Senoia been doing? When I get back to Senoia I want to take you out. I just pray to God I make it back. Sweetie do me a big favor and call Perry Bishop and tell him that I am [in] the Marines, Okay. Are you going steady with anybody? I sure hope not and if you are whoever he is sure is lucky. I haven't heard from anybody in a long time, please write as soon as you can because when I receive a letter from you it makes me feel good to hear from you.*
>
> *Well sweetie, I got to be going, they don't give us no time at all to write as you can see, but I promise the next letter will be longer. Please write soon.*
>
> *Love always,*
> *Bill*
> *USMC*

By the time Bill had completed his training, his stepfather had been transferred to Reese Air Force Base in Lubbock, Texas. So, Bill headed there to visit with family. He saw his sister Paulette, who lived in Detroit, and Gayle in Louisiana. Gayle's husband decided to take Bill out on the town one evening, and when they returned, Bill got sick all over the family's hardwood floor. Gayle was furious. She made Jess, her husband, clean up everything and get Bill into bed.

While in Lubbock, Clara spent time cooking for him. He loved black-eyed peas and cornbread and ate massive quantities of them while there. He went out to the movies with friends. His larger muscles from Marine training impressed everyone and caused much comment. As he departed Lubbock, Clara felt that this would be the last time she would ever see him.

Bill had trained as a radio-telegraph operator (RTO) and might have received extra training in his MOS after he visited Lubbock.

Regardless, by early December of 1969, he was on his way to Vietnam.

Bill was assigned to and served with Headquarters and Service Company (H&S Company), 2nd Battalion, 1st Marines, 1st Marine Division upon arrival in Vietnam. Bill was destined to be there for four months. His battalion conducted combat operations around the city of Danang. Because of his youth, the veteran Marines tried to keep him away from the most dangerous areas and ensure he was doing safer work at the base camp. However, the family was later informed that Bill had volunteered for everything. But keeping Bill at the base camp finally changed in March of 1970.

Marine Vietnam Veteran Bob Balogh recalled when things changed.

> *I remember sharing a warm beer with him before he went out that night... And that night, his Jeep hit a land mine. Thomas, in the passenger seat, absorbed the full impact of the bomb. The driver and the machine gunner survived.*
>
> *Barry Sadler from Texas [not to be confused with the popular Green Beret with the same name] was the radio man in the other Rat Jeep, and he called in the medevac. Bailey Eames was in the rear area with me, and I think Mike Clayton was working with Echo Company at the time.*

Interestingly, Eames remembers things a little differently than Bob Balogh.

Marine Vietnam Veteran Bailey Eames recalled Bill's last day this way:

> *The day he died was his 1st day to actually go to the field. It was a position on the Rat Patrol. I had been riding the Rat Patrol for about 6 weeks. L/Cpl Thomas worked for me as a Radio Operator for several months and each day he was like a kid as he bugged me to send him to the field. (That's the area that 2/1 was assigned to protect.) Many of my Operators liked the bush (Field) and they didn't want to give up their position as a Company Radio Man. Now at about 1430 (2:30PM) My OIC (Officer in Charge) told me to pick*

someone to take my place on Rat Patrol as I was needed more in the rear to take care of my Radio Platoon. CPL Mike Clayton and Cpl Bob Balogh were the last of my men to see Lcpl Thomas and Bob actually had a beer with Thomas. I picked Thomas to ride so he could stop fussing about not getting to go to the field. When I told him he was going to ride RT [radio-telegraph operator], he jumped up on me and gave me a big hug. He told me he would not let me down.

LCPL Thomas was so happy and he died doing what a Marine does best—taking care of his other brothers of the Corps. You see I was supposed to be in that Jeep seat that Lcpl Thomas was in when the Rat Patrol lead jeep hit a mine on the MSR route that leads out of Nue Kim San (BAD spelling) At about 1830 (6:30PM) I was actually taking a shower under a 55 gal water barrel when I hear an explosion. One of my men came running out of the hootch and hollered telling me that Rat Patrol had gotten hit. I ran to my Hooch and grabbed my boots and utilities actually running naked out of the hooch. As I saw this Jeep with a Lt driving it he stopped for me to get in. He had come from the COC bunker and was heading out to the position where RP got hit. LCPL Thomas was killed instantly. By the time I had gotten to the location with the LT from S-2, they had Thomas on a stretcher and were loading him onto a Chopper. The men who were in the 2nd Jeep told me that the first Jeep hit this mine and that Lcpl Thomas flew out of the Jeep and my best guess is that he died from the concussion from the artillery round that was buried at the location of the explosion. His body was not torn up very much, and the way I saw him he had many bones broken as when they picked him up he looked like a rubber doll.

I have cried many nights about him. So many people take the United States freedom for granted. Men like the kid from GA may have been a lawyer, banker or even the President of the United States. I have thought many times what would his life have been? I keep a picture of him at my home. Just a pic. Chest hi with that big grin on his face. He had sandy blond hair. He was a small Marine; At times I chewed his

> *ass out for him trying to be so salty. I would gladly give my life if I could bring him back.*

According to the casualty report, Bill Thomas "Died 25th March 1970 in Quang Nam Province, Republic of Vietnam as a result of multiple fragmentation wounds when the vehicle in which he was a passenger detonated a hostile explosive device while on patrol." Bill was the only Marine killed.

The news of Bill's death spread rapidly. Waldemar and Clara were driving to Georgia to take up his new post at Warner Robins Air Force Base. They planned to stop and visit their daughter Gayle in Shreveport, Louisiana. However, since they were on the road and unreachable, the military first contacted James and Inez Duke, Ronnie's parents, in Atlanta. Ronnie was working on a construction job when his oldest brother drove out to the site with the news of Bill's death.

"It was not a happy time for the family," Ronnie said.

In Louisiana, Waldemar and Clara finally made it to Gayle's door. Shortly afterward, the Marines walked up to that same door. Her mother "was beside herself. She had to go lay down on the bed. That is about all I remember of that day," said Gayle.

Bobbie, married and living in Topeka, Kansas, was nine months pregnant with her first child. Local law enforcement knocked on her door that day and requested that Bobbie contact home, saying that there was a family emergency. She immediately thought of her mother and stepfather traveling to visit her sister. Bobbie soon found out what the crisis entailed. She said she threw herself on the bed and her pregnant belly. She felt like she was smothering. She couldn't sleep.

The funeral took place at H.M. Patterson & Son Funeral Home in Atlanta. Bobbie got there even though they didn't usually allow pregnant women to fly if they were past their seventh month.

Waldemar and Ronnie identified the body when it arrived in Atlanta. Ronnie made them recomb Bill's hair because he knew that Bill didn't wear it that way, and he didn't want Clara to see it like that. Ronnie could see that most of the damage was to Bill's head. Waldemar got a military plot at Arlington Cemetery in Sandy Springs, and Bill was laid to rest there.

"It is tough to lose somebody that young," said Ronnie, the combat veteran. "It makes you appreciate life more than most people."

Waldemar Zimmerman left the Air Force in 1971. He and Clara moved to Fayetteville, Georgia, where their son Mike graduated from Fayette County High School. In 1978, Mike joined the Marine Corps. Waldemar and Clara moved to Acworth and eventually retired in Blue Ridge, Georgia. Waldemar died in 2003.

Gayle, Bobbie, and Clara lived in McDonough, Georgia, for many years. Bobbie made sure that her brother was listed on the local Veterans Wall of Honor. The family has not forgotten.

Bill Thomas died on March 25, 1970. He had just turned nineteen a few weeks before. Two months later, fifty-two students from East Coweta's Class of 1970 received their diplomas and threw their caps into the air. They had just graduated from high school.

***Born**: March 10, 1951*
***Home of record**: Senoia, Georgia*
***Died**: March 25, 1970, in Quang Nam province of South Vietnam*
***Coweta servicemen who died in the same province**: Daniel Post, Larry Pinson, Mike Watson, and Jerry Smith*
***Unit on Death**: H & S CO, 2nd BN, 1st Marines, 1st Marine Division*
***Decorations:** Purple Heart, National Defense Service Medal, Vietnam Service Medal, Vietnam Campaign Medal*
***Buried:** Arlington Memorial Park, Sandy Springs*
***Vietnam Memorial, Washington, DC:** Panel 12W Line 44*

Sources:
Interview with Clara Thomas Zimmerman, mother
Interview with Barbara Thomas Jenkersen, sister
Interview with Patricia Gayle Thomas Griffith, sister
Interview with Ronnie Duke, cousin
Interview with Deberah Williams, childhood friend
Interview with Betty Banks, childhood friend
Interview with Vicki Hill Whitlock, childhood friend
Interview with Freddie Cox, childhood friend
Email interview with Bob Balogh, USMC

Email interview with Bailey Eames, USMC

References

Coffelt Database, "William Thomas." Accessed June 16, 2018. http://coffeltdatabase.org/index.php

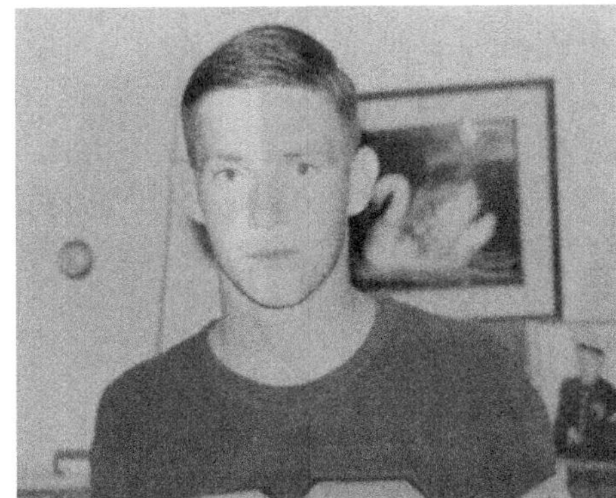

Bill Thomas, dates uknown.

Bill Thomas, USMC, 1969-1970.

*Photos courtesy of Bobbie Jenkerson. *

CHAPTER TWENY-THREE

John Tillman Dozier II

Sharpsburg/Palmetto, Georgia

We think of you often but always on August 23rd, our anniversary. We look at the pictures and smile. Holly and Venda laugh when we talk about swimming in the creek. Your girlfriend Mary named her boy after you. We all look forward to seeing you again in the next life. You were more than just my best man. You were a great friend.

—Joseph McKeon

Wanda McKeon didn't have long to live. She knew it. Her disease was progressive and terminal; her husband had hospice brought in to assist. But at least she would die at home, surrounded by her husband, children, and those she loved. Her husband, Joseph, was taking care of her around the clock. During the lucid times, he held her and talked to her about their family and memories. He was in anguish but wouldn't leave her. Joseph and Wanda McKeon had been married for forty-six years. They had met while Joseph was serving in the Army during the Vietnam War.

The day before she died, Wanda regained consciousness. Joseph was right there. She was unable to speak, but Wanda and Joseph held on to each other's hands. The love that had carried them through the good and bad times was still fierce. Neither wanted to let go of the other. Joseph finally said, "Wanda, let me tell you, if that angel [who picks you up after you die] is John Dozier, you tell him to keep his damn paws off you!"

Wanda laughed. John Dozier had once said that if Joseph didn't marry Wanda, he would.

Wanda McKeon died the next day.

"Maybe John's got her now, which would suit me fine," Joseph said. "I certainly hope that she has reunited with him and all of the wonderful, beautiful people we have had in our life."

Wanda's sisters all knew John Dozier. They loved him. Every Memorial Day, they contact each other and reminisce about John. Even now, Joseph and Wanda's children all know about John Dozier.

"I firmly believe John was there to welcome her back to the place from which we all come," said Joseph. "He's been gone over fifty years now, and I still think about him often. John once told me that 'the human race is really disgusting. All we seem to do is kill each other.' He was right."

John Tillman Dozier, named after his grandfather, was born on March 24, 1951, to James Thomas Dozier and Katie Belle Singleton Dozier. James Dozier was a veteran of the Marine Corps and the US Army and was a career soldier who spent thirty years in military service. He had served in World War II and Korea, garnering two Purple Hearts. Katie Belle, originally from Alabama, was named by her mother after her two favorite mules, Katie and Belle. John was the fifth of eight children and the first boy. The children included Priscilla Ann, Ramona, June, Judy, John, Westly, James, and April. When John was five, his father was stationed in Japan, followed by two tours in Germany, where he moved his family.

John's sisters Ramona and June described their brother as soft-hearted and gentle growing up. However, John's father was tough on him, even when he was young. He used to call him a "sissy" because he played with only girls, his four older sisters. The children used to get scared when their parents drank too much alcohol; neither handled it well.

Among his adventures in Germany, John on one occasion wandered away from home, and the family dog, Snodgrass, followed. His mother frantically tried to locate John but to no avail. She eventually called the police. They found young John, accompanied by his canine companion, a fair distance away from the house and crossing a bridge. They convinced John to get into the patrol car but said they didn't intend to take the dog. John protested and refused to go with them unless Snodgrass was included. Finally, the officers relented, and both renegades returned home.

The Dozier family spent eight years in Germany then returned to northern Virginia before landing in Atlanta's Five Points community.

As John grew up, his personality asserted itself. He was a jokester who enjoyed dancing and singing.

"He was a really, really good person. There wasn't anything that he wouldn't do for someone and nothing he wouldn't give to someone," said June Dozier, the third daughter and John's sister. "If it meant that he would go without, he would give it to someone else. That is just the kind of person he was. He loved his brothers and sisters."

John went to school in Germany then in Atlanta through the eighth grade. Afterward, he stopped attending school. Instead, he worked at a Burger King in the West End area of Atlanta, living with June, who had recently married. His mother, father, and younger siblings moved to West End then to Palmetto. After John's death, they moved to Sharpsburg and lived in a trailer that John had purchased for them while in the military. Two of John's younger siblings, Warren and April, attended East Coweta High School.

In the spring of 1968, John Dozier turned seventeen. The United States was in an uproar over the Vietnam War with the Tet Offensive ongoing. President Lyndon Johnson had declined to run for a second term. The Civil Rights Movement had taken a blow with the assassination of Martin Luther King. Despite the turmoil and the prospect of the draft looming, John Dozier decided that he needed to do his part and join the US Army. His father signed for him to enlist but told him that he would never make it. According to June Dozier, James Dozier told his son, "You don't have what it takes."

"John stood up to him," said June. John told his father that he would be a better soldier than James had ever been.

John Dozier entered the service in July of 1968. After completing Basic Training that summer at Fort Benning, he spent the fall at Fort Polk, Louisiana, for Advanced Infantry Training. After AIT, he was assigned to Fort Campbell, Kentucky, as an assistant gunner, bouncing between several units. Finally, in November 1969, he became the assistant range sergeant.

An assistant range sergeant was assigned to the area of Fort

Campbell known as Range Central. This area controlled all activities in the rear of the base, including drop zones for paratroopers and rifle ranges. Approximately thirty different rifle ranges were in that part of the base alone. Dozier did various tasks while assigned there. He took soldiers to a rifle range to police the area, cut the weeds and high grass with swing blades, and tested pop-up targets to ensure everything was working correctly.

John Dozier met Joseph McKeon at Range Central that fall of 1969. While McKeon had grown up on Long Island, like Dozier, he had dropped out of high school and enlisted in the Army in 1968. But unlike Dozier, Joseph had already served a tour in Vietnam, working as a crew chief in the 199th Recon Aircraft Company in the IV Corps area of Vietnam. He had flown in Birddogs and Hueys. Upon returning from Southeast Asia, he was stunned to encounter a tremendous change in attitude back home. McKeon was appalled at how the American people seemed to have turned against their soldiers. The year he had spent in a war zone now felt like a lifetime ago. While on leave, McKeon visited Atlanta, his mother's birthplace and his grandmother's home. He found that people in Georgia were more tolerant.

"Ironically, that is where John Dozier is from," McKeon said. So when he met John Dozier at Fort Campbell, even though Dozier had not been to Vietnam, McKeon found a sympathetic ear and a buddy. They seemed to bond instantly.

"He was really well-liked by everyone," said McKeon.

Fort Campbell was the home base for the 101st Airborne, but the division was in Vietnam, so the Fort was operating as a basic combat base. A variety of military personnel from different areas of the country worked there—lifers and draftees, soldiers who had been to Vietnam, and soldiers who had not been to Vietnam. All of them seemed to get along with John Dozier.

"He had a shit-eating grin," said McKeon. "You couldn't help but like him."

McKeon, Dozier, and a couple of other soldiers often went to Atlanta for long weekends in Dozier's neck of the woods. They wore wigs when they went to the Varsity or clubbing at night. They didn't want people to see the length of their hair, as it would be evident that they were in the military. They also went to the area of

Peachtree Street where, according to McKeon, the “hippies” hung out.

“It was great,” McKeon said. “We had a good time.”

A devout Catholic, John also had a religious side. McKeon said that John worked with the Catholic chapel at Fort Campbell. He enjoyed studying the Bible and had even considered becoming a priest.

While at Fort Campbell, McKeon dated a local girl who grew up in a farming community near Clarksville, Tennessee. Fort Campbell straddles the state lines of Kentucky and Tennessee, close to Clarksville. Wanda Lou Phillips had gotten a job at Fort Campbell out of high school then worked as a telephone operator in Clarksville. One evening, Joseph McKeon, John Dozier, and another sergeant were there in McKeon’s new Dodge Charger. Wanda was out with two of her three sisters in her new Chevy Malibu. The sisters drove by the soldiers. The guys shouted at them but got no response. The soldiers watched as the car full of girls pulled up into the Shoney’s drive-in and parked to order. Naturally, the guys pulled up beside them and began conversing with the sisters. Joseph asked the driver, Wanda, for her phone number.

“She told me her number was 615-2333,” Joseph said. “I wrote it down, and a little while later, after the girls had left, John looked at me and said, ‘You’re a damn fool. That’s not a real number. She made it up.’ So the next day, I called the number, and it really was her number!”

The pair met up with John and his girlfriend at the NCO Club. They ate and danced, and “it just took off from there,” Joseph said.

Wanda Phillips was the oldest of seven children. She had three brothers and three sisters. Dozier started going along with McKeon to hang out with the Phillips family.

“John was the only guy I would trust with my girlfriend,” McKeon said. He even loaned Dozier his car to pick up Wanda if she needed a ride, as he didn’t have a car. Instead, Dozier drove military trucks around the base and got a ride if he needed to go elsewhere.

“John was more than a friend,” Joseph said. “We got him set up with some gals that my wife knew, did some dating, spent time with him, and everyone really liked John.”

Joseph and John frequently double-dated, especially enjoying the NCO club. Joseph took Wanda, and John brought along whoever was available. John loved to dance and listen to Janis Joplin songs. "If he could have, John would have married Janis," Joseph said with a laugh. "He was nuts about her. So when a Janis Joplin song came on, John was all over it."

In August 1970, Joseph and Wanda married at a crowded Blooming Grove Baptist Church in Woodlawn, Tennessee, where Wanda had grown up. John Dozier served as best man. The Phillips home was the site of the reception. One of Wanda's sisters married a week later and used the same flowers.

June recalled her brother being in John's wedding and thinking that his wife, Wanda, was great.

"He really has a good woman," John told her. "I want to marry one like that."

John had an attractive blond girlfriend named Mary, whom he dated casually. He wasn't looking to get serious; he didn't think it was right to take a chance on making any young woman a widow so early in her life. He wouldn't get serious with someone until after returning from Vietnam. Also, according to June, John loved children. He was the "cool uncle" to June's son Johnny, who adored him. As the calendar moved into the fall of 1970, everyone waited for John to settle down.

John received his orders to Vietnam that fall. In 1970, the military bases got a "levy" every month. They needed to select a certain number of soldiers to go to Germany, Korea, or Vietnam. John was chosen for Vietnam in September. He planned on a career in the Army, so he didn't try to avoid the deployment.

Joseph McKeon talked to him about Vietnam. "Are you sure you want to do this? Because the people back home don't give a shit about us. You're not going to get any admiration from your friends in Georgia," Joseph told him.

John replied by mentioning the "band of brothers" and said he felt "more comfortable with these soldiers than with civilians." He said he wanted to serve in Vietnam as part of his career in the Army and needed to "walk the walk" so that he could "talk the talk."

John told June the thing that he was most worried about was the possibility of losing limbs or pieces of his body over there. He didn't want to come home like that and said he would rather die.

On John's last night at Fort Campbell, before he drove to the Atlanta area to visit with family then leave for Vietnam, Joseph and Wanda took him to Paris Landing State Park, about forty miles from Fort Campbell in Buchanan, Tennessee, for dinner. John had just reenlisted in the Army. Joseph again tried to talk him out of going, which Dozier wouldn't consider.

"I think he had something to prove to his daddy," Joseph said.

In early November 1970, John Dozier departed for Vietnam after a one-week training course to prepare for his deployment. Upon arrival in-country, he was assigned to the First Cavalry Division. However, the First Cav was sent home from Vietnam, so John was reassigned to Company A, 2nd Battalion, 502nd Infantry Regiment of the 101st Airborne Division and stationed at Camp Eagle in Thua Thien province. (Charles Walthall and Robert Webb served at Camp Eagle and died in Thua Thien province. See Chapters 11 and 24.)

Dozier wrote home to Joseph McKeon, his mother and siblings, and to his sister June.On occasion, he recorded tapes to send home. June remembers him sending her some coffee packets from his C-Rations. John Dozier's odyssey in Vietnam is revealed in his letters to June and her family, for which the grammar and spelling have been copied verbatim and reflect his lack of education and the rush in which they were frequently written.

But they also give a glimpse into his daily life in Vietnam.

November 21, 1970. Letter to John's sister, Mrs. June Dozier Murdock. Excerpts.

> *I am now assigned to Camp Eagle... Tomorrow I will draw my weapons and gear. My first sergeant seems ok. He said they are short on squad leaders so I hope to take over one when I get to my camp in the field.* [Camp Eagle was controlled by the 101st Airborne. Multiple servicemen from Coweta spent time in Camp Eagle.]

December 8, 1970. Letter to John's sister, Mrs. June Dozier Murdock. Excerpts.

> *The other day we had one of our men shot in the foot by one of our other men. They sent him back to the rear for a*

court martial. Nothing else has happened over here worth talking about. Just the same old rout teen. Hump [to walk or go on patrol], set up, eat, sleep, guard and go on patrol. Our squad is suppose to go on patrol sometime today.

Later the same day, John added on to the letter.

I am now walking slack man in our squad. There is two other Sgts before me so I should be squad leader around March. That is when they leave. Slack man is the second man to walk when we are humping. I am suppose to watch out for the point man while his is cutting the way threw.

December 25, 1970. Letter to John's sister, Mrs. June Dozier Murdock. Excerpts.

June, I received your long letters and in one of them you said I was brave. Glad someone thinks so. Vietnam esent as bad as most people think it is. If you spend your time worrying about getting shot and stepping on mines all the time you won't make it. Like you said I am safter over here than in the United States. For the month of November we had 40 men died of an overdose of drugs then you have your men who shoots themselves and by [illegible]. Charlie is causing not as many deaths over here as most people think. June, if anything should happen to me out here it wasn't for nothing because I believe in what I am doing and I am glad I can do something for my country.

January 5, 1971. Letter to John's sister, Mrs. June Dozier Murdock. Excerpts.

Today, two of our squads had to go out and buryed C rations. The rice crops had been bad this year and the enemy is going hungre. We are leaving C rations on another hill hoping the enemy will see us do it. When we leave they are suppose to come and dig them up while all along we have radar set up on that hill top. Then we will call air strikes on them. Cool huh. The type of radar we have can pick up human sweet far as a mile.

January 9, 1971. Letter to John's sister, Mrs. June Dozier

Murdock. Excerpts.

> *About the end of this month I will be squad leader. The squad leader now will be leaving the end of February and his is going to let me take over the end of this month so he can help me out. The job really esent all that hard and my men is all good and know what is going on over here since each and every one has already been in a fire fight.*

January 11, 1971. Letter to John's sister, Mrs. June Dozier Murdock. Excerpts.

> *This morning someone was playing jokes by putting C.S. gas in our hootches* [shelter]. *I started coughing and I spit up some blood. It is not the first time I have ever done that but the guy who hutch with me saw it and asked me if I was sick. I laughed and told him no, that I do it sometime when I cough a lot. (Which is all ways sence I have been in Vietnam. Well he told me to act like I was dying and that would get me some shame time* ["sham time," which indicates avoiding a task or goofing off]. *He went and got the medic and the medic took it all in. The medic went to the company commander and told him that I needed to go in. Before I knew it I was on a bird going to the hospital. They took chest ex-rays and I guess some things was wrong because, the doctor gave me a long speech on how important it was for me to stop smoking. It had something to do with the tubes going from my lungs is slowly [illegible] up and if I don't stop smoking it will turn into some type of decease. I am not worried about it and I should get 10 days shame time. I have to go back to the doctor tomorrow. Be good and June please write me soon.*

The CS gas Dozier mentioned is more commonly called tear gas. This was often used as a form of fragging (an attack by American troops on their officers, often by use of a fragmentation grenade) by disgruntled troops without killing anyone. It is unclear from his letter whether Dozier realized that it wasn't a joke or why he even included that in his letter to his sister.

Late January or February 1971. Undated letter John sent to his nephew, Johnny Murdock. Excerpts.

> *The Army has it for up where we [the men in Vietnam] can come back to the United States for two weeks on leave. You have to pay your way to home and back which will add up to about $600. Do you think it will be worth it. If I do decide to do it I will come home around June. You and your mother will have to get together and let me know.*

This leave was mentioned more than once in the letters John Dozier wrote home.

February 26, 1971. Letter to John's sister, Mrs. June Dozier Murdock. Excerpts.

> *Dear June and Family,*
>
> *Just a few lines before I go out and put my claymores and trips out. Hope the family and yourself is in the best of health and Ron and you is not working to hard on your jobs.*
>
> *I am about six miles from the DMZ now. Our company was [illegible] yesterday. We are suppose to be here until stand down. I don't know when that will be because they keep on changing it. They say it will be the 8 of March but can't say for sure. We have a new company commander and he is one big joke. He has us dig foxholes everywhere we go which is fine but he also has us to dig sleeping positions. We are humping two or three klicks [two or three thousand meters] a day now.*
>
> *In 26 more days I won't be a teeney bober no more.*

Dozier's mention of "trips out" referred to putting a tripwire attached to a claymore mine to create an automatic ambush (see Glossary in the appendix). The reference to no longer being a teenybopper was because his birthday was coming up, and he would turn twenty.

March 24, 1971. Letter to John's sister, Mrs. June Dozier Murdock. Excerpts.

> *What do you think about your big brother turning 20 today? I don't feel a year older. Yesterday we did a combat assault into a new A.O.* [area of operations] *and I came from 15 feet from losing half a leg. Our squad had to go on recon*

after we got to the L.Z. and where I put my rucksack a man step on a booby trap 15 feet from it. He lost half of his leg. The medic said that he doesn't think he will live because he went into shock after it happen. The man that was beside him was saved by his knife. The schrapnel hit his knife instead of his leg. We had a guy in my squad break his foot from jumping out of the bird. He was the assent M-60 gunner so I had to take his place. So now I am the assent M-60 gunner. The LT asked me if I wanted to take over 1st squad but I told him I would take over the squad I am in now when the Sgt goes in.

March 30, 1971. Letter to John's sister, Mrs. June Dozier Murdock. Excerpts.

Dear June and Family,

I am back in the field once more after spending two great days at Eagle Beach. June you wouldent believe it. After sleeping on the hard ground those state side bunks look real good along with hot baths and food. We was really treated like kings. I went swimming in the ocean and the water look so good I took a big drink without knowing it was full of salt. I took over 60 pictures. Quite a few of them are of me and will send them to you and mom to fight over when I get them developed. The floor show was great.

April 8, 1971. Letter to John's sister, Mrs. June Dozier Murdock. Excerpts.

We are humping more than usual. June sometimes I cannot understand this place. I guess the Army must think we are robots. They get us up at 6:30 in the morning. They send you out on recon about 500 hundred meters out you come back and start humping. In all you hump about 4 thousand meters a day. We will make another C.A. [combat assault] *after re-supply the 9th. They say our stand down will be the 1st of May but I cannot count on it. June they are having a hard [illegible] for everybody to get pack up so we can go on re-con. Hope to hear from you soon.*

April 18, 1971. Letter to John's sister, Mrs. June Dozier

Murdock. Excerpts.

My Battalion is on fire base Jack now after spending nine days in the rear on stand down. Our stand down was ok. We had a lot more training because of the mission we are on now. Our Battalion will be pulling raids in the A Shau Valley on known N.V.A. supply points. Our first raid is supposed to be on the 25 of April. We will be raiding a truck park on Tiger MT. The 22 we [our platoon] will repelle in to Tiger MT with engs and pull security for the engs while they plant mines on the roads.

A Shau Valley was notorious in Vietnam lore because of how tough it was to root the communists out of that location. "Engs" referred to engineers.

April 30, 1971. Letter to John's sister, Mrs. June Dozier Murdock. Excerpts.

I am in the rear once more. This time to go to C.L.C. [Combat Leadership course] *I will get about 10 days shame [sham] time out of it. In C.L.C. you learn more about maps, what to do in contact and you have to repell out of a bird. Repelling is when you go down on a rope from a bird about a hundred feet high. I will miss the mission my company is going on tomorrow. Company D & B, CA* [combat assault] *into [illegible] today. They got 2 birds shot down and got mortar and rockets. Tonight we will air strike 3000 meter from squad and tomorrow my company and C company will CA in and sweep it to find out if the air strikes did any good.*

Estimated mid-March 1971. Letter sent to John's nephew, Johnny Murdock. Entire Letter.

Dear Johnny-

Hope these few lines find my little man in good health and taking care of his mommy. As for Uncle John, I am in good health and miss his little man a whole bunch.

Your mom sent me a picture of you, herself and Great Granny Dozier and boy you sure have grown into a good looking, tough little man. Have you been doing much playing with your bear lately? I know I don't have to worry about my

> *sister (your mom) and my mother and BoBo (granny) when you are with them because you will fight anybody what tries to hurt them.*
>
> *Uncle John might come home in May for a two week leave to see his little man. I can't say for sure though. I only have 7 1/2 more months to go over in Vietnam and I will be home for good,*
>
> *Johnny I shall close for now and let you go. Tell mommy I will write her tonight. Uncle John is very proud of you Johnny and I love and miss you very much. Stay sweet but tough and write when you have the time.*
>
> *With love always your uncle*
>
> *John*
>
> *Ten Hup* [John always put this at the end of letters to his nephew. It is a misspelling of Ten-Hut, which is short for atten-tion, often barked by drill sergeants in the military.]

Undated, 1971. Letter to John's sister, Mrs. June Dozier Murdock. Excerpts.

> *Last night we had contact so we were all up most of the night. It sure was supkey* [spooky] *not knowing what is in front of you. I just got threw pulling four hours of guard. Like I told Dad and mom in their letter I don't have the time to write so much as I use to. The A.O. we are in is all open and we have to dig in each night. If we dident have a hole to jump in, in case of a rocket attack it would only take about 2 rockets to wipe us all out. I know it doesent take all day to dig a fox hole but we pull a lot more protrols and we are humping most of the day. I hope you understand and that it doesent keep you from writing. I told mom to send me $500 before May. I put in my request for a two week leave in May so if it does go threw you can expect me home some time in May. What do you think?*

John did go home to visit his family in May of 1971. However, before going back to Vietnam, he was notified that his squad had taken many casualties and was combat ineffective. John was distraught. "If I had been there, I could have done something," June remembers him saying. At that point, he just wanted to get back over there.

This attitude exemplified how John's military service had changed him, June said. "He became a leader. He became protective of the guys in his unit."

Unfortunately, on June 18, 1971, his leadership cost him his life. He probably moved to another unit because of the loss of his squad. The medic who treated him that day said John had not been with them for long. He explained what happened to John Dozier, who was in the A Shau Valley.

> *In conversations he and I had, he expressed the intention to have a career in the Army and wanted to acquire command experience as a squad leader. He quickly got the opportunity he wanted and took over one of our squads when the regular squad leader rotated out a few weeks later. He had been squad leader just for a couple of weeks when he died.*
>
> *Our company had been combat assaulted into an Area of Operations north and west of F.S.B. Tennessee because of intense enemy activity in the area. On June 17 and 18, our platoon was hit three times in two days. I had to medevac six people, including John and our platoon leader, during that two-day period.*
>
> *On the day John was killed, we had to set up in an old abandoned C.P. (Command Post) on top of a heavily wooded hill. Setting up in an abandoned C.P. is always risky, but we had little choice that night. John's squad was on point that day and so we were tasked with clearing the area before the rest of the platoon moved in to set up our night defensive perimeter. Unfortunately, the NVA had placed a fresh mechanical ambush with a grenade and a tripwire on the edge of the perimeter and that is what got John. He had been pretty close to the blast and had a very severe wound in his forehead as well as some other injuries. John had a bad habit of wearing his pot back on his head when patrolling and I have always theorized that that is why his forehead was exposed to the shrapnel. He was not conscious and clearly*

never knew what had happened. Another man in his squad was hit in the stomach by shrapnel from the same blast and had crawled into a foxhole by the time I got to him. He was badly injured but did not have immediately life-threatening wounds, so I spent most of my efforts working on John. We had to blow down some trees to clear an L.Z., and by the time that was ready it was almost dark. Our Colonel happened to be flying in the area in a loach [pronunciation of the acronym LOH, which stands for light observation helicopter] and his pilot offered, over the Colonel's protest, to fly John and I to the hospital in Phu Bai just as night was starting to fall. A very pissed-off colonel got out and I rode in the back of the loach with John's head in my lap while at the same time trying to hold up an IV above him. He was still breathing when I handed him over to hospital personnel on the tarmac in Phu Bai. I was pretty sure from his condition that he was not going to make it and the lonely ride back to the platoon was one of the most painful memories of my life. At about 3:00 in the morning, our platoon sergeant came over to my hole in the dark to tell me that H.Q. had just notified him that John had died, as I already knew he would. I was sitting up on radio watch when he told me, and even though I expected it, I just sat there and stared into the darkness and sobbed uncontrollably.

John loved the Army far more than most of us did in those days and was doing what he wanted to do, leading a squad when he died. He was serving his platoon and his sacrifice undoubtedly saved someone else in the platoon from a similar fate. As squad leader, he could have assigned someone else to do the dangerous job of sweeping our N.D.P. position [Night Defensive Position] but John took the risk himself that day, undoubtedly out of the strong sense of duty I mentioned before. I have thought about him many times over the years. When I first got back from Vietnam I wondered if I should try to find his family to tell them how he died but did not know how to do so. I probably could not have pulled it off emotionally in any case and sometimes things like that are better left alone.

I recently got an email from another former soldier who knew John very well and had actually attended his funeral in Atlanta. He told me quite a bit about John's background and gave me a lot of closure. He had visited John's parents' house in the southwest area of Atlanta while on leave with John and came to know them pretty well before John was shipped to Vietnam. It may interest you that our C.O. in Alpha Company at the time John was killed was Drew Dix, the first Green Beret enlisted man to win the M.O.H. It is unusual for the Army to reassign M.O.H. recipients to combat in the same war, but Captain Dix pulled some strings (he received a field commission for his action) and got a line company (Alpha, 2/502) in April of 1971. It was a real privilege to serve with him. I was very lucky with my commanding officers in Vietnam.

Drew Dix received the Medal of Honor in the same ceremony as Stephen Pless and Joe Jackson, both of Newnan.

"Dozier was doing what we all were trying to do, serve with dignity and honor and make it through a difficult year," said J. S. Staley, one of the members of Dozier's squad. "Doc and I were with him shortly after his misstep, and he never suffered, but we do continuously. John proved to me that freedom is not a hollow word."

June believes her brother could have sent one of his men out to do what he was doing that evening, but John was a leader, his squad's "protector."

"As usual, he was taking the chances himself, leading his squad," said Doc Cooper.

On Sunday, June 20, 1971, Father's Day in the United States, two men in military uniform went to see John Dozier's parents in Palmetto. After receiving the news, they called John's siblings. When June's husband answered, she immediately knew something was wrong. As her husband hung up, she stared at him, asking, "What is wrong?"

He replied, "John's dead."

She fell apart. "I will never forget that," June said.

On Tuesday, June 22, Joseph McKeon had just gotten home from the base when the phone rang. It was John's father. Joseph knew immediately what had happened. Initially, he held out hope that John had just been wounded. But after speaking with John's father, his hopes dashed, he called the guys at Range Central, Fort Campbell, and let them know.

John Dozier's funeral was held on Saturday, June 26, at Venetian Hills Baptist Church in Atlanta. Joseph and Wanda McKeon headed to Atlanta on Friday, along with another friend of John's. The two soldiers didn't wear their uniforms on the trip down from Kentucky because they feared the reaction they might encounter. They arrived and visited with John's family. They stayed overnight with McKeon's grandmother in Atlanta. The uniforms remained in the trunk until they were ready to attend the funeral. While John had converted to Catholicism, the Dozier children had been raised as Baptists, according to Joseph McKeon.

"I remember that day. It is etched in my soul," he said. "We were in our uniforms, we went to the church, and it was an open casket. When I looked at him, I knew his whole head had been reconstructed. He looked like a wax figure. It was incredible. I told Wanda not to go up and look at John. You want to remember him the way he was when we were together, with that smile. I remember when his sister came in, I can't remember which one, and went up and looked at John. She put both hands on the coffin and dropped to her knees, put her head against the casket, and cried out in anguish, 'My God, John, what did they do to you?' I thought, what a waste. What was this all for? That was one of the most traumatic experiences I ever had. Many people died in Vietnam that were friends of mine, many were Long Island friends, but when John went, it was bad."

Joseph McKeon stayed in touch with John's family afterward. His own family never forgot John Dozier.

John's girlfriend, Mary, had not become a widow. She later fell in love and married, and she had a son and named him John. She later told McKeon that she "thought the least I could do for John was name my son after him."

The captain and sergeant in charge of Range Central at Fort Campbell decided to do something to honor John Dozier. They had the Army bring in a large spruce tree, and they planted it by the driveway entrance to the facility and posted a sign reading, "This tree planted in memory of Sgt. John Dozier, 101st Airborne, Killed in Vietnam, June 18, 1971."

Joseph McKeon noted, "That didn't happen for just any soldier." McKeon visited Fort Campbell and the site around 2015. The buildings and the sign are gone, but the tree is still there, still honoring John Dozier.

After John's death, Katie Belle looked around and decided to place her trailer on a lot in Sharpsburg, which she thought was a nice area. Unfortunately, the trailer was damaged by fire years after John's death. Her other children offered to get her a new trailer. She wasn't interested; instead, she had the trailer redone because John had purchased it for her.

"My son got this for me, this is my home, and this is where I will die," she said. Katie Belle Dozier died in 2006 and rests at Westview Cemetery beside her John.

James Dozier died in 1995 and was buried at a veterans cemetery in Columbus, Georgia.

"For years and years, it was hard for me to believe that my brother was gone. Even though I saw him and all, it was still hard for me to really believe it," said June. "I kept thinking that he was over there somewhere and that really wasn't him, you know, even though I saw him. I just refused to believe he was dead."

"I want people to know that he was just a good human being, and he believed in his country," she said. He told June that he didn't understand what they were fighting for, but he said, "I do believe in my country."

**To see the catalog of original letters to and from John Dozier, visit www.bettermencoweta.com.

***Born**: March 24, 1951*
***Home of record**: Atlanta, Georgia*
***Died**: June 18, 1971, in Thua Thien province of South Vietnam*
***Coweta servicemen who died in the same province**: Charles Walthall, Robert Webb, Eddy Couch, Wayne Vessell, and Johnny Calhoun*
***Unit on death**: A CO, 2nd B.N., 502nd Infantry, 101st A.B.N.*

Division
Decorations: *Bronze Star Medal with Oak Leaf Cluster, Purple Heart, Air Medal, Good Conduct Medal, National Defense Service Medal, Republic of Vietnam Military Merit Medal, Vietnam Service Medal, Vietnam Gallantry Cross with Palm Unit Citation, Republic of Vietnam Campaign Medal*
Buried: *Westview Cemetery, Atlanta*
Vietnam Memorial, Washington, DC: *Panel 3W Line 80*

Sources
Interview with June Dozier Murdock, sister
Interview with Ramona Dozier Morey, sister
Interview with Joseph McKeon, US Army
Email interview with Charles Cooper (Doc), US Army
Email interview with J. S. Staley, US Army

References
Coffelt Database, "John Dozier." Accessed December 29, 2021. http://coffeltdatabase.org/index.php

John Dozier, dates unknown.

John Dozier, US Army, 1968-1970.

Photos courtesy of June Murdock.

CHAPTER TWENTY-FOUR

Robert Mitchell Webb Jr.

Newnan, Georgia

When he came home, he was a very different person than when he went, since the last time I had seen him. He was more serious, he was more nervous, and he had very curly hair, and his hair had not been curly before he went to Vietnam.

—Diane Webb Tillman

It was a Sunday.

Mike Webb was lying on the floor as he watched television. His sister, Debbie, plus his niece and nephew, Raine and Robin, also lounged around the living room, eyes glued to the screen. Suddenly, the ring of the doorbell pierced through the noise from the TV. None of the kids moved. In all likelihood, it was just a salesman. Mike knew that his sister-in-law, Edna, would go to the door and take care of whoever it might be. The doorbell rang again. He looked around but didn't see Edna. As the oldest child in the group, he reluctantly dragged himself off the floor and headed toward the door.

It was the summer of 1971, and Mike Webb was fifteen. His older brother, Bobby, was twenty-six and married. Bobby's children, Raine and Robin, were still in the other room with his sister and the television. When he got to the door and opened it, two soldiers stood there in uniform. Mike didn't think anything about it. Mike and Bobby's father was a World War II veteran and had made a career in the military. The family had already been on more military bases than Mike could count. Bobby had joined the Army eight years earlier. Soldiers were a common sight for the Webb family.

"They asked for Mrs. Webb," Mike said. "I told them that my mom and dad were in Texas, and they were. My dad and mom had taken a trip to Oklahoma and Texas to visit my sisters, Judy and Linda, so when they asked for Mrs. Webb, it never dawned on me that they were asking for Pete [the nickname for his sister-in-law, Edna] because she still is and always has been my sister. I never thought of her as a sister-in-law or Mrs. Webb. That was just Pete, my sister. She came up behind me and said, 'I am Mrs. Webb.' That's when they broke the news to her, and she collapsed in a chair next to the door. I will never forget that."

Bobby's brother-in-law, Robert Burgess, escorted his body to Newnan but not without some misadventure. The military lost his records, and they couldn't find the body in Germany. Finally, once the situation was resolved, Burgess met the casket in New Jersey then rode first-class to Atlanta. Edna was at the airport when her husband arrived. She had told Bobby before he left for Vietnam that she would meet him at the airport, dead or alive, and that is what she was determined to do. So she stood silently by the Eastern Airlines plane and watched as the coffin came off the aircraft.

Night had fallen. It was raining, which seemed to reflect the family's mood and the mood of the entire country. The casket was retrieved from the aircraft, put on a carrier, and taken to a waiting hearse. Edna met it before it got to the hearse. Burgess didn't see anyone but Edna that night, but she had been driven to the airport by a military driver and accompanied by a survivor assistance officer.

"I was quite emotional," Burgess said. It was Thursday, October 28, 1971.

When Bobby's siblings walked into McKoon Funeral Home that Saturday, October 30, they saw the coffin with a flag across it to the left in a small room.

"My mother was crying, and she had her head on the coffin," said Diane Webb. "She was patting the coffin like you would pat a baby, to calm a baby, and she was talking to him, and my father was consoling her. It is something that I will always remember because my mother and dad just looked so little and broken up."

When the funeral began in McKoon's chapel around 2 p.m., the family looked out, stunned. The chapel was packed. They looked at each other in confusion; they didn't know many people in Newnan.

Edna's mother and stepfather, Wesley and Marjorie Hall, had lived in the Hollis Heights neighborhood for some time. Edna and the children had come to live with them when her husband left for Vietnam. Nevertheless, the Webbs had anticipated a small gathering, but this was completely unexpected.

"It was just amazing what the people in Newnan did for us," Diane Webb said with a smile.

In Springfield, Missouri, Robert Webb Jr. was born on July 11, 1945, to Mary Katherine (Kat) and Robert Webb Sr. Their six children were Diane, Judy, Bobby, Linda, Mike, and Debbie. Bobby's father was a veteran of World War II. He had served in Patton's Army in North Africa and was wounded in Sicily by machine-gun fire. After the war, Robert Sr. spent four years in and out of various hospitals, trying and eventually succeeding in saving his left arm.

"It seemed that every time he had to leave a hospital, my mother came up pregnant," Diane said.

Even though he lost the ability to straighten out his injured arm, he had a career in the military, staying in the Army for thirty-five years. As a result of his injury, Robert Sr. became a cook. Robert's Army career meant more traveling for the family.

"Traveling was just something that we thought was normal," said Diane. "It was difficult to leave people that we loved and places that we loved, and we learned how to handle that. Mainly, we became very close as brothers and sisters. We were also friends. We fought a lot like kids do, but the family was our core. We didn't have a lot of relatives around us because we moved so much. We learned to feel that wherever we were was temporary, but our family was permanent."

The family moved from El Paso, where Diane and Judy were born, to Oregon, then to Missouri, where Bobby was born, and to Michigan, where Linda was born. In Michigan, Bobby was playing with matches next to the garage and started a fire. The fire department was called, and the garage was ruined, but the house was saved. Bobby got a spanking.

After Michigan, the family went to Germany. As a small child, Bobby seemed afraid of everything in the foreign country, and his sister Judy was his protector. She would run out of the house to defend him if she thought anyone was picking on him.

When they returned from Germany, the Webbs went to Washington State, where Mike was born. The family's most prominent adventure was the transfer to Alaska. They were housed at Camp Denali, which had served as a Japanese internment camp during World War II. The family was the first to move into the camp and lived in Quonset huts made of galvanized and corrugated steel. The military used Quonset huts extensively because they were lightweight and easy to assemble.

Debbie Webb was born in Anchorage. Bobby seemed to thrive in Alaska and was elected president of his junior high class. He went camping on the Eagle River, where he gigged salmon. He had his first girlfriend, Jenny. He enjoyed playing bongos, and he wrote poetry and songs. He participated in a variety of activities and had many friends. When it came time to leave Alaska, it seemed to affect Bobby more than his siblings, and Diane said he wasn't the same after that.

It was on to Columbus, Georgia, the home of Fort Benning.

Bobby started high school at Baker High in Columbus.[1] While not a large guy, Bobby was very athletic. According to his sister Judy, he was an excellent baseball player, the team's star. He broke his dominant arm playing baseball but still competed in a bowling tournament soon afterward. Using his unbroken arm, he bowled well, and his team won. Linda Webb, one of Bobby's younger sisters, met Edna Hall in school, and the two became friends. Edna first met Bobby at a party when she was sixteen and Bobby was eighteen.

Bobby's initial reaction to Edna? "You're too skinny to be a girl. I'll call you Pete."

It might also have been that he couldn't remember her name. Regardless, from that point on in the Webb family, she was "Pete," and they began a relationship that influenced the rest of "Pete's" life.

Bobby's high school experience didn't go as well as the family had hoped. According to Diane and Judy, Bobby was in and out of trouble, though nothing serious. His younger brother, Mike, believes that a judge suggested to his parents that military service might be an excellent option to get Bobby on the correct path. Bobby would undoubtedly have been influenced by his father's military service, as the military was all the family had known. Whether or not a judge influenced the final decision, Bobby Webb left high school and joined the US Army. He joined on the buddy system with his friend Pat McKinney. The buddy system allowed a male to join the Army and undergo Basic Training with a friend. Occasionally, there were promises of the two going even further together, but that rarely worked out.

"When he was growing up, he was a little bit of a delinquent, but when he decided to grow up, he was a self-made man," Edna said.

In July 1963, around his eighteenth birthday, Bobby Webb began Basic Combat Training at Fort Gordon, Georgia, just a few hours away from his family. Once Basic was over, he went to Fort Polk, Louisiana, for Advanced Infantry Training. Vietnam was still a blip on the horizon. Upon completion of AIT, Bobby volunteered for Airborne Training. Then it was back to Fort Benning in January 1964.

According to Webb's military records, he completed Airborne Training, qualifying him as a US Army paratrooper. He also trained as a Senior Scout Observer (SSO) and was assigned to the 87th Infantry, based at Fort Benning. He would be stationed at Fort Benning for the remainder of 1964. Returning to Fort Benning allowed him to pick up where he had left off with Edna Hall.

Bobby and Edna married in the summer of 1964, just before Edna's eighteenth birthday. Bobby was twenty, and he and his best friend, Pat McKinney, married in the same ceremony. (Pat later had an accident in training, broke his back, and was discharged from the Army.)

The couple spent the next six months together, getting accustomed to married life. In January 1965, Bobby entered Ranger School at Fort Benning, some of the military's most challenging training. The two-month program was divided into three phases—crawl, walk, and run. Bobby completed Ranger School successfully and looked forward to his next challenge. He would find it in a country on the other side of the world.

On August 19, 1965, he was assigned to the First Cavalry Division (Airmobile) and became a squad leader. The First Cavalry was an experimental unit then, the first US Army unit to utilize the concept of "air mobility." The air mobility concept involved helicopters moving troops to and from a battlefield. In March 1965, units of the Marine Corps had landed in Vietnam and, shortly afterward, begun to engage in combat with communist forces. On July 28, 1965, President Lyndon Johnson announced that he had ordered the First Cavalry to Vietnam. Bobby Webb was assigned to the division amid frantic preparations for deployment to Vietnam. The division traveled to Vietnam in groups, with Bobby's group, Company C, 1st Battalion, 12th Cavalry arriving in Vietnam by ship on September 20, 1965. The 1st Battalion wasted little time getting into combat, and Bobby was likely involved in several operations and saw considerable action while in Vietnam. However, his unit wasn't engaged in the Ia Drang Valley campaign, which involved the 1st Battalion of the 7th Cavalry. This was the group highlighted in the Mel Gibson movie *We Were Soldiers*. In this regard, he was fortunate.

Bobby and his squad spent a lot of time in the jungle. The Webb family sent him care packages with little bottles of wine, which he certainly shared with his comrades. The twelve soldiers in any squad, living with each other and facing danger daily, would have formed a bond unimaginable to civilians. They would do anything to make sure their brothers came home alive. Bobby's son, Robin, was born during this first tour in Vietnam. His brothers in arms would have wanted him to go home to that child.

Bobby was wounded, likely in June of 1966, just a few months before he rotated home. Bobby and his unit got into a large firefight with communist forces, losing several men. Bobby was wounded in the back of one leg. He returned home in July.

When Bobby got home, he appeared wracked by survivor's guilt.

"When he came home, he was a very different person than when he went, since the last time I had seen him," Diane said. "He was more serious, more nervous, and had very curly hair, and his hair had not been curly before he went to Vietnam."

Judy Webb described Bobby as "mentally wounded."

"Daddy used to tease him and say it was because he was so scared that the pores clenched up and caused his hair to grow out curly," said Diane.

Mike Webb said that when Bobby came back from his first tour in Vietnam, he and their father, who was wounded in Sicily during

World War II, talked about the experiences in Vietnam.

"It was really harrowing," Mike said. "I mean, it was pretty gruesome what he saw and what they did. I remember as a kid that it burned into my mind. And also, I think if I'm not mistaken, the idea was at the time of him going to Ranger school and jump school and then finally aviation is that maybe his odds would increase survival-wise because, at the time, I don't think that the North Vietnamese surface to air was as strong as it ended up being. So I certainly think that he wanted to get off the ground, let's put it that way, having served as a grunt."

Whatever Bobby's wound entailed, it wasn't severe enough to force his discharge from the Army. Upon returning home, however, he was placed on reserve status and spent time in St. Louis, Missouri, and Fort Dix, New Jersey, between July and October.

If a soldier had less than 180 days remaining on his enlistment, he had the option to be placed in the active or inactive reserve for the time remaining on his military service or stay on active duty. An enlistee (three-year active-duty commitment) as opposed to a draftee (two-year commitment) could very well be sent to other bases, depending on the needs and desires of the Army. These soldiers could volunteer to rejoin the active Army or stay in reserve status at any time, according to Joe Loadholtes, US Army and Vietnam veteran.

In October 1966, Bobby Webb and his family were stationed in Germany. The last time Bobby had been to Germany, his older sister made sure no one picked on him. But that wasn't going to be a problem now.

"He had ended up just the opposite of that now. He was a very tough young man," said Diane Webb. "He was fearless when he got older."

Judy agreed. "When he grew up, he was something else again. He was a warrior."

Bobby and Edna stayed in Germany for the next two years. Their daughter was born in a military hospital there, and Bobby got his GED. When the Webbs returned to the United States in August 1968, they reported to Jacksonville, Florida, then moved to Montgomery, Alabama, in March of 1969. Bobby's job was the same at both places: recruiting young men to join the US Army.

During 1968 and 1969, this couldn't have been easy.

Mike Webb was thirteen and stayed with Bobby and his family during Bobby's stint as a recruiter. Bobby created an indelible impression on his little brother when he bought Mike his first electric guitar and amp.

"He probably didn't have much money, but he went right up to a pawn shop," said Mike. "That was just a great moment for me."

In December 1969, the Webbs reported back to Fort Benning. Bobby was to attend Officer Candidate School (OCS). Until this point in Bobby's military career, he had been an enlisted man. His current staff sergeant rank made him a non-commissioned officer (NCO). The NCO is the backbone of the US Army and is close to the enlisted soldiers, the privates, specialists, and corporals. He works on soldiers' military etiquette, skills, and tactical abilities. He communicates with the officers to maintain open communication between the enlisted man and the officer ranks. A soldier must go through Officer Candidate School (OCS) to become an officer.

Bobby was influenced to become an officer by his brother-in-law, Robert Burgess. Robert had joined the Army in 1959, had married Bobby's younger sister Linda in 1965, and was a career soldier. He had also done a tour in Vietnam as a crew chief in fixed-wing aircraft, so he and Bobby had this in common, though they rarely discussed their experiences. Greg Gandy, a Green Beret, was another of Bobby's friends in OCS who had already served in Vietnam. Their platoon leader leaned on these experienced soldiers to help the young officers-in-training learn what was needed to survive in Vietnam.

The next three months saw Bobby Webb excel and graduate first in his class. He and Greg Gandy left OCS in the spring of 1970 as second lieutenants, the first commissioned officer rank. Webb was the only serviceman among the Coweta group killed in Vietnam who was an officer. (See the hierarchy of US Army units and ranks in the appendix.) Unfortunately, many officer candidates didn't make it through. Of the 260 who started the course, only 61 graduated.

In June 1970, Bobby was activated from the Reserves and launched into a new venture, pilot training, to become a helicopter pilot.

Greg Gandy said, "We decided that since we had already walked the jungles of Vietnam for one tour and knew that we were headed back to Vietnam as infantry second lieutenants after graduation, we would apply to flight school."

The Webbs' first stop was at Fort Wolters in Mineral Wells, Texas, the home of Army, Marine, and Air Force Basic and Primary Flight Training. Bobby would have trained with various training helicopters to learn the basics of flying a helicopter. One of the most challenging would have been the TH-55 Hughes 300.

"If you learn to fly that, you can fly anything in the world," said Gandy.

After completing training at Fort Wolters, Bobby was sent to Fort Rucker, Alabama, to learn to fly Army helicopters.

There were several Army helicopters that servicemen might learn to fly, but the most common and most recognizable was the Utility Helicopter-1 (UH-1), commonly called the Huey. The Huey helicopter became iconic during the Vietnam War, not only to the soldiers in Vietnam but also to the general public in the United States and worldwide on nightly television broadcasts. To the soldier in Vietnam, it was the machine that took you into the intensity of combat, but it was also the machine that brought you supplies and got you out of the muck, whether you were finished with the mission, wounded, or dead.

From December 1970 until April 1971, Bobby Webb learned to do things with this flying machine that Leonardo DaVinci would have envied. At this stage of their training, they focused on more advanced topics than at Fort Wolters. They trained to fly using only their instruments, formation flying, emergency procedures, and combat tactics that they could incorporate in Vietnam. Many servicemen who completed the training would be sent to Vietnam even in 1971, as the war seemed to be drawing to a close. Bobby Webb was no exception. He would return to Vietnam in June 1971 as a Huey helicopter pilot.

May 1971 saw Bobby on leave, preparing to ship out. Edna and the children moved to Newnan, where her mother and stepfather now lived. She stayed with them while Bobby served his tour.

Diane remembered, "They had spent some time up there, and Bobby loved the place, thought it was beautiful, and they had made the decision that they were going to live there."

As Bobby prepared to return to Vietnam, he and his brother-in-law, Robert Burgess, made a promise to each other. If either of them were killed in Vietnam, the other would escort the body home. Bobby was on the way back. Robert had been selected for fixed-wing flight school and would be in training.

The last night before leaving on his trip to Vietnam, Bobby had a surprise for his family. He explained to everyone his vision for his return from Vietnam. He wanted to buy land in Newnan and build a house for him and Edna. In fact, he had already purchased enough land to build a family "compound."

"Bobby and Pete both loved Newnan," said Diane. "Bobby said before he left for Vietnam the second time that when he returned, he was going to buy some land in Newnan and build a family compound where we would all live as neighbors. That's why he's buried in Newnan. Newnan was going to be his forever home."

Mike remembered how the family tried to keep everything normal on Bobby's last night at home. The family enjoyed television, so they decided to watch TV. They piled onto the living room furniture and on the floor and made a big bowl of popcorn. As they watched, they passed the big metal bowl around to everyone. Mike and Bobby passed the bowl, and it spilled all over the floor. Mike said they couldn't stop laughing, so they ate the popcorn off the floor. That night was the "last time I saw him," he said.

In early June 1971, Bobby Webb was in California, preparing to depart for Vietnam. According to Diane, he didn't want to go. She described her last phone call with her brother, in which Bobby called from an airport in California and told her that he didn't want to go and proceeded to get very emotional.

"My dad got on the phone and told him that is what servicemen do," Diane said. "We didn't want him to go either, but he had to go. He told my mother that he didn't think he would ever come back. My mother used to say that she wishes she had shot him in the foot or broken his leg or something so he wouldn't have to go."

When Bobby Webb arrived in Vietnam, he was assigned as a Huey aircraft commander to the 101st Airborne Division, the Screaming Eagles of World War II fame. D-Day. Operation Market Garden. The Battle of the Bulge. The Band of Brothers. One of the most recognizable Army Airborne divisions in American military history had been converted to an Airmobile Division in the vein of the First Cavalry. He became part of A Company of the Aviation Battalion, nicknamed the *Comancheros*, stationed at Camp Eagle in the Thua Thien province of South Vietnam. Interestingly, Greg Gandy had been in the 101st during his first tour, while Bobby Webb had served in the First Cav. Greg was in the First Cav on their second tour, and Bobby was in the 101st.

It was 8:30 p.m. on October 17, 1971. The *Comancheros* were needed for a flare mission. These helicopter crew members kicked flares out of the chopper when needed for an infantry unit that was under attack. The flares bathed the area in light, allowing the American units to see what was in front of them.

It was Bobby's turn to pull standby, and the standby crew was called out for the mission. The crew headed toward the aircraft and did their preflight inspections as the pilots got all the information to fly the mission. Finally, the flares were loaded. The aviators boarded the aircraft, slowly lifted off, and turned to an American firebase that needed assistance. Bobby Webb, the co-pilot on this mission, was joined by Jack Searing, aircraft commander; Al Barrington, crew chief; Wallace Depreo, crew chief; and Barry Brown, gunner. They hoped that they would be back in time to get some sleep.

It didn't take the helicopter long to get over the besieged fire support base code-named Birmingham. Webb's Huey was joined by a Nighthawk, an unusual Huey equipped with a spotlight and a mini-gun.

The two helicopters orbited the firebase for about twenty minutes, waiting for an artillery strike on the ground, but eventually, both aircraft needed to refuel. So the Hueys turned and headed back to Camp Eagle.

After refueling, the helicopters headed to Birmingham at 9:30 p.m. They orbited overhead as an artillery barrage took place. Once the artillery fire lifted, the choppers continued with their missions. Searing and Webb positioned the helicopter, probably at an altitude of 2,000 feet, and began the flare drop. The crew members would have been responsible for pulling the lanyards on the flares and getting them out of the helicopter. The lanyard opened up a small parachute, and when the parachute deployed, the flare lit the night sky into daytime. Suddenly, a violent rainstorm struck the chopper and cut off all visibility. Webb and Searing would have fought with the controls, scanning the instruments and talking on the radio.

"Once the flare drop began, it is believed that the aircraft commander became disoriented," said Greg Gandy.

Vertigo may also have played a part in what went on in the cockpit that night. They breathlessly called out the Mayday distress signal. Then silence. Shortly afterward, the Nighthawk aircraft returned to base, and the people at Camp Eagle tried to figure out where the chopper had gone down.

"When I came in that next morning, I came into operations. They said, 'Look, a bird crashed up at Eagle last night.' So I called up to Eagle and found out it was Webb," said Gandy. "I tried to get permission to fly him back to the States, but they wouldn't let me go."

He recalled, "I not only lost a brother in arms that night, but I also lost a good friend."

The crash site was deep in the jungle. It took soldiers several days to get to the crash site and recover the bodies. Diane Webb was working at a paper company in El Paso, Texas. Coincidentally, Diane's supervisor's son was an infantry captain in Vietnam. He led the patrol to find and eventually recover the entire crew.

Mike Webb remembered wrestling with Bobby before he went back to Vietnam. As they had wrestled, Mike realized the physical strength his brother had acquired.

"I was thinking that he could snap my neck if he wanted to. We were just starting to bond because I was almost sixteen, I was just starting to drive, and he would let me drive the 1955 T-Bird that he owned. We started talking about girls, you know, how brothers start bonding."

Mike Webb has always remembered his brother. He has paid his respects at the Wall in Washington, DC. He attended the fiftieth anniversary of Bobby's Officer Candidate School class and spoke to the veterans who had known his brother. He has told his children and grandchildren about Bobby. He will never forget.

On the day of Bobby's funeral in Newnan, Mike met a young lady he recognized as a babysitter for Bobby and Edna's children. Today, that young lady is his wife.

Robert Webb Sr. had a tough time with Bobby's death.

"We never even thought it was a possibility. At least, I didn't," said Diane. "It was a wake-up call, I think to every one of us, that one of our siblings, one of our group, had died, and it had a big impact on all of us. But we loved him a lot. That goes without saying. We all did. He was very tender and sweet-natured."

"In a lot of ways, he was just an all-American boy," said Judy.

Robert Webb Jr. was buried at Oak Hill Cemetery. After staying in Newnan with her parents, Edna and her children eventually moved away. Edna never remarried and today lives in Columbus, Georgia.

On October 14, 2015, this post was left for Robert Webb Jr. on the VVMF Wall of Faces Site by his brother-in-law, Captain (Ret) Robert Burgess:

> *I remember our deal that the survivor will bring the other one home. I always dreaded that I would be the one to get the phone call. When I got it, I actually didn't think that I could do it. Every October, I relive that time. I can honestly say that that mission to bring you home was the most honorable and the very hardest thing that I have ever been asked to do. I have buried a mother, father, and brothers and sisters, but nothing was that hard. You have been missed. You would be so proud of your children and what they have become. Rest in Peace, my brother, until the next roll call.*

**See end notes in the appendix for additional details.*

***Born**: July 11, 1945*
***Home of record**: Columbus, Georgia*
***Died**: October 17, 1971, in Thua Thien province of South Vietnam*
Coweta servicemen who died in the same province: *Charles Walthall, Eddy Couch, Wayne Vessell, John Dozier, and Johnny Calhoun*
***Unit on death**: A CO, 101st AVN BN, 101st AVN Group, 101st ABN Division*
Decorations: *Bronze Star, Purple Heart, Air Medal, Good Conduct Medal, Army Commendation Medal, National Defense Service Medal, Vietnam Service Medal, Vietnam Campaign Medal*

Buried: *Oak Hill Cemetery, Newnan*
Vietnam Memorial, Washington, DC: *Panel 2W Line 42*

Sources

Interview with Edna Hall Webb, widow
Interview with Mike Webb, brother
Interview with Diane Webb Tillman, sister
Interview with Judy Webb Moshell, sister
Interview with Robert Burgess, brother-in-law
Interview with Greg Gandy, US Army
Assistance from Joe Loadholtes, US Army
Assistance from William Killian, researcher

References

Coffelt Database, "Robert Webb." Accessed February 4, 2022. http://coffeltdatabase.org/index.php
Wings of the Eagle. "Helicopter UH-1H 67-19497." Accessed July 17, 2015. https://www.comanchero.org/67-19497.htm
Vietnam Veterans Memorial Fund Wall of Faces. "Jack Edward Searing." Accessed July 17, 2015. https://www.vvmf.org/Wall-of-Faces/46492/JACK-E-SEARING/
Vietnam Veterans Memorial Fund Wall of Faces. "Robert Webb Jr." Accessed February 9, 2022. https://www.vvmf.org/Wall-of-Faces/54940/ROBERT-M-WEBB-JR/

Robert Webb in Vietnam.

CHAPTER TWENTY-FIVE

Coweta County and the 132nd Helicopter Company

The people there were so nice. They still are, for Pete's sake. They are patriotic as well.

—Bill Millican, member of the 132nd Helicopter Company

The year 1968 has been described as one that "rocked the world." Historians call it a "watershed," a year that marks a turning point. This year would come to distinguish the 1960s from the 1950s. The year began with the Tet Offensive that shook America's support for the Vietnam War and its outcome. That event half a world away even unsettled the race for the presidency, as Eugene McCarthy showed LBJ to be politically vulnerable. Johnson eventually withdrew from the race to save the Democratic party from a bruising primary battle, which occurred anyway. In addition, Martin Luther King and Robert Kennedy were assassinated months apart, the Democratic Convention became a battle in the streets of Chicago, the Soviet Union invaded Czechoslovakia, and Richard Nixon was finally elected president. Extreme cultural changes were also engulfing the nation. An increasingly agitated Civil Rights Movement began moving away from Martin Luther King's nonviolent approach to more combative tactics. Youth rebelled against their parents' values and enjoyed the sexual freedom made possible by the birth control pill. That, along with questions about American society and its political system, combined in a cauldron of toxic witches' brew that brought into question the very survival of the Republic.

Coweta County, meanwhile, continued to hold fast to the old-fashioned ideals of God and country. These ideals were not overwhelmed by the havoc of 1968 and in many ways have never been "rocked" at all.

Thirty-seven years later, in 2005, I was speaking to the Atlanta Chapter of the Vietnam Helicopter Pilots Association regarding the Vietnam War class I taught at Newnan High School. After the presentation, one of the pilots approached me.

"I remember Newnan…" he started, and I smiled. I fully expected to hear about how his family used to stop at Sprayberry's Barbeque on their trips to Atlanta. However, I was taken aback when he continued, "In 1968, my helicopter unit was adopted by the City of Newnan before we left for Vietnam."

My interest was piqued. I had never heard anyone in Newnan speak of a connection with a helicopter unit serving in Vietnam. Within a few weeks, I visited the public library and found the article I knew would be in the *Newnan Times-Herald*. This fascinating piece of local history appeared to be almost completely forgotten. Initially, no one I asked remembered it.

In October 1967, Major Jack Joiner was part of the 10th Aviation Brigade stationed at Fort Benning, Georgia. Joiner had been in the military since 1953 and had already done one tour in Vietnam when his commanding officer called him into his office. Joiner was surprised when the CO asked if he was ready to return to Vietnam. Since he knew that his answer was irrelevant, Joiner agreed.

The CO then proceeded to astonish Joiner a second time. "I'm going to give you a choice," he began. "You can attend safety school at the University of Southern California or take command of a company of Chinooks."

Joiner was stunned. The Chinook helicopter is a large, versatile, twin-bladed machine specializing in carrying large amounts of cargo or people and recovering aircraft. Safety school meant investigating aircraft accidents and a lot of paperwork. Southern California meant great weather, but a college campus during this time wasn't particularly inviting to the men in the US military. On the other hand, being in command likely meant promotion and the responsibility for running a unit the way an officer thought it should be run. All of this flashed through Joiner's mind. "I'll take the squadron, sir," he replied.

Joiner was handed a piece of paper—an activation order. He wasn't taking command of an established Chinook company; he would start one from scratch. He had six months to get the unit up and running and ready to pass an operational readiness test to ensure it could do its job. As Joiner left the office, his mind raced.

Virl Martin had joined the military in 1953 and ended up at Fort Rucker, where he trained in helicopters. While stationed there, he met a woman whom he subsequently married. He spent time in Korea and Okinawa and did a tour in Vietnam from 1965 to 1966. After that, Virl was a flight instructor at Fort Benning, where he was recruited into the 132nd Helicopter Company, the new unit commanded by Major Jack Joiner.Martin's brother-in-law, James Sellers, had lived in Newnan since the early 1960s. Martin was visiting Newnan with his wife and was impressed with the town. It wasn't large, but it had a lot of history, and the people seemed pleasant and patriotic. Then, a thought struck him—military units had been "adopted" by towns in the United States, and the 132nd had been discussing the idea. Newnan wasn't far from Fort Benning, and while the country seemed to be growing more hostile to the American military, Newnan seemed supportive. He explained the concept to his brother-in-law, who quickly embraced the idea.

"I think he jumped on it right away," Martin said.

Sellers contacted Newnan Mayor Nat Glover while Virl Martin made contact with Major Jack Joiner.

"I had heard that one other unit had been adopted by a community, and I had heard good comments from the hierarchy that this is good public relations. We need more of this," said Joiner. "If you were there at that time, you were knowledgeable about the fact that the war in Vietnam was not very popular, and we were worried about public relations. The military was very interested in a relationship with the civilian world so they would know what we were doing and what was going on over there. So I put the word out that if anyone was interested or if anyone knew of any communities that were interested in adopting us, that we would look favorably upon it and try to work something out. I think that Virl came to me about Newnan."

Bobby Welch, former Coweta school system superintendent, was a principal at the time of the adoption project. He described Newnan as a "very patriotic place" in 1968. "I don't remember any of the ugliness that often accompanied the troops coming home from Vietnam," Welch said.

Wilkins Kirby, Coweta County Commission chair in 1968, agreed, saying there was "no animosity toward the troops" in Coweta County as there seemed to be in so many parts of the country. Another participant in the event, Dr. Charles Barron, added that "there was a lot of patriotism in Newnan. I don't think that we were the typical town for veterans to return to."

Nat Glover and other city officials were intrigued but wanted to know more. They weren't sure exactly what was involved and how they could help. At the end of February 1968, Joiner, Martin, and a few other 132nd officers flew a Chinook to Newnan to meet with city and county officials and answer their questions.

Joiner and his officers explained what they were looking for, how they would communicate with the city and county while in Vietnam, and how Coweta County could "be a part of what we are doing. It developed from that."

The meeting went splendidly, and Newnan and Coweta County embraced the idea wholeheartedly. The planning on both sides kicked into high gear. Neither side wanted to let the other down.

Wednesday morning, March 6, the 132nd flew two Chinooks to the Newnan-Coweta Airport and picked up a group of local businessmen and civic leaders. The Company had invited dignitaries from Coweta County to visit their training area at Fort Benning. The Company was in a more isolated section of Fort Benning while training for their Operational Readiness Test. However, the visitors would be the unit's focus that day.

The Coweta group arrived and disembarked to find the unit lined up in formation. Mayor Glover said a few words then was taken on an area tour with the other men from Coweta. The group witnessed a flight demonstration with the Chinooks picking up sling loads of different weights and various other activities. The Company hosted a lunch for the visitors and took them home that afternoon.

One of the community leaders who rode to Fort Benning that day, Dr. Charles Barron, recalled the event. "They even carried us down in a Chinook helicopter. I recall putting a helmet on inside the helicopter, and I didn't know what it was for until they cranked it up. You really needed it! Once we were there, they showed us how they evacuated soldiers and how they dropped them in by ropes. I was completely fascinated by it. It was a day to be remembered."

Bobby Welch agreed with Barron, especially regarding the noise from the Chinook. "I remember they gave me some earplugs, and I didn't want them. I always enjoyed flying. The Army guy told me I would come back to them later, and sure enough, it didn't take long before I wanted them!"

Welch described an interesting conversation with one of the ground personnel while at Fort Benning. "I tried to keep track of the Chinook that brought us from Newnan, and during one of the demonstrations, I noticed smoke coming from one of the engines. I got the attention of one of the military guys there and asked him if that was the aircraft that brought us down. He said that it was. I asked him if it was going to take us back. He replied that they would probably get another one to take us back."

"They flew us around Newnan for about thirty to forty minutes. We went all over Coweta County, the downtown area, pretty low at times," recalled Kirby.

"They knew we were there," Barron said.

The men remembered the unit fondly. "We were treated royally," Welch said, and Barron agreed that "they were fantastic to us."

Kirby added, "I think they really appreciated what we were willing to do, and we appreciated what they were doing for us."

On Monday, March 11, the City of Newnan and the Coweta County Commissioners adopted a joint resolution in support of the 132nd Helicopter Company.[1]

On Tuesday, March 19, Major Bill Millican of the 132nd spoke to the Newnan Kiwanis Club in the place of previously scheduled Major Bill Martin. Millican was the section leader of the second flight platoon at the time. He told the Kiwanians about the organization and mission of the 132nd and the role the company would play in Vietnam.

The adoption ceremony was held on Sunday, March 24.

"It was customary for a unit that was being adopted to have a day with the city," said Virl Martin. "We decided that we would take two Chinook helicopters up there."

A barbeque lunch was held in the National Guard Armory, where more than two hundred people from the 132nd and Coweta County ate and mingled. At 2:30 p.m., a formal adoption ceremony was conducted at the Newnan-Coweta Airport with more than 3,500 people attending. The Key to the City and County was presented to the Company commanders, Major Joiner of the 132nd and Major Dale Hurst of the 16th Transportation Corps (TC) Detachment. Chinook tours, rides, displays, the Fort Benning band and honor guard, and, according to the *Newnan Times-Herald* of March 28, 1968, even the Sport Parachute Club of Fort Benning "thrilled the crowd with a series of high-altitude parachute jumps."

"We gave anyone that wanted to ride in a Chinook the opportunity," said Martin.

"As long as they signed a waiver," Joiner said with a laugh.

The rides continued most of the day, and many took advantage of the opportunity.

"I remember going up," said *Newnan Times-Herald* reporter Billy Thomasson. "They flew us around Newnan. It was the first time that I had ever seen Newnan from that perspective. I think the people really enjoyed it. For some, it was the first time they had ever flown anything."

Many Coweta political leaders were involved. Mayor Bill Roesel of Senoia, Mayor Weston Tidwell of Moreland, Newnan City Manager Earl Joiner, and City and County Attorney Walt Sanders were all on the dais. Mayor Glover and Commissioner Kirby gave speeches. Glover declared the members of the 132nd and 16th "the newest citizens of the greatest city in the nation."

Kirby said no other project by either the city or the county had ever met with so much favor and enthusiasm.

Major Joiner spoke without notes. He told the crowd about the unit and its mission and recognized the 16th TC Detachment, the unit that maintained and serviced the helicopters. For security reasons, however, he was hesitant to say exactly when they would be going to Vietnam. Joiner and Hurst also said they would be proud to call Newnan and Coweta County home and would do their best to make everyone proud.

The 132nd had a good crowd of people here, "wives and all," according to Commissioner Kirby. "They mingled in with all the Newnan people that were there. It was a big event for Newnan."

Mayor Glover and Commission Chair Wilkins Kirby were presented with a wooden model of a Chinook. These models came from the Boeing factory that had built the helicopter, and these models signified the bond between the 132nd and Coweta County.

Major Joiner couldn't say enough good things about that day. "The band played. It was a real celebrating thing, wives, children, and everything. There were quite a few people there. It turned out beautifully."

The following Wednesday, Joiner returned to Newnan by automobile and discovered that Newnan had two flat-bed trailers loaded with donated equipment ready to be delivered to the Chinook company. Power tools, washing machines, ice makers, generators, freezers, electric fans, plumbing materials, hammers, and air conditioners were just some of the equipment donated by the city, the county, local businesses, and individuals in Coweta County.

"We were just flabbergasted by the generosity of the people," Joiner said.

"It all came in handy, believe me," said Bill Millican of the 16th TC Detachment.

"Most of us were going over for our second time, and as far as I know, none of us had those things the first time," said Virl Martin.

Meanwhile, the 132nd continued to train and prepare for their time in Vietnam. Upon getting the assignment to form the new Company, Major Joiner had felt it necessary to be able to fly a Chinook, which he had never piloted before. He attended Chinook pilot training and recruited some of the instructor pilots for the new helicopter company. "We had the best and most efficient pilots that I have ever been associated with in my career in the Army," said Joiner.

The Company passed the Operational Readiness Test without difficulty. They were heading to Vietnam in May 1968 with sixteen B model Chinooks, and the 132nd was the first unit with this new model.

Before the Company left for Vietnam, they realized they were short of "tugs" to move the Chinooks around on an airfield. There were none to be found, and the Company's departure was nearing. Finally, some men in the Company found three retired jeeps at Fort Benning that were about to be sold as surplus. The 132nd claimed them, rebuilt them, and had them ready to use as tugs when they arrived in Vietnam.

The 132nd became operational in Vietnam on June 5, 1968, and was assigned to the Americal Division, stationed at Chu Lai, in the I Corps area of South Vietnam.[2] They were given the call sign "Hercules." Two days later, the Chinooks recovered a downed Huey helicopter. After being in-country for a month or two, they finally received the tugs they needed, and the jeeps became surplus again. They traded one jeep to a supply unit for a case of lobster.

Major Bill Millican had served with the First Cavalry when it had first formed as an Airmobile Division in the early 1960s. Having already done a tour in Vietnam from 1965 to 1966, he was experienced in working in a war zone. Assigned to the 132nd in November 1967 as a pilot, he left with the 132nd for his second tour in April 1968. Millican and many men assigned to the 132nd were transported to Vietnam by ship.

When Millican arrived at Danang, he and others were transferred to a smaller craft to move down the coast to Chu Lai. Upon arrival, they unloaded the vessel. Millican stood at the ship's bow, smoking a cigarette, when someone ran up and told him that Colonel Clopp, commanding officer of the Chu Lai base, wanted to see him. Millican reported as ordered and was subsequently put in command of the 16th TC Detachment. He was now in charge of the maintenance crews on the ground that would support the 132nd.

All military branches used the airfield the 132nd was assigned to in Chu Lai, and the maintenance crews were told to find a place to work. Fortunately for the 132nd, the revetments were already there, which the Company appreciated. A revetment was a barricade on three sides of an aircraft parking space. It served as protection from damage or destruction from incoming mortar, rockets, or artillery fire.

There was an ideal building that would have been perfect for the maintenance team, but the Marine Corps was using it to store their beer. So the 16th TC Detachment set up their maintenance shop in some used Conex containers. Unfortunately, they were hot and unsuitable for nighttime work; any lighting they might use in the container at night would show, giving the enemy a target.

One day, that all changed for the detachment. A Marine sergeant in a jeep drove recklessly headlong into one of the Conex containers the 16th TC Detachment used. The maintenance crew assigned to that container was still inside. Suddenly, the airfield commander decided that the Marines didn't need that building for their beer and turned it over to the detachment.

The 16th moved into the building quickly. Now they had lights and the room to work. The heat was still extreme, however, so this building was one of the locations where the air conditioners from Coweta County came into play.

Bill Millican acquired one of the donated air conditioners and a generator. "I built a room in that building to put one of those air conditioners in so that the guys would have a room to go to cool off [in]," he said. "It really helped with morale. There were days out on the ramp where the air temperature would get way over a hundred degrees. I think I saw it once at one hundred thirty. It gets pretty hot there."

Millican made sure the mechanics and maintenance workers had a break every Sunday. The squadron would take a group to a small island off the coast of South Vietnam, leaving the group on the island for the day to enjoy the beach and the peace. Morale remained high. Eventually, the 16th TC Detachment was incorporated into the 132nd Company and wouldn't be regarded as a separate unit.

Major Joiner, who was promoted to lieutenant colonel in July 1968, wanted to ensure that the squadron stayed in touch with Coweta County. He assigned that task to his public affairs officers, who began sending bimonthly squadron newsletters back to Newnan to be published in the *Newnan Times-Herald.* The newsletters highlighted individual unit members, the first unit casualties, Company statistics on downed aircraft recovery, people transported, hours flown, and total sorties.

While there, the 132nd joined several other aviation units and adopted a local orphanage. Information about the orphanage and a plea for children's items was published in the *Newnan Times-Herald.* According to the June 30, 1968, newsletter, the An Tanh orphanage held sixty-one children, 99 percent of them orphaned by the war.

Coweta County responded again, and items were collected and sent to the children in South Vietnam. Typewriters, school supplies, and money all found their way to Vietnam to support the orphans. In addition, the aviators took children back to the squadron area to walk through the helicopters.

"The kids were excited about that," said Joiner.

In the newsletter dated November 1, 1968, the Company requested clothing and toys for a Christmas party for the children. The newsletter said, "We have the desire and the money but no place to purchase these items."

Mayor Glover and the Newnan City Council started the "City of Newnan Orphanage Fund" to support the 132nd. However, Newnan found it impossible to get the items to their adopted unit in time for the Christmas party, regardless of how hard they tried.

The January 7, 1969, newsletter thanked the Newnan Junior Service League for the fruitcakes that did manage to arrive for the Christmas party. However, the local newspaper explained the problems to its citizens a few months later. According to the *Newnan Times-Herald* of March 13, 1969:

> *They appealed to the citizens of Newnan for needed gifts of clothing for the children as well as some "extras" including toys and candy.* [However, problems began to arise with the shipping of the items to Vietnam.] *City officials ran into snags and snarls of official red tape from every source of transportation. They contacted high military officials, Senators, Congressmen, and every conceivable branch of the government and were told the same story-there was no possible way for the government or the military to transport supplies to an individual institution in the Republic of South Vietnam. It was utterly impossible to get the gifts to the orphanage in time for the 132nd Helicopter's Christmas party. After three frustrating months of appealing for help, Mayor Glover and City Manager Earl Joiner assigned the task of purchasing gifts and shipping them by regular Parcel Air Lift to Douglas Dorsey, Urban Renewal Director and an officer in the local National Guard Company. Mr. Dorsey had previously tried to get the gifts delivered to the orphanage through the Georgia National Guard but was unsuccessful. This week, with the help of*

> *volunteers from the Junior Service League, Mr. Dorsey shipped approximately $1,000 worth of gifts to the orphanage from the people of Newnan, Georgia. The gifts were paid for by money contributed by interested local individuals and the city.*

In the middle of the company area, the 132nd erected a large bulletin board. A separate wooden arrow was nailed to the upper left corner. It read, "Newnan Georgia 12,397," indicating the number of miles from Chu Lai to Newnan. Major Joiner thought that Virl Martin had the sign put up. Virl Martin thought that Major Joiner had posted the sign. The sign stayed in place until a typhoon virtually destroyed the base in 1971. At that point, the 132nd was preparing to return home.

"There were so many nice things done. It was just like the community now," said Joiner. "The way y'all support the military and the way you honor the military. For those of us that were involved, it means so much."

When the Wall That Heals came to Newnan in October 2011, the 132nd Company was invited back to Newnan to be honored. Forty-three years and seven months after their previous visit to Newnan and Coweta County, more than fifteen Company members returned. The Coweta Commission on Veterans Affairs recognized them at the Sunday ceremony that honored the men from Coweta who died in Vietnam.

As a class project, the Vietnam War class at Newnan High School made plastic Chinook models and mounted them to a wood base in honor of the Chinook models given to Mayor Glover and Commissioner Kirby by the 132nd in 1968. Woodworker extraordinaire Mark McLean made the bases for the models. Just as they were forty-three years ago, the members of the 132nd were honored and given something by which to remember this county. Each member of the 132nd who visited Newnan that day left with a model Chinook—and thanks.

"That was such a nice gesture. I just can't get over that because it came as such a shock to me," said Joiner. "My goodness. They made one of these for everybody here? I couldn't believe it."

This adoption of this helicopter company in 1968 gives us the essence of what Newnan was and still is more than fifty years later. In a year that was "rocking" the history of the United States and the world, Newnan supported the young men going where their country asked them to go. They supported their local young men and the young men of this helicopter unit not because everyone else was doing it but because it was right.

**See end notes in the appendix for additional details.*

Sources

Interview with Jack Joiner, CO, 132nd Helicopter Company
Interview with Daryl Anderson, 132nd Helicopter Company
Interview with Virl Martin, 132nd Helicopter Company
Interview with Bob Millican, 132nd Helicopter Company
Interview with Bobby Welch, City of Newnan
Interview with Wilkins Kirby, City of Newnan
Interview with Dr. Charles Barron, City of Newnan
Interview with Billy Thomasson, *Newnan Times-Herald*

References

"Helicopters, Skydivers Perform at Newnan-Coweta Airport Sunday." *Newnan Times-Herald,* March 28, 1968.
"Newnan Sends Gifts to Orphanage in Vietnam." *Newnan Times-Herald*, March 13, 1969.

The adoption ceremony in Newnan. Left to right, Major Hurst, Major Joiner and Mayor Nat Glover.

The Coweta group that flew to Fort Benning, March 1966.

The 132nd bulletin board in Chu Lai. Top left there is an arrow that says Newnan, Georgia, 12, 397miles.

CHAPTER TWENTY-SIX

Jackson, Pless, and the Medal of Honor

When you receive the Medal of Honor, your life changes, and it changes dramatically. I have to represent the thousands of Americans who have served their country. You have to make them proud of what you have done and what they have done. And that's a tough job.

—Joe Jackson, Newnan Medal of Honor recipient

Having a career in the Marine Corp meant the world to him [Stephen Pless], and he wore it for all to see like a tiger wears stripes. Cut from the same mold as many legends of the old Corps, once you came to know him, it only became too evident that this was a man who would not die of natural causes.

***—Thomas Petri in* Lightning from the Sky, Thunder from the Sea**

On Thursday, January 16, 1969, Lyndon Johnson walked into the East Room of the White House with the recipients of the Medal of Honor close behind, and the crowd applauded. The inauguration of Richard Nixon as the thirty-seventh president of the United States was four days away. Johnson speaks.

Please be seated.

Members of Congress, Secretary Resor [Secretary of the Army],

Secretary Ignatius [Assistant Secretary of Defense], *Secretary Brown* [Secretary of Defense], *Distinguished members of the Joint Chiefs of Staff, members of the families, ladies, and gentlemen. For the final time during my Presidency, this house is graced with the company of heroes who have scaled heights known only to a very few men in this land.*

The courage of the bravest in war is a very rare and very special quality. It knows no rank or station. Generals and Privates have worn the Medal of Honor. Riflemen and sailors and pilots and priests have all worn it on their breasts. It has gone to every kind of man that our country has ever produced. They have come from the cities and the farms and every section of our land, from very humble homes and from families of great wealth.

At this point, President Johnson looks up from his prepared remarks and begins to smirk. He sticks his tongue out the right side of his mouth as he briefly looks over at the four men. Then he speaks again, not looking at his text, obviously off the cuff.

I don't know what there is in this Georgia water, but there is something very special about this ceremony. Two of the recipients today come from the same little town in the great state of Georgia. And it really made me sorry that my grandfather had left Georgia. (laughter) I would like to go back there because I take such pride in the accomplishments of you gentlemen, whose families have been friends before you even entered the service.

We have had workers and scholars and businessmen and professional soldiers, they have lived in different times, and they have fought in different battles on different fields. They have demonstrated their bravery many, many times in different ways. But they have all shared one noble distinction, each man heard the call of duty in an hour of hard challenge. And each man answered that call with a courage beyond the man.

So now the names of Jackson and Pless and Lassen and Dix are added to this roster of the very brave. And the record of their deeds, at the very summit of human testing, will forever now be part of the history of valor. The words above and beyond the call of duty would never sound again in the world that we want and work for. Never again would war summon the best that men can give, but when that day comes, there will always be a high place of honor for the men that have bought it.

For all the good and gallant fighting men who took their duty as they found it. And they discharged it always with the courage of giants. Such men are with us here today. And we who owe them and their comrades so much all stand tall in their presence.

I should say that the thing that has given me more strength, as well as more comfort and confidence, in the five years of the responsibility that I have carried has been our men in uniform. From those distinguished, outstanding members of the Joint Chiefs of Staff down to the lowest sailor and airman, Marine and Army, they have never disappointed me once. And they have preserved freedom for us, many times with their own blood.

Newnan's Joe Jackson and Stephen Pless were both at the Medal of Honor Ceremony in Washington, DC, but the two men didn't know each other.

"I had never met him before," said Jackson.

Didn't the two meet just before receiving the Medal of Honor?

"I remember meeting him then, but until the president announced it, I didn't know he was from Newnan," Jackson said. "President Johnson was just talking off the top of his head."

Joe Jackson

Joe Madison Jackson was the youngest of seven boys. He was born on March 14, 1923, to James and Effie Jackson inside the Heard County line near Powers' Crossroads. Effie was born in Atlanta, but when she was six, her family moved to Heard County. She became a teacher and met James, also a teacher. At five three, Effie wasn't large physically, but she had a giant of a personality.

"She had the Bible in one hand and a peach tree switch in the other," one of her grandsons, Lee Jackson, said with a grin, "though I never saw her without a smile on her face." And despite the switch, he said, "She was a wonderful Christian woman."

When Joe came along, his father was an instructor at Western School in the Welcome area. The Jacksons also rented a farm in Heard County, and James worked at a sawmill during the summer. Around 1930, James had a stroke while working at the mill. A year of disability followed, then he was gone. The two oldest sons had already graduated high school, but Joe was only eight years old.

Effie raised James, Garrett (Buddy), Roy, Dan, Phillip, Frank, and Joe. Being the youngest, Joe was closest to his mother. Joe recalled that the first fourteen years of his life, the family moved around the countryside of western Coweta County, renting farms and barely getting by. Then his older brothers began working at the mills in Arnco and a wool mill in downtown Newnan, bringing home the money earned.

"They were just a hardworking country family," said Jane Jackson, niece of Joe Jackson. (Jane is the daughter of Dan Jackson, the sister of Denise Jackson, and the sister-in-law of Alan Jackson.)

While not all the brothers could complete high school because of the family's economic situation, as a teacher, Effie certainly saw the value of education. Most of the brothers either graduated from high school or got their GED. As he grew up, Joe wanted to drop out of high school and work to help the family, but his mother insisted he stay in school.

Effie Jackson moved to Second Avenue in Newnan, where Joe attended Atkinson Grammar School then moved on to Newnan High School, located on the property beside McKoon Funeral Home, today the home of Newnan's Veterans Park. Joe Jackson graduated from Newnan High School with the Class of 1940.

Effie Jackson "was a lovely, sweet lady," said Winston Skinner, then a reporter for the *Newnan Times-Herald*. "She was obviously very proud of all of her family."

The grandchildren all called her "Mama Jack" and adored her.

"When Mama Jack said that 'we're fixing to pray,' you knew what that meant. It meant you got on your knees," recalled Jane Jackson. "She prayed over her children, and she prayed over her grandchildren. A lot of days, I think I'm still running on Mama Jack's prayers."

When Joe graduated from Newnan High School, the Depression

had seemingly eased up, but jobs still weren't plentiful. So Joe went to trade school in Toccoa Falls. Joe had always been good with his hands, so he became an airplane mechanic. Even after earning his certification, however, he couldn't find a job; he lacked experience. To obtain that experience, Joe decided to join the Army Air Force in March 1941. There was no Air Force during that time, only the Army Air Force and the Naval Air Force. The USAF wasn't established until 1947.

Joe Jackson entered the US Army, and when Pearl Harbor was attacked, he was stationed at Orlando Army Airfield as an airplane mechanic. In January 1942, Joe was transferred to Westover, Massachusetts, and became a crew chief on a B-25 Mitchell Medium Bomber. (This was the same type of plane used in the famous Doolittle Raid in April 1942. Joe Jackson became friends with Jimmy Doolittle after receiving the Medal of Honor.)

A few months later, Joe was asked by one of his fellow airmen if he could serve as the flight engineer on an anti-submarine patrol. While on patrol, one of the engines on Joe's B-25 caught fire. Joe successfully instructed the pilot on how to put out the fire, saving the lives of all on board.

"I just had him feather the prop," Jackson said. "He didn't know what to do."

That day, Joe Jackson determined he could be a pilot. Once World War II began, the Army Air Corps waived the requirement for aviation cadets to have college degrees. In September 1942, Joe Jackson entered pilot training as an aviation cadet. Before World War II, a candidate to be a pilot was required to have a college degree.

While Jackson was stationed at Westover, he went on a blind date and met a local woman named Rosamund "Rose" Parmentier. They went skating, and neither could stay upright, which they laughed about later in life. They married on September 7, 1944.

Jackson went through all the stages of flight training—Primary, Basic, and Advanced. According to Joe's nephew, Lee Jackson, Joe did some flight training near Newnan, though Joe was stationed at Napier Field in Dothan, Alabama, for Advanced Flying School.

Lee Jackson recalled that Uncle Joe would fly over Newnan once or twice a week and buzz First and Second Avenue, where his mother and two of his brothers lived, including Lee's family.

"The whole ground would vibrate," Lee said. "Everyone in town knew who it was."

In April 1943, Joe finally graduated from training with his pilot wings. He expected to be sent into combat either in the European or Pacific theater. Disappointingly for Joe, this was not to be. Instead, working out of Eglin Air Force Base, he became a gunnery instructor for fighter pilots and eventually bomber crews destined for combat. However, this assignment didn't mean that he didn't fly. By the war's end, Joe was engaged in an unusual and little-known program at Eglin that went by the code-name *Pinball*. Jackson and some of the other instructors flew modified P-63 Kingcobra fighter aircraft and attacked bomber crews involved in the training. The bomber crews fired breakable bullets at the fighters, working on their marksmanship. As a result, Jackson would claim that he was shot at only by Americans during World War II. When the war ended, he was flying B-24 Liberators. Even though he never got into combat, this is where he believed he really learned to fly.

Jackson finally got overseas after the war, assigned to a P-47 squadron stationed in the American Zone of Germany from 1946 to 1947. He and his wife witnessed the devastation of Europe firsthand. In 1947, on his return home, Jackson decided to join the newly formed United States Air Force. He got to fly an unusual airplane called the P-82 Twin Mustang before transitioning into jets, starting with the F-84 Thunderjet. Jackson flew 107 combat missions during the Korean War, making up, at least in part, for staying in the United States during World War II.

In 1949, Joe and Rose had a daughter they named Bonnie, and a son, David, was born in 1953.

During the 1950s, Jackson was an operations officer and then a squadron commander at Turner Field outside Albany, Georgia. By 1957, he became the deputy squadron commander of the 4080th Strategic Reconnaissance Weather Squadron in Texas, which was flying U-2 spy planes. Joe was the second pilot to "check out" as a pilot of this unique aircraft. As a U-2 pilot, Jackson befriended Francis Gary Powers, who in 1960 would become famous for being shot down over the Soviet Union. Many locals are aware that Powers married his first wife in a house on East Washington Street in

Newnan.

By 1961, Jackson had put twenty years into the military. Finally, retirement was at hand. He had been assigned to Strategic Air Command and was attending the University of Omaha, working on a degree in education. Jackson planned on being a teacher when he graduated. After completing his degree, however, he was selected to attend the Air War College in Montgomery, Alabama, and work on his master's degree. He stayed in the military, got his graduate degree, then owed the military three more years of service.

During the 1962 Cuban Missile Crisis, Joe Jackson flew U-2s over Cuba. After one of the flights, he was ordered to Washington, DC, to brief military and political leaders. As he left, another U-2 pilot, Rudolf Anderson, spoke with him. Anderson was worried. He was scheduled to make the next flight over Cuba and had a premonition that he wouldn't survive. As predicted, Anderson was shot down and killed by a surface-to-air missile, fortunately piloting his plane away from Cuba before crashing. This incident bothered Joe for the rest of his life. He felt like he should have done something, but instead, he allowed himself to be rushed out the door to Washington, DC.

After serving with the U-2, attending the Air War College, and just missing nuclear war, he was assigned to work at the headquarters of the US Air Forces in Europe and stationed at Wiesbaden, Germany. From there, he received orders to Vietnam, where he became commander of the 311th Air Commando Squadron out of Danang, Republic of Vietnam.

Some of the children in Effie's neighborhood later told Jane Jackson that they spent a lot of time on their knees praying over Joe.

The 311th flew the C-123 Provider transport aircraft due to its short takeoff and landing capabilities. Similar to the Army/Air Force Caribou aircraft, it was used to supply and assist far-flung Special Forces camps dotted around South Vietnam, which had short and rudimentary airstrips.

When Joe Jackson took off in aircraft number 542 on Sunday, May 12, 1968, Mother's Day, he wasn't planning on doing anything heroic. He had no thought of participating in the event that would forever change his and his family's life. He was forty-five, and this was his third war.

That Mother's Day, he had decided to complete his check ride and demonstrate that he was still proficient in using the checklists associated with the plane, dealing with emergencies, and flying the C-123. This was standard Air Force practice. Joe Jackson wasn't flying as much as he had in the past, serving in more of an administrative role. However, all pilots must stay sharp and prove themselves continuously to fly a modern aircraft. Therefore, check rides were required every six months. His call sign that day was *Bookie 771*.

Meanwhile, a battle was taking place a few miles from the Laotian border at a base called Kham Duc. The American military wanted to strengthen the camp, as it had become the only camp along the border that was still operational for them to use to monitor the Ho Chi Minh Trail. However, the North Vietnamese wanted to eliminate it for the same reason.

On May 10, Military Assistance Command, Vietnam (MACV) ordered more than 1,500 South Vietnamese and American reinforcements into Kham Duc. On May 11, they changed their minds and ordered the soldiers to evacuate. They sent transport planes to retrieve everyone as the North Vietnamese closed in for the kill. As the evacuation began on May 12, nothing seemed to go right. Jackson was in the air when an all-call went out to every cargo plane in the vicinity. He responded immediately. Jackson watched seven planes attempt to save the men and families at Kham Duc. Four had been shot down and 140 people killed.

Like bees to honey, Kham Duc had attracted all types of aircraft to the scene. Transport and fighter planes were stacked up for thousands of feet in the air, waiting to see if they might be needed. Through a series of unfortunate circumstances, three men from a combat control team had been left on the ground near the airstrip while attempting to rescue anyone who might still be in the area. One plane had gone down to see if they were still alive, and it had been riddled with small arms fire. As they took off, they spotted the men near the airfield and passed the word to the airborne command post in the sky. To his credit, the pilot offered to make another attempt, but the plane was damaged and low on fuel. So they turned and limped back to Danang.

Jackson's radio squawked. The airborne command post asked if they had heard the last report. Major Jesse Campbell, the co-pilot giving Jackson his check ride, replied in the affirmative. Then, almost apologetically, they asked, "Do you want to go in?"

It wasn't an order. The colonel had a choice. But three Americans were down there, and Joe Jackson saw no other possible course of action. He felt Campbell's eyes on him, and he nodded. Major Campbell's reply to the airborne command post was simply "Roger. We are going in." He checked his torso restraints to make sure they were secure.

"I knew things were bad on the ground. You could see it," Jackson said. "We didn't have any trouble finding the base. It was all on fire."

Joe Jackson prepared to rescue three men, and consequently, he became one of only fourteen members of the Air Force to receive the Medal of Honor for their actions.

"People were wondering what to do," Jackson said. "You just can't leave three guys at the mercy of the VC and NVA if you know they're alive."

Those three servicemen were Major John Gallagher, Sergeant James Lundie, and Sergeant Morton Freedman. They had only recently realized their predicament.

Jackson decided that he couldn't take a standard, long approach to the runway. He had to get there quickly to avoid some of the devastating fire that he had seen strike so many of the previous aircraft that had flown down on the runway. So he pushed the nose over and screamed down toward the runway at Kham Duc.

In a transport plane.

The combat control team, trying to hide in a ditch beside the runway, suddenly heard the screech of an airplane in a dive. When Jackson's aircraft popped out of the fog and touched down on the runway, Sergeant Lundie muttered, "This guy is crazy. He's not going to make it."

"From the time we came in range, they opened up, firing from the bunkers and from below us as we approached," Jackson recalled.

He touched down and hit the brakes, desperately holding them down while guiding the aircraft around debris that littered the airstrip. The men on the aircraft heard the roar of the enemy guns. Incredibly, the transport plane came to rest a short distance from the three combat controllers. Jackson revved the engines and turned the C-123 in preparation for an attempted takeoff. Jackson and Campbell's mouths fell open as a 122mm rocket hit the concrete in front of their aircraft, bounced, then skidded to within a few feet of the nose wheel of the cargo plane, broke into two pieces, sizzled, but did nothing more. It was a dud.

The three Americans sprinted up the back ramp and into the plane. Fire from the enemy was everywhere. Once they got word from the crew that the control team was on board, Jackson navigated around the rocket and started down the runway. As they pulled away, a volley of mortars landed behind them, at the very spot where they had been sitting during the agonizing wait for the men to board the plane.

Jackson didn't wait around to see what else the communists might throw his way. Instead, he pushed the engines to the max and went down the airfield, lifting off with the sound of enemy weaponry slowly fading into the distance. "We were on the ground somewhere around forty to fifty seconds," he later recalled, but "that was an eternity."

In his statement to the awards and decorations officer, Sergeant Freedman said, "The aircraft touched down, saw us as we ran out together, motioned us to the rear as it turned around, and there the miracle was. We jumped aboard and took off. I couldn't believe what had happened. We were dead, and all of a sudden, we were alive."

Once the plane landed, Sergeant Lundie entered the cockpit, glanced at Jackson, then said, 'I just wanted to see how you could sit in that little seat with balls as big as you've got!'

The three combat controllers were sent to the hospital to get checked out while Jackson and Campbell filed their report on the day's events. Soon, one of two crew members who had been on board the aircraft came to find the two pilots. He looked like he had seen a ghost.

"I have gone over the plane inch by inch, sir," he said, his eyes large. "There's not a bullet hole in the bird. They didn't hit us once."

Joe Jackson Medal of Honor Citation

For conspicuous gallantry and intrepidity in action at the risk of his life above and beyond the call of duty. Lt. Col. Jackson distinguished himself as a pilot of a C-123 aircraft. Lt. Col. Jackson volunteered to attempt the rescue of a three-man USAF Combat Control Team from the Special Forces camp at Kham Duc. Hostile forces had overrun the forward outpost and established gun positions on the airstrip. They were raking the camp with small arms, mortars, light and heavy automatic weapons, and recoilless rifle fire. The camp was engulfed in flames and ammunition dumps were continuously exploding and littering the runway with debris. In addition, eight aircraft had been destroyed by the intense enemy fire and one aircraft remained on the runway reducing its usable length to only 2,200 feet. To further complicate the landing, the weather was deteriorating rapidly, thereby permitting only one air strike prior to his landing. Although fully aware of the extreme danger and likely failure of such an attempt, Lt. Col. Jackson elected to land his aircraft and attempt to rescue. Displaying superb airmanship and extraordinary heroism, he landed his aircraft near the point where the combat control team was reported to be hiding. While on the ground, his aircraft was the target of intense hostile fire. A rocket landed in front of the nose of the aircraft but failed to explode. Once the combat control team was aboard, Lt. Col. Jackson succeeded in getting airborne despite the hostile fire directed across the runway in front of his aircraft. Lt. Col. Jackson's profound concern for his fellow men, at the risk of his life above and beyond the call of duty, are in keeping with the highest traditions of the US Air Force and reflects great credit upon himself and the Armed Forces of his country.

When Jackson's plane was on the ground at Kham Duc, an overhead aircraft snapped a photograph of the plane sitting on the runway as the three combat controllers ran to get aboard. This photograph is the only picture ever taken showing an action that resulted in a Medal of Honor.

Stephen Pless

An old school bus was winding its way through rural south Alabama, abuzz with conversation and occasional whoops of laughter. The aviation cadets aboard the bus were still in relax-and-unwind mode from the night before. To provide a diversion from the intensity of their training at nearby Pensacola Naval Air Station, the Navy would occasionally bus the trainees to a girls' school in Mississippi for dancing and socializing with the Southern belles there. The cadets would stay over until the next day, when they would be returned to the base. Cadet Stephen Pless was sitting on that bus, staring out the window, deep in thought.

Cadet Pless already looked like a consummate Marine. His haircut was "high and tight," and his eyes were icy-blue and piercing. Others couldn't help being captivated by them. Few remember what happened at the dance the night, but many people recall what happened on the way home the next day.

Alongside the road near Summerdale, Alabama, stood a high school girl. According to her daughter, Cindy, she was an innocent, lovely young lady. Pless spotted her and was electrified by her allure. Somehow, he managed to get the bus to stop and let him off to speak with the attractive female on the side of the road. It isn't clear whether she got a ride on the bus, but what is clear is that Stephen Pless walked away with her contact information. He later told his buddy Frank Ritchie, "That's the girl I'm going to marry." In June 1961, he did precisely that.

The young lady was Jo Ann Smith of Summerdale, an isolated town in Southern Alabama. She was still in high school, an A student, but Pless was determined to win her over. He visited her and her family every chance he had. He flew over her house in a helicopter and dropped letters to her. His friends would ask how he found this girl, and he always replied, "I drove a car as far as I could, I walked as far as I could, and swung on vines the rest of the way."

Stephen Pless was born to Travis Pollard and Nancy Lassetter Pollard in Newnan, Georgia, on September 6, 1939. He was born on

West Broad Street, just a few blocks from downtown Newnan, behind the Glover pediatric office and across the street from Central Baptist Church. Travis Pollard was an Air Force mechanic from Haralson, while Nancy was the daughter of a Douglas County minister. The couple had settled in Newnan in 1938 and had two sons—Travis, born that year, and Stephen.

Within three years of Stephen's birth, the couple divorced and went their separate ways. Nancy moved to Atlanta, where she met and married Berlin Pless, who adopted the two boys. Travis and Stephen Pollard became Travis and Stephen Pless.

The Pless boys attended Decatur High School, but at the start of his junior year, Stephen transferred to Georgia Military Academy in College Park. While a senior in the fall of 1956, he joined the Marine Corps Reserves. Pless was assigned to the 1st Motor Transport Battalion in Atlanta until graduating high school in the spring of 1957. After graduation, he reported to Parris Island for his Recruit Training, finishing in October 1957. He then served in the 10th Marine Regiment of the 2nd Marine Division until he volunteered for Flight Training in Pensacola, Florida, in 1958. His desire to fly led to his chance encounter with Jo Ann Smith.

Stephen Pless graduated from Flight Training in 1960 and was promoted to first lieutenant. According to his daughter Cindy, her father was color-blind and faked his way through flight school. Pless and his wife were stationed along the East Coast, spending a good deal of time at the Marine base in New River, North Carolina. Pless came to the attention of fellow Marine aviator Chuck Feaselman during the spring of 1960 while at New River. Feaselman had gotten word that an inspection was coming, and he had to ensure that Pless's squadron was ready. So he went to Pless and explained the situation, and the unit was prepared when the inspector general arrived.

"From then on, we were buddies," said Feaselman. The two enjoyed spinning flying tales in the Officers' Club in the evenings. "He liked his drinks," Feaselman recalled as he shook his head.

This was characteristic of the military culture then and now; they drank often and often drank a lot. Pless's drink of choice was bourbon. This drinking culture would have momentous consequences for his future.

On December 29, 1961, Jo Ann was rushed to the Naval Hospital at Camp Lejeune, not far from New River. There she gave birth prematurely to a child they named Stephen Wesley Pless Jr. He died the same day.

Between 1960 and 1962, Pless served aboard the USS *Wasp* and the USS *Shadwell* as part of the assigned Rotary Wing squadrons. Pless also deployed on the USS *Boxer*, which traveled to Africa during the crisis in the Congo. After each deployment, he returned to New River. In 1962, Pless was transferred to HMM-162. HMM is an acronym for Helicopter Marine Medium, and the squadron flew Chinooks. He spent time in Thailand and South Vietnam as part of the American forces assisting with the counter-insurgency mission against the communist guerillas. Pless got his first taste of combat during this time. He would never be the same.

"He was born to fly," said fellow Marine Tom Petri. "But he was an adrenaline junkie."

After the tour in Southeast Asia, Pless returned to Pensacola as a flight instructor and eventually became the officer in charge of the Aviation Officer Graduate School. In April 1966, he was sent to Kaneohe Bay in Hawaii as a helicopter platoon commander. However, he was there for only a few months when he received orders for Vietnam. His wife was four months pregnant when he gave her the news, and she was devastated that he was being deployed again.

The child Jo Ann Pless was carrying at that time would be born in Pensacola in December 1966. It was Steve and Jo Ann Pless's third child, Cynthia Jeanette, or just Cindy. Paul Harding was born in November 1962 at New River, and Tina Marie was born in December 1964 in Pensacola.

September 1966 saw Stephen Pless in Vietnam, assigned as the brigade air officer to the Korean Marines stationed at Chu Lai.

"When we first arrived in-country, Steve was my CO at the Korean Marine ANGLICO Detachment," said Tom Petri. "We spent a lot of time together. That man was literally hell on wheels. If he could have calmed down just enough to survive his youth, many Marines in the know think he had a good chance to become commandant of the Marine Corps." ANGLICO stands for Air Naval Gunfire Liaison Company. Their mission is to coordinate close air support, artillery, and naval gunfire for Allied forces.

In March 1967, Pless was transferred to VMO-6 in I Corps. The stage was now set for the birth of a legend.

Chuck Feaselman happened to be at the same airfield when Stephen Pless arrived at VMO-6 and was delighted to learn that Pless was in the neighborhood. Feaselman was with air control and airfield administration. Anything that had anything to do with running an airfield was now in Feaselman's bailiwick. The chopper squadrons were on the other side of the airfield, including VMO-6.

Feaselman would frequently head to that side of the base, eat at the Officers' Mess, then stop at the tent that contained a homemade bar. He saw Pless when he wasn't flying. The problem for Feaselman was that Pless was flying a lot. By the time Pless left Vietnam, he would have 780 combat missions to his credit. He was shot down twice.

"He pulled my bacon out of the fire every couple of weeks," Petri said with a laugh.

"I just found a good friend in Steve," said Feaselman. "He was a squared-away Marine. He was a good pilot and good administrator."

Tom Petri agreed. "He was a by-the-book Marine. He told anyone who asked that he would stay a Marine until he was too old to walk."

The Pless combat missions ranged from the mundane to the terrifying. Once, he was involved in supporting a surrounded Studies and Observations Group recon team. He returned to help them eight times over three days, including making gun runs on the enemy with one of his rocket pods on fire. These undertakings garnered Pless the Silver Star. Another mission saw Pless come to the aid of a Marine outpost under heavy attack with a badly wounded Marine who needed a hospital. Bringing his gunship into position and ignoring enemy fire, he destroyed the enemy then picked up the injured Marine, saving his life. This action brought him a Distinguished Flying Cross.

On August 19, 1967, after his preflight walk-around, Stephen Pless mounted his UH-1 Huey helicopter alongside a crew with whom, except for John Phelps, he had never flown. Improbably, only Pless and Phelps knew each other or had ever flown together. They were just routinely assigned to that aircraft that day.

Nevertheless, co-pilot Captain Rupert E. Fairchild, Door Gunner Gunnery Sergeant Leroy N. Poulson, and Crew Chief Lance Corporal John G. Phelps followed Pless into the helicopter and got settled into their area of the aircraft. They were assigned to escort a Marine medical evacuation helicopter. Their call sign was *Cherry-6*.

Along the Vietnamese coast, an Army Chinook paralleled the coastline. Larry Allen was on board, catching a ride back to his base after taking care of some administrative business in Chu Lai. Two other men from his unit were with him. Twenty-five members of a United Service Organization (USO) troupe were also on board, including several American women.

Suddenly, the Chinook veered wildly. The pilot regained control but decided to put the chopper down on a nearby beach to investigate the problem. The helicopter lowered onto the earth, with the rotor wash flinging sand across the beach. The back door lowered, and the crew chief ran out. Larry and his mates filed off to provide security. One of the USO girls wanted to get out and walk around, but Larry insisted she stay aboard the Chinook. The four men stalked down the helicopter's sides, looking for a possible cause of the problem. They had converged at the front when they saw a single bullet hole in the plexiglass of the nose. As they studied the bullet's path, they concluded that it had struck the pilot's controls and knocked them out of his hands, causing the Chinook to go off course.

"Just about this time, *bam*! Off goes a grenade right behind us," said Allen. "The four of us just hauled butt from one end of that helicopter to the other." However, it was too late. The pilot had jerked the aircraft into the sky, and as they reached the back ramp of the chopper, it was just out of reach. Larry Allen looked frantically around. The crew chief was lying in the sand, twitching. Allen said he believes the crew chief had still been connected to the Chinook via his communication cord, and when the aircraft leaped into the sky, the cable broke his neck. The Viet Cong later cut his throat to make sure he was dead.

The three men scrambled behind a rise in the sand that provided scant cover. Allen had only a .38 revolver, but his two buddies had M-16s. The three engaged the Viet Cong, who seemed to be coming from everywhere. They ran toward the three Americans while shooting then threw a grenade and retreated. The Americans returned fire and threw many of the grenades back. The grenades that went off seemed less effective because of the soft sand.

Soon, the three Americans ran out of ammunition. Larry, with a bullet wound in his shoulder, was in the middle of the three, and he watched as one of his friends pulled out a knife. He looked at him, puzzled. Then the Viet Cong, realizing the Americans' situation, rushed the three from either side, and Larry's two companions seemed to take all the bullets. As the Viet Cong engulfed the three, he played dead.

Cherry-6 never completed the assigned escort mission. Instead, moving ahead of the delayed evac helicopter, Pless and Fairchild had been monitoring radio traffic. The Chinook that had left the four behind on the beach was frantically broadcasting for assistance. Pless pulled out a map and checked the coordinates. The Americans were on a beach not far from Pless. *Cherry-6* arrived at its scheduled evac site before the Dust-Off chopper. There appeared to be no problems, so Fairchild notified the Dust-Off helicopter that they were diverting to an emergency.

"Captain Pless asked the crew, 'Shall we help them?' We all put our thumbs up," said Leroy Poulson.

"He [Pless] was a man of action," said John Phelps. "We fed off of his courage."

When *Cherry-6* arrived at the beach, the Chinook was still flying back and forth off the coast. They saw the men in US Army uniforms prone on the beach, being beaten and stabbed by a large group of Viet Cong.

As Pless hovered over the Viet Cong, they taunted him. Finally, he saw Larry Allen raise his hand. Pless ordered Poulson to open fire. Poulson did so, careful not to hit any of the Americans. The VC scattered and headed toward the tree line, thirty meters from the shore.

Pless maneuvered the aircraft quickly and fired fourteen rockets into the VC. The smoke from the rockets obscured the VC, but Pless wouldn't give them a moment to recover. He flew into the smoke with the four machine guns blazing away and Poulson throwing grenades out the door. He was so low that his windscreen darkened due to the mud blown up by the rotor wash.

"This guy, you just can't believe how good a pilot he was," said Leroy Poulson. "I mean, he was just outstanding."

"He did things you couldn't do with a helicopter," agreed John Phelps.

After expending almost all his ammunition, Pless landed his helicopter between the VC and the wounded Americans. The Viet Cong regrouped. A new helicopter and crew were on the beach in front of them, and destroying both would be a great victory. As Poulson jumped out of the Huey, two thoughts struck him almost simultaneously—it was his daughter's seventh birthday, and he was going to die on this beach.

Over the next ten minutes, Poulson, Phelps, and Fairfield jumped out of the aircraft to protect it from oncoming Viet Cong and to rescue the three Americans, two of whom were unconscious and heavy. The struggle on the beach was extraordinary. Pless used his pistol to kill multiple Viet Cong within feet of his aircraft. Lawrence Allen, the first man pulled from the beach and into the Huey, spent some time on the M-60 machine gun, protecting the bird. As they pulled the third man into the Huey, they were vulnerable. Fairfield got into the co-pilot seat. Poulson and Phelps tried to ensure that they had everyone inside the helicopter. At that moment, an Army Huey slick flew directly over them, utilizing a mini-gun. The crew remembered the shell casing raining down on their bird.

"They probably saved us," said John Phelps.

When *Cherry-6* finally lifted off, the chopper was seriously overweight, even though they had left behind the crew chief, who was obviously dead. The helicopter skimmed across about a mile of beach, seemingly unable to obtain the lift it needed, and finally turned toward the South China Sea and departed. A South Vietnamese UH-34 helicopter attempted to pick up the dead crew chief remaining on the beach after Pless left but was driven off by heavy gunfire. Several hours later, a force of soldiers landed and retrieved the body.

"Our aircraft was at least five hundred pounds heavier than the maximum takeoff weight," said Fairfield. "Our skids hit the water before we finally got airborne."

The crew tossed everything they didn't need off the aircraft, and the Huey finally made it into the air.

"If it hadn't been for Captain Pless's flying ability and being able to maneuver that aircraft the way that he did, we would have never made it," said Poulson.

They landed at the hospital in Chu Lai and quickly carried their passengers inside the hospital. Larry Allen felt rain on his face as he lay on the stretcher. He later said it was the greatest thing he had ever felt. Unfortunately, he was the only one of the four to survive the ordeal.

Poulson wrote a letter to his wife that night. He told her that "nothing exciting happened today." He quickly corrected it the next day, but the local newspaper had already called her and asked for a comment.

The next day, the crew was required to fly to Danang for a news conference. The story of their heroics had spread quickly. Pless rolled in on a tree line on the way there because he thought he saw something. The fact that the bird had no ammunition on board was irrelevant.

One of the pilots from the Army helicopter later wrote, "In my opinion, this undoubtedly was the most heroic action I have witnessed in my eight months in-country. The Marine ship's crew did their utmost to save four Americans while under fire from the enemy nearly all the time. I highly recommend that this crew be properly rewarded for their unselfish act of heroism."

Pless returned from Vietnam a month later and was assigned to the Officer Candidate School at Naval Air Station Pensacola. In 1968, Steve Pless received the AVCO-Aviation/Space Writers Helicopter Heroism Award. The award recognized "uncommon bravery and superior aeronautical ability." In November 1968, he was promoted to major, the youngest in the Marine Corps.

"There is no doubt that I think that Steve could have retired as a three-star general," said Chuck Feaselman.

"I heard the story about the rescue on the beach, but I did not realize it was Steve," Feaselman said. "When I heard that he was to receive the Medal of Honor, I was so proud for him, I really was. He was a daredevil. He did things that other pilots probably would not have done."

Pless's Marine commander might not have been as understanding. Pless's daughter said he was furious that he had diverted from a Marine mission to save the Army guys stuck on the beach. He wanted Pless court-martialed. So it wasn't the Marine Corps that nominated Pless for the Medal of Honor but the US Army. Stephen Pless was the only Marine Aviator to receive the Medal of Honor during the war in Vietnam.

Rupert Fairfield, Leroy Poulson, and John Phelps each received the Navy Cross, the second-highest medal awarded by the US Navy. These four men are the most highly decorated helicopter crew members of the Vietnam War.

Pless believed the entire crew deserved the Medal of Honor for their willingness to attempt the rescue and their courage on the beach that day. They were all fortunate to be alive.

The beach where these heroics occurred had a group of hamlets and villages nearby that would become infamous a few short years later. One of those hamlets was My Lai.

Stephen Pless Medal of Honor Citation

> *For conspicuous gallantry and intrepidity at the risk of his life above and beyond the call of duty while serving as a helicopter gunship pilot attached to Marine Observation Squadron 6 in action against enemy forces. During an escort mission Maj. Pless monitored an emergency call that four American soldiers stranded on a nearby beach were being overwhelmed by a large Viet Cong force. Maj. Pless flew to the scene and found 30 to 50 enemy soldiers in the open. Some of the enemy were bayoneting and beating the downed Americans. Maj. Pless displayed exceptional airmanship as he launched a devastating attack against the enemy force, killing or wounding many of the enemy and driving the remainder back into a treeline. His rockets and machine-gun attacks were made at such low levels that the aircraft flew through debris created by explosions from its rockets. Seeing one of the wounded soldiers gesture for assistance, he maneuvered his helicopter into a position between the wounded man and the enemy, providing a shield which permitted his crew to retrieve the wounded. During the rescue the enemy directed intense fire at the helicopter and*

rushed the aircraft again and again, closing to within a few feet before being beaten back. When the wounded men were aboard, Maj. Pless maneuvered the helicopter out to sea. Before it became safely airborne, the overloaded aircraft settled four times into the water. Displaying superb airmanship, he finally got the helicopter aloft. Maj. Pless' extraordinary heroism coupled with his outstanding flying skill prevented the annihilation of the tiny force. His courageous actions reflect great credit upon himself and uphold the highest traditions of the Marine Corps and the US Naval Service.

Recognition

On January 14, 1969, Joe Jackson and Stephen Pless arrived in the nation's capital. They didn't go together. All four servicemen to be honored stayed in different hotels and didn't meet until before the ceremony. Each man was assigned an Army first lieutenant as an escort.

The escort told Drew Dix, one of the four men, "Whatever you want, it's on us. I have plenty of money."

"We didn't have to do anything," Dix said.

Though the men were told to limit their guest lists for the ceremony in the White House East Room, that limit didn't seem to be enforced. Dix took his wife, two boys, parents, grandfather, and in-laws. A few members of his infantry unit were also in the crowd. He was under the impression that the other men also had members of their units there. Jackson's mother, Effie, his six brothers, and their wives were invited. All attended except Effie, who was in her late eighties and didn't feel she could make the trip. Five of Jackson's brothers and their wives, who had never flown before, were flown to Washington by the US Air Force out of Dobbins Air Force Base. The Air Force treated the group like royalty the night before flying them to Washington, giving them a tour of the Dobbins facility, a formal dinner, entertainment, and an excellent breakfast the following morning. The sixth brother, Frank, decided to drive to Washington with his wife. Pless's family was there, along with Larry Allen.

Having four recipients at the ceremony also made it unique. In addition to more family and friends in attendance, there was also more congressional and military representation.

"It was pretty packed," said Drew Dix.

On Thursday afternoon, January 16, 1969, the four men met shortly before the ceremony kicked off. Dix said the other three recipients were all aviators and officers, and he was the only enlisted man to be honored. He said that all the recipients were treated the same way. The order in which the men were honored was determined by rank. Lieutenant Colonel Jackson was first, followed by Major Stephen Pless, Lieutenant Clyde Lassen, and Staff Sergeant Drew Dix.

President Johnson made his off-the-cuff remarks, which certainly surprised Jackson, though he didn't show it. No source could explain what Major Pless thought, but he took the remarks in stride as well. Watching the ceremony, observers couldn't tell that the two men had been, in a small way, bushwhacked on the biggest day of their lives. They were experienced, professional military men and had learned to expect the unexpected.

After the ceremony, the recipients and their families attended a small reception. It can be assumed that Jackson and Pless spoke about Newnan and their family backgrounds at that time.

That evening, a formal dinner was held for the recipients and their families.

During the dinner, a young girl walked up to Joe Jackson with a rose. She gave it to him and said, "Thank you for bringing my daddy home."

It's unlikely there was a dry eye at that table. Two men Jackson had saved during the mission came to the table later and met the Jackson family.

"Stephen Pless was a pretty sharp Marine," said Drew Dix. On the other hand, Jackson was more "laid back" and older than the other recipients. "He was more aware of what was going on. Him being forty-some years old and me being twenty-five, there's a lot of difference in experience. I got the impression that he was kind of looking out after me because I was the young guy."

Drew Dix has one additional memory from that day—meeting President Johnson's family. One of Johnson's daughters went upstairs and got some cookies for his two boys. She told Dix and his wife that there was "not much in the kitchen because you know we are moving." The Nixon inauguration was in four days.[1]

While in the capital, the Jackson family toured the White House and visited the Air and Space Museum, where a picture of Joe Jackson was unveiled. The Air Force flew the Jackson family back to Georgia before the inauguration. Drew Dix stayed and attended Nixon's inaugural on January 20.

Over the years, Drew Dix saw Joe Jackson many times at various Medal of Honor functions and events.

"He still wanted to look after me," Dix said with a laugh. "He's a gentleman and a wonderful person." Dix never saw Stephen Pless again.

On Thursday, January 16, the *Newnan Times-Herald* headlines read "Two Cowetans Get Medal of Honor" and proceeded to describe the missions that both Jackson and Pless flew, allowing them to receive the Medal that day. Behind the scenes, people from Coweta began to move to get the two men to visit and allow the Coweta community to honor them.

Wednesday, January 29, was a cold, foggy, and almost dreary day. The weather threatened Coweta's plans. The Second Marine Aircraft Wing's band from Cherry Point, North Carolina, couldn't get to Newnan because of the weather. There was a fallback plan for the day, however. Jackson and Pless arrived safely, and the locals refused to allow their plans to be derailed.

Everyone in downtown Newnan was asked to display American flags for Jackson-Pless Day and to "tidy up."

The two local men whose exploits had already become the stuff of legend were first feted at the Newnan Country Club early that afternoon. The Newnan Kiwanis and Rotary Clubs honored the pair and their wives, interrupting their remarks with several standing ovations.

"It is my pleasure to be here with you today," Joe Jackson said, according to the January 30, 1969, issue of the *Newnan Times-Herald.* "Never in my life have I received a warmer reception than upon my return home this week. I thank all of you from the bottom of my heart."

Major Pless told the crowd that Dr. Howard Glover, brother of Mayor Nat Glover, gave him his "first kick in the pants" when he was a baby and expressed his pride in returning to the place of his origin. "In this wonderful country," Pless said, "you can be anything you want to be regardless of how humble your beginning."

"Both men said it was a privilege to fight for America," according to the *Newnan Times-Herald* article.

After lunch, the program, the greetings from local dignitaries, and the taking of photographs, the group was whisked to Pickett Field near downtown Newnan, where the parade was to begin. Georgia Governor Lester Maddox and a variety of Marine and Air Force officers joined the group. The parade kicked off at 3 p.m. with the honored guests settled into their convertibles. This was undoubtedly the grandest parade in Newnan's history, even without the Marine Band. The lineup included a dozen automobiles carrying Jackson, Pless, their wives, mothers, and an entourage of military and civilian dignitaries. Those participating included the United States Air Force Band with pipers from Warner Robins, a thirty-five-man marching unit from Dobbins Air Force Base, a marching unit from the Newnan National Guard, the Air Force Drum and Fife Corps and the marching unit from Forest Park High School, members of the local Civil Air Patrol, Boy Scouts, Girl Scouts, and the Newnan High School Marching Band. The group marched up Wesley Street, turned right, and headed into the Court Square filled with people. Adults and school-skipping children crowded the west side of the Court Square as the procession advanced. The parade continued down LaGrange Street and finally broke up at the National Guard Armory on Armory Road, beside Newnan High School. The convertibles drove around the block and onto the track at Drake Stadium.

People poured into the home side of the new stadium, and the platform on the football field was filled with local notables and visiting VIPs. Joe Jackson and Stephen Pless were on the platform with their wives and mothers. Joe Jackson was surprised when asked to say a few words since he hadn't been told that he would be expected to speak. It is likely that Stephen Pless spoke as well. The *Newnan Times-Herald* reported on Governor Maddox's speech. (Maddox, a Democrat, was governor from 1967 to 1971 and was an outspoken segregationist.)

Maddox told the crowd that it was one of the proudest days of his life "because of the privilege to share the same platform with these two brave men." He brought laughter to the crowd when he said, "There are fifty governors in the United States, and I was the only one invited."[2]

At the conclusion of the ceremony, there was a memorial service for Coweta's men who had fallen due to the Vietnam War. This was the first time the boys killed in Vietnam had been recognized. The ceremony was conducted by the pastor of First Baptist Church of Newnan, Bob Baggott. Those honored were Terry Allen, Grady Elder, Michael Watson, J. C. Cofield, Eddy Couch, Bobby Freeman, Arthur Hines, Tommy Huddleston, Donald Lowery, Daniel Post, Wayne Vessell, and Charles Walthall. The ceremony concluded on that note. A flyover of Marine, Air Force, and Lockheed aircraft had been scheduled but was canceled due to weather.

After the event at Newnan High School, the luminaries moved to the National Guard Armory beside the school, where there were a lot of introductions and more photographs and back-slapping. G. D. Hendrix was in command of the National Guard unit stationed there. The Newnan Junior Service League had decorated the building to the point that it was almost unrecognizable. Sprayberry's Barbeque catered the meal, and the National Guard unit served it. Finally, Mayor Nat Glover presented the two men with the key to the city—made by Bonnell Aluminum, according to the *Newnan Times-Herald*—and an engraved silver tray that read, "In grateful appreciation from the people of your hometown of Newnan, GA."

Billy Thomasson of the *Times-Herald* said, "The city was heavily involved in organizing this event." He also recalled Mayor Glover as "an outstanding figure in the town." Thomasson said, "The armory was pretty well packed. They had a lot of people there."

After the dinner at the Armory, there was a patriotic worship service at First Baptist Church, where special recognition was given to the parents and families who had young men and women in military service.

The Jackson children—Bonnie, nineteen, and David, fifteen—had come to Newnan with their parents, but they focused on spending time with their cousins.

"I just remember it was a fun day," said Jane Jackson.

The Pless children were younger and spent the day with an uncle and aunt in Arnco.

Between the Medal of Honor award ceremony on January 16 and the Newnan event on January 29, a plea had gone out for local merchants to contribute gifts for the two men and their families. Donations flooded in, with thirty-four businesses contributing items for Joe Jackson and Stephen Pless. The *Times-Herald* noted one special gift—an Accutron Astronaut wristwatch for each man, donated by R. S. Mann Jewelers.

That evening, the Jackson family retired to Dan Jackson's son's home on Dogwood Road in Lake Hills. There, they opened gifts given by the community. Jane Jackson remembered that the gifts were practical and that "it was almost like a wedding shower. It was things for the home and that kind of stuff."

"The people of Newnan were very generous," said Joe Jackson. "They gave us several gifts when the dinner was over. It was very thoughtful of them. They kind of take you by surprise by doing that, but we enjoyed it. As a matter of fact, we still have a couple of gifts that were given to us forty-three years ago."

"It was quite a thing for a town this size to have two Medal of Honor recipients at the same time or ever, really," said Billy Thomasson. "I thought they were real heroes, and most people in town thought they were as well."

This Issue is Dedicated to Jackson, Pless

Newnan Times-Herald, Thursday, January 30, 1969

If this is indeed the first time in history that two men from the same town have received the Medal of Honor, this nation's highest award, at the same time, it is also the first time in the history of the Times-Herald *that two men have consistently dominated the front page for three consecutive weeks!*

The news made recently by Air Force Lt. Colonel Joe M. Jackson and Marine Major Stephen W. Pless, however, is of prime importance to their native city, which, incidentally, boasts a population of 15,000 instead of the "under 5,000" stated by former President Johnson at the time he made the awards.

Throughout this issue will be found numerous articles and pictures concerning these two brave men and their deeds.

The publishers are delighted and proud to dedicate this issue to Col. Jackson and Major Pless as another tribute from the people of Newnan the City of Homes and Friendly People.

Afterward: Stephen Pless

When Pless finished his tour in Vietnam in September 1967, he was assigned to work on the staff at the Naval Aviation Officer Candidate School, where he had served before being deployed to Vietnam. It was back to Pensacola for Steve Pless. However, after the Medal of Honor ceremony, he was also in demand for various Marine and Georgia events, including the celebration in Newnan. As a result, he spent the July 4 holiday in Atlanta, meeting the demands of the press and joining the parade downtown.

On July 20, the entire Pless family had been relaxing on Pensacola Beach. The family had just purchased a home in Pensacola. Jo Ann was pregnant with the couple's fourth child, a son she would later name for her husband. When the family departed for home, Steve said he would catch up with them later. He had recently purchased a motorcycle and was going to hang out with some of the flight students from the Naval Air Station. The guys met at a local bar. Unfortunately, the drinking culture so prevalent in the military was about to have severe consequences for the Pless family.

On the way back to Pensacola that evening, Pless and a group of men on motorcycles came to the drawbridge that connected Pensacola Beach to the City of Pensacola. It was a horizontal drawbridge, and when they arrived, it was in the process of opening. It had been 185 days since Pless had received the Medal of Honor at the White House.

The exact sequence of events that night is murky. Cindy said she thought he was "dared" by some of the other guys, also on motorcycles. She said that her father was "a daredevil and loved the attention" and would have stepped up to that type of challenge. The fact that he was highly intoxicated would have played into his swashbuckling personality. Riding his new motorcycle, Pless accelerated up the bridge, faster and faster. He launched out over the water and into the night sky. He didn't make it to the other side.

July 20 was the day of the first moon landing, which eclipsed everything else, including the death of a Marine hero.

Pless's service was a closed casket funeral, as were many funerals of men killed in Vietnam. Representatives from Newnan and Coweta County took a small plane from the local airport to attend the services.

Tom Petri wasn't totally surprised to hear how Pless died. "You could talk to him for five minutes and realize that he was not going to die in a bed," he said.

A few months later, Jo Ann gave birth to the couple's fourth child and named him Stephen Lawrence Franklin Pless, after his father and his father's flight school buddy, Frank Ritchie.

Jo Ann was shocked at the loss of her "protector," as Cindy Pless put it. Her mother remarried quickly and became Mrs. William Smith. However, the family fortunes continued to spiral downward. Cindy was fourteen when their home was lost because of the family's inability to make the payments. People came in and took the furnishings. "It was pretty awful to watch," she said. Cindy ran away from home a short time later, eventually finishing high school in San Antonio, Texas, as an emancipated minor at nineteen.

The Huey that Pless flew on his Medal of Honor mission made it home from the war. It has been restored and is in the National Museum of the Marine Corps near Quantico, Virginia.

"I was surprised and elated to see the UH1-E that he flew on that mission hanging from the ceiling in the Vietnam Gallery," said Tom Petri. "I am very grateful that the Marine Corps Heritage Foundation recognized my old buddy in the presence of the greatest of the great. I know in my heart that he would consider that to be the best honor the Marine Corps could bestow on him and am equally sure he is very pleased by that gesture."

Afterward: Joe Jackson

Joe Jackson flew 298 combat missions during his time in Vietnam, all overshadowed by the mission on Mother's Day of 1968. After his return, Jackson served in the Pentagon and the Air War College in Alabama, where he taught classes and retired in 1974 as a full colonel.

On April 22, 1978, a ceremony was held at the National Guard Armory alongside Newnan High School. Nine years earlier, the armory had been the site of the dinner held in honor of Joe Jackson and Stephen Pless. Now, thanks to the efforts of Mayor Joe Norman, the armory would be named in honor of the local Medal of Honor recipients.

Jackson returned for the honor, as did Mrs. William Smith, the widow of Stephen Pless. Georgia Governor George Busbee was the keynote speaker.

"To place their names on this armory for all posterity to observe is a fitting tribute to these heroes," the governor said. He also pointed out that in 1978, Georgia had only twenty-three Medal of Honor recipients, and two were from Newnan. At the conclusion of the ceremony, four F-100 Super Sabre jets and a Huey helicopter from the Georgia Air National Guard did a flyover to honor the two men.

Jackson and his wife moved to Washington State after his retirement in the mid-1970s, as he went to work as a consultant for Boeing Aerospace Company, headquartered in Seattle. His first assignment was a training program for the Iranian Air Force, just a few short years before the revolution and hostage crisis. He returned to Washington in 1977 and worked for Boeing until the late 1980s.

Jackson's mother, Effie, had moved to Powell Place in Newnan, to a home that Joe had purchased for her. When she spoke about getting old, her grandchildren always told her that she would live to be one hundred. She continued to live alone in her home until, in her mid-nineties, she sent messages to the family to report to her house. As they arrived, she told them to get whatever they wanted; she was moving to a nursing home. She had already arranged to move to Beaulieu Nursing Home on East Broad Street and share a room with her sister. Upon moving in, she insisted on cleaning her room. She told the staff to "take care of the old people." She died in early 1983 after living to be one hundred, just as her grandchildren had prophesied.

In 1985, Joe Jackson attended a reunion of his pilot training class in Las Vegas. One evening while swapping stories with some of his old friends, one of the pilots, Charlie Brown, told them an intriguing tale of a combat mission he had flown over Europe during World War II in a B-17 Flying Fortress. During that mission, his aircraft had suffered extreme damage, with crew members wounded and dead. The plane had been separated from the squadron and was almost defenseless, easy prey for a German fighter pilot wanting to pad his score of shootdowns. Instead, a German fighter came along, flew around the damaged B-17, saluted the pilot, and left. The story is fully recounted in Adam Makos's book *A Higher Call*. What is also interesting is what happened at this reunion and afterward. Makos wrote:

> *Charlie stunned his Scotch-sipping buddies when he casually remarked, "You'll never believe this, but one time I was saluted by a German pilot." Jackson and the others were so intrigued that they prompted Charlie to reveal the full story. Charlie told them about the German pilot who had spared him and his crew. "You should look for him," Jackson urged Charlie. "He might still be out there."*

Charlie Brown followed Joe Jackson's advice and began hunting to see if the pilot survived the war and was still alive. The big break he received was when the most famous living German ace of World War II, Adolf Galland, agreed to help him get a letter to the editor printed in Jagerblatt, the journal for the association of German fighter pilots.

Incredibly, the pilot was still alive and living in Canada. He had often wondered about the American plane he had let go that day. So when he saw the letter to the editor, he was electrified. The two pilots eventually agreed to meet in Seattle in June 1990. Makos continued the story.

> *Charlie's wife had been unable to travel with him to meet Franz, so he had brought a friend—Joe Jackson, the Medal of Honor recipient who had first suggested that he look for Franz. The following morning, Jackson joined Franz and Charlie as they sat in Charlie's hotel room and talked. Jackson had brought his video camera and filmed their discussion. He knew he was watching history in the making.*

Jackson was undoubtedly watching history in the making. But Jackson did more than watch history. Jackson made history his entire life.

Joe Jackson could never be described as arrogant. To him, the fact that he had received the Medal of Honor only signified that he had done the right thing.

"He didn't take himself too seriously," said Winston Skinner, a former reporter and editor at the *Newnan Times-Herald*, who interviewed Jackson on many occasions. Skinner said that once, he mistakenly referred to Jackson as a general in an article. The next time Jackson saw Skinner, he looked at him, shook his head, and chuckled. Jackson told him that he "could never be cooperative enough to be a general," and the two laughed, with Skinner quickly apologizing for his mistake.

"He could speak very movingly about patriotism, but he was no stuffed shirt, not in any form or fashion," Skinner said. "He was an extremely smart man."

Jackson and his wife found a home in Kent, Washington, part of the Seattle metropolitan area. He enjoyed helping his wife, a master gardener, with her horticultural projects. Over the next thirty years, he also got involved with volunteer work in the local area. He enjoyed giving tours at the air and space museum in Seattle. Jackson also became more involved in the Medal of Honor Society and traveled around the country speaking on patriotic themes to community groups and school children.

"He loved to talk to children," remembered Jane Jackson. Joe even visited Newnan High School and spoke to the students there on multiple occasions.

On November 1, 1995, two ceremonies were held to rename State Highway 34 in Coweta County for Stephen Pless and Joe Jackson. Joe and Rose returned to Newnan for the honor. Nancy Pless flew in from Arizona, where she was then living. Local veteran G. D. Hendrix, who had hosted Jackson and Pless in the National Guard Armory in 1969, chaired the dedication committee and served as master of ceremonies at both events. The first ceremony, in honor of Stephen Pless, was held that morning at East Coweta High School. Pastor Travis Eidson of Arnco Baptist Church, an area where some of the Pless family had lived, led the service. Marine Colonel Jim Hardin, a Coweta native, gave a eulogy for Stephen Pless. Jim Hardin knew Pless personally and had worked with him in planning the honor paid to him by Coweta County in January of 1969. He told the audience that Pless was a "'very pleasant person to know; quiet and unassuming.' Pless 'wore the uniform well and looked the part of an officer,' Hardin continued. Hardin described Medal of Honor recipients as quiet, efficient people who love to be with others. He concluded by saying, 'All of us here in Coweta County took great pride and still do' in Pless' selection for the nation's highest award for bravery.'"(Skinner,1995).

Nancy Pless then spoke. She recalled other honors paid to her son over the years. According to the *Newnan-Times Herald* of November 4, 1995, "Mrs. Pless said that on each of those occasions, she felt she was experiencing the high point of her life. Pless had the same feeling on Wednesday. "I feel like I'm standing on sacred ground, she said. How very, very grateful I am. How proud I am to be here.

After lunch, the group moved from East Coweta to Newnan High School, Jackson's alma mater. During the ceremony, the road signs were unveiled simultaneously in the school gymnasium and on the road itself. The community supported this honor, as evidenced by the extensive list of sponsors and the involvement of many city and county officials.

The special guest that day was Georgia Secretary of State Max Cleland, who had helped dedicate the plaque on the west side of the courthouse that Memorial Day in 1988. As a horribly wounded soldier in 1969, Cleland had met both Jackson and Pless. He spoke at Newnan High School and applauded the community for remembering the two Medal of Honor recipients. According to the *Newnan-Times Herald*, "'I had the greatest admiration for them then, and I do now.' He also spoke of the rarity of having two Medal of Honor recipients from the same community. That occurrence is testimony to 'the degree to which the people of this community are dedicated to this nation and willing to do anything, even give their lives, to protect and preserve it,' Cleland said" (Skinner, 1995).

Nancy Pless "spoke of Wednesday's Medal of Honor Highway observance as a tribute to two great men. She added, 'This is their day, and we are all proud to be a part of it'" (Skinner, 1995).

Nancy Pless would move back to Newnan the following year.

"'Having received this great honor is extremely humbling,' Jackson said. 'When I think of the millions of men and women who have served our country and have never been recognized, I feel very small in comparison'" (Snow, 1995).

Six weeks later, the two Medal of Honor markers on the west side of the courthouse were revealed to the public. At noon on December 15, 1995, county officials, alongside relatives of the honorees, again gathered to commemorate their service to their country. The Coweta County Ambulance Service and private donations from citizens of Coweta County paid for the two markers. In addition to the road dedications just a few weeks earlier, these monuments had been organized by the same man who served as master of ceremonies during both occasions, G. D. Hendrix.

Two of Joe Jackson's brothers, Buddy and Phillip, reflected on their brother and his service. Stephen Pless's nephew spoke for his uncle and moved the crowd with his words.

Regarding President Johnson's comment about there being something in the water, Matthew Pless said, "I would respectfully disagree with President Johnson. It's not the water. What creates heroes like these are values taught in places like Newnan. What is most important about these men is what's most important about our country."

Also attending were County Commissioners Lawrence Nelms, Vietnam veteran Robert Wood, and Jim McGuffey. All made comments, with McGuffey stating that when he sees the monuments in the future, he would view them "as a reminder of the freedom I have."

Winston Skinner recalled how excited Nancy Pless was when she relocated to Newnan and discovered the new marker honoring her son. "For years, she had a flat floral arrangement that clipped on the top of the one for Steve," Skinner said. "She would change it out over the course of the year and have a new one put on."

Nancy was determined to see that her son was not forgotten.

In April 2002, the Air Force named a transport plane *The Spirit of Colonel Joe M. Jackson* in honor of Newnan's native son. Joe is quoted on the McChord Air Force base website: "I flew fighters for 17 years, and nobody ever called me a fighter pilot. I flew reconnaissance airplanes for 3 years, and nobody ever called me a reconnaissance pilot. I flew C-123s for one year, and I'll forever be known as a transport pilot."

The transport aircraft, a C-17 Globemaster built by Boeing, is one of the largest transport aircraft in the Air Force today.

As early as 2004, Mark and Jenelle Byrd visited the city of Newnan and Newnan High School to talk about a statue to honor Pless and Jackson. Mark was a Vietnam helicopter pilot turned artist who, along with his wife, created statuary to honor American military members as part of his Valor Remembered Foundation. While citizens were interested in the project, the cost and the lack of a suitable location for the statues kept the project from advancing. In 2007, a committee was formed at the behest of the City of Newnan to develop a city park in honor of the city and county's veterans. The location was the park where veterans had already been gathering for several years, the old site of Newnan High School, the corner of Temple Avenue and Jackson Street. The late Rob Tornow, US Air Force, chaired the group. The idea of a statue for the local Medal of Honor recipients resurfaced during the creation of the park. They had the place; they just needed the money.

By Memorial Day 2009, the park was ready to be dedicated. Funds had been allocated by the City of Newnan and Coweta County. Local individuals and businesses had also contributed, and the sale of engraved bricks had added to the park's development.

"This year, while we remember those men, we celebrate this wonderful community achievement that tells the world that Cowetans cherish the memory of their sacrifices," said Jeff Carroll, commander of the local VFW (Skinner, 2009). Military displays were set up around the park then moved to the downtown train depot, where the public could visit with local veterans and discuss their service.

An estimated two thousand people attended the dedication ceremony. "This is a testimony to Coweta County's and Newnan's support of its veterans," Jeff Carroll said as he looked out over the crowd (Skinner, 2009). The only thing missing from the park was the statues of Pless and Jackson.

Six months later, on Veterans Day, the statues were in place. Joe Jackson came home to attend the Veterans Day service at the park and be a part of the unveiling. The statues showed Pless and Jackson talking to children, which was appropriate, especially for Joe Jackson. He is depicted talking as a pilot, his hands guiding the position of the aircraft he was describing. He loved to talk about airplanes and how they worked.

"That statue was so him. That is what he loved to do," said Jane Jackson.

In 2010, NBC *Nightly News* featured Joe Jackson, at eighty-seven, volunteering in Kent, Washington. They described what Jackson was doing as "an act of service, born of routine." The news spot told of Jackson going to the Covington Safeway Grocery Store in Kent every Monday for the past eighteen years to pick up donated groceries and take them to the local Lutheran church to be prepared for the church's evening meal for locals in need

"And until last night, most of the people served by the church's food ministry were unaware that the man who collects the food for their meal is a military hero, recipient of the nation's highest award for combat valor," the newscast reported.

In 2006, the City of Kent dedicated a new bridge over the Green River, along Veteran's Memorial Drive, in the name of Colonel Joe M. Jackson.

The week before he died, Jackson visited with one of the men he rescued at Kham Duc. Joe Madison Jackson died on January 12, 2019. His body was taken to Virginia and buried in Arlington on

March 26. The family witnessed military precision at its finest as the Air Force honored one of its most revered pilots. The body was taken to the funeral on a caisson, and there was a military band and a twenty-one-gun salute.

"It was very precise and impressive," said Jane Jackson. A "missing man" flyover added to the pageantry, but the flyover by the *Spirit of Col. Joe M. Jackson* had the most significant emotional impact. The big plane flew very low and dipped its wing. "It was just beautiful," said Jane.

Afterward, the Air Force held a reception for the family. They sat around and told "Uncle Joe" stories.

"We just had a real good time remembering," Jane said.

Mayor Dana Ralph spoke about Joe during the Kent City Council's January 15, 2019, meeting. "Joe was a Medal of Honor recipient and a veteran of World War II, the Korean War, and the Vietnam War," she said. "He was a native of Georgia but called Kent home. He retired here and lived here for many years. We are very sorry to hear of his passing. I want to recognize the contributions that Joe made to our entire country and our city as well."

Joe Jackson always spoke to students about their decision-making and doing the right thing. "The right thing may not be what you as an individual would like, but if it is the right thing, then do it. Major decisions become a lot easier when the right thing is used as a benchmark."

Please note: Someone who is awarded a Medal of Honor should not be called a "winner." They should be referred to as a "recipient." They did not "win" as one thinks of a game or a sporting event. Instead, they received the Medal because of their courage and willingness to sacrifice for others. The Medal of Honor is bestowed on a deserving recipient. In Pless and Jackson's case, both were awarded the Medal for rescuing others.

**See end notes in the appendix for additional details.*

Joe M. Jackson

***Born**: March 14, 1923*

***Died**: January 12, 2019*
***Decorations and honors:** Medal of Honor, Legion of Merit, Distinguished Flying Cross, Air Medal X3, Air Force Commendation Medal, World War II Victory Medal, Army of Occupation Medal, Korean War Service Medal, Vietnam War Service Medal, Air Force Longevity Service Award, numerous Campaign Medals, and unit citations. Inducted into the Georgia Military Hall of Fame, the Georgia Aviation Hall of Fame, the Airlift/Tanker Association Hall of Fame, and the Combat Airman Hall of Fame. Newnan National Guard Armory is named after Pless and Jackson. In addition, roads in Washington State and Newnan, Georgia, are named for Joe Jackson.*
***Buried:** Arlington National Cemetery. Section 34, Site 465-A*

Stephen W. Pless

***Born**: September 6, 1939*
***Died**: July 20, 1969*
***Decorations and honors:** Medal of Honor, Silver Star, Distinguished Flying Cross, Bronze Star, Purple Heart, 38 Air Medals, Navy Commendation Medal with Valor, Korean Order of Military Merit, multiple Service and Expeditionary Medals, Georgia Military Hall of Fame, and Georgia Aviation Hall of Fame. Newnan National Guard Armory is named after Pless and Jackson. The Headquarters building at Marine Corps Air Station Camp Pendleton is named for Stephen Pless. A cargo ship of the Navy's Military Sealift Command is named* Major Stephen W. Pless*, and a Marine Corps League Chapter in Griffin, Georgia is named for Stephen Pless. A road in Newnan, Georgia, is also named for Stephen Pless.*
***Buried:** Barrancas National Cemetery, Pensacola. Sec 21 Grave 929A*

Sources
Interview with Joe Jackson
Interview with Lee Jackson, nephew of Joe Jackson
Interview with Drew Dix, US Army and MOH recipient
Interview with Tony Armstrong, US Army

Interview with Chuck Feaselman, USMC
Interview with G. D. Hendrix, US Army
Interview with Cindy Pless, daughter of Stephen Pless
Interview with Billy Thomasson, *Newnan Times-Herald*
Interview with Winston Skinner, *Newnan Times-Herald*
Interview with Louise Howard, friend of Nancy Pless
Interview with Jane Jackson Johnson, niece of Joe Jackson
Email interview with Thomas Petri
Assistance from Winston Skinner, Susan Mullins, Carolyn Turner, Susan Smith, Beth Neely, Sybil Coggins

References

"Veteran of the Day Air Force Veteran Joe M. Jackson," VAntage Point, last modified January 15, 2019, https://blogs.va.gov/VAntage/55661/air-force-veteran-joe-m-jackson/.

Pete Mecca, "A Veterans Story: There must be something in the water," *Henry Herald*, last modified August 27, 2017, https://www.henryherald.com/news/a-veteran-s-story-there-must-be-something-the-water/article_f02427a3-8016-5e0f-a117-42236bc40fc6.html.

Matt Schudel, "Joe Jackson, who received Medal of Honor for rescuing three men in Vietnam, dies at 95," *Washington Post*, last modified January 19, 2019, https://www.washingtonpost.com/local/obituaries/joe-jackson-who-received-medal-of-honor-for-rescuing-three-men-in-vietnam-dies-at-95/2019/01/19/b5ed8080-1a6a-11e9-88fe-f9f77a3bcb6c_story.html.

City of Kent. In Memoriam, last modified January 16, 2019, https://medium.com/@CityofKent/in-memoriam-air-force-col-joe-jackson-411d835b4277.

Home of Heroes, Joe Madison Jackson, accessed May 19, 2022, https://homeofheroes.com/heroes-stories/vietnam-war/joe-m-jackson/.

McChord Air Museum. Our History, accessed June 12, 2022. http://www.mcchordairmuseum.org/REV%20B%20OUR%20HISTORY%20%20C-17%200184.htm

"Joe Jackson, "Lieutenant Colonel, US Air Force," video, 4:40,

https://www.youtube.com/watch?v=7hcISjvEdOI.
Stephen Pless Chapter, Marine Corp League. Vietnam War Congressional Medal of Honor Recipient Major Stephen Wesley Pless, USMC, accessed May 23, 2022, http://www.mcleague1196.org/index1.html.
Kevin O'Rourke, "Beyond the Call: The Saga of Major Stephen Pless." Chronicle of War: Vietnam, Fall, 1989.
"Two Cowetans get Medal of Honor." *Newnan Times-Herald*, January 23, 1969.
"Newnan Welcomes Two War Heroes." *Newnan Times-Herald*, January 30, 1969.
Wayne Snow, "Highway is named for two war heroes." *Atlanta-Journal-Constitution,* November 9, 1995.
Winston Skinner, "Highways dedicated to Jackson and Pless." *Newnan Times-Herald,* November 4, 1995.
Winston Skinner, "Nancy Pless died Sunday at age 89." *Newnan Times-Herald,* February 14, 2006.
Winston Skinner, "Veterans Plaza Dedication today at 11." *Newnan Times-Herald*, May 25, 2009.
Winston Skinner, "'Fantastic Turnout' for dedication of Coweta's Veterans Memorial Plaza." *Newnan Times-Herald,* May 26, 2009.
Makos, Adam, *A Higher Call* (New York: Penguin Press, 2012), 357-364.
Petri, Thomas, *Lightning from the Sky Thunder from the Sea* (Bloomington: AuthorHouse, 2009), 157-165.
Larry Smith, *Beyond Glory* (New York: W.W. Norton & Company, 2003), 334-349.
Undated interview with Larry Allen, Leroy Poulson, and John Phelps at PopaSmoke Reunion, circa 1999.

The Pless crew. Left to right, Phelps, Pless, Fairfield, Poulson.

Joe Jackson, left, at the Newnan National Guard Armory accepting the engraved tray from the people of Newnan.

The parade in Newnan honoring Jackson and Pless.

People gathering in Drake Stadium for the honoring of Jackson and Pless.

At the NHS Student-Vet Connect program. Left to right, G.D. Hendrix, Joe Jackson, and Joe Brooks.

Photos courtesy of the Shapiro Collection, Jane Johnson, USMC and Steve Quesinberry.

CHAPTER TWENTY-SEVEN

The Wall That Heals

Newnan, Georgia

Memorials are not really for the dead. They are in name, but their real purpose is to serve the living that are left behind. It gives them somewhere to put their pain and sorrow of not having that someone in their lives any longer. When people come and find the name of that person, it touches something inside them. They can leave behind something for that young man, a flag, a teddy bear, or maybe a letter. But most importantly, they can leave the pain. No one will ever know exactly why Maya Lin's Wall is so powerful in this way. It mends broken hearts and reminds us today of the truly great sacrifice that those men made in a country far away.

—Ellen Rayburn Whitlock

A little after noon on Tuesday, October 18, 2011, the bell rang at Newnan High School and, by design, kept on ringing.

It was a fire drill. Many students rolled their eyes but were glad for the break as they headed for the classroom door. A fire drill causes many high school classes to move immediately onto the front lawn bordering LaGrange Street, but not all classes are assigned to evacuate to the front.

That day, however, it quickly became evident that everyone was headed out to the front lawn of the campus. Many students went where they were directed. They were more worried about the classwork they had left behind or perhaps the girl or guy walking in front of them. Some students might have wondered why they were going in an unusual direction. Some students already knew about this alteration to the schedule, which had been explained earlier by their teacher. So that Tuesday, the students in the Vietnam War class knew exactly where they were going, and the group hurried out of the school door, clenching the American flags they had brought from home. They quickly gathered at the intersection of Armory Road and LaGrange Street. They knew what was coming and its significance.

Traditionally, when one of the various Traveling Walls enters a community, it is escorted by motorcyclists. Many cyclists are veterans and deeply understand the Wall's meaning. On that Tuesday, riders from Coweta County met the tractor-trailer containing the Wall That Heals at Shannon Mall, located at the Union City exit off I-85 just south of Atlanta. They escorted it down Interstate 85 South to Exit 47 and turned west onto Bullsboro Drive, heading toward downtown Newnan. The clamor of the truck and motorcycles caught people's attention as they roared down Newnan's main thoroughfare. As they flashed by Oak Hill Cemetery, many riders were jarred by the sight of a solitary woman holding a homemade cardboard sign outside the cemetery's front gate. The sign read "Marine Lance Corporal Joseph Michael Watson."

Then they moved into the hub of Newnan.

People stood along the sidewalks as the caravan entered downtown. They waved and cheered. The fire department had hung an enormous American flag at the West Broad Street and Jackson Street intersection, allowing the cyclists and truck to roll underneath. The vehicles should have continued onto Greenville Street, which would have taken them straight to the Coweta County Fairgrounds, their final destination. However, instead of curving left to the end of Jackson Street, then turning onto Greenville Street, they went straight ahead onto LaGrange Street.

The students on the front lawn of Newnan High School could hear the vehicles before seeing them. Soon the motorcycles came into view, followed by the truck. The Vietnam War students began waving their hands and flags to the people in the procession. Soon, most of the students on the front lawn were waving. Many riders waved back, and the truck honked its horn. Then they turned left at Waterworks Road (now Cougar Way) and, in another moment, were gone.

The Wall That Heals had arrived in Newnan!

The arrival of the Wall That Heals can be traced to a passion for local history, the number of veterans in the West Georgia region, the strength of the Coweta Veterans Club, and the History and Social Studies Department at Newnan High School.

And let's not forget the two veterans with a vision.

The Newnan-Coweta Historical Society, the Newnan Carnegie Library, and the Senoia Area Historical Society all share credit for preserving and promoting the local history of Coweta County. Individuals such as Norma Haynes, Elizabeth Beers, and Jimmy Davenport have advocated, spoken, and written about the history of Newnan and Coweta County for years.

The Coweta Veterans Club is one of the strongest clubs in the state of Georgia and supports all of our veterans, regardless of their club membership. They have gained prominence with distinguished national and state leaders and are heavily involved in the community. These men and women all support our schools. During the mid-1990s, the Newnan High School History and Social Studies Department aimed to become more involved in the community, especially its veterans. Its Student-Vet Connect program, begun in 1995, brought students together with local veterans to learn modern history from the people who lived it, many of them from the Coweta Veterans Club. By 2011, at the end of each semester, approximately seventy-five veterans would descend on the National Guard Armory next door to the high school, set up displays, and tell students about their time in military service. Away from the typical classroom setting, history students engaged with the veterans one on one and loved it.

In 2009, two attendees began talking about the Student-Vet Connect program and how it had become increasingly meaningful for the students at Newnan High School. Through their conversations emerged the idea that Student-Vet Connect might also benefit the public. These discussions gave birth to the Coweta Commission on Veterans Affairs (CCVA). Malcolm Jackson and Joe Brooks believed in community involvement and served together in a local Kiwanis Club. Now they turned their considerable talents to promoting veterans and their military service to the local community.

Malcolm Jackson served with the Air Force from 1959 to 1963. He was trained in weather equipment repair and stationed at

Hanscom Field in Bedford, Massachusetts. He was assigned to the Weather Research Laboratory and worked with NASA during the earliest period of the space program. One problem that NASA encountered in attempting to launch a man into space was lightning. So Jackson and others from the Weather Research Laboratory flew in a C-130 over Cape Canaveral, measuring atmospheric electricity to determine if it was safe to initiate a launch.

Joe Brooks had served in the Navy from 1956 to 1958 then transferred to the Army. He became a specialist in Chemical Warfare and served in that role with a variety of units. Eventually, he moved into the Transportation Branch and finally retired in 1992 from the Army Material Command with the rank of brigadier general. His last major assignment was the command of seaport operations during Operation Desert Shield and Desert Storm.

Jackson and Brooks had a unique combination of leadership, talent, strength, and personal contacts that they now applied to this new organization. They were also great friends.

The idea of a Veterans Commission wasn't new; Brooks had served on one while living in Maryland. The Commission in Maryland had worked on educating the population about the service of the American military, especially after September 11, 2001. Brooks would continually stress that only 1 percent of the population served in the military and that they protected the other 99 percent. It was the other 99 percent that Brooks saw as needing to know what the 1 percent was sacrificing on their behalf. He discerned that the Student-Vet Connect program might be an avenue to help educate that 99 percent. One of the lessons he drew from his experience in Maryland was that there needed to be some "umbrella" organization that coordinated these types of educational activities for the community. However, there would be struggles to get this off the ground in any region, and Coweta County was no different.

The local VFW and American Legion initially reacted with suspicion to the idea of a Veterans Commission. Jackson and Brooks had to convince them that "we were more in the education business," said Brooks, while the veterans organizations were more in the business of supporting veterans. "We struggled with how to do this without alienating the veterans," Brooks said. "I think Malcolm's contacts and the way he was able to interact and bring them on board was absolutely critical. It was key."

After getting the veterans organizations on board and receiving approval from the county commission, the newly formed Coweta Commission on Veterans Affairs began planning its first educational event.

A Veterans Muster, a gathering of troops for inspection, was the first event, and it was held in downtown Newnan on a beautiful Saturday, October 16, 2010. It started with a service in the Veterans Memorial Park, highlighted by the Newnan High School Band, the Atkinson Chorus, and the Men's Ensemble from First Baptist Church. Local Air Force Brigadier General Don Harvel spoke, and the ceremony concluded with a flyover by a Vietnam-era Huey. Afterward, the activity moved from the park to downtown Newnan, where veterans from World War II to the local National Guard unit displayed memorabilia and interacted with old and young alike, just as they did in the Student-Vet Connect program. Local high school JROTC drill teams performed. Local veterans who were authors signed copies of their books. Tours were given of the newly renovated Coweta County Courthouse. The event ran smoothly and was a great success.

Between that event and the end of the year, the Commission began to think about the future. There was individual discussion and an exchange of emails about possibly doing the same thing again or trying to surpass what had been done that October. By January, the group was investigating the possibility of bringing one of the Traveling Walls to Newnan. In addition, the Department of Defense had declared 2011 the first year of the fiftieth anniversary of the Vietnam War, which could dovetail with a plan to honor our local Vietnam veterans, bringing us back to the idea of a Traveling Wall.

As the discussion began to center on a Traveling Wall, many members thought we should focus on scheduling the Wall That Heals from the Vietnam Veterans Memorial Fund (VVMF), the original Traveling Wall. We discovered that the VVMF had specific criteria about where the Wall could be placed, the security that would be necessary, how it would be taken down, and more. Those benchmarks had to be met before the CCVA could apply to host the Wall. Fortunately, Coweta County had just created an area that would fit the bill perfectly—the new Coweta County Fairgrounds on Pine Road. After securing permission to use the site, the Commission sent the application to Washington, DC. Within a month, the approval was obtained, and Coweta County was put on the Wall's schedule. Several Walls travel the country each year. The one associated with the Wall in Washington, DC, is called the Wall That Heals and is the only Wall certified by Congress.

The Coweta County Veterans Commission went to work. First, appropriate activities were discussed, investigated, incorporated, or discarded. Additional people were brought in to work on different aspects of the project.

"We dreamed pretty big, and it took on a life of its own," said Malcolm Jackson.

Brooks and Jackson recruited talented, organized, and community-minded people who believed in the undertaking to join the Commission then assigned them to committees based on their knowledge and skill sets.

The committees and assignments included:
Policy/Publicity/Ceremony Committee: Joe Brooks and Malcolm Jackson
Fundraising: Don Harvel and Hank Berkowitz
Volunteers: Hank Berkowitz
Wall Committee: Tom Downey and Steve Quesinberry
Grounds Committee: Jeff Carroll and David Jessel
Muster Area Committee: Steve Quesinberry and Frank Henderson
Veteran Service Organizations Committee: Dick Stender
Communications: Lynn Geddie

Don Harvel and Hank Berkowitz, assisted by Brooks and Jackson, worked on raising the thousands of dollars needed to host the Wall and stage events to accompany its visit to Coweta. They made presentations to the Newnan City Council, the Coweta County Commission, local businesses, civic clubs, and anyone else interested in the vision of the CCVA. While most of the donations were made by individuals and weren't huge, Sargento Foods made a significant donation that the CCVA used to put a down payment on the visit of the Wall That Heals. The local Harley-Davidson club, which counted many veterans among its membership, held a ride to raise money for the project. The Coweta Community Foundation donated accounting services to keep up with the Commission's funding and expenditures. Joe Brooks and Malcolm Jackson worked on the ceremony to honor the local boys killed in action in Vietnam and served as overall spokesmen for the project.

Tom Downey, a Vietnam veteran, and Newnan High School teacher Steve Quesinberry organized all aspects of the Wall visit. This included the opening and closing ceremonies, events held near the Wall, coordination with the school system, the search for family members of the young men who died in Vietnam, and the subsequent contact with those families. Each family was asked to submit a photograph of their lost serviceman. These photographs were used in presentations and videos recognizing the young men during the visit of the Wall That Heals. They were also posted on the Virtual Wall, the online version of the Wall in Washington, DC, controlled by the VVMF. For twenty years, the VVMF has attempted to have people across the country post on this website the pictures of the men and women killed in Vietnam to "bring them to life" once again. By the time the Wall arrived, the committee had posted a photograph of every young man from Coweta County who died in Vietnam.

Jeff Carroll and Dave Jessel, both Coweta Veterans Club members, ensured that everything needed was at the right place at the right time. Tables, chairs, sound systems, medical assistance, and golf carts all fell under their purview. They also worked on parking issues. It doesn't sound remarkable, but the job was paramount to the venture's success.

Steve Quesinberry and Frank Henderson from the Newnan High School History and Social Studies Department worked to move the Student-Vet Connect program to the fairgrounds that Saturday.

Dick Stender, one of the most visible and vocal members of the Coweta Veterans Club, ensured that organizations offering services to veterans were also out on Saturday, offering resources and answering questions.

After meeting Jackson and Brooks at a Northgate ROTC program, Lynn Geddie volunteered her services. She promoted the event via Facebook and other social media and assisted in tracking down members of the KIA families.

Joe Brooks later said that "this group could cure cancer."

One man who was not considered part of the CCVA but, at a minimum, should have been an honorary member was *Newnan Times-Herald* reporter Alex McRae. Alex promoted the visit of the Wall That Heals through the newspaper at every opportunity. He also wrote a series of articles on local Vietnam veterans and their experiences. He requested and collected the names of local Vietnam veterans so they could be honored by having their names printed in the *Newnan Times-Herald.* Most importantly, Alex wrote articles that assisted the CCVA in finding family members of the locals killed in Vietnam.

On Sunday, October 16, 2011, Wall Week began at the school system's Donald W. Nixon Centre for Performing and Visual Arts with a one-person stage production of *The Things They Carried*, based on the book by Tim O'Brien. *The Things They Carried* was hard-hitting and sometimes challenging for the audience to comprehend. Some of the audience members were shocked by the language and topics that were brought up. However, Tim O'Brien was a Vietnam War veteran, and the book was in many ways autobiographical. The work had been praised across the country as an important piece of literature. It certainly got the attention of the audience. Before the play, photographs of men from Coweta who had died in Vietnam flashed in a loop in the front of the auditorium, and Malcolm Jackson called out each name, with members of the Vietnam War class at Newnan High School holding a framed picture of each. Those pictures were placed under the honorary seats in the front row before the students withdrew

On Tuesday, the *Newnan Times-Herald* ran an article titled "Truck carrying Wall arrives in Newnan about noon today."

"It's going to be a great week," Malcolm Jackson, co-chair of the CCVA, told the newspaper. "The group of patriotic motorcycle riders escorting the Wall into town is going to be quite a show all by itself. I can't wait to see it all happen. This whole event is something I feel sure everyone will appreciate and enjoy, especially our veterans."

Principal Doug Moore of Newnan High School had agreed to allow the students to view the procession of the Wall That Heals that

Tuesday, and he decided to double down and make it a fire drill. Not only did the students see the Wall That Heals arrive, but so did a huge crowd in downtown Newnan. The woman holding the sign at the entrance to Oak Hill Cemetery was identified as Sandra Jordan Vaughn, Lance Corporal Joseph Michael Watson's fiancée when he was killed in Vietnam on January 8, 1968. (Sandra and Mike's story is in Chapter 8, Joseph Michael Watson.) After the convoy arrived at the fairgrounds, the truck was secured, and the riders dispersed. Many of them would be back at the fairgrounds on Wednesday morning.

That evening, the school system's performing arts center witnessed an emotional event. A large crowd showed up to see the documentary film *In the Shadow of the Blade*, the story of a restored Vietnam Huey helicopter that had traveled ten thousand miles around the country to reunite Vietnam War veterans and the families of the men killed in action with the helicopter that symbolized their lost youth. One of the film's highlights involved a woman from Marietta, Georgia, who had served as a nurse in Vietnam. She had saved an infant's life while there, and through the filmmakers, she reunited with the infant, now grown and living in California. After the story of the nurse and infant played on the screen, the film was paused, and the Marietta nurse, Mrs. Donna Rowe, and the infant, Mrs. Kathleen Epps from California, were introduced and spoke about their experiences and what the Wall That Heals meant to them. After they finished to a standing ovation, the film was played to its conclusion, and Donna and Kathleen greeted veterans and well-wishers. It was an outstanding success and set the mood for the week.

Both the play on Sunday and the film on Tuesday began by recognizing any KIA families in attendance. This recognition led to standing ovations on both days.

The morning of Wednesday, October 19, saw a horde of volunteers descend on the fairgrounds in cold and windy weather. Under the direction of the Wall That Heals supervisor and truck driver Bob Dobek, the group spent the morning assembling the Wall. Individual signs listing the exact location for each Coweta KIA were posted in front of the panel where their names could be found.

On Thursday morning, October 20, the Wall That Heals opened to the people of Coweta County and the West Georgia region. It would be open around the clock for the next three days. The opening ceremony was held at 9 a.m. to great fanfare and saw two Vietnam-era Huey helicopters land and become static displays for the weekend. The trailer that the Wall arrived in also opened out to a small museum, allowing people to view the history of the memorial. Students from all three public high schools visited and were guided to the Wall by local veterans of the Vietnam War. Every evening, a military chaplain held candlelight ceremonies at the Wall along with the playing of "Amazing Grace" by a bagpiper and taps from a bugler. These vigils were organized by veteran and business owner Curt Grayer.

On Friday morning, October 21, school buses rolled into the fairgrounds, delivering Gifted students from every elementary and middle school in the county. They came to learn about the Vietnam War, the significance of the Wall, and the local men who could be found there. During the weeks leading up to the Wall's arrival, Gifted teachers from each school taught lessons on the Vietnam War, the Wall, and the local boys who had died. Watching the children leave items created in their classes at the base of the Wall was genuinely moving. These visits continued into the afternoon. That night, a Chinook helicopter from Fort Stewart landed at the fairgrounds and set up as a display for Saturday. Many students at the Newnan High School football game heard the chopper pass overhead as it made for the fairgrounds. They cheered.

Saturday, October 22, saw the largest crowds of the week. The weather was sunny and warm. People from all over West Georgia visited the Wall, found family and friends' names, and honored their sacrifices. A wreath-laying ceremony got the day off to a noteworthy start. Seven wreaths were laid at the Wall by various local organizations. These included the Gold Star Mothers, the American Veterans (AMVETS), the American Legion, Coweta County, the Marine Corps League, the Veterans of Foreign Wars, and the Sons and Daughters of the American Revolution. It was a poignant way to start the day.

Along with the helicopters on display were other Vietnam-era vehicles. Several jeeps, a two-and-a-half-ton truck (known as a deuce and a half), and a vehicle called a "mule" made up a fascinating display. More than forty veterans from the Student-Vet Connect program displayed their memorabilia and spoke with visiting children and adults. Local authors sold and signed their books, artist Marc Stuart displayed his impressive military art, and the Coweta Veterans Club and the Newnan Rotary Club staffed fair booths to sell refreshments. Students from Newnan High School volunteered to help veterans with their displays and visit the Wall for themselves.

"When I think about the Wall coming, I get tears in my eyes. That experience was a once-in-a-lifetime opportunity," said Taylor Cornelius, one of those students. "That Wall meant so much to so many of our veterans. I saw grown men on their knees with tears in their eyes because they recognized a name on the Wall. Words cannot describe that heartbreak. It was an indescribable experience."

Local volunteers, primarily veterans, worked together to create a first-class experience for visitors to the Wall. All volunteers gave up a Saturday morning for training and were assigned different time slots and jobs during that week and weekend. Assembling the Wall, disassembling the Wall, guiding students on tours of the Wall, parking, providing golf carts for the elderly and handicapped, picking up trash, and many other tasks were essential to the smooth running of this endeavor. There were more than one hundred of these first-layer volunteers. In addition, local Civil Air Patrol, Sea Cadets, and especially the Newnan High School Air Force ROTC were essential participants. Working as a Color Guard and as greeters, wreath layers, and manual laborers, these young people stood out. The second volunteer layer came from people at local churches who provided food and drink to those working at the Wall. This was much appreciated. All the team members thought the event was significant and worked diligently to ensure they were prepared and on time. It was indeed a community effort.

The final day of the Wall That Heals visit to Newnan, Sunday, October 23, was the most poignant. While the memorial remained open for guests, the CCVA prepared for the Families Ceremony to be held at 2 p.m. This ceremony, conducted by veteran Malcolm Jackson and the two generals, Army Major General Joe Brooks and Air Force Brigadier General Don Harvel, was held to honor and thank the families of the twenty-three Coweta fatalities from the Vietnam War. Parents, siblings, cousins, wives, fiancées, and friends packed the ballroom. They listened to special singing by the L. C. Lane Chorus Group and a short address by Reverend Robert Certain, a Vietnam War POW from Georgia. The families were recognized individually while photographs of their loved ones were on the screen. Brooks and Harvel were joined by State Representatives Billy Horne and Lynn Smith as each family was presented with a framed plaque containing a picture of their loved one and the name rubbing from the Wall in Washington, DC.

During the ceremony, the 132nd Helicopter Company, adopted by Coweta County and the city of Newnan in 1968, was invited back to Newnan to be recognized. As part of this recognition, the Newnan High School History and Social Studies Department purchased plastic Chinook models, which students from the Vietnam War class assembled. To honor the unit's aircraft and the models given to local officials in 1968, these models were now presented to the 132nd members in attendance. These models were a small way of reconnecting the two groups after forty-three years.

After the ceremony, a reception was held, and many families visited the Wall That Heals for the final time.

The Wall That Heals closed at five p.m. that evening with a closing ceremony led by VFW and CCVA member Dick Stender. As the colors were retired and the last notes of the bagpiper's rendition of "Amazing Grace" gradually faded into stillness, the emotion was palpable. The Wall That Heals had done its job.

The objects and mementos left at the Wall were tagged and collected each evening. Those objects are now owned by the Newnan High School History and Social Studies Department, and the items are used to teach local youth about the war in Vietnam and the great sacrifices that any war entails. Any sealed envelope left at the Wall has never been opened and will forever remain secure.

Volunteers were out again on Monday morning to disassemble the Wall and pack it into the trailer to visit another community. The visit had finally concluded.

However, it wasn't quite over.

One of the families of the deceased had not been found in time to be invited to the Sunday ceremony. A few weeks later, after the

Wall's departure, Deberah Williams at the *Newnan Times-Herald*, who had been assisting with the family search, found the family of Bill Thomas. Bill's mother and sister were living in McDonough, Georgia. The Commission made contact, and in early December, Joe Brooks and Steve Quesinberry drove to McDonough and held a presentation ceremony for Bill's mother. She was thrilled to describe her son and his service to the two men and was grateful for their visit.

Now it was finally over.

"I don't know how many people came during the four days the Wall was here," said Dick Stender, a member of the CCVA. "But the turnout was huge. It really meant a lot to all our local vets, especially our Vietnam vets" (McRae, 2011).

"It went beyond my expectations, almost beyond my comprehension," Brooks said.

Thousands of people visited the Wall That Heals that week in October 2011. Many came because they knew someone whose name was on the Wall. A few came because they were curious. Students came because their teachers took them or convinced them it was important. Some family members and friends of the Coweta boys had traveled back to Newnan, in some cases for the first time in years. For some of those family members, the Wall visit had allowed them to find the closure they desperately needed.

"The whole week was just fantastic," Brooks said in the *Newnan Times-Herald*. "The support from the community was just overwhelming. But what really brought it home was when we were passing out plaques to the families of the Coweta soldiers killed in Vietnam. I could see the emotion and expressions on their faces and began to understand what we had really accomplished."

For Steve Quesinberry, the visit from the Wall That Heals convinced him to begin the project that resulted in this book.

Sources

Interview with Joe Brooks, CCVA Co-Chair
Interview with Malcolm Jackson, CCVA Co-Chair
Interview with Taylor Cornelius Jarvis, student volunteer
Steve Quesinberry, CCVA Member

References

Winston Skinner. "Veterans will be honored Saturday at muster." *Newnan Times-Herald*, October 15, 2010.

Alex McRae. "Truck carrying 'Wall' arrives in Newnan about noon today." *Newnan Times-Herald*, October 18, 2011.

Alex McRae. "The Wall Arrives." *Newnan Times-Herald*, October 19, 2011.

Alex McRae. "Wreath-laying ceremony honors fallen." *Newnan Times-Herald*, October 23, 2011.

Alex McRae. "Honoring our fallen Heroes." *Newnan Times-Herald*, October 24, 2011.

Alex McRae. "The Wall moves on after an emotional salute to Veterans." *Newnan Times-Herald*, October 25, 2011.

Alex McRae. "Newnan High School students share essays on Vietnam War." *Newnan Times-Herald*, October 2, 2011.

The truck carrying the Wall That Heals in downtown Newnan.

The Vietnam War Class on Lagrange Street to welcome the Wall that Heals

The CCVA. (front row, left to right) Steve Quesinberry, Hank Berkowitz, Malcolm Jackson, Lynn Geddie, Tom Downy (back row, left to right) Don Harvel, Jeff Carroll, Dick Stender, Joe Brooks.

Students from the Vietnam War class at the Performing Arts Centre as part of the visit of the Wall That Heals.

The Wall That Heals

The Hines family (left) and the Smith family (right) after the Sunday ceremony honoring their loved one.

Photos courtesy of Paul and Susan Conlan. All rights reserv

CHAPTER TWENTY-EIGHT

The Vietnam War Class at Newnan High School

Newnan, Georgia

In my class, a remarkable thing took place: the young were united with the old. The students grew to see the veterans as brave and honorable men, and the veterans grew to see the students as intelligent and enthusiastic young adults. I am filled with deep emotions when I think about the Vietnam War. It has come alive for me. I do not feel it is a topic to avoid. The war had a monumental impact on the United States, and it should be discussed. This subject is controversial, and people have very different views concerning our involvement. I, for one, had listened to the views of others and taken them as my own without knowing any facts. Such an assumption is a mistake I will never make again. People need to discover for themselves what went wrong, what went right, and how America got through this chaotic time... as I did.

—Christie McDonald

On April 28, 2016, Newnan High School History and Social Studies Department Chair Steve Quesinberry gave opening remarks at the Certificate of Honor ceremony held in the school's historic auditorium:

> *Good evening. On behalf of Dr. Chase Puckett, principal of Newnan High School, VFW Post 2667, American Legion Post 57, and the Newnan High School History and Social Studies Department, I want to welcome you to Newnan High School. It is an honor and a privilege to host you and your family tonight.*
>
> *The Certificate of Honor is sponsored by the Georgia Department of Veteran Services as part of the 50th Anniversary Commemoration of the Vietnam War. We are honored to have members of that department, as well as Commissioner Mike Roby, in attendance here tonight. Their goal is to award every veteran in the state of Georgia a Certificate of Honor. We have worked together this year to find and enlist Vietnam and Vietnam Era veterans from our area eligible for the Certificate of Honor. Our first award presentation was spearheaded by the VFW and American Legion this past October at Unity Baptist Church.*
>
> *We wanted this presentation to be held at Newnan High School. This school has a history that goes back more than a hundred years. The building that we are sitting in was opened in 1952. The school has been an integral part of the community for a long time. I would guess that many of you attended school here, or your children did. We want this school to continue to be involved in the life of this community now and into the future.*
>
> *Teaching history isn't about the textbook. It isn't about every date or every detail. It is about engaging our students in a story about the world, our country, and our local area. Good and bad. The story is about people. Part of that story is about you.*
>
> *You have seen the entire History Department staff in white shirts out here this evening. They are not here because they are getting paid a lot of money to do this or because I gave them some pizza a few hours ago. They are here because of you and the families that supported you.*
>
> *You have seen students in white shirts this evening*

helping with this program. The entire Vietnam War class, spring 2016. They weren't here at 7 p.m. because of any textbook. They aren't here because I have taught them every detail about the Vietnam War. They are here because of you and the families that supported you.

This is what we want to teach our students and why we wanted you to visit our school. We want you to understand that our staff is committed to this community and teaching your story. We want our students to appreciate the community they live in and the sacrifices that so many made before them. While I certainly hope that you leave here and tell your family and neighbors that we did a great job, tonight will not be the biggest or the best thing we will ever do for you. That will come tomorrow in class when the staff and I stand in front of thirty teenagers every hour and relate to them what you and your family did for our country.

In the Spring of 2003, I taught my first class on the Vietnam War. Twenty-three students. Eighteen weeks. Ninety minutes per day. Those twenty-three students became my proving ground. I was concerned that I would have difficulty filling the time allotted; I was wrong. I figured it would take about three years to get the class where I wanted it to be. I was also wrong about that. In both cases, being wrong wasn't a problem. Instead, it was the best thing to have happened. Even though those twenty-three students wouldn't recognize the Vietnam War class today, I'm grateful to them for taking the chance. If there hadn't been enough students the first year, the course might never have taken off, and this story and book would never have been written.

There is no state-mandated curriculum for a class on the Vietnam War, so I had a degree of freedom that few high school teachers ever enjoy. I could create lesson plans that made the class interactive, engaging, enjoyable, and hopefully, memorable. Naturally, I believe this should be any good teacher's goal. However, the scope and expanse of the state curriculum and high-stakes testing limit this type of freedom and lessons simply due to time. I spent most of my time in my World History classes teaching the lessons, telling stories, providing visual and literary reinforcement, then going back over the topic to ensure students' mastery of the material. I managed to squeeze in something different on occasion, but I was always conscious of the time involved. In the Vietnam class, time was also at a premium, but not because I was concerned about covering the state curriculum and preparing for a state-mandated test. I just had so many compelling opportunities with which to involve my students!

I set out to create more than a class; I wanted to create an *experience*. I wanted it to be real. I wanted the students to reach out and touch their own history. I wanted the class to impact the students long after it was over.

The Vietnam War class at Newnan High School was heavily influenced by a course taught in North Carolina called the Lessons of Vietnam (LOV). After my class had been approved in 2002, I contacted the teacher of Lessons of Vietnam, Lindy Poling, via email. Lindy, now retired, was an extraordinary teacher at Millbrook High School and had won numerous awards for her innovative teaching methods. She graciously responded to my email and, over the following weeks, gave me ideas and advice that assisted me in getting started. In addition, I met her and her husband at an education conference hosted by the Vietnam Veterans Memorial Fund (VVMF) that summer, and she was just as kindhearted in person. We have stayed in contact to this day.

Another crucial influence on my teaching of the class was the 50th Anniversary Commemoration of the Vietnam War. After being contacted by a gentleman who worked for that group, I signed the History and Social Studies Department on as a Commemorative Partner. Joining as a partner would present me with various speakers and create even more opportunities to engage the students. In September 2017, General James Jackson, the individual in charge of the Commemoration program, visited Newnan High School to meet with my Vietnam War students. It was an honor I still look back upon fondly.

I had to recruit students to take the class, especially in the beginning. This class wasn't required, and there are many options for electives at high schools in Coweta County. Over the next few years, I had additional student interest once word got around that the class was different. Students took the Vietnam War class for a variety of reasons. During interviews, students explained why they signed up for the class.

> *I didn't know a lot about Vietnam, but hearing about history from my dad, he always talked about how important that time period was, so I had a little interest going into it but not a lot of information. —Alaina McLarin*

> *I always enjoyed history, and I was a big WWII guy, and I didn't know much about Vietnam, but I had heard how cool of a class it was, so I said why not? —Andrew Copeland*

> *I love history, and I was interested in the idea of a whole class about the Vietnam War. —Casey Stillwell*

> *I knew it was a cool and unique concept. It was not something I was going to get anywhere else, even at a university.—Jake Oldham*

> *It was a once-in-a-lifetime opportunity. —Logan Hudson*
> *I have always loved history. History and Social studies are like real life. Vietnam, it was specifically one class about one war that meant a lot to our country, but not a lot of people know about it. —Shelby Stillwell*

> *I always had a passion for history. I felt like I would never get a chance to study, in-depth, what happened in Vietnam again. So, I was excited to get the opportunity to learn about it. —Taylor Cornelius*

The class formula I gradually implemented encompassed many elements that the Lessons of Vietnam contained and the 50th Anniversary Commemoration offered. I also found that Coweta County and the Atlanta area provided many additional possibilities to get students involved in Vietnam War history. As the instructor, I saw my role as setting the stage, the first phase, for all that might follow. I would provide the background, the visuals, the stories, and the discussion. While I knew much about the war, I needed to learn more. So I began a reading program on all aspects of the 1960s that continues to this day. I wanted my students to know as much as possible as they moved into the second phase of the class.

The second phase involved students interacting and engaging with the men and women involved in what they were learning. The Vietnam veterans, as a group, were not treated particularly well when they returned home from their military service. Some didn't talk about it then. In countless cases, their families stopped asking. Now, they were moving into their retirement years, and I thought many of them might want to relate their stories. I was correct. But would they want to tell their story to a group of teenagers they didn't know? Fortunately, they did.

Starting about the third week, the class hosted, on average, two speakers a week. Speakers were carefully selected and scheduled to augment the knowledge students had gained in regular class sessions. This comprehension was a critical part of the class, and just like in any military operation, logistics is the key to success. By bringing in the veteran *after* we had covered the topic, I found students were prepared to receive and understand the information. They frequently knew the references the speaker touched on and understood enough about the subject to ask intelligent questions, maximizing their learning. The speaker reinforced what they had already learned and added in-depth stories of their experiences that a high school student would never obtain in a textbook or from their instructor.

I had also worked on varying the way the speakers came into the class so that the course would stay vibrant and engaging. I didn't bring in all the speakers solo. One of my favorite things was to bring them in with a partner. I stumbled on to this technique accidentally, but I worked to have some sessions featuring two to three speakers at a time. Changing speakers in the middle of the class kept students more alert and processing the information. Students enjoyed the banter between the class visitors. Often, one veteran would tell the students about an incident, and the partner would remember a similar or very different story about the topic that they had not thought about in years. That was the point at which history genuinely came alive!

Going a step further, we hosted group sessions. Group sessions had four to six veterans conversing with students in smaller groups, each at a different table in our Media Center. In groups of five, students spent approximately fifteen minutes with each veteran. These methods allowed students to be exposed to a variety of people in a limited amount of time. The group sessions also forced students to look the veteran in the eye. There was no hiding behind the person in front of them as some students did while attempting to be inconspicuous in class. This also brought variety to the course, which students appreciated.

In addition to the contact with veterans in the classroom, phase three had students correspond with a Vietnam veteran from across the country via email. They communicated with their assigned veteran once every two weeks, asking questions about themes the class had studied during the previous fortnight. This allowed students to get an additional viewpoint, reinforcement, and stories about each subject we covered. For example, if I covered the topic of letters and communication between the servicemen and home, the students would then begin to ask the class visitors about the significance of mail to them while in Vietnam. They would also ask their email partner the same question, ultimately hearing about the importance of home communication in multiple ways and by various people. The email project was a great way to get students to write, communicate in an adult fashion, and think.

None of these phases were chronological. They were all integrated into the class almost simultaneously. During a week, I could go over background on a topic, host a veteran speaker who talked about his experience with the subject, and then have students email their veteran contact and ask additional questions about the same thing. The following week might be similar, or it might be different. This variety kept students engaged throughout the semester.

During interviews, students reacted vigorously to this segment of the class.

> *I thought the variety of experiences was really interesting. One of the more impactful speakers was the anti-war protester, which balanced things in regard to what some of the country thought at this time. Getting their personal*

experiences really made the class meaningful.
—Alaina McLarin

They could have come in and given us the G-rated version of it, but I appreciated how real they were when they came in and told their story. They also answered all our questions, just like our pen pals on the email did. There is something really cool about not just learning the history, seeing it in the book, but actually talking to someone who was there.
—Andrew Copeland

That is something that a textbook can never teach you, those first-hand experiences. I had a lot of fun getting to know my veteran through the email project. It was really cool because she shared her experiences as a nurse with me. Especially a female in Vietnam, when there were mainly males that came in to speak to us. It was another perspective, what she saw and how she felt about it.—Anna Grace Rogers

Just hearing their stories, I thought, was so special. It's just not the same as reading it in a textbook.
—Casey Stillwell

They were just phenomenal. That is what connected me to wanting to know more about history and to major in it in college. This is what brought it to life for me. They also showed me different perspectives and experiences and the fact that there is not just one narrative. That was the first time that it hit home with me; those multiple perspectives are what make up history. There were so many ways to learn and make those connections, and the email project helped make it a little more personal. That personal connection was cool.
–Ellen Rayburn

It provided a really cool lens to separate the conflict itself from the people that were in it. —Jake Oldham

It engages students more. It engaged me more. I like the

emphasis on respecting, having a professional connection with the speakers, like shaking their hands and saying thank you. I think it is just incredible how having a speaker enhances the learning. —Jensen Fitzgibbon

That was one of my favorite parts of the class, hearing from people that were there, deep down in Vietnam, talking to us in Newnan in our classroom, face to face. You never got to do that anywhere else in school. —Logan Hudson

Having history tangibly available to you changes how you learn. It's so much different than learning from a textbook. It really sticks with you. It gave me a broad insight into the Vietnam War. Sometimes we left the class in tears. The entire experience is so personal. —Romina Subia

My favorite part of the entire curriculum. I really liked hearing their stories. It's different than reading it in a book. —Shelby Stillwell

Every story was different, and every story touched me in a different way. I loved the opportunity to learn from these individuals. I will never forget the opportunity to say thank you. —Taylor Cornelius

It makes a big difference. You can read it in a book or hear about it in a lecture, but having someone who actually lived it and is able to describe it in more detail just helps bring it to life. —Stephen Quesinberry

It makes it more real because a lot of history stories sound just like... stories. But when you talk to someone who was there, it makes it feel like it happened to an actual person. —Ashley Quesinberry

It made it more engaging. To hear all the different perspectives and roles that were a part of that conflict gave you the sense that history is all around us. It gave us a more solid appreciation for those men and women in all the services. —Sarah Hinkemeyer

You can read about it in any other class, but when you have the actual guys in front of you that lived it, it impacts you a lot more. Also, the stories they related would never be put in a textbook. —Patrick Boren

It makes you see how it was instead of just reading it in a book or seeing it in a movie. It looks interesting in a movie, but what those guys have is even more special. It's really cool to know people who have experienced things like that before. —Mason Bervaldi

It was cool to hear all the veterans' different points of view. Not all of them have the same opinions on the same things. We got to hear from a lot of people from different backgrounds, and I thought that was really cool.
—Spencer Matthews

By 2011, more people had become aware of the class and were intrigued by what was happening at Newnan High School. I had already begun taking advantage of local opportunities to get students involved with the Vietnam War. Still, after the Wall That Heals came to Newnan in the fall of that year, the opportunities seemed to multiply. These opportunities were due, in part, to the fact that 2011 had been designated as the first year of the 50th Anniversary Commemoration of the war, and Newnan High School had joined as a Commemorative Partner. I tried to take advantage of every occasion and every opportunity that I thought would help connect students with the war and the people who had served. The school administration worked with me, and the teenagers embraced every activity presented.

"Getting outside of the classroom just enhanced the learning," said Jensen Fitzgibbon, a Vietnam War student.

"The opportunities the class offered us were incredible," said Romina Subia, another student. "I even met the governor. Every single aspect melded into a class that you never forget."

Some of the more memorable activities of the class included the following:

Connecting with the Vietnam War: Vietnam Helicopters

In 2004, local veteran Terry Garlock and I traveled to Hampton, Georgia, to visit the Army Aviation Heritage Foundation (AAHF). The foundation is a nonprofit organization dedicated to telling the story of Army Aviation. To tell the story, they have acquired and maintained a fleet of Army helicopters and small aircraft. They have owned multiple Hueys and Cobras and, at various times, a LOH, Caribou, and Birddog. Garlock knew some of the men who worked there, and he was kind enough to introduce me. Soon, I was taking the students on trips to the AAHF hangars, where the group had veterans waiting who had flown the various aircraft in Vietnam. They allowed the students to climb into the cockpits just like the crew members had done decades earlier.

"The trip to the hangar made everyone's entire week," recalled student Shelby Stillwell.

The group was so impressed with the students I brought that they eventually agreed, on multiple occasions, to fly some of the choppers to Newnan High School for an even more immersive experience. Those flights to Newnan High School developed into interdisciplinary events. History, math, and physics classes were all involved in studying the helicopters before their arrival then watching them land, climbing aboard, and hearing the veterans describe their use.

That trip with Terry Garlock began a relationship between the AAHF and Newnan High School that continues to this day.

> *My grandfather was a Huey guy, so I took a bunch of pictures with me in the cockpit and sent those to him, and he had a great time with that. Of course, I had a great time with it too. —Jake Oldham*

> *Seeing the Hueys was one of the coolest experiences. You have history in your hand. You can imagine what the soldiers were going through. —Romina Subia*

State History: The Trips to the State Capitol

In 2014, as part of the 50th Anniversary Commemoration, the Georgia Department of Veterans Services held a ceremony to honor and remember the soldiers still listed as Missing in Action (MIA) in Vietnam. The Department of Veterans Affairs contacted me in the hope that I could help extend the invitation to Johnny Calhoun's family. (See Johnny Calhoun, Chapter 10.) I obliged and contacted the family. They had moved to Roanoke, Alabama, and Johnny's mother was elderly. They appreciated the tribute being paid to their son and husband but didn't feel they could make it to Atlanta. They requested that I accept the honor for the family. I had been with them when Johnny had been inducted into the Georgia Military Hall of Fame. It had been an exceptional evening, and the family had reacted with grace and dignity. Now, however, I was overwhelmed with the enormity of their request.

I wasn't sure I could represent the family in something of this nature. But how could I tell "Granny," Calhoun's mother, that I couldn't do it?

I hesitantly agreed. I contacted the Department of Veterans Affairs to make sure they approved. They did. Then I dropped the bomb. What would they think about my Vietnam War class attending the ceremony? To their credit, they took a leap of faith and agreed to having thirty teenagers attend.

The school backed the trip, and when I explained it to my students, they were buoyant. Even after I explained that they would be required to don jackets, ties, and dresses, their enthusiasm didn't abate. That trip to the Capitol was outstanding. The adults there were impressed with the students' appearance and behavior. They met Governor Nathan Deal and had their picture taken on the steps inside the building.

The *Newnan Times-Herald* interviewed some of the student participants. They reported, "'By being here, they (the veterans) can see that people of our generation care about what happened in the past,' said Jada Smith, an NHS senior. 'I think it is an honor to be here and watch these veterans who have given so much for our country,' said Kait Nichols, an NHS senior. 'Even though they are MIA, it is awesome to honor them.' They also enjoyed experiencing the history they learned about in class. 'I think it's an honor to be able to come here and honor these people we learn about in class,' said NHS senior Mary Margaret Boyd. 'It's just an honor to witness the things we see in class in real life,' added another senior, Heys Rowan. 'It's also an honor to see the commemoration of Vietnam Veterans'" (Shortt, 2014).

Those students set the stage for all the Vietnam War students to follow.

Almost every semester afterward, the Department of Veterans Affairs invited the Vietnam War class to attend the 50th Anniversary Commemoration ceremony held under the rotunda of the Capitol. They often chose different Vietnam veteran groups to honor, like the MIAs or the Prisoners of War (POWs). Sometimes it was just Vietnam veterans in general.

Each class continued to amaze the adults, who seemed obsessed with the idea that teenagers couldn't behave and didn't care. By 2018, the Department of Veterans Services began asking the class to participate in the ceremonies. The students were honored.

> *In the class, you gain an appreciation for veterans that fought in Vietnam and had an impact on our world at the time. To see that our state still recognizes those individuals and applauds them was an amazing experience. We got to meet other Vietnam veterans as well as the governor. Overall, it was an awesome opportunity to show them that we care. —Anna Grace Rogers*

Connecting with the Veteran: Medal of Honor Recipients

We hosted various Medal of Honor recipients in 2007, 2009, 2012, and again in 2017. The students spent time with American heroes Bruce Crandall, Wesley Fox, Gary Wetzel, and Bennie Adkins. Colonel Joe Jackson, a native son, visited with Vietnam War and World War II students multiple times, explaining the mission that led him to receive the Medal of Honor and his philosophy of community service. These visits brought our students face-to-face with our nation's heroes. These men were heroes not just because of what they did in Vietnam but also because of how they lived their lives afterward.

Connecting with the Veteran: The Speaker Series

When the History and Social Studies Department became a Commemorative Partner in the Vietnam War's 50th Anniversary, we committed to holding at least one special event a year to honor veterans of the war. While I felt I was already doing that in the Vietnam class, a series of circumstances caused our department to begin bringing in speakers for our students and community. We started hosting one speaker each semester, one of the speakers being from the Vietnam War. We asked them to visit students in the Vietnam War class, World War II class, or both, depending on their area of expertise. While we've hosted several guests who weren't affiliated with the Vietnam War, such as a Civil Rights Freedom Rider and a World War II fighter pilot, we also hosted many prominent Vietnam veterans. Paul Longgrear (Green Beret) and Donna Rowe (Army nurse) both spoke, as did Steve Ritchie (Vietnam Air Force Ace), Jason Sehorn, Wayne Waddell, Kevin Cheney (Vietnam POW), and Joe Galloway (UPI reporter during the Vietnam War).

Connecting with the Veteran: Certificate of Honor Presentations

In 2015, the Department of Veterans Affairs, again in concert with the 50th Anniversary Commemoration, started a decidedly ambitious project of awarding every Vietnam or Vietnam-era veteran in Georgia a Certificate of Honor. They wanted local organizations to spearhead these presentations, and department members would make every effort to award the certificates personally. The Coweta Veterans Club, also a 50th Anniversary Commemorative Partner, organized a presentation led by Auxiliary member Janet Alford. The Newnan High School History Department, united with the Veterans Club, started registering veterans to receive the certificate. We also planned the who, what, where, when, and how of presenting these certificates. I had worked closely on projects with Miss Janet in the past, and I enjoyed working with her on the Certificates of Honor immensely.

Over several months, we signed up close to six hundred local Vietnam or Vietnam-era veterans. We held ceremonies during the fall of 2015 and spring of 2016, and each veteran chose which to attend. The fall 2015 presentation was held at Unity Baptist Church, hosted by the Coweta Veterans Club and assisted by Newnan High School. The spring 2016 ceremony was held at the Newnan High School Auditorium, hosted by the History Department and aided by the Veterans Club.

The fall ceremony went beautifully. I took students to assist, but the Veterans Club did all the heavy lifting. In the spring at Newnan High School, the responsibilities were reversed. The entire History staff and Vietnam War class were outfitted in unique polo shirts for the evening. They proceeded to register, guide, drive, and seat veterans and their families, assisted by the Coweta Veterans Club. State Commissioner of Veterans Affairs Mike Roby gave out the Certificates of Honor, just as he had in the fall. Our staff and students impressed the veterans who entered the building that evening, and the veterans impressed them in return.

I was responsible for welcoming the families gathered that evening. As I spoke, I wanted them to feel good about the upcoming recognition, which for many was long overdue. However, I also wanted them to grasp the importance that we placed on their position in our community. I wanted them to understand that this wouldn't be a recognition we hosted and then forgot. While they might have been ignored on their return home fifty years ago, I needed them to know that Newnan High School, the flagship high school in Coweta County, remembered them that night and would remember them in class each semester.

They should never be forgotten.

Connecting with the Veteran: The Trip to the VA Hospital in Atlanta

Another notable event that caused students to interact with history was our trip to the Atlanta VA Hospital in 2018. I met one of the hospital's administrators at a Certificate of Honor ceremony. As a result, the Vietnam War class was invited to visit the hospital and interact with veterans there. I drove to the hospital, which I had never seen before, with local Vietnam and Coast Guard veteran Mike Johnson. We met with the administrator. He gave us a tour and described what he would like our students to do, and it was on.

Back at Newnan High School, I tracked down our Department of

Labor representative and Jobs for Georgia Graduates (JGG) coordinator, Mr. Gaines Coker. Gaines had driven the bus for me on various trips, including those to the helicopter hangar and the State Capitol among others. We had known each other for thirty years and worked well together. I wanted him to drive us to the hospital, and he wanted his JGG students to be involved. It wasn't a hard sell for either of us.

The students were enthusiastic about the project, and before the trip, we formed an assembly line in class to stuff bags full of items for the patients. I knew we would need to break into groups to cover the hospital in the time constraints we were working under, so I recruited our two instructional coaches, Elizabeth Doster and Kelley Finger, to come along. They jumped at the chance.

The trip was marvelous. I was astonished at how those students went out of their way to engage with the patients. They shook hands, encouraged them, and thanked them for their service to our country. When veterans spoke, they looked them in the eye and listened to what they had to say.

Frank Henderson once said that "kids discovered a sense of service by taking the Vietnam War class." I remember thinking on the way home that people who worry about our country's teenagers would be reassured if they had seen our group in action that day.

Local History: The Trip to the Veterans Park

After each semester, starting around 2012, the Vietnam and World War II classes combined for a "walk to the park." The Newnan Veterans Park, completed in 2009, was our destination. Our goal was to teach the students about Newnan's local heroes and the importance of remembering the sacrifices of many young men, especially those from Coweta County, Georgia. We would head down LaGrange Street toward downtown Newnan and the park as soon as class began. Upon arrival downtown, the Vietnam War class would divert to the courthouse for a short lesson at the monuments to Colonel Joe M. Jackson and Major Stephen Pless, plus the plaque on the courthouse wall that lists the men from this county who were killed in Vietnam. Frank Henderson, the World War II instructor, kept his students going to the park. Once we gave the students time to eat lunch, we moved into the lesson. We usually started at the statue of Jackson and Pless, and I spoke to the students about these local heroes and the creation of the statue by the Vietnam veteran from Texas. Frank then took the students onto the terrace to discuss the lists of those killed in action from the 20th century. He also noted the significance of everything located in the park. We wrapped up that section by looking at the bricks purchased to help finance the park's renovation. (One of those bricks was purchased by my spring 2007 Vietnam War class on their own initiative.) This trip was focused on the local history experience and the sacrifices of our local families. It was a sobering and reflective moment with the students and an excellent activity for the end of the semester.

> *So, this is Newnan, and this is our heritage. That connection to the community really shaped me as a person in regard to patriotism and my role in society. That is what pushed me to be a teacher and to push other people to have that connection. —Ellen Rayburn*

> *That was a special thing. I had never looked over there or taken the time to read that stuff or know the history. That was a really cool, really insightful, and a very educational piece, literally in our downtown, I had never thought about before. —Logan Hudson*

In 2021, toward the end of the pandemic, I decided it was time to retire. I had completed thirty-six years of teaching, and while I still loved it, there were other things I wanted to accomplish, including this book. Unfortunately, a tornado pummeled the school approximately a month after I had told the History and Social Studies Department that I was leaving. It made the building I had worked in for those thirty-six years uninhabitable. It seemed to be a sign that I had made the correct decision. However, I didn't want the Vietnam War class to fall by the wayside. I felt it had become too important to the school, students, and the community. The administration agreed, and I asked Frank Henderson to continue the class.

Frank taught the World War II class at the school for fifteen years. When he arrived at Newnan High, the Student-Vet Connect program was on the verge of being discontinued. Since then, he has worked diligently with me to keep that program alive. Frank has also been involved with the Speaker Series, the Medal of Honor speakers, and he started the Student-Vet Connect 5k, which raised $50,000 to help local veterans in need. He already knew many of the veterans I worked closely with concerning the class, and as the time approached for my retirement, I made sure he knew everyone. When I asked him to keep it going, I didn't ask him to do it exactly as I had; I asked him to make it his own and improve it.

"The biggest reason to keep it going is that it has been an established class for so long, and the kids really, really love the class," said Frank. "They not only learn the history, but they meet the veterans, interact with the community, and learn things that they would never otherwise get an opportunity to learn."

"History isn't something that happened eons ago and that is completely unrelated to who students are. There are events that are recent enough to have people that lived it that can tell them about it," Frank said. "We used to say, 'bringing history to life,' and this class does that. I hope that we have created a generation of kids that love history. For the veterans, it is cathartic to speak to students who are interested in what happened and are sympathetic to their experiences.

"Everything was real. Bringing the veterans into class, taking the students to Student-Vet Connect, traveling to the Capitol and the hospital made it real," said Frank.

Most importantly, Frank Henderson *believed* in this approach to history education.

Keeping it real also involved teaching our youth about the guys who preceded them and had died in service to their country, as we did at the Veterans Park. As I reviewed information on the class in preparation for writing this chapter, I found an article in the *Newnan Times-Herald* that I had forgotten. It had been written a few months before I began that first Vietnam War class. In that article, I was quoted saying, "We want to strive to ensure that our native sons are more than just names and dates." That first semester, I contacted some families who were still living locally, and they came to school one day to be interviewed by my students. We scanned the photographs they brought in and posted them on the VVMF Wall of

Faces website. As the years passed and I heard from few people regarding that project, that original goal faded. Its revival began when the Coweta County Veterans Commission started its work to bring the Wall That Heals to Newnan.

From that fall semester of 2011 until I packed them up post-tornado in 2021, those photographs of each of Coweta's Vietnam dead, framed during the visit of the Wall That Heals, hung on my classroom's back wall. I told the students that those men watched me each day to ensure they weren't forgotten. During the ten years the pictures hung in my room, I taught my students about those boys who, at about their age, had died on a foreign battlefield. I explained to them the grief of their families. I had people who knew those boys tell the students a little of their story. Student Mason Bervaldi shared how these photographs and the discussion about these men impacted him during the class.

> *What was really special to me was those twenty-three guys in the back, on the wall. They are from our hometown, so you can relate to them. It was interesting to know that we had guys from Newnan, Georgia, that went and fought in that war. You wouldn't think so because we are just a small little town, but it was interesting to know that.*

Frank Henderson has those pictures on display in his classroom today.

They should never be forgotten.

My goal from the beginning was to make the class an "experience." I wanted to make it real. I wanted my students to reach out and grab their history by the collar. I wanted to impact the students long after they left high school.

> *The class deeply impacted me as far as the way I view history. It really set off a spark that made me interested in studying history. —Alaina McLarin*

> *Folks that were in the Vietnam War, I go out of my way to talk to them. Every time. That was driven into us in that class. It wasn't that hard of a sell because of what we*

learned. —Andrew Copeland

It's that appreciation. It's showing the older generation that I care and am forever in debt to them and what they did for our country. For me, the Vietnam War class was by far my favorite. It felt like I was living back in the moment —Anna Grace Rogers

I was just empowered by the female perspective and what she went through. It sparked my interest in medicine and caused me to be a nurse today. So that was very near and dear to my heart to have her come and speak to us. —Casey Stillwell, referring to Captain Donna Rowe, a nurse

It gave me the chance to view globe-changing events from individual perspectives. I think that has helped me in a lot of other situations, to be able to look at big topics, but also what is going on with the people. The individual is important. That was a central theme looking back on it. —Jake Oldham

Being respectful to veterans. It gives me chills to think about what they went through and what they experienced. Every time I see a Vietnam veteran, I say thank you. —Shelby Stillwell

The level of respect after taking that class skyrocketed. I never truly understood what a sacrifice being in the military could be until I heard some of these stories. Now, I thank every service man that I see. —Taylor Cornelius

You know what everyone else went through before you. It puts your experience more in perspective. You are more grateful. —Stephen Quesinberry (Stephen spent eight years in the US Army)

As a nurse, I have many patients who were in or have relatives who were in the Vietnam War. The class gave me a better understanding of what they or their family has gone through.—Ashley Quesinberry

It stuck with me to show more appreciation to those men and women, as they don't get the appreciation they deserve. But it also gave me an understanding of how that war changed so many things in our country. It also gave me the information to be more of an informed citizen and voter. —Sarah Hinkemeyer

You get a better perspective and respect the veterans so much more. You go out of your way to talk to them. It also made us realize how different the culture was back then. It let us know that when you look at your grandparents and think they never had fun, they did have fun. It was just a different kind of fun. —Patrick Boren

Sources

Interview with Sarah Hinkmeyer, Newnan High School graduate, 2007 *(Sarah is now a Chemist/Technical Specialist at Yokogawa Corporation in Newnan.)*

Interview with Stephen B. Quesinberry, Newnan High School graduate, 2008 *(Stephen spent eight years in the US Army and is now the Director of Acquisitions for a Real Estate Company.)*

Interview with Jake Oldham, Newnan High School graduate, 2011 *(Jake is now a math teacher at Newnan High School.)*

Interview with Ellen Rayburn Whitlock, Newnan High School graduate, 2011 *(Ellen is now a history teacher in Florida.)*

Interview with Ashley Quesinberry Hover, Newnan High School graduate, 2011 *(Ashley is now a nurse and a small business owner.)*

Interview with Andrew Copeland, Newnan High School graduate, 2012 *(Andrew is now a member of the Coweta County Board of Education.)*

Interview with Casey Stillwell Hurley, Newnan High School graduate, 2012 *(Casey is now a nurse.)*

Interview with Taylor Cornelius Jarvis, Newnan High School graduate, 2012 *(Taylor is now a legal assistant.)*

Interview with Alaina McLarin George, Newnan High School graduate, Class of 2015 *(Alaina is now a history teacher at Newnan High School.)*
Interview with Shelby Stillwell Rogel, Newnan High School graduate, 2016 *(Shelby is now a nurse.)*
Interview with Jensen Fitzgibbon, Newnan High School graduate, 2017 *(Jensen is now an analyst for Georgia Pacific.)*
Interview with Romina Subia, Newnan High School graduate, 2018 *(Romina is a college student.)*
Interview with Anna Grace Rogers, Newnan High School graduate, 2019 *(Anna Grace is a college student.)*
Interview with Logan Hudson, Newnan High School graduate, 2019 *(Logan is a college student.)*
Interview with Patrick Boren, Newnan High School graduate, 2019 *(Patrick is a college student.)*
Interview with Mason Bervaldi, Newnan High School graduate, 2019 *(Mason is a college student.)*
Interview with Spencer Matthews, Newnan High School graduate, 2020 *(Spencer is a college student.)*
Interview with Frank Henderson, Newnan High School graduate, 1990, and Vietnam War Instructor, starting in 2021.

References

McDonald, Christie. My Vietnam. October 20, 2008.
"Students to study Vietnam War." *Newnan Times-Herald,* November 25, 2002.
Celia Shortt, "Vietnam War class at NHS attends ceremony honoring those MIA." *Newnan Times-Herald,* September 26, 2014.

MOH visitors to the Vietnam War Class. Bruce "Snake" Crandall (left) and Joe Jackson (right). Both are shown with NHS students.

Vietnam War Class at the Capital (left)-honoring MIA Johnny Calhoun, school year 2014-2015. A selfie with Governor Brian Kemp (left), school year 2019-2020.

Vietnam War Class visits from Joe Galloway (left), school year 2018-2019, and Steve Ritchie (right), school year 2017-2018.

Vietnam War students working at the Certificate of Honor ceremony at NHS (left), school year 2015-2016. Students at the VA Hospital (right) in Atlanta, school year 2018-2019.

Vietnam War Class and JGG students at the VA Hospital in Atlanta, school year 2018-2019.

APPENDIX

While I have spent innumerable hours researching and writing these narratives, I understand that there is more to each story; there is more to discover about the people and events chronicled in this book.

Please get in touch with me if you believe you have any anecdotes that might add to this volume and are willing to share.

Please let me know if you have proof that I've made a factual error. I can't correct anything without that proof, whether it's in the form of a newspaper article, military document, school report card, or whatever. For substantiated assertions, I will certainly make the necessary changes with much appreciation for your assistance.

I didn't include all the photographs I have amassed over the past ten years, but I am always looking for more. If you have any photographs that you are willing to share of the people or events related to the Vietnam War in Coweta County, please get in touch.

I have set up a website to add information and pictures that I was unable to include in the book itself. You can also contact me by visiting this website, www.bettermencoweta.com.

I appreciate your interest in the history of Coweta County.

Quick Reference Guide

Quick Reference Guide: Coweta Vietnam Killed in Action Chronological by Death

Name	Town	Branch	Rank	DOD	Age	MOS	Wall
Grady Elder	Grantville	Army	SGT	6/11/1966	30	11D	Panel 08E Line 036
Daniel Post	Newnan	Marine Corp	CPL	7/31/1966	23	0311	Panel 09E Line 092
Donald Lowery	Newnan	Army	PFC	2/15/1967	19	11B	Panel 15E Line 033
Jesse Cofield	Newnan	Army	CPL	9/13/1967	21	11B	Panel 26E Line 065
Thomas Huddleston	Newnan	Army	SP4	11/18/1967	21	11C	Panel 30E Line 027
Jerry Smith	Newnan	Army	SGT	1/3/1968	20	11C	Panel 33E Line 032
Joseph Watson	Newnan	Army	LCPL	1/8/1968	19	3371	Panel 34E Line 002
Arthur Hines	Grantville	Army	PFC	2/10/1968	27	11B	Panel 38E Line 072
Johnny Calhoun	Newnan	Army	SFC	3/27/1968	22	05B4S	Panel 46E Line 045
Charles Walthall	Palmetto	Army	PFC	5/21/1968	20	11B	Panel 65E Line 003
Terry Allen	Newnan	Army	CPL	6/23/1968	20	11B	Panel 55W Line 020
Wayne Vessell	Senoia	Marine Corp	PFC	7/14/1968	24	0311	Panel 52W Line 032
Bobby Freeman	Grantville	Army	SGT	8/12/1968	22	11C	Panel 49W Line 053
Timothy Cole	Newnan	Army	WO	10/18/1968	21	062B	Panel 41W Line 072
James Kerr	Palmetto	Army	SGT	12/6/1968	20	36K20	Panel 37W Line 051
Robert Couch	Senoia	Army	SGT	12/30/1968	19	11B	Panel 35W Line 008
Leavy Solomon	Palmetto	Army	SP4	1/11/1969	22	91A20	Panel 35W Line 073
Edgar Pittman	Moreland	Army	SP4	6/23/1969	19	36K20	Panel 21W Line 001
Larry Pinson	Grantville	Marine Corp	LCPL	9/19/1969	19	0351	Panel 18W Line 114
Warner Hughie	Newnan	Army	CPL	3/12/1970	21	11B	Panel 13W Line 118
William Thomas	Senoia	Marine Corp	LCPL	3/25/1970	18	2533	Panel 12W Line 044
John Dozier	Sharpsburg	Army	SSGT	6/18/1971	20	11B	Panel 03W Line 080
Robert Webb	Newnan	Army	1LT	10/17/1971	24	1981	Panel 02W Line 042

Map

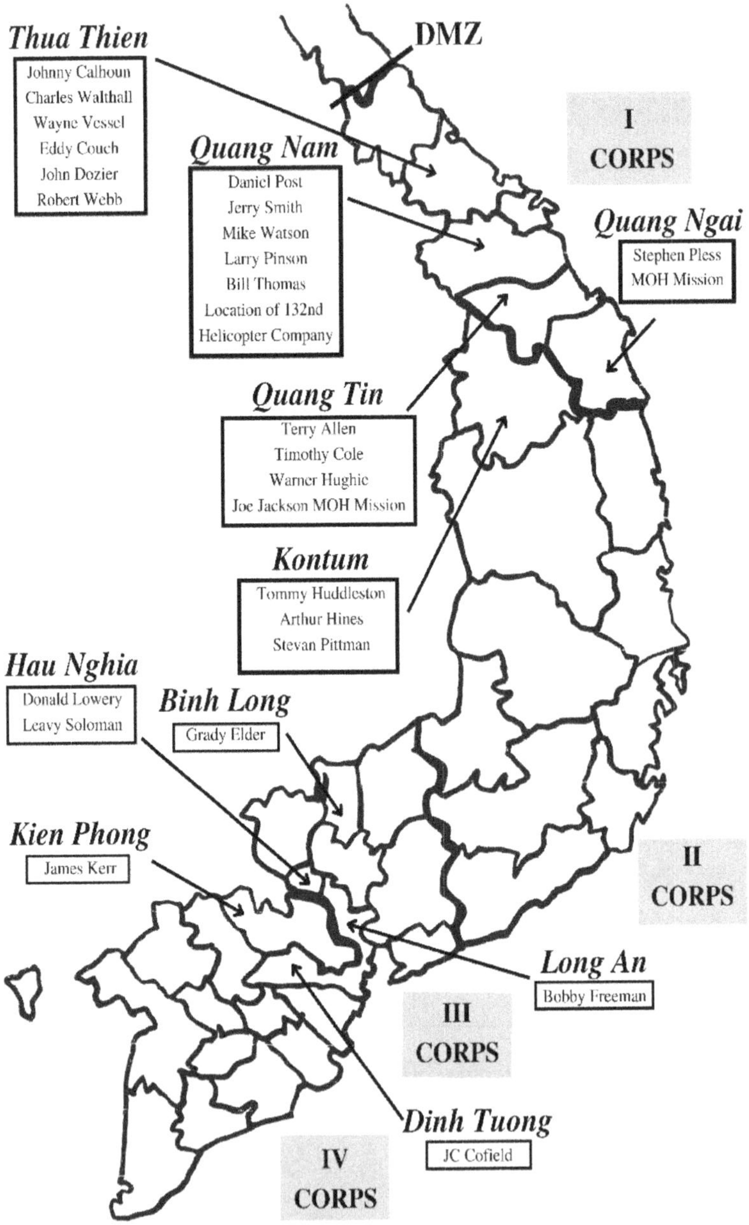
Thua Thien
Johnny Calhoun
Charles Walthall
Wayne Vessel
Eddy Couch
John Dozier
Robert Webb
DMZ
I CORPS
Quang Nam
Daniel Post
Jerry Smith
Mike Watson
Larry Pinson
Bill Thomas
Location of 132nd Helicopter Company
Quang Ngai
Stephen Pless
MOH Mission
Quang Tin
Terry Allen
Timothy Cole
Warner Hughie
Joe Jackson MOH Mission
Kontum
Tommy Huddleston
Arthur Hines
Stevan Pittman
Hau Nghia
Donald Lowery
Leavy Soloman
Binh Long
Grady Elder
Kien Phong
James Kerr
II CORPS
Long An
Bobby Freeman
III CORPS
Dinh Tuong
JC Cofield
IV CORPS

Map courtesy of Jodi Hobbs and Ashley Quesinberry. All rights reserved

Glossary

AC: Aircraft commander.

AHC: Assault Helicopter Company.

AIRBORNE: Paratrooper.

AIRBURST: The explosion of munitions in the air.

AIRMOBILE: People or materials moved around by helicopter. Helicopter technology had civilian and military uses, but the idea of moving service people and supplies by helicopter just happened to come about at the same time we went to war in a country with few roads.

AIR CAVALRY: Helicopter-borne infantry. As part of the airmobile concept, helicopters are viewed as taking the horse's place.

AIT: Advanced Individual Training, the period following Basic Training where a soldier trains for his Military Occupational Specialty (MOS).

A-O: Area of Operations.

ARVN: Army of the Republic of Vietnam (South Vietnamese Army).

ASH AND TRASH: Helicopter mission flights that are considered non-combative.

A SHAU VALLEY: Located in Thua Thien Province of I Corps near the Laotian border. One of the entry points to South Vietnam for NVA soldiers coming from the Ho Chi Minh Trail.

BASE CAMP: The field headquarters and resupply base for a brigade or division-sized unit. Base camps usually contain all or part of the unit's support elements (artillery, air, etc.).

BERM, BERM LINE: Hedgerow or built-up area which divided rice paddies; also, a rise in the ground.

BIRD: A nickname for any aircraft.

BIVOUAC: A temporary camp.

BOONDOCKS, BOONIES, BRUSH, BUSH: Expressions for the jungle or any remote area in Vietnam.

BX: Base Exchange.

C & C: Command and Control.

CENTRAL HIGHLANDS: A large plateau at the southern edge of the Truong Son Mountains.

CHARLIE, CHARLES, CHUCK: American slang for the Viet Cong (VC). This came from the NATO phonetic alphabet, V being Victor and C being Charlie.

CHICKEN PLATE: Body armor worn by helicopter pilots and gunners. It provided some protection against shrapnel but was not bulletproof.

CHIEU HOI: (Choo Hoy): "Open arms." The program under which South Vietnam offered amnesty to members of the NLF and VC.

CHINOOK: A CH-47 cargo helicopter.

CIB: Combat Infantry Badge. To receive this badge, one must be in an infantry unit and engaged in ground combat.

CLAYMORE: A fan-shaped, antipersonnel mine. It is placed on the ground and detonated by command or a trip wire. If not used, it is picked up to be employed at another time.

CO: Commanding Officer.

COBRA: Army attack helicopter during the Vietnam War. They are used by the Marine Corps today.

CONTACT: The condition of being in proximity to the enemy in addition to involving a firefight.

CP: Command Post.

CREW CHIEF: Huey crewmember who maintains the aircraft and supervises the ground crew.

CROSSCHECK: When everyone checks everyone else for things that are loose, make noise, light up, etc., before going on patrol.

C's, C-rations, C-rats, Charlie rats, or combat rations: Easily transportable canned meals used during military operations.

DEROS: Date Eligible for Return from Overseas; the date a serviceman's tour in Vietnam was estimated to end.

DMZ: Demilitarized Zone. The dividing line between North and South Vietnam.

DOC: Nickname for any field medic.

THE DRAG: The squad in the back of the platoon or company to ensure rear safety.

DUFFEL BAG: The bag in which troops stored all their various gear as they moved from one assignment to the next. Not the bag they would take on a patrol.

DUSTOFF: Call sign for a medical evacuation helicopter or mission. This call sign originated with Major Charles Kelly, considered the father of "*Dustoff*" because of his role in its inception.

ELEPHANT GRASS: The sharp-edged grass found in the highlands of Vietnam; can grow as tall as 7 feet.

EXTRACTION: Withdrawal of troops from an area via helicopter.

FAC: Forward Air Controller.

FIGHTING HOLE: Another word for a "foxhole;" sometimes has an elevated sheet metal roof reinforced with sandbags.

FIREBASE: An artillery firing position. These bases dotted Vietnam and usually comprised four howitzers with crews and a company of Infantry.

FIREFIGHT: Exchange of small arms fire between opposing military units.

FLAK JACKET: A heavy fiberglass-filled vest worn for protection from shrapnel or "flak."

FRAG: A slang term for a grenade.

FREEDOM BIRD: Any aircraft on which an American soldier left Vietnam and returned home (home being "the world.").

FRIENDLIES: US troops or allies.

FRIENDLY FIRE: Describes air, artillery, or small-arms fire from American or Allied forces mistakenly directed at American or Allied positions and/or service people.

GREEN BERETS: Special Forces of the US Army. They were awarded the Green Beret headgear as a mark of distinction.

GRUNT: A popular nickname for an infantryman in Vietnam; derived from the sound one made from lifting his rucksack due to its weight.

HAMMER & ANVIL: A strategy used by US forces, that involves placing a "blocking" unit at one point (the Anvil) and then putting in a unit at another location (the Hammer) to sweep the enemy into the blocking force.

HOOTCH: Small living quarters or native hut.

HORN: Radio.

HOT: Dangerous.

HQ: Headquarters.

HUEY: Nickname for the iconic UH-1 (utility helicopter); used for everything imaginable during the Vietnam War.

HUMP: To be on patrol.

I CORPS: The northernmost military region in South Vietnam. Also known as "Eye" Corps.

II CORPS: The military region that contains the Central Highlands of South Vietnam. South of I Corps.

III CORPS: The military region between Saigon and the Central Highlands. South of II Corps.

IV CORPS: The southernmost military region in South Vietnam, located in the Mekong Delta. South of III Corps.

ILLUM: Illumination. Flares dropped by aircraft and fired from the ground by hand, artillery, or mortars.

INCOMING: Receiving enemy mortar or rocket fire.

IN-COUNTRY: When you were "in-country," you were in Vietnam.

INSERTION: Helicopter placement of combat troops.

IN THE FIELD: Any forward combat area or any area outside of a town or base camp.

JUNGLE ROT: A skin abrasion caused by heat, sweat, and friction. It can also be acquired by bacteria, common in the tropics.

KIA: Killed in Action.

KLICK: Slang for kilometer.

KP: Kitchen Police.

LAAGER: A night defensive position.

LIFER: A career soldier.

LIGHT UP: To fire on the enemy.

LOH (LOACH): Light Observation Helicopter.

LP: Listening Post. A two-man or three-man post placed outside the barbwire surrounding a firebase. They were the early warning for the troops inside the perimeter. This goes back to World War I.

LZ: Landing Zone.

M-16: The standard American rifle used in Vietnam after 1966.

M-60: Standard issue machine gun carried by the infantry during the Vietnam War. A door-gunner would also use it on a Huey.

MACV: Military Assistance Command, Vietnam. The American headquarters in Vietnam.

MACV-SOG: Military Assistance Command Vietnam Studies and Observations Group. This highly classified group did reconnaissance missions into Laos, Cambodia, and along the Ho Chi Minh trail.

MAMA-SAN: An elderly Vietnamese woman.

MASH: Mobile Army Surgical Hospital.

MECH: Mechanized infantry. Infantry going into battle in or with Armored Personnel Carriers. (APC)

MEDEVAC: A medical evacuation by helicopter; call sign "*Dustoff*."

MIA: Missing in Action.

MOH: Medal of Honor.

MONTAGNARD: "Mountain man" in French. The nickname for the indigenous people that live in the Central Highlands of Vietnam. They worked closely with the American Special Forces during the war.

MOS: Military Occupational Specialty; a soldier's job specialty.

MP: Military Police.

MRF: Mobile Riverine Force. The MRF includes the 2nd Brigade of the 9th Infantry Division and River Assault Flotilla 1.

NATO: North Atlantic Treaty Organization. Created in 1948 as an alliance of Western European countries and the United States to protect the freedom and security of the allied nations. It was formed during the Cold War to safeguard against possible Soviet aggression. It is still functioning today.

NCO: Noncommissioned Officer. (See Army/USMC Organization)

NDP: Night Defensive Position.

NLF: National Liberation Front, the political arm of the communist party in South Vietnam. The military component was the Viet Cong.

NUMBER ONE: The best.

NUMBER TEN: The worst.

NVA: North Vietnamese Army.

OCS: Officer Candidate School.

PAPA-SAN: An elderly Vietnamese man.

POINT MAN: A lead soldier on patrol.

PONCHO LINER: A nylon insert to the military rain poncho, primarily used as a blanket.

POP: To initiate something, such as in "pop a flare" or "pop a smoke."

POW: Prisoner of War.

PTSD: Post-Traumatic Stress Disorder.

PX: Post Exchange.

RECOILESS RIFLE: Allowing some gases to escape out of the rear of the gun makes this small, shoulder-fired artillery piece recoilless.

RECON: Reconnaissance.

RF/PF: Regional Forces and Popular Forces; also known as "Ruff-Puffs." Recruited to protect the areas where they lived in South Vietnam.

RPG: Rocket-Propelled Grenade; Russian-manufactured antitank rocket.

R&R: Rest-and-Recreation or Recuperation. A week-long break was usually taken mid-way through a one-year tour in Vietnam. Out-of-country locations were Bangkok, Hawaii, Tokyo, Australia, Hong Kong, Manila, Taipei, Kuala Lumpur, and Singapore. In-country R&R was usually awarded to service people who had done something that deserved a reward. Vung Tau, Cam Rahn Bay, and China Beach were all in-country choices for R&R.

RTO: Radio Telephone Operator. The serviceman who carried the unit's radio in the field.

RUCK, RUCKSACK: A backpack issued to infantry in Vietnam.

RVN: Republic of Vietnam (South Vietnam).

SAPPERS: North Vietnamese Army or Viet Cong demolition commandos.

SEARCH AND DESTROY: Offensive operations designed to find and destroy enemy forces, not to take and hold land.

SEMPER FI: The USMC motto, short for "Semper Fidelis," Latin for "Always Faithful."

SEVENTEENTH PARALLEL: temporary division line, also known as the DMZ, between North and South Vietnam. This line was established by the Geneva Accords of 1954.

SHAM TIME: To avoid a task or goof off.

SHRAPNEL: Large/small pieces of metal scattered about after an explosion of a bomb, shell, or grenade. Shrapnel accounts for many deaths and even more wounded during combat.

SHORT, SHORT-TIME, SHORT-TIMER: An individual with little time remaining in Vietnam due to the conclusion of his twelve-month or thirteen-month tour of duty.

SIT-REP: Situation Report.

SKATE: To avoid a task or goof off.

SLACK MAN: Second man in a patrol, behind the point man.

SLICK: Huey helicopter used for troop and supply transport. There are no guns on the side of the aircraft; thus, the sides are "slick." Two door gunners protect the slick.

STAND-DOWN: A unit being pulled back to the rear for a period of rest, refitting, and training.

STAY BEHIND (LEAVE BEHIND): Ambush tactic wherein a small group is left behind after a unit breaks camp to ambush any enemy who might be following.

STERILIZED: To restore a site to its original condition before leaving it.

SUPPRESSIVE FIRE: Also called "covering fire," this type of fire is used to keep the "enemy's heads down," allowing the friendlies to move without being shot.

TET: Vietnamese Lunar New Year holiday period. It also refers to the nationwide NVA/VC offensive during the Tet Holiday in 1968.

THUMPER (THUMPGUN): M-79 grenade launcher.

TOC: Tactical Operations Center.

TRIP-WIRE: Thin wire used by both sides strung across an area someone may walk through. It is usually attached to a mine, flare, or booby trap.

TRIPLE CANOPY: Thick jungle, plants growing at three levels - ground level, intermediate, and high levels.

TU DAI: The VC used to warn the locals of booby-trapped areas by posting little wooden signs with those words on them, just at the edge of the wood line. Ironically it was pronounced, "To Die."

USO: United Service Organization.

VILLE: Short for a village.

VN: Vietnam. In the Vietnamese language, no word is larger than one syllable. Therefore, Vietnam is actually two words: Viet and Nam. Thus, VN.

VVMF: Vietnam Veterans Memorial Fund.

WEB GEAR: The canvas belt and shoulder straps used by the infantry for packing equipment and ammunition.

WIA: Wounded in Action.

(THE) WORLD: Slang term for the United States or any place outside Vietnam.

XO: Executive Officer. The second in command of a unit the size of a Company and up.

YARDS: Slang for Montagnard soldiers.

NOTE: The source for some of the preceding definitions was the Dictionary of the Vietnam War, edited by James S. Olson; published by Greenwood Press, Inc.; New York, 1988.

End Notes

Chapter Two: Grady Elder

[1] While the Elder's address was technically Grantville (3.4 miles from Grady's home and in Coweta County), they were closer to the town of Lone Oak (1.5 miles from Grady's home and in Meriwether County). Hogansville was less than ten miles to the southwest. (7.5 miles from Grady's home and in Troup County). All three of these communities would play a part in Grady's story.

[2] Grantville Brown still stands in Grantville; it is now occupied by the Regional Educational Service Agency or RESA. The Coweta County School System built a new elementary school in Grantville in 2004 named Glanton Elementary after long-time Grantville Principal Thomas Glanton.

Chapter Four: Donald Lowery

[1] According to the Post Museum website, "A successful on–the–fly exchange depended on many factors, including the clerks' experience, strong mail pouches that would not burst open when snatched by a fast-moving iron crane or kicked off a moving train, postmasters who attached the pouches correctly and well-maintained equipment that worked as expected. Retrieving mail from the crane was only one-half of the job. As many clerks learned, kicking the mail pouch out could be just as difficult. One clerk booted an outgoing pouch with so much force that he sent it flying through the railroad terminal window. The clerk who did not kick hard enough watched helplessly as the pouch was sucked under the train and mail torn to shreds by the train's wheels. Clerks had a name for that. They called it a "snowstorm."

Smithsonian National Postal Museum. "Railway Mail Crane." https://postalmuseum.si.edu/collections/object-spotlight/railway-mail-crane

Chapter Eight: Michael Watson

[1] Mike was born when his mother lived in Moreland, though he

did not live there long. Newnan was really his hometown.

[2] The location of Union Station was at the intersection of the Central of Georgia track and the A&WP track. The Central of Georgia line ran from Rome, Newnan, Macon, and Savannah. The A&WP went from East Point to West Point, Georgia. The two tracks crossed in Newnan at the location of Union Station. The station was shaped like an L so that passengers from each train had their own platform. There was a park on Savannah Street beside the station, likely the only park in Newnan. A small motel just down Dunbar Street would have housed Railroad and Postal workers. Union Station was torn down sometime during the 1970s.

[3]Spencer's Skating Rink was in the area behind Wadsworth Auditorium in Newnan.

Chapter Ten: Johnny Calhoun

[1]During the early 1970s, Faye composed this poem to honor and remember her missing husband.

Our Husband, Father, and Son

It was long ago that we first met
And not for a moment do I regret
That we fell in love and later married
And now our name our daughter carries

We were very happy the time we had
But the day you left was very sad
For Vietnam has made her cries
And left this family with nothing but sighs

You were patriotic, so I knew you must go
But a year without my love will pass very slow
You felt it your duty, so I would do my best
To make this year go as fast as the rest

I wrote you a letter each night that went by
And in between lines, sometimes I would cry
But only because I love you so deep

And hoping that soon at the airport we would meet

I too looked forward for the postman each day
For I knew how sweet your words would say
"I love you and Teresa with all of my heart"
And hope that we never again have to part

Then November came and in Hawaii we met
Only for a week was my only regret
For the days and nights went by so fast
And before we knew it our week has passed

It was Thanksgiving Day, day after my return
We heard of Tommy, with all great concern
For "Missing in Action" he was declared
None other around could Tommy be compared

It was Saturday after, the worst news arrived
That could not stop the tears from our eyes
For Tommy had died while saving another
Except in the hearts of wife, mother, daddy, sister and brother

The Red Cross did help for home you did fly
But on December 11th, again we did sigh
"God Bless You and I love you" were words we did say

Christmas came next and it was very sad
For it was the first Teresa didn't have her dad
I knew the next months would go so slow
But thank God we only have four more to go

On March 29, the sad news arrived
All plans of you we thought were deprived
For "Missing in Action" again we did hear
About our love one we all love so dear

I thought the first year went by very slow
But how very long a year could be, I did not know

For almost three years have passed without a word to hear
Not knowing what year will again bring you near

It has been hard on everyone to be without you
And especially not knowing what you may be going through
But in God we must trust all the way to the end
For he is the guidance of all the day that we spend

The ending of this poem for which I chose
Is a prayer with which I will close

Thank you, Dear God, for all you have done
For he is our "Husband, Father and Son"
We all love him so dear and miss him so much
His thoughts in our hearts we will always clutch

Take care of him Dear God wherever he may be
And do bring him home so we all may see
The one we all love so true and so dear
And hope and pray that soon he will be here

Thank you again Dear God for all you have done
For you know that he is "Our Husband, Father, and Son"

Chapter Twelve: Terry Allen

[1] Howard Warner was a highly educated African American who moved to Newnan in 1914 and worked with black students to help them acquire job skills. The school was built in 1934 as the Savannah Street School and later renamed Howard Warner. It has been renovated and reopened as a community center and a Boys and Girls Club branch. Central High School is now the Central Education Center, the most renowned educational initiative of the Coweta County School System.

[2] Arquette played Charley Weaver on Dragnet, The Tonight Show, The Roy Rogers, and Dale Evans Show, and even hosted Charley Weaver's Hobby Lobby on ABC.

[3] Douglas-Lomason has been torn down, but you can see pollution monitoring equipment if you drive by the site today on

Hwy 16 West. According to local accountant Rick Melville, the business contaminated the soil at that location and the surrounding area. Werner Hughie worked there as well. See Chapter 21.

[4] Hattie Thurman's married name is Dunn; she worked for many years in the Coweta County School system and was an exceptional educator and administrator.

Chapter Thirteen: Wayne Vessell

[1] The Marine base in Albany was only five years old when William Vessell was assigned there. Their primary responsibility is to repair and rebuild equipment for the Marine Corps.

Chapter Fifteen: Timothy Cole Jr.

[1] The Cole family had initially migrated from the Blount Mountain area to Coweta during the depression. Blount Mountain is southwest of Gadsden.

[2] Phillip Smith could not remember if the whole school or specific grades did this.

[3] The county schools at this time included Madras, Moreland, Grantville, Western, Arnco-Sargent, East Coweta, and East Newnan. Unfortunately, no one remembers if Skip's team won their race.

[4] Five months earlier, in June 1968, Terry Allen from Newnan had been killed in this same general area by friendly fire. See Chapter 12.

[5] Sonnet from Senior Tigers, Newnan High School Empyrean, 1964

Our Newnan Tiger Class of sixty four,
Who rambling down the halls in many ways
To pass their leisure time throughout the days.
Are leaving through our Alma Mater's door;
Four years of grueling work that's always hard
Still left us hours to play our youth tricks;
We talked and sang and laughed to get our kicks
And always kept our teachers on their guard;
For all posterity, we leave our gift,
And may our followers take this to heart,
For now their senior leaders have to part;

And you in turn must give to yours a lift;
Farewell we say now in a saddened state-
We hope the legacy we left is great!

[6]Timothy Cole Jr. Honors and Recognitions

Medical Service aviation suffered a tremendous loss in October with the death through hostile action of WO1 Timothy Cole Jr. WO1 Cole was transferred from the 1st Flight Platoon of the 45th to the 54th Medical Detachment in Chu Lai during late October and was killed as his aircraft went down less than one week later during a medical evacuation mission. Tim, 'Dust-Off 19,' was highly decorated for his actions with the 45th and was a true professional in every sense of the term. His memory will long be honored by those privileged to serve with him.

—III & IV Corps Dustoff Quarterly Newsletter, 1968

Warrant Officer Tim Cole served his country with dignity, honor, and valor in Vietnam, flying over 800 missions and evacuating over 1,600 wounded personnel. Tim was a dedicated pilot who earned the Silver Star, 5 Distinguished Flying Crosses, the Vietnamese Cross of Gallantry, the Purple Heart, and multiple Air Medals during his 9 months in combat. Tim was assigned to the 45th Medical Company (AA) in early 1968 and shortly became an Aircraft Commander in the war-torn III Corps Tactical Zone. A typical mission found Tim and his crew swiftly responding, landing in a hot landing zone, ignoring hostile fire, and saving multiple Soldiers in harm's way. His flying abilities as a highly decorated DUSTOFF pilot immediately became legendary. Tim was transferred to the 54th Medical Detachment (HA), which was short of pilots, and only a few days later, was mortally wounded by hostile fire. He always gave freely to others without regard for his own safety. Tim will always be remembered as one of the greatest DUSTOFF pilots. Tim Cole was inducted into the DUSTOFF Hall of Fame on 21 February 2009.

—Dust-Off Hall of Fame Website

Warrant Officer 1, Army, Newnan. In 1968 in Vietnam as a Dust-Off Helicopter Pilot, he displayed great courage while flying unarmed aircraft into battles to save lives, evacuating over 1,600 and flying over 800 combat hours. On 5,8 & 9 May, 18 June, and 30 July 1968, he saved many lives flying through heavy enemy fire. He was awarded five Distinguished Flying Crosses (Valor) for these five missions. On 18 October he was Killed in Action and was awarded the Purple Heart and the Silver Star.

—Georgia Military Hall of Fame Website

DUST-OFF PILOTS

The Dustoff pilot is a strange breed of man,
Going places no one else can.
A big red cross is his weapon of war,
One on the front and one on each door.
The Dustoff man has one belief
Which many times brings grief.
Through enemy fire like a cold steel knife,
Get the wounded out and give him life.
The enemy sees a red cross in the air,
He aims his rifle with very great care.
The big red cross means one thing you see,
A big red bull's eye he shoots at for free.
He fires his rifle again and again,
Knowing the ship is for wounded men.
Sometimes they live and sometimes they die,
But from these brave men there is never a cry.
A dedication to the deadly task,
They wear emotions behind a mask.
Afraid, yet above it, ever ready to go,
Dustoff, the brave ones, ask the wounded, they know.
Afraid tho proud ever near-death's grip,
Above the best in their cross-bearing ship.

By CW2 David G. Alderson
45th Medical Company (AA) 4th platoon RVN 1968

Chapter Sixteen: James Kerr

[1] She met another young woman in the airport waiting for her husband to arrive from Vietnam. She had a baby that the husband had never seen. Shelia was holding the baby for her when James walked in from an earlier-than-expected flight. His immediate reaction was, "I've got a baby!" In all the confusion, Shelia couldn't find the baby's mother. James later told her that the first thought when he saw her was that he didn't believe she was pregnant when he left! "It was just a really funny incident!" said Shelia.

[2]IN MEMORIAM

To James C. Kerr, who died on Vietnam December 6th, 1968
A TRIBUTE AND A REASONING

We know that time will ease the pain
And the hurt we feel today.
But time nor man can ever erase
The memories, which tend to stay.

He was here only yesterday fulfilling his job
To man and to this day;
But he knew the source of his destiny, and he knew God planned it this way.

We ask ourself why (it's human discrepancy).
Though an answer will never come;
But never doubt that God has a reason,
And never doubt that God's will be done.

God has a purpose in all the he does;
Though his will is not to cause pain:
Who are we ---to question God?
Acceptance is all that remains.
But in God you'll find the courage and strength to face this trial and loss.

And remember, James died for the lives of men; Such as Jesus died on the cross.

One little drop in the fountain of life
If lost, is surely missed,
For without that drop and its contribution the pond will never exist.

One small life in this world of men
If lost, most surely is missed,
For the lives of men have made this world and without them a world wouldn't exist.
(*Written by Janice Burdette to Sheila Kerr on the death of her husband, James Kerr, December 6, 1968.*)

When the traveling Wall came to Newnan in 2011, Jimmy Hines gave Bubba's sister, Judy, this poem. He had never told anyone about it before. "I wrote this when my youngest daughter Emily was in high school doing a project on Vietnam," said Jimmy. "She had to find a poem as part of the assignment. I told her of visiting the Wall in Washington on a business trip and looking up Bubba's name. She began to ask about Bubba, so we spent a lot of time discussing childhood things. Out of that assignment came these words."

MY DAD TOLD ME THIS STORY
ABOUT HIS BOYHOOD FRIEND

WHO LIVED DOWN THE ROAD
JUST AROUND THE BEND

GROWING UP WAS FUN
EACH DAY WAS FILLED

WITH SWIMMING AND BASEBALL
AND KING ON THE HILL

BUBBA WAS STRONG AND COULD
HIT A BALL HARD

ACROSS THE STREET AND INTO
THE NEIGHBORS YARD

THE YEARS ROLLED BY FAST
AS TIME SEEMS TO DO

TWELVE YEARS IN SCHOOL
HOW'D WE EVER MAKE IT THROUGH

OFF TO WORK OR COLLEGE PERHAPS
TIME TO GIVE UP THE BALLS
AND THE BATS

FINDING REAL WORK WAS NOT EASY TODAY
CAUSE OUR DRAFT STATUS WAS
THE DREADED 1-A

WE BOTH GOT A NOTICE TO
COME ON DOWN

REPORT FOR A PHYSICAL
TO SEE IF YOU'RE SOUND

JUNE 16th THE DRAFT LOTTERY CHOSE
IT WAS TIME FOR BUBBA TO GIVE UP
HIS CIVILIAN CLOTHES

INTO THE ARMY
AND OFF TO WAR

DID ANYONE KNOW WHAT WE WERE
REALLY FIGHTING FOR?

PROUD YOUNG MEN
A JOB TO DO

PROTECTING THE RIGHTS
OF ME AND YOU

I CAN SEE BUBBA NOW
AS HE STEPS TO THE PLATE

HOME RUN BALL OVER
THE LEFT FIELD GATE

I CAN SEE BUBBA NOW
AS HE LAY ON THE GROUND

THIS GIANT OF A MAN
A BULLET HAS FOUND

IF GIVING ONE'S LIFE
IS IN GOD'S PLAN

I WANT TO SAY THANKS TO
THIS BRAVE YOUNG MAN

FOR THE MEMORIES, THE FUN,
GREAT TIMES AS THEY WERE

AND THE FRIENDSHIP GIVEN ME
BY JAMES CLAYTON KERR

BUBBA---------YOU'RE UP NEXT--------AND WE NEED A HIT!

Chapter Seventeen: Eddy Couch

[1] One day, the two boys were in the house, wrestling without let-up. Elna was exasperated. It didn't matter what she did; they kept after it. Finally, inspiration struck when they seemed to be at a break in the contest, and she insisted that they keep fighting. They went back to it. When they finally seemed to finish, Elna announced that they had to keep wrestling and fighting; once they

stopped, she told them, "I am going to whip you!" Finally, they got tired and told Elna that they didn't want to fight any longer, precisely what she wanted to hear!

[2] McKnight recalls being in Physical Education class with Eddy during their senior year during the last period of the day. The Coach would often split the students into groups; he would take a group to work on the skill for that day, and he would have Ray and Eddy take another group. Ray also remembers skipping school the Tuesday before Thanksgiving break and spending the day at the pool hall in Newnan. (author's note: Thanksgiving break was always Wednesday through Sunday during this time.) In addition, the "group" once went to the Coweta County Fair on Temple Avenue and avoided paying the entrance price by jumping the fence. "We thought it was funny," discloses Ray. "We won some teddy bears for the girls."

Chapter Nineteen: Stevan Pittman

[1]I tried cornbread and syrup and liked it. It was like eating pancakes!

[2] After German reunification in the early 1990s, the base was turned over to the German government and redeveloped. As a result, there is almost nothing left that Stevan Pittman would recognize today.

[3] Having a soldier remain with the body through the funeral was commonplace during the Vietnam War, and many of the Coweta families who suffered through this tragedy remember it well.

Chapter Twenty: Larry Pinson

[1]October 9, 1969, Newnan Times-Herald. "Funeral Held Sunday for Former Central Player" column by Johnny Brown (Sports Editor)

Young men are dying daily on the fields of Vietnam, and it is impossible to pay tribute to each one. However, occasionally news of a death in Vietnam strikes more sorrow than others. Gunnel Pinson is dead; killed in Vietnam, and the news of this death probably passed unnoticed here except for a handful of people. I got the news late and like many of the young men I have known who lost their life in this police action- the news of Gunnel's death was indeed sad. This young man was a part of one of Central High School's finest football teams a couple of years ago. They won the region championship and played a great game against Spencer of Columbus at Drake Stadium in the play-offs. This Panther team was spearheaded by Rayford Patterson, a standout athlete who accepted a scholarship to Minnesota after being sought after by many colleges. Foes of the Panthers that year had to worry about more than stopping Patterson. Coach Henry Seldon had a number of great athletes on that team. Several of them went to college on grants but five of them decided to join the Marines. These included Sammy Davis, Walter McCrary, Allen Strozier, Willie Barber and Jackie Adams. Gunnel Pinson also chose to cast his lot with Uncle Sam. So while Patterson went off to Minnesota in a hail of football glory- Gunnel Pinson went off to war.

Patterson and Pinson Both Came Back

The events of the past few days have a dash of irony that borders on the Hollywood scriptwriter. Both these young men were good athletes- Patterson was the star and was good enough to make anyone's all-star team. Pinson was a good, rugged player, but one who failed to gain the spotlight of glory. They both came home recently. Patterson, who made the Minnesota Frosh team last year and was a defensive starter this season on the Big Ten team's varsity, quit the squad and came home to Newnan. No one knows for sure- some say he had a spat with his coach and decided to quit. A few days later Gunnel Pinson came home. The trip from Vietnam was in a government casket. Gunnel was dead. Gunnel didn't quit- he was in a game that requires a man to play the fourth quarter as hard as the first. This young man gave all he had for his country. Coach Seldon and the Panther-mates of Gunnel were not surprised. He played the game of football the same way. Sunday he was buried and his mates served as pallbearers.

Willie Barber Came Back- Served as Pallbearer

This past Sunday was a sad day for the athletes of that great Central team. They got together for the first time in many months- they had rather the occasion be for reasons other than serving as pallbearers for Gunnel Pinson. Willie Barber was one of the youngsters who went to Vietnam but he returned in good health in time to serve as a pallbearer this Sunday. Davis, McCrary and Adams are still in Vietnam and their game is in the fourth quarter, they should be home soon. Many of the players on this year's Central team started their football days as yearlings when this region-winning team played as seniors. They served as pallbearers Sunday- Steve Shavers, Lonnie Freeman, James Pitman, Gordon Mitchell, Barber, Ricky Hill, and the star of the team- Rayford Patterson. It's odd to say but Patterson played second string to Gunnel Pinson in this final contest. Gunnel was the star as he met with his former teammates for the last time Sunday afternoon.

Chapter Twenty-One: Warner Hughie

[1] Newnan High School and Newnan Junior High School were located at the intersection of Temple Avenue and Jackson Street, on the spot that is now the Veterans Park in downtown Newnan.

[2] Interested in this trick? Google "how to flip your eyelids inside out."

[3] East Newnan Road the intersects of Poplar Road, Turkey Creek Road, East Newnan Road, and McIntosh Street, renamed Martin Luther King Jr. Drive. That intersection is known as Five Points. They are now all connected by a round-a-bout.

[4] According to local accountant Rick Melville, the business contaminated the soil at that location and the surrounding area. Douglas-Lomason has been torn down, but you can see pollution monitoring equipment if you drive by the site today on Hwy 16 West.

[5] This song was on the final Supremes album that included Diana Ross, called *Cream of the Crop*. Of the three members of the Supremes, only Diana Ross sang on this track, along with one of the song's writers, Johnny Bristol. Ross was in the process of leaving the Supremes at the time.

[6] The Americal Division is the only US Army division with a name, not a number. The name came from World War II when an American Army Task Force was stationed on the island of New Caledonia in the southwest Pacific. The name derives from Americans in New Caledonia.

Chapter Twenty-Four: Robert Webb

[1] Baker High School was open for almost fifty years. It was closed in 1991.

Chapter Twenty-Five: 132nd Helicopter Company

[1]Resolution Adopted by the city of Newnan and the county of Coweta. March 11, 1968.

On motion duly seconded, the following resolution was adopted:

WHEREAS, the citizens of the City of Newnan and the County of Coweta, State of Georgia, take great pride in their devotion to and love of their country, of which they are an active and vital part; and

WHEREAS, the citizens of the City of Newnan and County of Coweta, State of Georgia, are acutely aware of the enormity of our country's debt to the members of her armed services for their loyalty and devotion to her; and

WHEREAS, the 132nd Aviation Company Medium Helicopter Unit through hard work and expert training has become an active and vital part of the Armed Forces of the United States of America, and under its country's colors will soon be serving her best interest in South Vietnam; and

WHEREAS, it is fitting that the citizens of this City, the County and the members of the 132nd Aviation Company Medium Helicopter Unit, being part of a team dedicated to the principles for which this country stands, should be identified together in the days and months to come;

NOW THEREFORE, BE IT RESOLVED by the Mayor and Council of the City of Newnan, and the Board of Commissioners of Roads and Revenues of Coweta County, Georgia, sitting in joint session, that the 132nd Aviation Company Medium Helicopter Unit be, and the same is hereby adopted as their official military representative.

BE IT FURTHER RESOLVED that from and after this date said Unit shall be affectionately known by the City and the County as the 132nd Newnan-Coweta Aviation Company Medium Helicopter Unit.

And May Godspeed.

This 11th day of March, 1968.

[2] The Americal Division is the only Army division with a name, not a number. It got its name during World War II when it was formed on the island of New Caledonia. The name comes from Americans in New Caledonia.

Chapter Twenty-Six: Pless, Jackson, and the Medal of Honor

[1] Both of Lyndon Johnson's daughters were in the White House on this day; Lynda Bird (25) and Luci Baines (21). It is impossible to know which one got the cookies for the Dix boys. According to Stephen Pless's daughter, Cindy, the Johnson girls also helped with their family that day.

[2] The list of expected VIPs was impressive: the Georgia Lieutenant Governor and Speaker of the House, the State Senator from Carroll County, both of Coweta County's State Representatives, Troup County's State Representative, and Coweta's Congressman.

The United States Army Organization

Smallest to Largest

(the numbers listed for each unit below are the maximum number that each unit might contain. Starting with a platoon and going up, the numbers may vary widely.)

FIRE-TEAM: 4 soldiers.
Commander: Corporal or Sergeant

SQUAD: 8 soldiers, made up of two fire-teams.
Commander: Sergeant. A Sergeant is a NON-COMMISSIONED OFFICER.

PLATOON: 45 soldiers divided into 4-5 squads.
Commander: Lieutenant (usually a 2nd but could be a 1st) A LIEUTENANT is a COMMISSIONED OFFICER. *

COMPANY: 150-200 soldiers divided into 3-4 Platoons. An artillery company is called a BATTERY.
Commander: Captain

BATTALION: 900 soldiers, 4-5 Companies.
Commander: Lieutenant Colonel

REGIMENT: 1500-2000 soldiers. 2 battalions.
Commander: Colonel

BRIGADE: 6,000-7,000 soldiers. 4-8 Battalions.
Commander: Colonel

DIVISION: Most historically recognizable American military unit. Divisions become famous and often have unique insignia that builds pride and esprit de corps in that division. A division consists of 15,000- 20,000 soldiers divided into 3 brigades.
Commander: Major General

CORPS: Two or more divisions. Corps has a dual meaning in the US military- it could also mean any group doing asimilar function, such as the Signal Corps or Medical Corps.
Commander: Lieutenant General

FIELD ARMY: Two or more Corps.
Commander: General

Enlisted Ranks: E1/E2: Private, E3: Private First Class, E4: Specialist, E4: Corporal, and E5-E9: Sergeant. The Corporal and the Sergeant are NCOs. However, the Sergeant has the most significant impact on the lower-ranking soldiers. A Sergeant works his way up from his enlistment into the military to various levels of the Sergeant rank. He is considered a **NON-COMMISSIONED OFFICER (NCO)** and *EXTREMELY* important in the army's functioning.

A **Warrant Officer** is a technical specialist; during the Vietnam War, this rank usually applied to helicopter pilots.

Sergeant Ranks: Staff Sergeant, Sergeant First Class, Master Sergeant, First Sergeant, Sergeant Major, Command Sergeant Major, Sergeant Major of theArmy.

Officer Ranks: **Commissioned**: 2nd Lieutenant, 1st Lieutenant, Captain, Major, Lt. Colonel, Colonel, General.
**A Commissioned Officer has gone to Officer Candidate School (OCS) as an enlisted man to graduate into the Commissioned Officer Corps or is commissioned through colleges that offer the Reserve Officers Training Corps (ROTC) as a source of commissioning. The Service Academies (West Point, Annapolis, USAF) also graduate their students into the Commissioned Officer Corps. All graduates, regardless of route, are Second Lieutenants upon graduation. The Coast Guard also has an Academy, and its graduates are given the rank of ensign, the equivalent of 2nd Lieutenant in the other branches.*

General Ranks: Brigadier General- 1 Star Rank, Major General- 2 Star Rank, Lieutenant General- 3 Star Rank, General-4 Star Rank, General of the Army- 5 Star Rank (only 5 men have achieved this rank- all WWII Generals.)

Assistance from Joe Loadholtes, US Army

United States Marine Corps Organization

Smallest to Largest

(the numbers listed for each unit below are the maximum number that each unit might contain. Starting with a platoon and going up, the numbers may vary widely.)

FIRE-TEAM: 4 Marines.
Commander: Corporal

RIFLE SQUAD: 3 Fire Teams + a squad leader = 13 Marines.
Commander: Sergeant. A Sergeant is a NON-COMMISSIONED OFFICER.

RIFLE PLATOON: 3 Squads + a Platoon Sergeant = 40 Marines.
Commander: Lieutenant (usually a 1st but could be a 2nd) A LIEUTENANT is a COMMISSIONED OFFICER. *

RIFLE COMPANY: 3 Platoons = 120 Marines.
Commander: Captain/Gunnery Sergeant (NCO)

INFANTRY BATTALION: 3 Companies = 360 Marines.
Commander: Lieutenant Colonel/First Sergeant (NCO)

INFANTRY REGIMENT: 3 Battalions or 1,080 Marines.
Commander: Colonel/Sergeant Major (NCO)

DIVISION: 3 Regiments/Brigades or 2916 Marines. Three Marine Corps Divisions, plus other Regiments, spent time in Vietnam. Today, there are three active divisions and one Reserve division.
Commander: Major General/Sergeant Major (NCO)

MARINE CORPS: Three or more divisions.
Commander: Commandant of the Marine Corps/Sergeant Major of the Marine Corps (NCO)

Enlisted Ranks: E1: Private, E2: Private First Class, E3: Lance Corporal, E4: Corporal, and E5-E9: Sergeant. The Corporal and the Sergeant are NCOs. However, as in the Army, the Sergeant has the most significant impact on the lower-ranking Marines. A Sergeant works his way up from his enlistment into the military to various levels of the Sergeant rank. He is considered a **NON-COMMISSIONED OFFICER (NCO)** and *EXTREMELY* important in the functioning of the military.

Sergeant Ranks: E5: Sergeant, E6: Staff Sergeant, E7: Gunnery Sergeant, E8: First Sergeant or Master Sergeant, E9: Master Gunnery Sergeant or Sergeant Major, Sergeant Major of the Marine Corps.

A **Warrant Officer** is a MOS specialist. They usually come from the Sergeant or Staff Sergeants rank and have real-world experience in their MOS.

Commissioned Officer Ranks: 2nd Lieutenant, 1st Lieutenant, Captain, Major, Lt. Colonel, Colonel, General.
**A Commissioned Officer has gone to Officer Candidate School (OCS) as an enlisted man to graduate into the Commissioned Officer Corps or is commissioned through colleges that offer the Reserve Officers Training Corps (ROTC) as a source of commissioning. The Service Academies (West Point, Annapolis, USAF) also graduate their students into the Commissioned Officer Corps. Since the Marine Corps is considered part of the Navy, Naval Academy (Annapolis) graduates can choose to enter the Marine Corps. The US Army, Air Force, and Marine Corps, regardless of route, are Second Lieutenants upon graduation. The Coast Guard also has an Academy, and its graduates, along with the Naval Academy, are given the rank of Ensign, the equivalent of 2nd Lieutenant in the other branches.*

General Ranks: Brigadier General- 1 Star Rank, Major General- 2 Star Rank, Lieutenant General- 3 Star Rank, General-4 Star Rank; there is no 5 Star Rank

Assistance from Rodney Riggs, USMC

Instructions for the Escorts of Deceased Personnel

(taken from Warrant Officer Albert Michaels's orders to escort the body of Timothy Cole Jr. home)

1. The selection of a military escort for the purpose of accompanying the remains of the late_______ to ________ may appear on the surface to have been made at random; however, this is not the case. Only the highest caliber of personnel are selected to perform escort duty. It is a compliment to you to be chosen to express the Nation's homage to its honored dead. You are, therefore, advised that your selection and assignment as a military escort places a responsibility upon you as a member of the Armed Forces.

2. It is desired to emphasize the importance of this assignment; particularly your maintaining neatness of appearance, sobriety, and certain acceptable intangibles which will preclude the possibility of any criticism being levied against you as an individual, or the Armed Forces. Needless to say, the duty of an escort is of a sensitive nature. One slip in your actions or a misplaced word or gesture made unwittingly or knowingly, can cause irreparable damage never to be overcome by any subsequent well-meaning words or gestures.

3. Tact and diplomacy are most essential in this assignment. Remember that you are representing the Armed Forces of the United States and the Department of Defense. Because of your position of responsibility, you will be looked upon as a model representative of the Armed Forces.

4. <u>GENERAL INFORMATION</u>:

a. Remains will be at the railroad depot or airport in ample time to meet your schedule. Arrangements for this will be made by the Mortuary Officer.

b. The next of kin and receiving Funeral Director will be notified by this office by telegram of the time the remains will arrive at your final destination. Receiving Funeral Director will be requested to meet your train or plane with transportation.

c. The envelope which will be attached to the shipping case of the deceased will contain the Transit Permit and Letter concerning Transportation Invoices. (This material is intended for the receiving funeral director)

d. You will hand-carry the following documents and present them to the next of kin.

   1. Request for Reimbursement of Interment Expenses (DD Form 1375) to include an instruction sheet for completion, with a self-addressed envelope to be used by the next of kin to return the form.
   2. Request for additional Death Certificates or Information concerning Death Certificates.
   3. Application for Headstone or Marker (DD Form 1330). Advised next of kin that this form will be completed and both copies (Original and Duplicate) will be forwarded to Chief, Office of Support Services, Department of the Army, ATTN: Memorial Division, Washington, D.C. 20024. (This form will be omitted when remains are consigned to a National Cemetery)

4. Condition of Remains and Casket at Final Destination (436 MAWHQ Form 0-99A) will be given to the receiving funeral director for completion.

e. Secure tickets and Special Orders from the Base Mortuary. Report to Mortuary at least one-half hour before departure to assure on-time departure.

f. Prior to departure, check the shipping case by reading the name on the envelope to assure you have the proper remains. Also, check the baggage form attached to the handle to insure proper destination.

g. DO NOT BECOME SEPARATED FROM THE REMAINS WHICH YOU ARE ESCORTING. Be particularly cautious when transfers are necessary.

h. Be sure to check with the conductor before arrival at any major stop to ensure that baggage car will not be removed from the train.

i. Upon arrival at final destination, after inspection of remains by receiving funeral director, request him to drape the flag (located on top of casket in shipping case) over the casket.

(1) When the flag is used to drape a half-couch casket (viewable remains), it should be placed in three layers (10-inch folds) to cover the closed half of the casket on the deceased's left.

(2) When the flag is used to drape a closed casket (non-viewable remains), it should be placed so that the union (blue field) is at the head and over the left shoulder of the deceased.

j. If you attend the funeral service, you should learn from the funeral director what is expected of you. You may be requested to present the flag to the next of kin at the end of the graveside service. You should present the folded flag to the next of kin with a remark such as, "This flag is presented by a grateful nation in memory of the faithful service performed by your loved one."

k. If the next of kin has expressed a desire for military honors, this activity will request the Commander of the nearest Base to your final destination requested and the Commander of the nearest Base to final destination does not have sufficient military personnel to render the honors, you may contact any patriotic organization (VFW, American Legion, etc.) to assist in rendering honors.

5. GENERAL INSTRUCTIONS:

a. You will have a smart, well-groomed appearance and maintain sobriety at all times.

b. Secure tickets and Special Orders from the Base Mortuary.

c. PERSONALLY check to see that remains you are escorting are placed in the baggage car or aboard aircraft.

d. Board the train or plane and occupy seat after remains are placed onboard.

e. Personally accompany remains if transferred enroute, from one station to another, or from one train to another. Stay with the remains until they are placed in the proper baggage car before you take your seat. DO NOT PAY ANY TRANSPORTATION COSTS OUT OF YOUR OWN POCKET, as they are paid by the Government upon receipt of a valid claim for same.

f. Notify, by collect wire, both the Mortuary Officer, Dover AFB, Del, and receiving funeral director of any deviation from scheduled arrival time.

g. Offer your services, through the receiving funeral director, to next of kin and assist them if they so desire. You will remain for funeral services unless the next of kin advises you that your services and not required.

h. Be sympathetic and understanding in dealing with relatives, and in conversation do not divulge information which should be safeguarded. Remember, the deceased is the most important person in the world to his surviving loved ones.

i. If the remains you are escorting are non-viewable but the next of kin desires to open the casket, there is no law prohibiting them to do so. However, as a member of the Armed Forces, you will neither encourage nor participate in the opening of the casket containing non-viewable remains.

j. If at any time any problem is encountered concerning religion, contact the nearest military chaplain, or, if not available, a civilian clergyman.

6. After carefully reading these instructions and following a briefing by a representative Mortuary Officer, you will complete a certificate indicating your full understanding of the contents of this letter.

Visit of 'the Wall that Heals' has special meaning

Thoughts on the Traveling Wall

Steve Quesinberry

Newnan Times-Herald, October 9, 2011

John Stuart Mill, a British philosopher and Member of Parliament, once said, "*The world consists largely of weak men made and kept free by better men than themselves.*" As you study the history of the world, this statement seems more and more inspired. People tend to see history as linear, yet there are numerous places where history could have been sidetracked and led to different outcomes that do not include the United States as a beacon of freedom. The battle at Tours, the defeat of the Spanish Armada, the rout of Napoleon's Imperial Guard at Waterloo, the confrontation at Yorktown, the desperate struggle at Midway Island, and the decision to invade the Norman coastline on June 6, 1944. In all these battles leading to or preserving the American way of life, you can see the "better men" Mills references. They should not be forgotten.

We see this same phenomenon at the Vietnam Memorial, whether we go to it, or it comes to us. This week is important to the students and the people of this community, not because of what the wall is made of, but the fact it reflects its surroundings or even its dimensions. It is important because it allows us to see and remember those "better men" that Mills references. Coweta County produced "better men" then, and I believe still does today. On no account should we forget.

This week is also significant to those that did not die but frequently came home to a hostile or a merely apathetic populace. Col. Hal Moore, commander of the 1st Battalion, 7th Cavalry, once stated, "Hate war, but love the American Warrior." These "better men" served and often took the brunt of the war's unpopularity. Politicians send our young men to war; we must never forget.

This event is imperative for our students as it helps bring them face to face with the past, whether you stare at the names that seem to go on endlessly or shake the hand of a veteran who returned safely. We attempt to connect students with history through these veterans and their stories at Newnan High School. Our *Student-Vet Connect* program forces students to reach back into the past and make a connection with these "better men." This is the way history should be; touched, not forgotten.

In a town that remembers and commemorates its history like Newnan, the war in Vietnam seems largely forgotten. It does not connect with local people today, perhaps because of the dramatic growth over the last two decades or because people have tried to put the ugliness of this period behind them. Yet Coweta County is very much represented in this era, with two Medal of Honor recipients, twenty-three killed in action, and more than five hundred men and women in Coweta County that served. We cannot forget.

When visiting the traveling wall this week, look closely, and see America's best. Then, look around for one of those "better men" volunteering, shake their hand and tell them, "Thank you." We should always remember.

Newnan Soldier Writes Poetry from Vietnam

Sp/4 Tim P. Willingham, son of Mr. and Mrs. Clyde Willingham, 253 Greenville Street, is now serving with Company B, 4th Battalion, 3rd Infantry, 11th Infantry Brigade, in Vietnam. He has written the following poem to his family here.

"The night is dark, the firing ceased;
The faith and hope seem to increase,
As soldier guard by night and day,
Hoping God will show the way.
We, the men in Vietnam,
Serve the mission we are on
Hoping soon the year will pass,
And we'll be home again at last.
Sometimes we ask what we're fighting for
Why this cruel and brutal war?
We fight for freedom in this land,
For our own freedom lies at hand
Some may be wounded, some may die,
The price at stake is very high;
If we believe with heart and soul
We'll surely reach our final goal.
May God let the firing soon to cease
And forever let us live in peace."

Newnan-Times Herald Thursday, April 11, 1968

Acknowledgments

The end of each chapter of this book lists the people I interviewed or assisted me in telling that story. It doesn't show my deep appreciation for each one of the people I interviewed. Because of them, I can tell a story that might otherwise have been overlooked. So many people assisted me with individual chapters; I am in your debt; thank you!

My wife Susan was the first reader of this narrative; she pointed out numerous errors, made suggestions, asked for explanations, and encouraged me to keep going! My love and gratitude have no limits. Thank you!

My daughter Ashley designed the front and back covers, worked on photographs, and lent her expertise in the publishing process. She was also quite selective about the photograph of me destined for the back cover. The picture that finally met her stringent criteria was taken by my daughter-in-law, Hannah. Thanks, Ash and Hannah; you guys are the best! (I know, you get that a lot!)

Thanks to artist Jodie Hobbs for the artwork on the book's cover and the map illustration in the appendix. I can't adequately express my appreciation!

My son, Stephen, a financial guru, has been an invaluable resource in analyzing the most efficient way to finance this book.

Alex and Angela McRae had much to do with this book; Alex helped me find families of the men from Coweta who were killed in Vietnam, and his gracious wife Angela did an incredible job cleaning everything up in the editing process. I appreciate both of you!

Thanks to Keith Dunnavant, a real author, for all the advice and assistance.

I extend my gratitude to Jimmy Davenport, Joe Loadholtes, Frank Henderson, Courtney Stillwell, Janet Alford, John Boren, Laurie Pope, Rodney Riggs, Deberah Williams, John Davidson and Pepper Copenhaver for their many and varied contributions to this book.

I am also indebted to Cathe Nixon of the Nixon Performing Arts Centre, for her enthusiasm and the work that she put in to launch the book at this venue. It was much appreciated!

I am much obliged for the assistance given by the Senoia Historical Society and especially by Mrs. Barbara Smith and Mr. Hal Sewell.

Thanks to Clay and Beth Neely and the Newnan Times-Herald, plus the variety of Civic Clubs around Coweta County, having allowed me to publicize these stories and ensure that they are remembered.

I would also like to recognize my two sons, Stephen and David, for joining the US Army on their own initiative. I appreciate their service to this country. I often thought of them as I worked on these narratives.

Thanks to others who just encouraged me in my efforts. My parents, Del and Ann Quesinberry, Ellen Quesinberry, Heath Hover, Reyna Fox, Kelley Finger, Elizabeth Doster, Gaines and Melissa Coker, Greg and Beth Travis, and Leo and Jan Harlan. I am also indebted to my in-laws, Dave and Pat Fox, for their encouragement and financial support of this effort.